Cincinnati, Ohio

PENGUIN REFERENCE BOOKS
R10
A DICTIONARY OF POLITICS

A DICTIONARY OF
POLITICS

By Florence Elliott and
Michael Summerskill

PENGUIN BOOKS
BALTIMORE · MARYLAND

Penguin Books Ltd, Harmondsworth, Middlesex
U.S.A.: Penguin Books Inc., 3300 Clipper Mill Road, Baltimore 11, Md
AUSTRALIA: Penguin Books Pty Ltd, 762 Whitehorse Road,
Mitcham, Victoria

—

First published 1957
Second Edition 1959
Third Edition 1961

—

Made and printed in Great Britain
by Unwin Brothers Ltd,
Woking and London

AUTHORS' NOTE

Modern international affairs are so complex that the task of selection of entries for inclusion in this Dictionary has not been easy. We hope that we can justify any particular entry either on the ground that there is frequent reference to it in political discussion or on the ground that it is important for a real understanding of international affairs, or on both these grounds. In particular, we must point out that, as far as politicians are concerned, we have adhered to our original decision only to include those who were alive at the time of going to press. The Dictionary includes no political developments which occurred after May 1961.

The letters *q.v.* are inserted after a term if a reference to that term might help the reader to understand better the subject under discussion. They are not inserted after every term elsewhere defined.

F.M.J.E.

M.B.S.

A

Absolutism. The principle of absolute government, the governed having no representation, vote, or other share in the administration.

Abu Dhabi. An independent state under British protection on the Trucial Coast, *q.v.*, in the Persian Gulf. It is the largest of the Trucial States, and of particular importance because the strategically significant oasis of Buraimi, *q.v.*, lies on the frontier between Abu Dhabi and Muscat and Oman, *q.v.* The mainland oil concession is held by Petroleum Development (Trucial Coast) Ltd, which has the same shareholders as the Iraq Petroleum Co., *q.v.* The ruler of Abu Dhabi, Sheikh Shakhbut bin Sultan, gave a sea-bed oil concession to the D'Arcy Exploration Co., a subsidiary of the British Petroleum Co.; his right to do so was contested by the I.P.C. interests, but upheld in an arbitration.

Abubakar. Alhaji Sir Abubakar Tafawa Balewa, Nigerian politician; born in 1912 in the village of Tafawa Balewa in Northern Nigeria, and educated as a teacher at Katsina College and at the Institute of Education, London University. He entered politics, on his return from London in 1946, as a member of the Northern People's Congress, and was elected to the federal House of Representatives in 1948, becoming a Minister in 1952 and Prime Minister of Nigeria in 1957, when the post was created. He was Prime Minister when Nigeria became independent in October 1960.

Abyssinia. *See* Ethiopia.

Activists. Those in a political group who want to take active steps towards the objectives of the group rather than merely to proclaim a programme.

Aden Colony. A British possession in southern Arabia; area 80 sq. m.; population (1955 census) 138,441, mostly Arabs. It is an important port of call on the route to the east, and has an oil and coal bunkering station and an oil refinery. It was first occupied by the British in 1839 and was for many years administered as part of India, but has been a colony since 1 April 1937. Government is by a Governor, with the assistance of an executive council and (since 1947) a legislative council, which became partly elective in January 1956. Since the elections in January 1959 the legislative council has consisted of 12 elected, 5 ex-officio and 6 nominated members, with an impartial speaker appointed by the Governor. The Aden Association, comprising merchants and professional men, aims at self-government within the British Commonwealth.

In 1951, when Persia nationalized its oil industries, the Anglo-Iranian Oil Co. (now the British Petroleum Co.) had already decided to set up a new refinery between Suez and India. A site was chosen at Little Aden, on the west side of the bay opposite the town of Aden, and construction began in November 1952. Oil began to flow through the refinery in August 1954. Aden is now an important bunkering port, most of the petroleum refined there being delivered in the form of bunkers to vessels using the port.

Aden Protectorate. A British possession in southern Arabia; area 112,000 sq. m.; population approximately 660,000. It is divided into the Western Aden Protectorate and the Eastern Aden Protectorate, which comprise two states, eleven sultanates, two amirates and nine sheikhdoms, all of which are in protective treaty relations with the U.K. Some of these communities accept British advice about their internal affairs and all agree to British management of their external affairs. In February 1959, 6 of the 17 Western Protectorate territories were formed into the Federation of the Arab Amirates of the South, also known as the Aden Federation, and the U.K. agreed by treaty to provide financial and military aid to help it to become, ultimately, an independent state. In October 1959 the Sultanate of Lahej joined the Federation, the capital of which is Ittihad City, north of the town of Aden. The neighbouring state of Yemen has opposed federation, regarding it as a breach of its 1951 agreement by which the U.K. promised to maintain the *status quo* in the disputed frontier areas.

Adenauer, Dr Konrad. West German Christian Democratic leader and Chancellor (Prime Minister); a Roman Catholic; born 5 January 1876. He studied law and economics at Freiburg, Munich and Bonn Universities and after holding a succession of local government posts in Cologne he became Lord Mayor in 1917. He was a member of the Provincial Diet of the Rhine Province from 1917 to 1933, and in 1919 supported the French attempt to detach the Rhineland from Germany. In 1933 he ordered the Nazi flags to be taken down on Hitler's visit to Cologne, and was removed by Hitler's supporter, Hermann Göring, from his post as Lord Mayor. Between 1933 and 1945 he was twice arrested by the Nazis but later released. At the end of the Second World War he became Mayor again, but was removed by the British occupation authorities for 'inefficiency'. He took part in the founding of the Christian Democratic Party in 1945 and was the President of the Bonn Parliamentary Council from 1948 to 1949. He has been a member of the Bundestag since 1949, when he was appointed Chancellor.

Afghanistan. An independent Central Asiatic state on the northern frontier of Western Pakistan; area 250,000 sq. m.; capital Kabul; the estimated population is 13,000,000, of which nomadic tribes constitute 2,000,000; the majority belong to the Sunni sect of the Islamic religion. In the eighteenth century Afghanistan conquered northern India but later declined in importance, and in the nineteenth century Russia and the U.K. decided that it should be a buffer state. In 1919 the U.K. agreed to recognize its independence, and this agreement binds Pakistan as the successor of the U.K. in that area. In 1927 and 1928 King Amanullah toured Europe and the Near East and on returning ordered the modernization of Afghanistan along Turkish Kemalist lines, including monogamy, European clothing, and abolition of women's veils. Accordingly the Mullahs, the powerful Moslem clergy, revolted in 1929 and expelled the King. After some internal disorder the head of the anti-Amanullah revolt, an Afghan chief, seized power, but was later defeated by other Afghans (with British backing) under General Nadir Shah. The General became King and introduced gradual reforms; he was assassinated in 1933. His son Zahir Shah (born 1914) is the present King. The King and his brother-in-law, the Prime Minister, Daoud Khan, have demanded the establishment of 'Pakhtunistan', *q.v.*, an enlarged Afghanistan which would rule the Pathans (Pakhtuns) in Western Pakistan, and incorporate all the territory west of the river Indus, down to the Arabian Sea. This plan is strongly opposed by Pakistan. Under the 1931 Constitution governmental powers are vested in the Council of Ministers; there is a Senate of 50 nominees, a National Council of 171 elected members, and a Grand Assembly which meets to make important decisions on policy matters. Nearly all the members of the Ministers' Council are related to the King. Only five per cent of the land is cultivated, and most of the population is engaged in agriculture and sheep-raising; there is a flourishing export trade in Persian lamb skins. Both the U.S.A. and the U.S.S.R. have given financial aid, and U.S. and German engineers have assisted in the construction of dams in the southern desert. Oil has been discovered near the Russian border and hydro-electric schemes are being developed. Afghanistan has one of the largest U.N. Technical Assistance missions.

A.F. of L. American Federation of Labour, *q.v.*

A.F. of L. – C.I.O. American Federation of Labour and Congress of Industrial Organizations, *q.v.*

Afro-Asian Conference. Held at Bandung, Indonesia, in April 1955, it was the first inter-continental conference of African and Asian peoples. The states represented were: Afghanistan, Cambodia, Ceylon, China, Egypt, Ethiopia, Gold Coast, India, Indonesia, Iraq, Japan, Jordan, Laos, Lebanon, Liberia, Libya, Nepal, Pakistan, Persia, Philippines, Saudi Arabia, Sudan, Syria, Thailand, Turkey, North Viet-Nam, South Viet-Nam, and Yemen. Observers included representatives from Cyprus (Archbishop Makarios, leader of the Enosis movement), the U.S.A. (a Negro Congressman), and the African National Congress. There were differences between the pro-western, pro-Communist, and neutralist blocs, but the Conference passed resolutions supporting economic and cultural co-operation, self-determination, the admission of Cambodia, Ceylon, Japan, Jordan, Laos, Libya, Nepal, and a unified Viet-Nam to the United Nations, and a resolution opposing colonialism, including French rule in Morocco and Tunisia and Dutch rule in Netherlands New Guinea. The Conference upheld the U.N. Declaration on Human Rights, in spite of Chinese objections.

Agent Provocateur. A French term meaning 'provoking agent'; a person sent, during political or social conflicts, into the adversary's ranks, in the disguise of an adherent, to provoke compromising actions. *Agents provocateurs* have been used in struggles between governments and revolutionary movements. In international politics *agents provocateurs* have been used to provide pretexts for interventions and wars by stirring up disorder and bringing about 'incidents'.

Aggression. An attack; but aggressors often deny any aggressive intention and claim to be acting merely in self-defence against an actual or anticipated attack, or more generally on behalf of law, order, and civilization. It was easy to name the aggressor in the cases of the Italian invasion of Ethiopia in 1935, the German invasions of Poland in 1939 and of the Low Countries and Norway and Denmark in 1940, and the Japanese onslaught on the U.S.A. in 1941. In other cases it is arguable whether or not there is aggression, particularly where there is a *coup d'état* with external aid.

Aggression was defined in the Convention for the Definition of Aggression of 3 July 1933 between Afghanistan, Estonia, Latvia, Persia, Poland, Rumania, Turkey, and the U.S.S.R. as existing wherever any of the following took place: (*a*) a declaration of war against another state; (*b*) an invasion by armed forces, without a declaration of war, of the territory of another state; (*c*) an attack by armed forces, without a declaration of war, on the territory, naval vessels, or aircraft of another state; (*d*) a naval blockade of the coasts or ports of another state; (*e*) aid to armed bands formed on the territory of another state and invading the other state, or refusal, despite the demands on the part of the state subjected to attack, to take all possible measures on its own territory to deprive those bands of any aid and protection. This definition was similar to one put forward in May 1933 by the Committee on Security Questions of the Disarmament Conference. The term is not defined in the United Nations Charter.

Åland Islands. A group of several hundred islands and islets in the northern Baltic Sea, half-way between Sweden and Finland, autonomous and administered with Finland since the Middle Ages; area 572 sq. m.; population (1959) 22,000, ninety-seven per cent Swedish-speaking. Mariehamn is the principal town. The islands could be used as a base for an attack on Finland, Sweden, or the U.S.S.R. Their holder could control the shipping route of Swedish iron ore to Germany. The Baltic powers therefore oppose their fortification. With Finland, they passed to Russia in 1809. Under an 1856 Convention between France, the U.K., and Russia, they were given a special international status and Russia, at Sweden's request, was forbidden to fortify them. After the Russian Revolution in 1917, the islanders by a plebiscite demanded annexation by Sweden. Swedish troops and later German troops occupied the islands until November 1918. Sweden and Finland disputed sovereignty over them and a treaty between ten states (excluding Russia) decided in 1921 that the islands belonged to Finland but should be granted self-government and demilitarized.

Alaska. A large peninsula on the north-western border of Canada and a member state of the U.S.A; area 586,400 sq. m.; population approximately 191,000; capital Juneau. Alaska was ruled by a Russian Governor in the nineteenth century until its purchase by the U.S.A. from Russia in 1867 for $7,200,000 at the instigation of Seward, the U.S. Secretary of State. 'Seward's Folly', as Alaska was known at the time of the purchase, produced sufficient gold in the subsequent twenty-five years to pay for itself forty-four times over. There are large forests and the minerals identified include gold, silver, oil, iron, coal, and tin. The question of the grant of statehood was hotly disputed for many years but in July 1958 the U.S. Congress finally agreed to admit Alaska to the Union; statehood was proclaimed on 3 January 1959, and formal entry took place on 4 July 1959.

Albania. An independent Balkan state on the Adriatic coast north of Greece; area 10,700 sq. m.; population (1959) 1,560,000 of whom more than half are Moslems; capital Tirana. The country was ruled by Turkey from 1467 to 1912, when it became an independent monarchy with a King, Prince Wilhelm of Wied, appointed by other European powers. From 1914 anarchy prevailed until a republic was proclaimed in 1925 under President Zogu who, as King Zog, reigned over the Kingdom of Albania from 1928 until the Italian invasion of 1939. The King of Italy then assumed the Albanian crown. After the defeat of Italy in the Second World War King Zog was deposed, and in 1946 a republic was again declared. The government is Communist; Enver Hoxha has led the Communist Party since 1945 and Haxhi Lleshi was appointed Head of State in 1953.

Albania is economically backward, but with aid from eastern Europe has developed oil refineries (it has its own oilfields), large textile factories, and a sugar refinery. Agricultural output by 1958 was more than twice the pre-war level and progress has been made with electric power schemes. The government is probably the first in Albania to establish its supremacy over every village.

Algeria. French North African territory; area 860,937 sq. m., most of it mountain and desert; capital Algiers; population 10,273,000, of whom approximately 1,100,000 are Europeans and the rest Arab and Berber Moslems. The number of Moslems is increasing at the rate of 200,000 per year. The territory was annexed by Napoleon III in 1865 and has since been part of France; it sends 66 deputies to the French National Assembly. The government and administration are centralized at Algiers in the person of the Governor-General who acts for the government of France. The territory comprises 13 Algerian and 2 Saharan departments.

The early French policy of confiscating land and settling French citizens (*politique de peuplement*), to provide French leaders and administrators for an Arab community, inspired hostility among the natives. Today Europeans farm 5,000,000 acres (one third of all the cultivable land) in the fertile coastal strip and produce early vegetables, wine and wheat for export to France at guaranteed prices, and virtually nothing for home consumption. Subsidies on Algerian wine and wheat are provided by metropolitan France. The introduction of mechanization and efficient farming methods has aggravated unemployment among Arab farm-workers; out of a working population of 2,300,000, Algeria has 400,000 permanently unemployed and a further 450,000 in seasonal employment. Attempts by the French government to extend to its Arab subjects the social services enjoyed by French citizens in France have been strongly resisted by the settlers. In 1947 an Algerian parliament was set up to deal with local affairs, French nationality was extended to all Algerians and posts in the civil service were opened to Moslems. The parliament never included supporters of the Arab nationalist movement as they withdrew from the elections which, they claimed, were controlled by the Europeans. Since it is treason to advocate nationalism in Algeria (as it is treason to attempt to overthrow the Republic on French soil), all nationalist organizations have been driven underground.

In 1954 the Front de Libération Nationale, *q.v.* (F.L.N.), the major nationalist movement, 'declared war' on France. Since then, despite the employment of modern weapons, of helicopters, and the admitted use of torture to extract information from suspects, 400,000 French troops have been unable to curb the rebellion. Considerable areas of the Oran and Constantine departments remain under the control of the nationalists. It is difficult to evaluate the true feelings of the largely illiterate native population who are terrorized both by the prospect of the penalties exacted by the French for treason and by fear of reprisal by the F.L.N. for collaborating with Europeans. However, the nationalists are known to have the support of the younger population, and they receive substantial unofficial assistance from the neighbouring Arab states of Tunisia and Morocco.

From the fall of Pierre Mèndes-France, *q.v.*, in 1955, until 1958, French governments failed to reconcile domestic demands for reduced taxes with increasing military expenditure in North Africa. They transferred the burden of the civil administration of Algeria to the army, but at the same time permitted the most violent criticism of army police methods to be circulated in France. The government disowned responsibility of the French aerial bombardment in February 1958 of the Tunisian village of Sakiet which, the army claimed, had been used as a supply base for Algerian rebels, and the French National Assembly on several occasions urged direct negotiation with the rebel leaders to secure a cease-fire. This was interpreted in Algeria as condonation of the rebellion, and a betrayal of French soldiers who were risking mutilation and death in order to keep Algeria within metropolitan France. On 13 May 1958 the military authorities, under General Salan, with the connivance of the former Resident-Minister, Jacques Soustelle, *q.v.*, and with the full support of the French settlers, refused to recognize the government of France. A Committee of Public Safety for Algeria was set up, and demanded the assumption of supreme power in France by General de Gaulle, *q.v.* This was successful in that de Gaulle was granted full powers by the French Assembly, but the proposals which he made for solving the Algerian problem were not acceptable to the settlers. These included: enough schools for all Moslem children by 1968;

the building of new industrial centres, the restoration of eroded and uncultivated land, and housing projects. Since these proposals could not be implemented without a cease-fire they would have to be preceded by complete military victory, for the F.L.N. has refused to negotiate a surrender except on the basis of independence, and not integration with France.

At a referendum held on 8 January 1961 the following question was put to the people of France and Algeria: Do you approve the draft law submitted to the French people by the President of the Republic concerning the self-determination of the people of Algeria and the organization of the public authorities in Algeria before self-determination? The draft law provided that, once peace was restored, the Algerian people would decide, by universal suffrage, what their future relationship with France was to be, and also that the administration in Algeria would be reorganized. Approximately 75 per cent of those voting approved of the draft law, and this was taken to signify approval, by the majority, of the principle of self-determination for Algeria. In April 1961 General de Gaulle suppressed an attempted *coup d'état* by French officers in Algeria.

France would have great difficulty in financing de Gaulle's policy of immediate social and political equality for Algerians without reducing, drastically, her own standard of living. At the same time, the discovery of oil deposits, estimated to exceed those of the entire Middle East, in southern Algeria in 1956, has made even more difficult French accession to nationalist demands for independence. France has invested substantial sums in oil development schemes, and work has begun on the laying of pipe-lines and the extension of railway tracks south from Touggourt, while wells at Hassi-Messaoud, near Ouargla, and at Edjelé, near the Libyan border, have been in operation since 1957.

Alternative Vote. An electoral system which gives a voter the right to state a second preference. If any candidate receives an absolute majority of votes at the first count, he is elected, and the second preferences are ignored. If no candidate gains an absolute majority at the first count, the second preferences of those who voted for anyone other than the first two candidates are added to the votes of those two candidates. The system was recommended for use in British elections by the 1911 Royal Commission on electoral reform, but has never been adopted. It should not be confused with Proportional Representation, *q.v.*

Alto Adige. An alternative description of the Italian Province of Bolzano (known as Bozen when under Austro-Hungarian rule).

The status of its German-speaking inhabitants is a matter of concern to the Austrian government, which describes the area as the South Tirol, *q.v.*

American Federation of Labour (A.F. of L.). A U.S. and Canadian labour movement with 9,605,840 members when it merged in December 1955 with the Congress of Industrial Organizations, *q.v.*, into a federation known as the American Federation of Labour and Congress of Industrial Organizations, *q.v.* The A.F. of L. was founded in 1881 by Samuel Gompers and Adolph Strasser, both members of the cigar-makers' union; its strength lay in the craft unions of the carpenters, cigar-makers, printers, iron and steel workers, and iron-moulders. It was their dislike of the emphasis on the importance of the craft unions that caused certain union leaders to form the Committee for Industrial Organization, and eventually the Congress of Industrial Organizations, as a seceding body, in 1935 and 1936. Though politically less radical in outlook than the C.I.O., the A.F. of L. generally supports the policies of the Democratic Party. It has been troubled, to a greater degree than the C.I.O., by inter-union raiding, racketeering (particularly in the longshoremen's union) and race discrimination. After the Second World War it refused to join the World Federation of Trade Unions, *q.v.*, on the ground that the Russian trade unions did not constitute a free and democratic movement. The President of the A.F. of L., George Meany, *q.v.*, signed the agreement for the merger of the A.F. of L. with the C.I.O. in February 1955.

American Federation of Labour and Congress of Industrial Organizations. A trade union movement established in the U.S.A. in December 1955 by the merger of the American Federation of Labour, *q.v.*, with the Congress of Industrial Organizations, *q.v.* The total membership is approximately 16,000,000. Each affiliated union of the A.F. of L. and the C.I.O. became an affiliate of the new movement. The merger marked the end of a split in the American labour movement which had lasted since 1936. George Meany, *q.v.*, became the President, and Walter Reuther, *q.v.*, became the leader of the Industrial Union Department, comprising most of the C.I.O. unions and some A.F. of L. unions.

Amnesty. From the Greek word meaning forgetfulness or oblivion; it is an act whereby the state pardons political or other offenders. Punishments threatened or imposed on them may be cancelled and those already in prison released. Amnesties are a frequent means of political reconciliation. They often occur after changes in the throne, presidency or régime. There are also amnesties for rebels and terrorists, and financial or tax amnesties, pardoning tax evaders on condition that they subsequently pay the taxes or subscribe to certain loans.

Anarchism. From the Greek word *anarchia* (non-rule), a political doctrine advocating the abolition of organized authority. Anarchists hold that every form of government is evil and a tyranny. They want a free association of individuals, without armed forces, courts, prisons or written law. Their methods have varied greatly; some have advocated peaceful transition to anarchy and others have demanded revolution. Anarchists murdered Tsar Alexander of Russia, King Humbert of Italy, President Carnot of France, Empress Elizabeth of Austria, and President McKinley of the U.S.A. Leo Tolstoy (1828–1910) was a religious anarchist. He said that the state was inconsistent with Christianity and that love should rule; people should refuse to render military service, to pay taxes or to recognize the courts, and the established order would collapse. His principles of non-violence and non-co-operation were adopted in India by Gandhi. International anarchist congresses were held in 1877 and 1907 but anarchism proper never succeeded in setting up a permanent organization. Syndicalism, *q.v.*, a modified branch of anarchism, became an organized mass movement in a few, mostly Latin, countries.

Andorra. A republic in the Pyrenees under the joint rule of France and Spain; area 175 sq. m.; population about 5,200, living in six villages, and speaking Catalan; capital Andorra. The Andorran valleys established their independence in the ninth century; in 1278 they were placed under the joint suzerainty of the Comte de Foix, whose rights passed to France on the accession of Henri IV in 1589, and of the Spanish Bishop of Urgel.

There is a General Council of the Valleys, of twenty-four members elected by some of the inhabitants, which can submit motions and proposals to the Permanent Delegations established by the co-suzerains. The franchise was extended by a bloodless revolution in April 1933 but restricted again in 1940. A French law nationalizing all French radio stations and thus abolishing radio advertisements has been ignored by the General Council of the Valleys, which continues to permit Radio Andorra to broadcast to Andorra and to a large area of south-west France. France claimed in 1953 that the General Council was not a representative body and for some time jammed Radio Andorra and closed the frontier.

Angola. A Portuguese territory, also known as Portuguese West Africa, on the west coast of southern Africa, to the south of the Congo

Republic (formerly the Belgian Congo) and north of South-West Africa; area 481,351 sq. m.; population 4,750,000, of whom 170,000 are white; capital St Paul de Luanda, also known as Luanda. Angola was a colony until 1951, when it became technically an overseas territory; it was incorporated as a province of metropolitan Portugal in 1955. There are believed to be considerable mineral resources.

The region was discovered by the Portuguese in 1482 and, except for the years 1641 to 1648 when it was held by the Dutch, has been occupied by them since then. For three hundred years it was exploited as a source of slaves, of whom several millions were exported to the Americas; now the main products are coffee, diamonds, and fishmeal, and forced labour is forbidden by law except for public service, punishment, or non-payment of taxes. The laws as to forced labour are, however, evaded with official sanction.

Annexation. The act whereby a state takes possession of a territory formerly belonging to another state, or to no state at all. It is a unilateral action without the consent, or at least the voluntary consent, of the former possessor. It confers full rights of sovereignty, and thus differs from other actions which practically or temporarily confer similar rights but are not annexations proper, such as military occupation, a United Nations trusteeship, or the establishment of a protectorate. The annexed population become subjects of the annexing state. Acquisition of territory by purchase or lease, as a bilateral action, is not spoken of as annexation.

Antarctic Continent. An area of approximately 5,000,000 sq. m. around the South Pole which has been the subject of conflicting claims. Most of its coastline has been charted but little is known of large portions of the interior. The claimants to various parts include: Argentina, Australia, Chile, France, New Zealand, Norway, the U.K., and the U.S.S.R.

The U.K., with sixteen bases in the Antarctic, claims the Falkland Islands Dependencies (South Georgia, South Orkney, South Sand-wich Islands, South Shetland Island, Coots Land, Graham Land, and some land adjacent to the South Pole). British claims are based on a number of acts of sovereignty between 1678 and 1843. Argentina, with eight bases in this area, claims sovereignty over most of these Dependencies. Chile, with four bases in the area, claims sovereignty over the western part of the Dependencies (including some of the land claimed by Argentina) and over a sector farther to the west. It claims that it is the rightful successor of Spain, and that Charles V in the sixteenth century regarded the area as Spanish and as coming within the jurisdiction of the Governors of Chile from 1555 onwards.

17

British offers in December 1954 to refer the matter to the International Court of Justice were not accepted by Argentina and Chile. In March 1956 the Court rejected a British request for the recognition of British sovereignty and for a declaration against Argentinian and Chilean 'pretensions and encroachment', on the ground that it had no powers in the matter since Argentina and Chile would not accept the Court's jurisdiction.

Norway claims Queen Maud Land, a sector east of the Falkland Islands Dependencies up to the 45th meridian of east longitude. Farther east lies the Australian Antarctic Territory of about 2,742,000 sq. m., said to be rich with mineral deposits including coal, and a valuable source of food supplies (whale, fish, seals, plankton, etc.). It was established by an Order in Council dated 7 February 1933 and comprises all Antarctic territories (except Adélie Land, claimed by France) south of the 60th parallel and lying between the 45th and 160th meridians of east longitude. From the 160th meridian of east longitude to the 150th meridian of west longitude lies the Ross Dependency, established under the jurisdiction of New Zealand by an Order in Council dated 30 July 1923. The U.S.S.R., whose ships have whaled in and charted parts of the Antarctic, stated in 1950 that it would regard no boundary decisions as valid unless it participated in such decisions.

In December 1959 the representatives of Argentina, Australia, Belgium, Chile, France, Japan, New Zealand, Norway, South Africa, the U.K., the U.S.A., and the U.S.S.R. concluded a treaty, the main effects of which were to suspend all territorial claims and disputes in the area, to establish free use of the Continent for scientific work, and to set up a mutual inspection system to prevent any military activities, including nuclear explosions. The treaty applies to all land south of the 60th parallel and is subject to review after 30 years.

Anti-Clericalism. Opposition to organized religion and, in particular, to the influence of the Roman Catholic Church in politics. It is not a coherent political doctrine, but anti-clericalists of different parties tend to unite in their opposition to the Roman Catholics on specific issues, such as the provision of state grants for Roman Catholic schools and facilities for divorce.

Anti-Semitism. Hostility towards the Jews. In the twentieth century religious anti-semitism has been replaced by racial anti-semitism; Germany under the Nazi régime was a centre of this doctrine. Racial anti-semitism emerged in the middle of the nineteenth century simultaneously with theories about the Aryan or Nordic race, which provided for it a pseudo-scientific basis. It arises partly from economic jealousy, the Jews having achieved important positions in many trades and liberal professions, and partly from a feeling of inferiority on the part of those who consider themselves to be failures, and wish to blame some easily identifiable group for this.

In Nazi Germany Hitler adopted the distinction between Aryans and non-Aryans, and made laws along those lines. The Jews were declared to be a foreign and inferior race, with a poisoned blood which made them criminals by nature; marriage and love-making between Jews and Aryans were forbidden. Jewish scientists, including Einstein and Freud, were driven into exile, and music by Mendelssohn and Offenbach was banned. The Jews were deprived of civic rights, banned from trades and professions, and sent to concentration camps.

Eastern Europe was also a centre of anti-semitism in the first half of the twentieth century. The post-1945 constitutions guaranteed racial tolerance, but there has been anti-semitism under the Communist régimes, though on a far smaller scale. In Poland and Rumania broadcasts and newspaper articles have attacked the Jews in general and the government of Israel in particular. The high percentage of Jews who were in cabinet posts immediately after 1945 has diminished. In the U.S.S.R., where there are approximately 2,200,000 Jews, and where after the 1917 Revolution Jews were treated well and promised a Jewish autonomous state, Yiddish theatres, books, newspapers, and journals have largely disappeared. Religious worship by Jews, however, is not discouraged.

A.N.Z.U.S. (Australia, New Zealand, and the United States). An expression used to describe the tripartite security treaty concluded between the three countries at San Francisco on 1 September 1951. Under the treaty, which remains in force indefinitely, 'each party recognizes that an armed attack in the Pacific area on any of the other parties would be dangerous to its own peace and safety, and declares that it would act to meet the common danger in accordance with its constitutional processes'. An armed attack is deemed to include 'an armed attack on the metropolitan territory of any of the parties, or on the island territories under its jurisdiction in the Pacific, or on its armed forces, vessels or aircraft in the Pacific'. The parties agree to maintain and develop their capacity to resist armed attack 'by means of continuous self-help and mutual aid'. The pact symbolized a re-orientation on the part of Australia and New Zealand towards the U.S.A. and away from the U.K., which, according to a statement made in Parliament in April 1951 by Herbert Morrison, then Foreign Secretary, wanted to be a party to the treaty.

Apartheid. Afrikaans word (literally 'apart-hood') meaning racial segregation as practised by the National Party which came to power in South Africa in 1948. There had been racial segregation in South Africa from the mid-seventeenth century when European colonization began, but the National Party in particular introduced a series of measures affecting nearly all aspects of the life of the non-whites, who form seventy-nine per cent of the population. The policy involves racial purity and segregation, and white paramountcy (*baaskap*). Ideally it means that the races should be given separate and equal opportunities, but supporters and opponents alike agree that this is almost impossible. The laws introduced by the National Party have affected the political rights of non-whites, and their rights of movement, choice of residence, property, choice of occupation and marriage. Other laws have established separate non-white territorial units, as part of the concept know as Bantustan, *q.v.* In 1953 it was made a crime for a native worker to participate in, or to instigate, a strike; regulations as to the mixing of races were altered after a court decision that facilities must be equal, so that segregation is now valid whether the facilities are equal or not; and responsibility for native education was transferred from the Provinces to the Minister for Native Affairs, who in introducing the law stated that teachers who believed in equality were not desirable teachers for the natives. *Apartheid* was debated by the General Assembly of the United Nations in 1952, it being suggested that the policy constituted a threat to peace and a violation of human rights. A commission of three (of which Dr Bunche, *q.v.*, was a member) was set up to investigate the problem, and, though refused permission to enter South Africa, reported its condemnation of the policy of *apartheid* and hoped that the South African government would change its views. The United Party, which is the main opposition party in South Africa, approves of the principle of *apartheid*, though disagreeing with some of the methods used to carry it out.

Arab Federation. A federation of the two independent states of Iraq, *q.v.*, and Jordan, *q.v.*, proclaimed on 14 February 1958 by the late King Faisal of Iraq and King Hussein of Jordan. The Federation agreement provided for the two states to have an army and defence ministry, a diplomatic service and a foreign ministry, a currency and customs system, an educational structure and a legislature in common. The head of state was to be King Faisal, with King Hussein as his deputy. Membership of the federation was to be open to any other Arab state.

The federation was widely interpreted as a reaction to the establishment of the United Arab Republic by Egypt and Syria. Its constitution was approved by the parliaments of Iraq and Jordan on 27 March 1958. After the necessary constitutional amendments had been passed in both countries, the federation became effective on 13 May 1958, when it became known as the Arab Union, *q.v.*

Arab League. A loose confederation of Arab states (Egypt, Iraq, Jordan, Lebanon, Saudi Arabia, Syria, and Yemen) established on 10 May 1945, as a result of the Arab Unity Preparatory Conference held at Alexandria in the autumn of 1944. The League reflects Arab nationalist sentiments which have become increasingly apparent in the twentieth century. It has been especially concerned with: (1) the crisis in the Levant in 1945, when it supported Syrian and Lebanese independence rather than continued French occupation, (2) Palestine, *q.v.*, which it wanted to remain an Arab land, and where it opposed the establishment of the state of Israel, (3) the French occupation of Algeria, where it believes that France has wrongly withheld self-government from the native population.

The League, and Egypt's leadership within the League, were greatly weakened by the adherence to the Baghdad Pact, *q.v.*, of Iraq, which had played a big part in the creation of the League in 1945. Strong opposition to the Pact was expressed in Egypt and Syria on the grounds that the Arabs should be an independent force in international affairs with a unified policy. On achieving independence Libya and Sudan joined the Arab League. The significance of the League increased with the creation in February 1958 of the United Arab Republic, *q.v.* In 1958 Morocco and Tunisia joined the Arab League.

Arab South. A term used by Arabs to describe Aden Colony, *q.v.*, Aden Protectorate, *q.v.*, and Yemen, *q.v.*, with the addition sometimes of the Sultanate of Muscat and Oman, *q.v.*, to the east of the Aden Protectorate

Arab Union. The name given to the Arab Federation, *q.v.*, uniting the two independent states of Iraq, *q.v.*, and Jordan, *q.v.*, when, after the necessary constitutional amendments, the Federation became effective on 13 May 1958. A Union cabinet was then established under the premiership of an Iraqi, the late General Nuri es-Said, who had resigned as Prime Minister of Iraq to take up the new post. In addition to a Jordanian deputy-premier, there were three ministers with responsibility for foreign affairs, defence and finance (which were federal matters) and two ministers without portfolio. After the *coup d'état* in Iraq on 14 July 1958, involving the murder of King Faisal and General Nuri es-Said, King Hussein claimed to have succeeded

King Faisal as head of state; Iraq thereupon formally announced its withdrawal from the Union. The Jordan government then issued a decree acknowledging that, as from 1 August, the Union had ceased to exist.

Arabia. The Arab peninsula, also described as Arabia proper as distinct from other Arab-inhabited countries. It comprises the independent states of Bahrain, Kuwait, Muscat and Oman, Saudi Arabia and Yemen, the independent states of the Trucial Coast, and the Colony and Protectorate of Aden.

Argentina. An independent republic and the second largest country in South America; area 1,112,743 sq. m.; population (1958) 20,435,000 of whom ninety-three per cent are Roman Catholics; capital Buenos Aires. It achieved independence of Spain in 1816; its government is based on the 1853 Constitution revised in 1860, 1866, 1898 and 1957, and modelled on the U.S. Constitution. The republic comprises twenty-three provinces and the federal district of Buenos Aires. A President, elected for a term of six years, controls the executive and selects the cabinet; the National Congress has a Senate representing the provinces and a House of Deputies elected on a population basis.

The republic produces large cereal crops and is the world's leading exporter of meat, but its economic situation is unhealthy. In 1955, according to a survey by the U.N. Economic Commission for Latin America, the national income per head was only 3·5 per cent higher than in 1945 and there was a serious balance of payments deficit caused by: (1) falling exports; (2) an increase in petroleum imports brought about by the country's failure to make the most of its resources; and (3) an emphasis on industrialization at the expense of agriculture, which had fallen behind technically and lacked man-power. The government had neither made the investments needed to provide the country with the fuel and power supplies required for its economic growth, nor created favourable conditions for private enterprise to make such investments. In October 1955 the government issued a number of decrees in immediate implementation of the United Nations survey.

From 1946 to 1955 the President was Juan Perón who, although he successfully submitted himself for re-election in 1952, established a dictatorship under which the National Congress, organizations of employers and employees, women's movements and youth movements, newspapers and universities, were deprived of their independence and made to support Perón. He had a considerable popular following, particularly among industrial workers whose real income he increased by forty-seven per cent during his nine years of office at the expense of agricultural and middle-class workers. The Confederation of Labour was one of the main supports of his régime. The whole of the population benefited, however, by some of Perón's social measures, which included a system of medical attention at low cost, based on monthly contributions; pensions for all; and a huge beneficent organization, the Eva Perón Foundation, founded by his wife, to which everyone was obliged to contribute two days' pay yearly. In 1954 Perón alienated the Roman Catholic Church, with which he was already on bad terms, by introducing laws to legalize divorce (for the first time in the country's history) and prostitution (which had been banned since 1936), to end religious instruction in state schools, to end tax exemption for religious institutions, churches and schools, and to authorize a national assembly to alter the constitutional rules linking Church and State.

The Perón régime was overthrown by a four-day revolt of the armed forces in September 1955; General Eduardo Lonardi, who had previously played no part in politics, became Provisional President, removed all outward signs of the former régime, and dissolved the National Congress, the Supreme Court appointed by Perón, and the Perónista Party. Lonardi was replaced in November 1955 by General Pedro Eugenio Aramburu, Chief of the General Staff, in the course of a *coup d'état* organized by liberal political and military leaders who thought that the Provisional President intended to govern as Perón did, but with a pro-Catholic programme. The Aramburu government confirmed the measures introduced by Lonardi, abolished brothels and made divorce illegal, and returned to its rightful owner the important newspaper *La Prensa*.

The overthrow of the Perón régime, the subsequent devaluation of the peso, and stringent foreign exchange regulations were not followed by economic recovery, and the presidential election in February 1958 produced a substantial majority for a radical lawyer, Arturo Frondizi, who received considerable support from the working masses who once favoured Perón. His policy was to cut imports, develop local industry, overhaul the economy, and invite foreign companies to help in the exploitation of Argentina's oil resources.

Aswan Dam. An important dam on the river Nile in southern Egypt, completed in 1899 by British engineers. Its name is often used to describe a new and larger dam farther south, which is known as the High Dam, *q.v.*

Atlantic Charter. A declaration made jointly by Franklin D. Roosevelt, President of the U.S.A., and Winston Churchill, Prime Minister of the U.K., after their meetings in mid-Atlantic in August 1941. It stated the common principles in the policies of the two countries on which the two men based their hopes for a better future for the world. These were: (1) the U.S.A. and the U.K. seek no territorial or other aggrandisement; (2) they desire to see no territorial changes that do not accord with the freely expressed wishes of the peoples concerned; (3) they respect the rights of all peoples to choose the form of government under which they live; (4) they will endeavour to further the enjoyment by all states, victor or vanquished, of access on equal terms to the trade and to the raw materials of the world which are needed for their economic prosperity; (5) they desire to bring about the fullest collaboration between all nations in the economic field; (6) after the destruction of Nazi tyranny they hope to see established a peace in which all nations can dwell in safety within their own boundaries, and which will afford assurance that all the men in all the lands may live out their lives in freedom from fear and want; (7) such a peace should enable all men to traverse the high seas without hindrance; (8) they believe that all nations must abandon the use of force and that, pending the establishment of a wide and permanent system of general security, the disarmament of nations which threaten or may threaten aggression is essential; they will aid and encourage all practicable measures which will lighten for peace-loving peoples the crushing burden of armaments.

Atomic Energy Acts, 1946 and 1954. U.S. laws providing for the development and control of atomic energy. The 1946 Act authorizes programmes: (1) to foster research and development in order to encourage scientific and industrial progress; (2) to disseminate as much information as is consistent with security requirements; (3) to make the benefits of the peaceful application of atomic energy available internationally; and (4) to ensure that the government should control the possession and production of fissionable material so as to make the maximum contribution to common defence and security. The Act established an Atomic Energy Commission to supervise these programmes. The 1954 Act allowed private enterprises to participate in the development of peacetime uses of atomic energy, and permitted international agreements to be made for the exchange of secret information.

Atomic Energy Commission. A term used to describe: (1) the body set up by the United Nations in 1946 in its attempt to obtain international agreement on disarmament, *q.v.*, and merged in 1951 with the Conventional Armaments Commission to form the Disarmament Commission; and (2) the body established in the U.S.A. to supervise the atomic energy programme authorized by the Atomic Energy Acts, 1946 and 1954, *q.v.*

Attlee, 1st Earl, Clement Richard Attlee, leader of the British Parliamentary Labour Party from 1935 to 1955; born 3 January 1883 and educated at Haileybury College and University College, Oxford. After practising as a lawyer for three years he moved to the East End of London, where he worked in settlements, including Toynbee Hall, and became an ardent Socialist. From 1913 to 1923 he was a lecturer at the London School of Economics. After serving in the First World War he was active in local government and entered the House of Commons in 1922 as the member for Limehouse. He was Parliamentary Private Secretary to Ramsay MacDonald, 1922–4, Under-Secretary of State for War in 1924, Chancellor of the Duchy of Lancaster, 1930–1 and Postmaster-General in 1931. He was then deputy leader of the Parliamentary Labour Party for four years and succeeded George Lansbury as its leader in 1935, in an election in which he defeated Arthur Greenwood and Herbert Morrison. During the Second World War he was successively Lord Privy Seal, Dominions Secretary and Lord President of the Council. He was Prime Minister of the Labour government which held office from 1945 to 1951. After 1951 he led the Labour Party in opposition in the House of Commons, and retired in 1955, when he accepted an earldom. He rarely committed himself publicly on the supposed policy differences between the right and left wings of the Labour Party, but contrived to remain undisputed leader as a result of his political shrewdness and a refusal to identify himself with any faction.

Australia. A Dominion within the British Commonwealth; area 2,974,581 sq. m.; population (1959) 10,008,665; federal capital Canberra. It comprises the six former British colonies of New South Wales, Victoria, South Australia, Queensland, Western Australia, and Tasmania which were federated, as states, under the name of the 'Commonwealth of Australia' on 1 January 1901. The Northern Territory was transferred from South Australia to the Commonwealth in 1911. Each state retained the constitution, subject to changes embodied in the Commonwealth constitution and subsequent alterations, by which it had been governed before federation, and the powers of the Federal Parliament, although they now embrace defence, foreign affairs, finance and social services, are strictly limited. Each state legislature consists of a Governor, representing the Queen, an upper and lower house of parliament (except in Queensland where the upper house was abolished in 1922), a cabinet led by a premier, and an executive council. The states have equal representation in the Senate, the upper house of the Federal Parliament, which comprises 60 senators chosen for six years with half the members retiring every three years. In 1958 there were 124 members in the lower chamber, the House of Representatives, but as they are elected in proportion to the population the number may increase or decrease; no state may send fewer than five. Since 1922 the Northern Territory has had one representative in the lower house who is not entitled to vote except on matters which directly concern the Territory. In 1948 similar representation was provided for the Australian Capital Territory (area 939 sq. m.) which includes Canberra. Both chambers are elected by universal adult suffrage and voting has been compulsory since 1925. The House of Representatives is normally elected every three years; in certain circumstances, for instance disagreement with the Senate, there can be an earlier dissolution.

The right-wing, conservative Liberal Party, led by Robert Menzies, *q.v.*, who became Prime Minister in 1949, forms a government coalition with the Country Party, which represents Australian farming interests and opposes any revaluation of the undervalued Australian pound. The coalition won 77 seats at the 1958 General Election, a gain of 2 seats. The Communist Party has no parliamentary representation. The Menzies government passed a Bill dissolving the Communist Party which was ruled as unconstitutional in the High Court and abandoned in 1951 after it had been submitted to a referendum. The Australian Labour Party (45 seats) is divided into two factions: a secular group which includes most of the trade unions, the Socialists and some intellectuals, and a Catholic, anti-Communist group which ran its own candidates at the 1958 elections and has two seats in the Senate. Approximately three-quarters of Australia's Catholic population of over 2,000,000 vote Labour, and Catholic Action organizations have tried to use the party as an instrument of Catholic social policy and as a method of influencing the trade unions. The party was last united under the late Joseph Benedict Chifley, who, while married to a Protestant, was a Catholic progressive; the present leader is Arthur A. Calwell, *q.v.*, who holds similar views.

Although the Australian economy is still dependent on the export of wool, manufacturing industries have undergone rapid expansion since 1945. The country does not attract enough capital to keep pace with the demands of a growing population for an increasing standard of living but there has been considerable U.S. investment and substantial borrowing by the state governments from private American investors. The U.K., however, remains Australia's most important trading partner and source of new immigrants, of whom 125,000 (all European) are admitted every year.

Austria. A Central European state between Italy and the German Federal Republic, and created after the First World War from the German-speaking Alpine provinces of the former Austro-Hungarian Empire; area 34,064 sq. m.; population (1954) 6,968,500, of whom eighty-nine per cent are Roman Catholics; capital Vienna. In 1934 a clerico-Fascist group seized power under Dollfuss and suppressed both a popular rising in defence of the republican constitution and a Nazi rising in which Dollfuss was killed. In 1938 German troops marched in and the German dictator Adolf Hitler annexed Austria. A majority of Austrians may have been ready to accept a federal relationship with Germany, but many Socialists, Catholics, and Monarchists resented the compulsory union. In 1945 the victorious allied powers occupied Austria and divided it into four zones which were occupied by France, the U.K., the U.S.A., and the U.S.S.R., and a provisional Austrian government restored the republic as it had existed before 1938.

In July 1955 Austria became a free and independent state for the first time since 1938, upon the ratification of the Austrian State Treaty, which was concluded in May 1955 by the four occupying powers. All occupation forces were withdrawn from Austria by 25 October 1955. A constitutional law was then passed by which Austria is pledged to remain permanently a neutral country.

A General Election was held in May 1959 to elect 165 Deputies to the National Assembly, the lower house of the Federal Parliament. The two large centre parties, the Roman Catholic, conservative, Austrian People's Party (led by Julius Raab) and the moderate left-wing Socialist Party (led by Bruno Pittermann), once more emerged as the dominant group. The Austrian People's Party, which represents business and peasant interests and believes in a deflationary policy, lost 3 seats, 79 of its candidates being returned. The Socialist Party, supporting the welfare state and policies similar to those of the British Labour Party, with which it has close ties, gained 4 seats, 78 of its candidates being returned. The right-wing Austrian Freedom Party won 8 seats. After the election the coalition formed by the People's Party and the Socialists, under Dr Raab, the Federal Chancellor or Prime Minister, continued in office. Dr Raab was succeeded, in April 1961, as Chancellor and as leader of the People's Party, by Dr Alfons Gorbach.

The proportion of the population engaged in agriculture fell from thirty-three per cent in 1939 to twenty-two per cent in 1956, and there has been rapid progress in the industries concerned with hydro-electric power, steel, and oil. In 1946 many businesses, including the three largest commercial banks, every oil-producing and refining company, and most coal-mining, steel producing, and iron and steel manufacturing firms, were nationalized.

The status of the German-speaking inhabitants of the South Tirol, *q.v.*, (alternatively known as the Alto Adige, *q.v.*) in Italy, is a source of friction between Austria and Italy.

Autarky. From the Greek word *autarkeia* (often spelt 'autarchy', self-rule, by mistaken analogy with 'diarchy', dual rule) meaning self-sufficiency. In the economic sense it conveys the idea that a country should produce at home everything it requires and should cease to depend on imports. The drive for autarky was particularly strong in Germany before the Second World War, being adopted with a view to making Germany blockade-proof.

Authoritarian. A term denoting a dictatorial system of government, as opposed to a democratic system based on popular sovereignty. Adherents of authoritarianism criticize the alleged delays and inefficiency of the democratic system, and praise the advantages of a strong state authority.

Autonomy. A word of Greek origin ('self-law') meaning self-government.

Awolowo, Obafemi. Nigerian politician; born in 1910 and educated at London University, where he took degrees in law and commerce. He then qualified as a barrister, and on returning to Nigeria was engaged in journalism and founded the *Nigerian Tribune* in Ibadan. He is Prime Minister of the Western Region of Nigeria, and founder and leader of the Action Group.

Azikiwe, Dr Nnamdi. Nigerian leader; born in 1904 and educated at Lincoln and Pennsylvania Universities in the U.S.A. At Lincoln University he became an instructor in history and political science. He has been Governing Director of the African Continental Bank, Ltd, and Chairman of Associated Newspapers of Nigeria, Ltd, and of the African Book Company, Ltd, a member of the Nigerian Legislative Council and of the Eastern Region House of Assembly, and Prime Minister and Minister of Local Government in the Eastern Region. He led a political party, the National Council of Nigeria and the Cameroons. In January 1957 a Tribunal reported the results of an inquiry into allegations of improper conduct arising from his government's acquisition of the African Continental Bank which he controlled. The Tribunal found that although Azikiwe's primary motive was to liberalize credit, his conduct had 'fallen short of the expectations of honest, reasonable people'; it added that he should have relinquished his interest in the Bank when the proposal to inject public monies into it was first made, and that 'he was guilty of misconduct as a minister in failing to do so'. He took office as Governor-General of Nigeria in November 1960, after the country became independent.

B

Baghdad Pact. A treaty concluded between Iraq and Turkey in February 1955 and open, for accession, to any member-state of the Arab League or any other state actively concerned with security and peace in the Middle East and 'which is fully recognized by both of the parties'. Israel, which is not recognized by Iraq, was therefore prohibited from joining the Pact. The U.K., Pakistan, and Persia acceded in 1955. Article One of the Pact stated: 'The parties will co-operate for their security and defence. Such measures as they agree to take to give effect to this co-operation may form the subject of special agreements with each other.' There was no provision that each member should regard an attack on another as an attack on itself, or that a member which was attacked must be helped. Iraq and the U.K. entered into one of the special agreements envisaged on 4 April 1955, when they renewed the Anglo-Iraqi treaty of alliance of 1930, which was due to expire in 1957, and the U.K. simultaneously acceded to the Baghdad Pact. Under Article Six a permanent council at ministerial level was to be set up when at least four powers had become parties to the Pact. The council held its first meeting at Baghdad in November 1955. A military committee, and an economic committee to plan regional developments, were set up.

The Pact had been described in the U.K. and the U.S.A. as a 'northern tier' of defence for the Middle East against any encroachments by the U.S.S.R. The Russian government stated in October 1955 that the Pact involved the formation in the Near and Middle East of a military grouping which was an instrument of aggressive circles who were not interested in the consolidation of peace and international security. In May and June 1957 U.S. representatives became members of the economic and military committees although the U.S.A. did not accede to the Pact itself.

Iraq ceased to take part in arrangements relating to the Pact after its revolution in July 1958, and formally withdrew in March 1959. On 21 August 1959 the organization was renamed the Central

Treaty Organization. Its headquarters had already been transferred, in October 1958, from Baghdad to Ankara.

Bahrain. An independent state on the west coast of the Persian Gulf, comprising a group of islands, area 231 sq. m., of which the largest is Bahrain; population 143,213, mostly Moslems of the Shia and Sunni sects, and a number of Britons, Americans, Indians, and Persians; capital Manama. It was ruled by Persia (which still claims sovereignty) until 1782, and thereafter by a family originating in Kuwait. It has been under British protection since 1861.

In 1932 oil was discovered by the Bahrain Petroleum Co., of which Standard Oil Co. of California, and Texas Co., each own fifty per cent. Profits were divided between the sheikhdom and the oil company on a fifty-fifty basis; of the sheikhdom's share, the family of the ruler (Sulman bin Hamad Al Khalifah, born 1895, and Sheikh since 1942) receives one third, and the government two thirds. Bahrain also has the world's fifth largest oil refinery. Although the oil revenue accounts for three quarters of the national income, Bahrain is not wholly dependent on oil; it has long been a centre of Persian Gulf trade, an entrepôt for trade from the interior of Saudi Arabia, and a base for the pearl-fishing industry. Its airport has an important position on international civil air routes. There has been considerable expenditure on education and public health during the last thirty years.

Balance of Payments. The balance between the cost of a country's imports and the receipts for its exports. The chief items will usually be visible imports and exports, but there will also be invisible imports (such as tourist expenditure in foreign countries and the interest paid on loans from foreign countries) and invisible exports (such as the expenditure of foreign tourists, the interest paid by foreign countries on loans made to them and payments for banking, shipping and insurance services performed for foreigners).

Balance of Power. The theory that the strength of one group of powers on the European continent should be equal to the strength of the other group, thus preventing any hegemony and ensuring peace. The maintenance of this balance was for many years the traditional object of British foreign policy, and the long period of peace from 1871 to 1914 was achieved by the balance between the German-Austrian-Italian group (the Triple Alliance) and the Anglo-French-Russian group (the Triple Entente). After the First World War the theory of the balance of power passed into diplomatic history; the U.K. appeased but did not oppose the most powerful continental state, Germany, until 1939. Since 1945 there has been no attempt by the U.K. to maintain a balance of power; its influence has been used in an effort to create a preponderance of power in favour of the western against the eastern nations.

Balfour Declaration. A letter from A. J. Balfour, then Foreign Secretary, to Lord Rothschild, Chairman of the British Zionist Federation, in which the founding of a Jewish national home in Palestine, *q.v.*, was promised. The letter, dated 2 November 1917, read as follows: 'His Majesty's Government view with favour the establishment in Palestine of a national home for the Jewish people, and will use their best endeavours to facilitate the achievement of this object, it being clearly understood that nothing shall be done which may prejudice the civil and religious rights of the existing non-Jewish communities in Palestine or the rights and political status enjoyed by Jews in any other country.' There was considerable dispute as to whether this Declaration contradicted the undertaking given to the Arabs in the McMahon Correspondence, *q.v.*, but Jews were admitted to Palestine, although only on limited annual quotas, between the First and Second World Wars. The independent state of Israel, *q.v.*, was established on 14 May 1948.

Balkan Pact. A military treaty of alliance between Greece, Turkey, and Yugoslavia, signed in Bled on 9 August 1954. It is a development of a treaty of friendship and collaboration, signed in Ankara in February 1953.

A Yugoslavian alliance has been a basic principle of Greek foreign policy since before 1914, in view of Greek fears of attack from Italy and Bulgaria. Since the fourteenth century there has been no serious conflict between Serbs and Greeks. The only exception has been the period 1944–8, when a pro-Russian Yugoslavia supported Bulgaria and Rumania, old enemies of Greece. Friction between Italy and Yugoslavia has made Italy oppose this friendship between Greece and Yugoslavia. In 1934, during the negotiations with Yugoslavia for the first Balkan Pact, the Greeks had to insist on 'the Italian clause', which automatically prevented Greece from going to war if Italy were involved in any conflict with Yugoslavia. The Pact marked an improvement in Greco-Turkish relations but these deteriorated as a result of the Cyprus dispute. Yugoslavia and Turkey were estranged in the period 1944–8 when the U.S.S.R., in alliance with Yugoslavia, appeared to be threatening Turkey; nevertheless both countries have much to gain from mutual trade.

Yugoslavia has been reluctant to strengthen the Pact as it considers that international tension has been reduced; Turkey has adopted a more cautious attitude towards developments in Russian policy and has demanded more military co-operation between the three countries. A Permanent Council was established under the Pact and held its first meeting in Ankara in February 1955. It adopted an earlier recommendation that a three-power Consultative Assembly should be set up, composed of twenty parliamentary delegates from each country, and to meet in each capital in turn. It also decided to hold a tripartite economic conference to discuss economic co-operation.

Bamboo Curtain. The barrier often said to be formed by the frontiers of China since the establishment of the Communist régime and the Chinese People's Republic. At the Afro-Asian Conference, *q.v.*, in 1955, the Chinese Prime Minister, Chou En-lai, denied the existence of a 'bamboo curtain' and said that the delegates to the Conference could all visit China. Those who believe that such a barrier exists allege that there is no freedom of movement in and out of China. The expression 'iron curtain', *q.v.*, may be compared with this term.

Banda, Dr Hastings Kamuzu, Nyasaland politician; born in 1905 and educated, after running away from home at the age of 13 to work in the gold mines of South Africa, at the Wilberforce University High School, Ohio, the University of Chicago, the Meharry Medical College in Nashville, Tennessee, and Edinburgh University, where he qualified as a doctor of medicine. He practised medicine for many years in London but his concern for the future of Nyasaland caused him to return in July 1958. There followed a series of meetings and riots which culminated in the declaration of a state of emergency on 3 March 1959, a declaration that the African National (later the Malawi) Congress was illegal, and the arrest of Banda, its President-General, with 166 of its members. He was released in April 1960.

Bandaranaike, Sirimavo. Ceylon politician; born 1916, the daughter of a prosperous Kandyan land-owning family, and educated at Roman Catholic convent schools, she is a Buddhist. In 1940 she married Solomon West Ridgway Diaz Bandaranaike (born 1909) who became Prime Minister in April 1956 as leader of the Sri Lanka Freedom Party (S.L.F.P.) and was assassinated by a Buddhist monk on 25 September 1959. She did not engage in political work during the lifetime of her husband, but instead took part in the Mahila Samiti movement, which tried to raise the living standards of women in rural areas; she has also been a strong supporter of birth control. She refused the presidency of the S.L.F.P. and took only a minor part in the elections of March 1960, but accepted the presidency in May and led the party at the further elections of July 1960, when it secured a majority; she then became the first woman Prime Minister of an independent state.

Bandung Conference. *See* Afro-Asian Conference.

Bantustan. Land in South Africa set aside for use and occupation by Africans under the Promotion of Bantu Self-Government Act, 1959. There are eight Bantu national units, each with limited powers of self-government, a white resident, and envoys to the white-occupied part of South Africa, where most of the Africans work. The units occupy approximately 14 per cent of the total area of South Africa, and represent one aspect of the application of the policy of apartheid, *q.v.*

Bao Dai. Former Emperor of Annam, the central province of Viet-Nam, *q.v.*; recognized by the western powers as head of the state of Viet-Nam from February 1950 until October 1955. A man of elastic political convictions, he abrogated all treaties between France and Annam in March 1945, and pledged his loyalty to the Japanese. On their surrender he abdicated in favour of Ho Chi-Minh, from whom he accepted the post of Supreme Political Adviser, calling on all parties to support unreservedly the Democratic Republic of Viet-Nam. In 1947 he left for France where he negotiated successfully for recognition as head of a French-controlled Viet-Nam. He signed the Auriol agreements which made Viet-Nam independent of France in all except foreign relations, finance, and defence, then returned to Indo-China in his new role with the diplomatic recognition of the western powers. A plebiscite held in Viet-Nam on 23 October 1955 deposed him.

Basutoland. *See* High Commission Territories.

Bechuanaland. *See* High Commission Territories.

Belgian Congo. The name by which the Congo Republic (formerly Belgian), was known when the area was Belgium's only African colony. It was created a state in 1885 under Leopold II as a result of a decision of the great powers at the Conference of Berlin, becoming a Belgian colony in 1908. Administration was by the Colonial Ministry in Brussels, through a Governor-General in the colony. The Belgian government tried to develop the economy and to improve standards of education while blocking political progress, and the United Nations condemned Belgium's refusal to allow the natives any political voice. This policy of 'paternalisme', in which the state was absolute, was modified and some literate Africans were enfranchised for the 1957 local elections. A legislative Council was established in 1959 and the country became completely independent on 30 June 1960.

Belgium. An independent state and the most densely populated country in Europe; area 11,779 sq. m.; population (1958) 9,078,635, partly Flemish (Germanic), in increasing numbers, and partly Walloon

(Latin), in decreasing numbers; a large number are Roman Catholic; capital Brussels. Belgium became an independent constitutional monarchy in 1831. Though it tried to preserve its independence (as guaranteed in the Treaty of London, 1839), it was invaded by Germany in the First and Second World Wars. Its position on the northern flank of France invited German attacks in 1914 and 1940; it has long been a principle of British foreign policy to resist any attack on the Low Countries, which consist of Belgium, Luxemburg, and the Netherlands. King Leopold III, who ascended the throne in 1934, abdicated in 1951 in favour of his son (born 1930) who became King Baudouin.

Since 1918 Belgium has been ruled by coalition governments, with the single exception of the Christian Social government of 1950–4. In the 1961 election the Christian Social (Catholic) Party lost ground which it had gained in 1958 and failed to obtain a majority in the Chamber of Representatives with 96 out of 212 seats. The Socialist Party (which ceased to call itself the 'Belgian Workers' Party' in 1945) remained unchanged, winning 84 seats. Also returned were 20 Liberals (representing small business men and shopkeepers), 5 Communists and 5 representatives of the Christian Flemish People's Union. In the Senate the Christian Social Party secured 47 of the 106 directly elective seats. Other results: Socialists, 45; Liberals, 11; Communists, 1; C.F.P.U., 2. From 1954 to 1958 a Socialist, Achille van Acker, led a coalition of Socialists and Liberals. Frequent disputes occurred over the education of Catholic children and the government angered the Catholic Church by increasing the grants to state secular schools. After the 1961 election Gaston Eyskens' Liberal-Christian Social coalition was succeeded by Théo Lefèvre's Socialist-Christian Social coalition. Belgium has had a customs union with Luxemburg since 1921, and with the Netherlands and Luxemburg, known as Benelux, q.v., since 29 October 1947.

A small country, and comparatively poor in natural resources, Belgium has been increasingly troubled by its failure to modernize and to re-equip its industries and by the tendency of Belgians to indulge instead in increased consumption and higher living standards. Successive Belgian governments have made determined efforts to stimulate a higher rate of fixed productive investment and to facilitate exports. These efforts included substantial investments in the Belgian Congo, q.v., which became independent in 1960 under the title of the Congo Republic. Belgium is responsible for the United Nations trusteeship territory of Ruanda-Urundi, q.v.

Ben-Gurion, David. Israeli politician, born in Plonsk, Poland, 16

December 1886; educated at a Jewish religious school, privately, and at Istanbul University, where he studied law. After promoting Zionism, *q.v.*, in Poland and Russia he settled in Palestine, then part of the Ottoman Empire, in 1906, and worked as an agricultural labourer and watchman. He advocated the adoption of Ottoman citizenship by Palestine Jews at the beginning of the First World War, and was exiled from Palestine as an undesirable Zionist in 1915, when he went to the U.S.A. There he edited and published a Yiddish newspaper and was active in recruiting for the American Jewish Legion, in which he served under General Allenby. In 1920 he became one of the leaders of the Jewish labour movement and of Zionism and as a member of the General Council of the Zionist organization he travelled extensively in Europe and America in support of these causes. He was Secretary-General of Histadrut, the General Federation of Jewish Labour in Israel, from 1921 to 1935. From 1935 to 1948 he was Chairman of the Executive of the Jewish Agency, *q.v.*, and leader of the Labour Wing in the World Zionist Organization. He was one of the organizers of Mapai, the Jewish Labour Party. He was in supreme charge of the Jewish fighting force, Haganah, until the creation of the Israel Defence Army. Upon his proclamation of the independence of Israel on 14 May 1948 he became Head of the Provisional Government of Israel and on 17 February 1949 he was appointed Prime Minister and Minister of Defence. He retired from the premiership and from political life in December 1953. He spent fourteen months living in the southern desert (the Negev) as a shepherd and agriculturist, but returned to politics, becoming Minister of Defence again in February 1955 and Prime Minister in November 1955, when sporadic fighting had begun once more on the frontier between Israel and Egypt.

Benelux. A Customs Union between Belgium, the Netherlands, and Luxemburg, it is the result of a convention concluded in London on 5 September 1944, and came into existence on 29 October 1947; a common customs tariff came into force on 1 January 1948. After unification of the tariffs an attempt was made to seek agreement on a unification of excise and indirect taxes, which varied greatly between the communities. It was then realized that the success of such negotiations would depend upon a considerable degree of economic integration, the reconciliation of the controlled economy of the Netherlands and the liberal economy of Belgium, and a greater degree of concentration by each state on those tasks which it performed most efficiently.

Measures taken to free the movement of goods from restrictions were for some time not coupled with any similar liberation of capital and labour. The restrictions on capital movements and the immobility of workers, combined with the exclusion of agriculture from the free trade principle, hindered development of the union, although there was a steady expansion of mutual trade. Difficulties were caused in particular by intensive Dutch competition in Belgian markets, and it became necessary to introduce special concessions by which a state could impose quotas and import duties as safeguards against foreign competition. The Dutch blamed the high costs of Belgium's industry, which had been insufficiently modernized and re-equipped since 1945; the Belgians blamed low Dutch wages.

In 1954 the members agreed to establish, between 1 March 1954 and 1 March 1956, a common trade and payments policy for Benelux in relation to other countries. This meant that treaties with other countries concerning quotas, financial arrangements, and other commercial details would be negotiated by Benelux on behalf of Belgium, the Netherlands, and Luxemburg. No separate treaties were to be concluded. Movement of capital was also to be made easier so that all capital transactions would be freed.

A Treaty establishing an Economic Union between the three countries was concluded at The Hague on 3 February 1958. It provided for a free flow of capital, goods, services and traffic, and free movement of people. A common commercial policy must be adopted in relations with other countries, and co-ordination of policy is to be sought on investments, agriculture, and social matters. The Treaty came into force on 1 November 1960.

Berlin. A city in the German *Land* (province) of Brandenburg, and until 1945 the capital of Germany. Under the Protocol of 5 September 1944 and the Berlin Declaration of 5 June 1945, it was agreed that whereas the rest of Germany was to be divided into four Zones of Occupation, Greater Berlin should be governed as a single entity by France, the U.K., the U.S.A., and the U.S.S.R. Though Berlin was within the Russian Zone, it would thus be impossible for any one power to claim that it occupied the former capital. Within Berlin itself the pattern of the quadripartite administration of Germany was reproduced, the city being split up into four areas; the three areas occupied by France, the U.K., and the U.S.A. are called the Western Sector, and the area occupied by the U.S.S.R. is called the Eastern Sector. The position of the Western Sector made it easy for the U.S.S.R. to cause difficulties for the western powers when international relations were bad, as it has always been dependent for its supplies on the main road through Eastern Germany to Western

Germany. After the failure of the Foreign Ministers' Conference in Moscow, the declaration of the Truman Doctrine, *q.v.*, and the announcement of the Marshall Plan, *q.v.*, all of which events took place in 1947, the Russian authorities introduced new traffic regulations in March 1948 which threatened to force the western powers to abandon the Western Sector. The Berlin airlift, by which supplies were flown into Berlin by day and night for several months, defeated this manœuvre.

When the German Federal Republic, *q.v.*, became independent and sovereign on 5 May 1955, the new régime did not apply to the Western Sector, but instead the western powers declared that they would normally exercise powers only in matters relating to: (1) the interests of their forces in Berlin; (2) disarmament and demilitarization; (3) occupation costs; (4) Berlin's relations with foreign authorities; (5) authority over the Berlin police in connexion with security matters. The treaty by which the U.S.S.R. gave independence and sovereignty to the German Democratic Republic on 6 October 1955 provided that the Republic should have control over traffic, except military vehicles, passing between Berlin and the German Federal Republic. The German Democratic Republic levies dues on western traffic and thus adds to the considerable expense of maintaining the Western Sector. This expense is borne partly by the German Federal Republic and partly by the U.S.A., which invested large sums in Berlin industries and reduced unemployment from 300,000 in July 1950 to 91,300 in the spring of 1958. There were 2,226,000 people in the Western Sector and 1,090,353 people in the Eastern Sector in 1958.

Bessarabia. An area between the rivers Dniester and Pruth in the extreme south-west of the European part of the U.S.S.R. It was part of the Turkish Empire until 1812, when it was ceded to Russia; after being defeated in war Russia was forced to yield most of the coastal area of Bessarabia to the principality of Moldavia (which was later united with Wallachia to form Rumania) under the Treaty of Paris in 1856, but recovered this part in 1878. When Russia collapsed as a military power at the end of the First World War, Rumania seized Bessarabia and incorporated it as a province. In June 1940 the U.S.S.R. forced Rumania to return Northern Bukovina and Bessarabia. The greater part of the territory was then incorporated in the Moldavian Soviet Socialist Republic. The rest, with Northern Bukovina, was added to the Ukraine, *q.v.* Bessarabia and Northern Bukovina have the densest population in the U.S.S.R. (approximately 4,000,000 in 20,000 sq. m.).

Bhutan. An Indian protectorate situated between India and Tibet, to the east of Nepal and Sikkim; area 18,000 sq. m.; population approximately 700,000; capital Punakha. The territory was annexed by the U.K. in 1865, but in 1910 the British government agreed not to interfere in the internal administration, while the Bhutan government agreed to be guided by the advice of the British government in regard to its external relations. The old arrangements were superseded when India, which had become independent in 1947, concluded a fresh treaty with Bhutan in 1949, but the relationship with India is similar to the previous relationship with the U.K. India pays an annual subsidy to Bhutan.

Bhutan is ruled by a hereditary Maharaja, Jigme Dorji Wangchuk, who was installed in 1952. Rice, timber, and wheat are exported, and there are valuable forests.

The government has been disturbed by the fact that China claims part of the country, and Chinese maps have shown approximately 300 sq. m. of eastern Bhutan as part of China.

Bilateral Agreements. Agreements between two parties, as opposed to multilateral agreements which are concluded by more than two parties.

Bipartisan Foreign Policy. A foreign policy on which both the government and opposition parties are agreed. The expression is used with special reference to the U.S.A. and the attempts of successive American Presidents to win opposition support for their foreign policies. A noted advocate of such a policy, after he had abandoned isolationism, was the late Senator Vandenberg, who stated on 5 January 1950 in a letter to a constituent: 'To me "bipartisan foreign policy" means a mutual effort under our indispensable two-party system to unite our official voice at the water's edge so that America speaks with maximum authority against those who would divide and conquer us and the free world. It does not involve the remotest surrender of free debate in determining our position. On the contrary, frank co-operation and free debate are indispensable to ultimate unity. In a word, it simply seeks national security as a partisan advantage. Every foreign policy must be totally debated (and I think the record proves it has been) and the "loyal Opposition" is under special obligation to see that this occurs.' A bipartisan foreign policy poses a dilemma for an administration when it seeks to renew its support at an election because in theory both administration and opposition are entitled to credit for any successes that the policy may have had. Critics say (a) that any fundamental differences of principle between parties should be reflected in foreign as well as in home affairs, and (*b*) that the Vandenberg statement shows how difficult it is to define bipartisan foreign policy; if argument is to be permitted while the policy is being formulated, it is difficult to say when it should stop, for a nation should always be ready to discuss the fundamental bases of its foreign policy in order to adapt itself to an ever-changing world.

Blockade. The prevention of supplies from reaching an enemy by sea, either by placing ships outside an enemy port or by an attempt to cut off an entire country. In international law neutral merchant ships which attempt to break a blockade can be confiscated. In the First and Second World Wars the U.K. attempted to blockade Germany. A pacific blockade may take place where there is no state of war; it consists of a temporary suspension of the commerce of an offending state, by the prevention of access to its shores, but without recourse to other hostile measures. In 1862 the U.K. instituted a peaceful blockade of Rio de Janeiro to exact redress for the plunder of a British ship wrecked on the Brazilian coast, but the blockade was confined to Brazilian ships.

Blundell, Michael. Kenyan politician, born in Yorkshire in 1907. He emigrated to Kenya in 1936 and became one of its wealthiest farmers, with business interests in breweries, canneries, and newspapers. In the Second World War he led an East African unit in the Ethiopian campaign. He turned to politics and became member for Nakuru in the Legislative Council and successively Minister without Portfolio and Minister of Agriculture in the Kenya government. He founded the United Country Party, believing that all races must be given a share in the government of Kenya, but the Party was dissolved voluntarily on 3 January 1957 following an agreement between all the European elected members in the Legislative Council that party affiliations should cease. He resigned from the Ministry of Agriculture in April 1959 to found the New Kenya Party, a party wishing to create a common electoral roll for all races and to redistribute land.

Bogota Conference. April to May 1948; the Ninth International Conference of American States, held at Bogota, Colombia, which set up the Organization of American States, *q.v.*, a stronger version of the Pan American Union, *q.v.* The Conference was interrupted by several days of violent rioting for which many blamed Communist agitators, but which was in any case symbolic of the political instability of many Latin American states.

Bolivia. An independent South American state; area 404,388 sq. m.; population 3,369,000, of whom two thirds are Indians, the rest mixed races or whites; capital Sucre; government centre La Paz: the Roman Catholic Church is established and subsidized by the state. The country's liberator was Simon Bolivar (1783–1830). Since the Pacific War (1879–82) Bolivia has had no outlet to the sea; it is barred from the Pacific by a strip of Chilean land and from the Atlantic by Paraguay, a fact which has caused several wars between Bolivia and Paraguay. There has been a number of revolutions in recent years; in 1952 the National Revolutionary Movement (M.N.R.) took over the government after heavy fighting, and suspended the Senate and the Chamber of Deputies. The M.N.R. government, supported by most of the peasants and tin miners, won the elections held in June 1956, and in June 1960; on 6 August 1960 Dr Victor Paz Estenssoro, who had been President from 1952 to 1956, again became President.

Bolivia is the world's third largest producer of tin, and also has oil, antimony, and silver deposits. One of the largest tin-mine owners was the Bolivian millionaire Patino, while American companies also had extensive interests in the mines. The tin companies are said to have been able to bring down any government that was hostile to them, but in 1952 their mines were nationalized by the M.N.R. government. This was the most important act of nationalization in Latin America since Mexico nationalized oil in 1938. To assist Bolivia after the 1952 economic crisis, the U.S.A. bought much of the tin surplus for its strategic stockpile and provided free wheat and economic aid. The M.N.R. government wishes to assert Bolivian economic nationalism, to make full use of mineral resources, and to integrate the Indians, who have been virtually slaves, into the life of the country. Bolivia imports fifty to seventy-five per cent of its food, and the fertile valleys east of the great central plateau are being developed and linked to La Paz by new roads. Efforts are being made to develop manufacturing industries and to institute agrarian reforms, by which land will be taken from large landowners. The chief opposition groups are: the Falange Socialista Boliviana, to which the right wing looks to overthrow the M.N.R.; the Partido Obrero Revolucionario (P.O.R.), one of the world's few important Trotskyite parties; and the Partido de la Izquierda Revolucionaria (P.I.R.), a pro-Communist group in popular disfavour for its previous opposition to the M.N.R. Bolivians of the left often profess pride in their Indian blood, while *mestizos* (persons of mixed white and Indian blood) of the right consider themselves to be white.

Bolshevism. An alternative name for Communism. When the Russian Social-Democratic Party split over the issue of radicalism or moderation in 1903, the radical faction, headed by Lenin (1870–1924, leader of the 1917 Revolution and first Head of State of the Soviet Union), polled a majority of votes at the Party congress. The Russian for majority is *bolshinstvo*, and hence the radicals were called Bolsheviki, meaning members of the majority. The moderate Socialists were called Mensheviki, derived from *menshinstvo*, meaning minority. In western countries the word Bolshevik is generally used in a derogatory sense, and sometimes to describe any radical.

Borneo. An island between the South China Sea and the Java Sea, belonging for the most part, under the name of Kalimantan, to Indonesia, but containing also, along its northern coast, the British colony of Sarawak, *q.v.*, the British protected state of Brunei, *q.v.*, and the British colony of North Borneo, *q.v.*

Bosphorus. The northern part of the straits which connect the Mediterranean and the Black Seas, the southern part being the Dardanelles, *q.v.*

Bourbons. Once the French royal dynasty, but banned from France upon the establishment of the Third Republic in 1871. After the extinction of the direct Bourbon line in the last decade of the nineteenth century, the Bourbon-Orléans branch was recognized by French royalists as the legitimate pretender to the throne. Its head is the Comte de Paris. The Spanish line of the Bourbons, represented by Alfonso XIII, was dethroned in 1931; however, Spain was declared to be a monarchy in 1947 and the Spanish government indicated that Prince Juan Carlos de Bourbon (born 1938) might become King on the death or retirement of the head of state, General Franco.

Bourgeoisie. French for 'citizen class'; a term used by Marxist Socialists to denote the class of proprietors (other than agricultural), capitalists, manufacturers, merchants, persons with a business of their own, and members of liberal professions, as opposed to the 'proletariat', *q.v.*, who live only by selling their labour. Under this classification the bourgeoisie are subdivided into the industrialists and financiers on the one hand and the petty bourgeoisie on the other, comprising small artisans, shop-keepers, and others who are not far above the proletariat in their standard of living. According to this analysis the bourgeoisie became the ruling class with the rise of modern factory production, overthrowing the feudal class or aristocracy and its obsolete economic system. The rise of the bourgeoisie was accompanied by the spread of liberal ideas necessary to break the feudal bondage. According to the Marxist theory the bourgeois class is doomed to be succeeded by the proletariat, and turns to dictatorial systems to defend itself against this inevitable successor. At this stage the petty bourgeoisie is gradually proletarianized while the other section of the bourgeoisie is reduced to a small number of capitalists who control the nation's resources.

Bourguiba, Habib. Tunisian nationalist leader; born 1904. Educated in France, a moderate Moslem, he is the leader of the Tunisian Neo-Destour Party, *q.v.*, and for many years advocated the departure of the French and complete sovereignty for Tunisia. He was permitted by the French authorities to return to Tunis in June 1955, after ten years spent partly in exile and partly in French prisons. He became Prime Minister on 8 April 1956, five days before Tunisian independence was declared. He was elected President and Head of Government in July 1957, and re-elected to these posts, under the 1959 Constitution, in November 1959.

Brainwashing. A treatment of persons designed to change their outlook. The expression was once limited to, and probably originated in, Communist treatment of prisoners aimed at altering their political and moral outlook on the western world. It is now often used loosely to describe any change in attitude on the part of a prisoner resulting in sympathy with his captors' views or a readiness to confess to crimes. There may be an apparent alteration in personality or a revision of opinions on certain topics. These changes may have been brought about by torture (mental, or physical, or both), rewards of preferential treatment instead of degrading circumstances, or propaganda and argument. Though there is no doubt that all these methods have been applied, there is little reliable information as to the effectiveness of each method or the extent to which each has been responsible for prisoners' altered outlooks. A U.S. governmental committee, which laid down a new code of conduct for prisoners, reported in 1955 that the failure of American officers to assume responsibility caused a decay of morale among U.S. troops in some Korean prisoner-of-war camps, and that the average American prisoner was under a serious handicap when faced with attempts to indoctrinate him. He was unable, the report said, to answer pro-Communist arguments with democratic arguments, and the committee attributed to this fact the readiness of some prisoners to accept Communist teachings.

Brandt, Willy. West German Social Democratic politician; born in 1914 in Lübeck, as Herbert Karl Frahm. His writings in Socialist newspapers made him unpopular with the Nazis, and in 1933 he fled to Norway, using the pseudonym which he has retained. He returned to Berlin in 1945 as a Norwegian citizen with the rank of Major, and became a German citizen again in 1948. He entered politics, being elected Mayor of Berlin in 1957, and is regarded as one of the leaders of the Social Democratic Party.

Brazil, United States of. The largest and most populous South American republic; area 3,287,842 sq. m.; population approximately 62,725,000; capital Brasília; language Portuguese. Eleven per cent of the population are black, twenty-seven per cent brown, and sixty-two per cent white or of white descent. Brazil was a Portuguese colony until it achieved independence in 1822. It is the world's largest producer of coffee. It is potentially a rich country, but is over-dependent on its vital coffee exports, in spite of the efforts to stabilize coffee prices which have been made by the cartel set up by twelve South American countries. There are large reserves of oil which are virtually untapped; the country produces less than ten per cent of the oil that it consumes, though an important strike made at Nova Olinda in Amazonia made it probable that Brazil would produce fifty per cent of its petroleum needs by 1965. The government oil monopoly, Petrobras, enforces a rule by which no interests in oil can be acquired by foreigners but it has insufficient resources fully to develop the reserves. There is a hydro-electric potential, particularly from the river Amazon, which is nearly as great as that of the U.S.A., and the country contains about one quarter of the world's known iron ore deposits. There has been investment by Japanese interests in Brazilian cotton mills, by American business in the automobile and rubber industries and by the Schneider–Creusot group in heavy industry.

The Brazilian political scene was dominated for thirty years by President Getulio Vargas, who for much of that time ruled as a dictator; he committed suicide in August 1954. His proclaimed pre-occupation was with the hardships of the under-privileged. Under the 1946 Constitution there are a President and a Vice-President, elected directly by the people for five years and ineligible for successive terms, a Senate of 62 members elected for eight years and a Chamber of Deputies of 324 members elected for four years. At the elections held in October 1955 for the term beginning on 31 January 1956, the pro-Vargas Juscelino Kubitschek was elected President. He was supported in his campaign by the Partido Trabhalista Brasileiro (the Brazilian Labour Party, created by Vargas and led by Goulart) and the Partido Social Democratica or S.P.D. (the Social Democratic Party, the largest party in the Chamber of Deputies), both pro-Vargas groups. At the elections held in October 1960 for the term beginning on 31 January 1961, Jânio Quadros, a member of the Brazilian Labour Party and a former Governor of São Paulo, was elected President. Though he defeated the candidate supported by Kubitschek, he was regarded as being a supporter of the Vargas tradition.

At the elections for the new Chamber of Deputies and for one third of the Senate seats, held in October 1958 while Kubitschek was still President, there had been a marked swing away from the pro-Vargas groups towards the centre parties and the conservatives, who include the União Democratica Nacional (U.D.N.).

Bretton Woods. A town in New Hampshire, U.S.A., where the United Nations Monetary and Financial Conference set up the World Bank (International Bank for Reconstruction and Development, *q.v.*) and the International Monetary Fund, *q.v.*, in July 1944.

British Cameroons. *See* Cameroons, British.

British Commonwealth. Formerly called the British Empire, it is an association of twelve independent states, Australia, Canada, Ceylon, Cyprus, Ghana, India, Malaya, New Zealand, Nigeria, Pakistan, Sierra Leone, and the United Kingdom, and their dependencies. Its total population is about 700,000,000. The Commonwealth is neither a state nor a federation; it has no single parliament or government, and no central defence force or executive power. The ten self-governing Dominions were formerly integral parts of the United Kingdom's imperial territories. Until 1925 the Colonial Office was responsible for all these territories except India, which was entrusted to a separate Department. In that year the British government created the post of Secretary of State for Dominion Affairs, with responsibility for the self-governing Dominions (which then comprised Australia, Canada, Newfoundland, New Zealand, and South Africa), for the self-governing territory of Southern Rhodesia, and for the South African High Commission Territories, *q.v.*, of Basutoland, the Bechuanaland Protectorate, and Swaziland. The 1926 Imperial Conference described the Dominions as 'autonomous communities within the British Empire, equal in status, in no way subordinate one to another in any aspect of their domestic or foreign affairs, though united by a common allegiance to the Crown, and freely associated as members of the British Commonwealth of Nations'. In 1931 the Statute of Westminster, *q.v.*, gave statutory force to the description of the Dominions as autonomous and equal in status. Newfoundland lost its Dominion status in 1933 and became part of Canada sixteen years later, but after the Second World War India and Pakistan (in 1947) and Ceylon (in 1948) became Dominions. The title of Secretary of State for Dominion Affairs was altered to Secretary of State for Commonwealth Relations in 1947, with the additional responsibility of handling the affairs of India and Pakistan and later Ceylon. Though India and Pakistan are members of the Commonwealth they are republics and owe no allegiance to the Queen, recognizing her only as the Head of the Commonwealth. Burma and Ireland became independent states and rejected offers of Dominion status. Southern Rhodesia, Northern Rhodesia and Nyasaland formed the Federation of Rhodesia and Nyasaland, *q.v.*, in 1953, but though this Federation is largely independent, the U.K. is responsible for its international relations, and it is not a Dominion. Ghana and Malaya became Dominions in 1957, Nigeria in 1960, and Cyprus and Sierra Leone in 1961, in which year South Africa left the Commonwealth.

The dependencies of the independent Dominions are part of the British Commonwealth, and may be divided into Colonies, *q.v.*, Protectorates, *q.v.*, Protected States, *q.v.*, and Trusteeship Territories, *q.v.* Australia, New Zealand, and the United Kingdom have such dependencies.

British Guiana. A British colony on the north-east coast of South America, seized from the Dutch in 1796; area 83,000 sq. m.; population approximately 539,940; capital Georgetown. The 1953 Constitution was suspended in October 1953 after it had been in operation for six months on the ground that there was Communist infiltration into the government, which comprised an Executive Council of 11 members, including 6 from the House of Assembly. The People's Progressive Party (P.P.P.), an extreme left-wing party led by Dr Cheddi Jagan and Forbes Burnham, had won 18 out of the 23 seats elected by universal suffrage in the House of Assembly and thereupon took up the 6 places on the Executive Council reserved for House members. The new Ministers immediately demanded full self-government, and objected to the reserved powers given to the Governor, and to the upper house or State Council, which was largely composed of members nominated by the Governor. They supported a strike on the sugar estates and introduced a Bill to compel employers to recognize specific trade unions. The Governor became convinced that the P.P.P. was planning to introduce a proletarian dictatorship, and recommended that the Constitution should be suspended. This advice was followed by the British government, which also landed armed forces to prevent public disorder.

The British government replaced the legislature by a wholly nominated Legislative Council of 27 members and an Executive Council of 11 members. No elected members were to be permitted and the Governor was given the right to reject the advice of the Executive

Council. An independent Constitutional Commission reported that the P.P.P. was Communist in its aims, organization, and methods, supported the action taken in October 1953 and stated that the large P.P.P. vote was the result of the backward economic condition of British Guiana.

In August 1957 elections were held under a new Constitution approved in 1956. The P.P.P. won 9 out of the 14 elective seats and the People's National Congress, an off-shoot of the P.P.P. under Forbes Burnham, won 3 seats. The Constitution provides for 3 *ex-officio* members of the legislature and gives discretion to the Governor to appoint 11 more. The elected members are entitled to 5 of the 10 places on the Executive Council.

The population, which is increasing rapidly, is in the main dependent on part-time employment on the estates which grow sugar, the colony's largest source of income. Bauxite and rice are the other chief products. The government plans to improve communications, organize land settlements, and electrify rural areas.

British Honduras. A British colony on the east coast of Central America, to the south and east of Mexico and to the east of Guatemala; area 8,867 sq. m.; population (1958 estimate) 88,156; capital Belize. The first English settlers came to cut wood in 1638 and the area became a British colony, under Jamaica in 1862, and independently in 1884. Until the risings against the Spaniards in 1821 Spain claimed the area; Guatemala, which achieved independence in 1839 on leaving the United States of Central America, has also frequently claimed the colony, especially since 1945. In January 1946 the U.K. invited Guatemala to submit the dispute to the International Court of Justice, but the offer was not accepted. The Mexican government, alleging that a treaty of 1783 between Britain and Spain conceded part of the area to Spain, claims to have inherited Spanish rights in that area.

Internal politics in the colony are affected by the territorial dispute. At the elections held on 1 March 1961 the People's United Party (P.U.P.), led by George Price, won all 18 elected seats in the Legislative Assembly. Price had opposed the idea of Caribbean Federation, *q.v.*, and spoke of 'the trend of concealed but constant drift into a West Indian economic orbit'. His views were acceptable both to those who disliked the prospect of distant rule from the West Indies, and to the many Catholics who found the Latin American countries more sympathetic. The British Colonial Secretary broke off financial and constitutional talks with P.U.P. representatives in London in November 1957 on the ground that Price had engaged in private discussions with the Guatemalan Minister in London about a possible association between the colony and Guatemala. Price agreed that the Minister had proposed a Central American Federation which would include Guatemala and British Honduras. The National Independence Party, comprising the National Party and P.U.P. dissidents, campaigned in the 1961 elections for independence within the British Commonwealth and closer economic links with the Caribbean Federation; it failed to win any seats. The non-elected members in the Assembly consist of five nominated and two official members. Under the new Constitution George Price became First Minister.

The colony produces cedar, mahogany, rosewood, pine, and many hardwoods and woods suitable for pulp. Over ninety per cent of the area is occupied by forests. There are also exports of citrus fruits, especially grapefruit and oranges. There is much seasonal unemployment, and Colonial Development Corporation attempts to diversify the economy by encouraging cattle breeding, banana growing and tourism, have met with little success. The colony cannot support itself and sufficient investment from the U.K. and U.S.A. has not been forthcoming.

British North Borneo. *See* North Borneo.

British Somaliland. The name of an area which from 1886 to 1960 was a British protectorate in East Africa on the Gulf of Aden, between French Somaliland and the former trusteeship territory of Somalia, area 68,000 sq. m.; population 600,000; capital Hargeisa. The population, which is almost entirely nomadic, consists of Somali tribes who are Sunni Moslems and whose life is centred exclusively on their camels, goats, and sheep. In 1884 the Egyptians withdrew from the Somali coast and in 1886 the tribes voluntarily placed themselves under British protection and undertook, in return, never to cede their lands to any other government. In 1897 the British government concluded a treaty with Emperor Menelik, the predecessor of the Emperor of Ethiopia, after his victory over the Italians at Adowa, by which Ethiopian territory was to include some of the traditional grazing grounds and wells of the tribes; the Somalis, however, who were not consulted, were given the right to enter Ethiopia to use these grounds and wells. The Ethiopian government never administered this area and after the liberation of Ethiopia and Italian Somaliland (now Somalia) from Italy, the British continued to manage the region which has an area of approximately 25,000 sq. m. and a population of some 300,000. In November 1954 an Anglo-Ethiopian agreement was signed, providing for the return of the area to Ethiopian administration, but still preserving the right of the tribes from British Somaliland to graze their flocks there. The Ethiopian government had refused an alternative offer of access to a port (Zeila) in British Somaliland in return for continued administration of the area by the U.K. After concluding the 1954 agreement Ethiopia opened negotiations with a U.S. firm which wanted an oil-prospecting concession in the grazing grounds. Somali representatives, regarding French Somaliland, British Somaliland, and Somalia as a national territory which might one day, as Greater Somalia, be self-governing, objected strongly to the 1954 agreement. The disputed area comprises the Haud and the Reserved Area.

The protectorate ended on 26 June 1960, when there was created the independent state of Somaliland, whose newly-established national assembly met the next day to pass an act of union with the Italian trusteeship territory of Somalia, *q.v.*, which itself became independent on 1 July 1960.

British West Indies. The colonies in the West Indies which belong to the U.K. They are Jamaica, *q.v.*, in the Great Antilles, and Barbados, the Leeward Islands, Trinidad, and the Windward Islands in the Lesser Antilles. In 1947 proposals were made for a close association between most of these colonies, together with British Honduras, *q.v.*, in Central America and British Guiana, *q.v.*, in South America. The proposed union was often described as the Caribbean Federation, *q.v.* It came into existence on 3 January 1958 when it became known as the West Indies Federation, *q.v.*

Brown, George Alfred. British Labour Party politician; born September 1914, the son of a lorry-driver, he left school at the age of fifteen and was in turn a junior clerk in the City of London, a shop assistant, and a fur salesman, continuing his education in the Workers' Education Association and at evening classes. In 1945, after working as a trade union official, he was elected to the House of Commons as member for the Belper division of Derbyshire. He became Joint Parliamentary Secretary to the Ministry of Agriculture and Fisheries in October 1947, and was Minister of Works from April 1951 until the Labour Party was defeated in the general election of October 1951. He was elected Deputy Leader of the Labour Party, in succession to Aneurin Bevan, in November 1960.

Brunei. A British protected state on the north coast of Borneo which, except for its coastal strip, is surrounded by Sarawak; area 2,226 sq. m.; population (1958) 80,277; capital Brunei. The state came under British protection in 1888, and the British government is therefore responsible for defence and external affairs. Under the 1959 Constitution, which is the state's first written Constitution, there is a Privy Council, an Executive Council, and a Legislative Council. The Executive Council is presided over by the Sultan and comprises 7 ex officio members, the High Commissioner (directly responsible to the British government) and 7 unofficial members. The Legislative Council, which has an unofficial majority, is presided over by the Mentri Besar (Chief Minister); it comprises 8 ex officio members, 6 official members appointed by the Sultan, 16 elected members, and 3 members nominated by the Sultan. It is intended to add 16 more members, elected by district councils.

Under the Constitution the Sultan may not, without the consent of the executive council, surrender or cede any part of Brunei, or amalgamate, federate or unite any part with another territory. Suggestions have been made, particularly by the Party Rayat or People's Party, that there should be a federation between Brunei, Sarawak and North Borneo but these have encountered resistance from those who wish to preserve the character of Brunei as a Malay Islamic sultanate.

Brunei is wealthier than its neighbours as a result of its oil industry, which employs three quarters of the working population, and which causes its exports to yield more than five times the cost of its imports. The oilfield, which is based on Seria but extends offshore, is controlled by the Brunei Shell Petroleum Company.

Sir Omar Ali Saifuddin Wasa'dul Khairi Waddin became Sultan on the death of his brother in June 1950.

Brussels Treaty Organization. Renamed Western European Union, *q.v.*, in 1955, it was created by a Treaty of March 1948, between Belgium, France, Luxemburg, the Netherlands, and U.K., by which the signatories promised 'all the military and other aid and assistance in their power' if one of them was the object of an armed attack in Europe. This is a stricter obligation than that laid down for members of the North Atlantic Treaty Organization, *q.v.*, which are bound to take 'such action as they deem necessary' if one of them is attacked. The Brussels Treaty also provided for meetings of the five Foreign Ministers every three months in a Consultative Council to co-ordinate foreign policies, a group of sub-committees on economic, social, and cultural matters, a Permanent Commission comprising the four ambassadors in London and a Foreign Office representative, a Permanent Military Committee, and a secretariat. In economic and social matters the parties agreed to the abolition of visas and the mutual recognition of social insurance benefits. As from 5 May 1955, Italy and the German Federal Republic entered the Organization, which then became the Western European Union.

Buffer State. A small state established or preserved between two greater states to prevent direct clashes between them.

Buganda. A kingdom and one of the four provinces of the British protectorate of Uganda, *q.v.*; capital Kampala. The Kabaka of Uganda, Mutesa II, was deposed and deported in November 1953 as a result of an alleged breach by him of the Uganda Agreement of 1900 which governed relations between Buganda and the British government. The government claimed that he had not fulfilled his obligation to co-operate loyally in matters of day-to-day administration. The underlying cause of the disagreement was the Kabaka's demand for the separation of Buganda, as an independent state, from the rest of Uganda. The Uganda High Court held in November 1954 that the 1900 Agreement did not bind the U.K. which could withdraw recognition at any time as an act of state. It stated, however, that if it were mistaken, and the agreement were binding, it was incorrect to say that the Kabaka had not co-operated loyally, although the government could have relied on a breach of another term in the agreement for the Kabaka had certainly failed to abide by a decision of policy.

Constitutional reforms for Buganda proposed by the Namirembe Conference in 1954 included recommendations that Buganda should continue to be an integral part of Uganda, that the conduct of public affairs in Buganda should be in the hands of six Ministers, and that, while all the traditional dignities of the Kabaka should be fully safeguarded, Kabakas should, in future, be constitutional rulers bound not to prejudice the security and welfare of the Buganda people (the Baganda) and the Uganda protectorate. The Buganda assembly, the Lukiko, and the Prime Minister, the Katikiro, suggested certain minor amendments and the new constitution came into force in 1955.

The exiled Kabaka returned to Kampala in October 1955, when he signed the Buganda Agreement which now governs his relationship with the British government. The Lukiko continues to oppose measures which might give a disproportionate voice on the Executive Council to the Asian minority, and it has on several occasions voted in favour of secession from Uganda.

Bulganin, Nikolai Alexandrovitch. Former Russian leader; born 1895. He joined the Communist Party in 1917 and served in the Cheka from 1918 to 1922. He held various industrial posts from 1922 onwards and in 1931 became Chairman of the Moscow Soviet, in which capacity he visited London. He became a member of the Central Committee of the Communist Party in 1935 and in 1937 represented the Moscow district in the Supreme Soviet, *q.v.* After the German invasion in 1941 he was an organizer of defence with the rank of Lieutenant-General, and became a Marshal of the U.S.S.R. in 1945. He was appointed as a Deputy Chairman of the Council of Ministers in 1949, a First Deputy Chairman in 1953 upon the death of Stalin, and Chairman (a post roughly equivalent to that of Prime Minister) upon the resignation of Malenkov in February 1955. He was replaced as Chairman in April 1958 by Khrushchev.

Bulgaria. Independent state on the western coast of the Black Sea between Rumania and Greece; area 42,796 sq. m.; population (1956) 7,629,254, of whom eighty-three per cent belong to the Eastern Orthodox Church which receives a state subsidy, and fourteen per cent are Moslems; capital Sofia. Already part of the Turkish Empire, it achieved more freedom by becoming a principality under Turkish sovereignty by the Treaty of Berlin, 1878; in 1908 it became an independent kingdom. Though successful in the first Balkan war against Turkey in 1912, Bulgaria was defeated in the second Balkan war in 1913 when its former allies, Greece and Serbia, turned against it, with Rumania. In the First World War Bulgaria supported Germany and collapsed in 1918. It lost the Dobrudja (to Rumania), Thrace (to Turkey and Greece), and Macedonia (to Greece and Yugoslavia). A radical peasant party came to power, only to be overthrown in 1923 by a *coup d'état* led by the army and four parties which merged to remove the agrarian reformers.

There was considerable social and political unrest between the two World Wars, when Bulgaria, a very poor country, suffered severely from the economic depression, and support for the Communists gradually increased. The German army occupied Bulgaria in the Second World War, and when it withdrew in 1944 there was another *coup d'état* which put into power the Fatherland Front, a coalition of the Communists, the Agrarian Party and the Social Democratic Party. In 1945 the Agrarians and Social Democrats left the government; in 1946 a referendum demanded and secured the abolition of the monarchy and the proclamation of a republic, and elections were held to the Grand National Assembly. With one deputy to every 30,000 electors, the Fatherland Front won 364 seats (277 for Communists) and the opposition 101 seats. In 1947 the Agrarian Party was suppressed, its leader, Nikola Petkov, being arrested (with twenty-three other Agrarian leaders) by order of the Communist Georgi Dimitrov, charged with conspiracy, and hanged. In 1948 some Social Democrats joined forces with the Communists, while others were arrested. No opposition Social Democrats were allowed to sit in the

National Assembly after July 1948. At the elections held on 18 December 1949, 97·66 per cent of the votes were cast in favour of the Fatherland Front; the Front still contained two political parties, the Communists and the remnants of the Agrarians. Elections held in 1953 and 1957 produced similar majorities in favour of the Fatherland Front.

By 1949 the economic structure had been radically altered under the 1947 Two-Year Plan and the Communists were in complete control. The private sector of industry dropped from 83·6 per cent to 5 per cent of the total number of enterprises, and between 1947 and 1948 industrial output increased by 44 per cent. A Five-Year Plan was completed in 1949–53 and a second Plan was concluded in 1957. Land was taken from the monasteries and private owners and divided among landless peasants and co-operative farms; the country is still essentially agricultural, in spite of increasing industrialization, which has included an iron and steel works and a chemical factory. In 1955 the Prime Minister, Vulko Chervenkov, said that agricultural progress had been disappointing in some respects and that greater emphasis would be placed on the development of heavy industry. In April 1956 Chervenkov resigned and was replaced by Anton Yugov.

A feature of the Bulgarian Communist Party has been the disputes between nationalist Communists and those who look to Moscow. The pre-war border disputes with Greece over Macedonia continued after 1945 and Bulgaria supplied arms to the Communist forces in Greece until 1948, but an agreement concluded in August 1955 provided for the avoidance, and settlement, of frontier incidents.

Bunche, Ralph Johnson. United Nations official; born 7 August 1904 in Detroit, Michigan. After a distinguished academic career, in which he specialized first in philosophy and then in social anthropology, at various American universities, the London School of Economics and Political Science, and the University of Capetown, he became in 1939 a staff member of the Carnegie Corporation's Survey of the Negro in America. He served with the U.S. Office of Strategic Services from 1941 to 1944 as senior social science analyst in charge of research on Africa and other colonial areas, specializing on the British Empire, and was appointed as an adviser to the U.S. Delegations to the Dumbarton Oaks Conference, q.v., in 1944, to the International Labour Conference in 1945, and the San Francisco Conference, q.v. in 1945. As a member of the U.S. delegations he attended the International Labour Conference in 1945 and the United Nations General Assembly in London in 1946. He then became U.S. Commissioner on the Caribbean Commission, 1945–7, and in 1948 was appointed as Principal Director of the United Nations Trusteeship Department. In the same year he became Principal Secretary of the United Nations Palestine Commission and personal representative in Palestine of the United Nations Secretary-General. From 1948 to 1949 he was the United Nations Mediator in Palestine, and in 1950 was awarded the Nobel Peace Prize; he is the only Negro ever to have received this award. In 1960 he represented the United Nations Secretary-General in the Congo Republic (formerly Belgian) during the disturbances which followed independence.

Buraimi. An inland Arabian oasis comprising nine villages on the frontiers of the Sheikhdom of Abu Dhabi, *q.v.*, and the Sultanate of Muscat and Oman, *q.v.*, two coastal principalities on the Persian Gulf and the Arabian Sea respectively. Most of the external relations of the principalities are in the hands of the British government; the greater part of the principalities themselves is in the concession area of Iraq Petroleum Co., *q.v.* The oasis is claimed by both Saudi Arabia and the two principalities. It is believed to lie near rich oilfields and is thus particularly coveted by Saudi Arabia and the Arabian American Oil Co., 'Aramco', which holds the Saudi Arabian concession. In August 1952 a Saudi Arabian force of some eighty men passed through Abu Dhabi, occupied part of the Muscat portion and distributed money. The British government protested on behalf of the Sultan. For a further two years there were skirmishes and accusations of bribery. In July 1954 the British and Saudi Arabian governments agreed to hold an arbitration to decide the correct frontier between Saudi Arabia and Abu Dhabi and in particular to determine who was sovereign over the Buraimi oasis. A court of arbitrators was set up which included one Saudi Arabian and one British citizen. In October 1955 the arbitration proceedings broke down following the withdrawal of the British arbitrator, Sir Reader Bullard, who resigned when it transpired that the Saudi Arabian arbitrator had been one of those previously handling the dispute for the Saudi Arabian government, and had been in touch with that government during the proceedings. The United Kingdom then accused the Saudi Arabian government of having offered £30,000,000 to the Sheikh of Abu Dhabi to leave Buraimi open to Saudi Arabia. The forces of the Sheikh of Abu Dhabi and the Sultan of Muscat and Oman, supported by the levies of the Trucial Coast, *q.v.*, then resumed their previous control of the oasis, and areas to the west of it, returning the Saudi Arabian forces, via Aden, to their bases.

Bureaucracy. A hybrid word, originally a satirical combination of

French *bureau* and Greek *kratein*, to rule, on the analogy of 'democracy' and 'aristocracy'. Now used as a serious term for (*a*) the rule of a caste of high officials, (*b*) this caste itself, hence the word bureaucrat.

Burma. An independent Asian state to the east of India and East Pakistan; area 261,789 sq. m.; population (1954) 19,242,000, of whom 84·3 per cent are Buddhists, 5·2 per cent Animists, 4 per cent Moslems, 3·9 per cent Hindus, 2·3 per cent Christians; two thirds of the population are Burmans, but there are also some 2,000,000 Karens, 700,000 Indians, 310,000 Chinese and Kachins, Chins, Shans, Mons, and Arakanese; capital Rangoon. In the eleventh and twelfth centuries Burma was a great empire but its power was destroyed by the armies of Kublai Khan. It later became part of British India, some self-government being allowed in 1937. In 1941 it was occupied by the Japanese who were regarded as liberators by the Burmans. An all-Burmese government was set up; however, there was no real independence until the withdrawal of the Japanese and the creation, in 1948, of the independent Union of Burma. The Union, which comprises Burma proper, the Shan States, and the Karenni States in the north-east, chose not to remain in the British Commonwealth. There is a Chamber of Deputies (250 members) and a Chamber of Nationalities (125 members). The Anti-Fascist People's Freedom League, commanding since 1951 a majority of the members of the Chamber of Deputies, is a confederation of parties, the most powerful of which is the Socialist Party, which preaches a Marxist-Leninist doctrine. Other A.F.P.F.L. groups include the All Burma Peasants' Organization, which is powerful in the countryside, the Trades Union Congress, and a number of communal organizations representing the Muslims, the Karens, Shans, and other frontier people. At the elections held in February 1960 for the Chamber of Deputies, the A.F.P.F.L. and its supporters, led by U Nu, won over 170 seats.

Under the Constitution the state is the ultimate owner of all land. The government pursues a policy of land reform, industrialization, and social welfare. For some time there was serious trouble from rebellious Communists, Trotskyites, army deserters and Karens, and from supporters of Chiang Kai-shek who used the Shan states as a refuge, but strong military action by the Burmese government has largely suppressed these. Burma has resources of teak, tungsten, tin, lead, petroleum and precious stones. The biggest source of income is rice, exports of which provide the country with about eighty per cent of its earnings of foreign currencies. The market has declined owing to increased production in countries like India, which once imported Burmese rice in substantial quantities. Burma is therefore looking for new markets, such as the U.S.S.R., and turning to other forms of production.

Bustamante, Sir William Alexander. Jamaican politician; born 24 February 1884. He was adopted in 1899 by a sailor and taken to Spain where he joined the Spanish army, and then served in Morocco. He joined the Cuban police force in Havana, then found employment with a tram company in New York, with an electricity company in Panama, and in a New York hospital. He returned to Jamaica in 1932. There he became involved in agricultural disputes and led a campaign against the introduction of water-meters. He became Treasurer of the Workers' and Tradesmen's Union in 1937 and was active in the widespread Jamaican strikes of 1938, when he founded the Bustamante Industrial Trade Unions. Because of this activity he was charged with sedition and his cousin, Norman Manley, Q.C., *q.v.*, later Chief Minister, appeared for him; the charges were later withdrawn. He organized another strike in 1939 at the outbreak of war and was interned under the Emergency Defence Regulations from 1940 to 1942. In 1943 he founded the anti-Socialist Jamaican Labour Party which won 22 out of 32 seats in the House of Representatives at the 1944 elections which were the first to be held on a basis of manhood suffrage. Bustamante himself was elected for Kingston West and made Chairman of the special committee of the House dealing with Transport and Communications, a post he held until 1953. At the 1949 election his party won 18 of the 32 seats and he was recognized as the unofficial Prime Minister. Under the revised constitution of 1953 he became Chief Minister of Jamaica and Minister of Local Government from which posts he resigned after the elections of January 1955 in which his party lost four seats, and its majority, in the House of Representatives. In 1958, upon the establishment of the West Indies Federation, *q.v.*, Bustamante became a leader of the newly formed Democratic Labour Party. He resigned from this post in May 1960 to emphasize his belief that Jamaica should secede from the Federation. A demagogic politician and fond of self-dramatization, he has declared that his recreations are conviviality, motoring, and speech-making.

Butler, Richard Austen. British Conservative Party politician; born 9 December 1902 and educated at Marlborough and at Pembroke College, Cambridge. He was a Fellow of Corpus Christi College, Cambridge, from 1925 to 1929, and has been the Member of Parliament for Saffron Walden since 1929. He has been Parliamentary Under-Secretary of State for India, 1932-7, Parliamentary Secretary to the Ministry of Labour, 1937–8, and Parliamentary Under-Secretary of State for Foreign Affairs, 1938–41, during which period he supported the Munich Agreement, *q.v.* As President of the Board of Education from 1941 to 1945 he guided the 1944 Education Bill through Parliament, stating his belief that 'education is the spearhead of social reform'. He was Minister of Labour in the 1945 Conservative 'caretaker' government until the return to power of the Labour Party. His powerful influence and his work in the Conservative Party research department did much to persuade his colleagues to accept the principles of the welfare state and to develop an approach which would win the sympathy of the British electorate. He became Chancellor of the Exchequer in October 1951 and held that office until the government reorganization of December 1955, when he was appointed Lord Privy Seal and Leader of the House of Commons. In January 1957 he added to these offices that of Home Secretary, and in October 1959 gave up the post of Lord Privy Seal and became Chairman of the Conservative Party.

Buy American Act. A U.S. law passed in 1933 requiring government departments to give preference in awarding contracts to domestic suppliers, unless their prices are substantially higher than those of foreign bidders.

Byelorussia, *or* White Russia. One of the fifteen constituent Republics of the U.S.S.R.; area 81,090 sq. m.; population 8,100,000; capital Minsk. It is situated in the western part of the European section of the U.S.S.R. and was set up on 1 January 1919. An area inhabited by approximately 2,000,000 Byelorussians was kept by Poland after its war with the U.S.S.R. in 1920 and reoccupied by the U.S.S.R. after the partition of Poland in September 1939. The Byelorussians or White Russians are a nation (speaking a language distinct from but akin to Russian and Ukrainian), not a political group; they should not be confused with the 'White' Russians of the civil war period who opposed the revolution. Byelorussia, like the Ukraine, *q.v.*, is a member of the United Nations Organization.

C

C.I.O. Congress of Industrial Organizations, *q.v.*

Cairo Declaration. A statement of policy issued on 1 December 1943 by the governments of China, the U.K., and the U.S.A. after a meeting at Cairo between Chiang Kai-shek, Winston Churchill, and Franklin D. Roosevelt, from 22 to 26 November. The three governments reaffirmed their policy of obtaining the unconditional surrender of the enemy forces and denied that they were seeking any territorial aggrandizement. They sought to relegate Japan to the status that it had occupied in 1895 and said that it was their purpose that Japan should be stripped of all the islands in the Pacific which it had seized or occupied since the beginning of the First World War in 1914, and that all the territories that Japan had 'stolen from the Chinese', such as Manchuria, Formosa, and the Pescadores, should be restored to China. Japan was also to be expelled from all the other territories that it had 'taken by violence and greed', and it was resolved that Korea should become free and independent.

Callaghan, Leonard James. British Labour Party politician; born 27 March 1912; educated at Portsmouth Northern Grammar School. He entered the civil service as a tax officer in 1929 and became Assistant Secretary of the Inland Revenue Staff Federation in 1936, a post which he held until 1947 except during the Second World War, when he served in the Royal Navy. In July 1945 he was elected to the House of Commons as the member for South Cardiff, and was Parliamentary Secretary to the Ministry of Transport from 1947 to 1950 and Parliamentary and Financial Secretary to the Admiralty from 1950 (in which year his constituency changed to South-East Cardiff) until the Labour Party was defeated at the General Election of 1951.

Calwell, Arthur Augustus. Politician and Australian Labour Party leader, a Roman Catholic; born August 1896 in Melbourne, Victoria, the eldest of seven children of a policeman and educated at the Christian Brothers' College. On leaving school in 1913 he entered the Victorian civil service, in which he became a member of the Federated Clerks' Union. He was president of the Victoria branch of the Labour Party from 1931 to 1940, when he entered the Federal House of Representatives as the member for Melbourne. At the beginning of the Second World War he led an unsuccessful opposition within the Labour Party to the Labour government's proposal to extend conscription to include service overseas. He became Minister of Information in 1943 and later, as Minister for Immigration from 1945 to 1949, was a strong supporter of the White Australia policy. He was elected Deputy Leader of the Labour Party in 1951 and Leader in March 1960, after the resignation of Dr Evatt.

Cambodia. An independent state, formerly of the French Union, *q.v.*, situated in south-west Indo-China; area 70,000 sq. m.; capital Pnom Penh; religion Buddhist; population 5,040,000, of whom five per cent are Chinese and the rest a mixture of Indian and Malay strains. In the ninth and tenth centuries Cambodia was the seat of the great Khmer Empire which ruled most of Indo-China; from the fourteenth century it was disputed territory between Thais and Annamites until the French established a protectorate in 1864. Although grateful for this protection the Cambodians have resisted all French influences, religious and cultural. In 1930 the French acknowledged the futility of their assimilation policy by founding the Buddhist Institute at Pnom Penh and the Institute of Cambodian Arts.

From 1949 to 1954 Cambodia was an Associate State of the French Union. A measure of independence was achieved in 1953 when King Norodom Sihanouk retired temporarily to 'political asylum' in Thailand until the French relented; this independence was guaranteed in 1954 at Geneva, where the eleventh-hour refusal of the Foreign Minister, Tep Phan, to sign the Agreements because they neutralized his country secured for Cambodia, and Laos, the right to make treaties and enlist foreign aid (other than French) in their own defence.

King Norodom Sihanouk (born 1922) succeeded to the throne on 26 April 1941. In 1947 he introduced a new constitution with an elective assembly and manhood suffrage, except for Buddhist priests and soldiers who are disfranchised. In March 1955 the King abdicated in favour of his parents, King Norodom Suramarit and Queen Kossamak, entered politics, and founded the Sangkum (Socialist People's Community) Party which supports a parliamentary monarchy, strong central government and provincial assemblies to administer local affairs. In the General Election of August 1955 the Sangkum won all the seats in the assembly, routing the chief opposition party, the Democratic Party, led by Sihanouk's cousin, Prince Phorissa, and the anti-French republican Son Ngoc Thanh. Between August 1955 and the General Election of March 1958 there were ten ministries, four of them headed by Sihanouk whose supporters dominated the assembly. In the Election the Sangkum won all the sixty-one seats. King Norodom Suramarit died on 3 April 1960, and the royal powers were then vested in a Council of Regency until a new King should be elected. Effective control remained in the hands of Sihanouk.

There are few industries and little commerce, although foreign aid has been used to build a new port on the Gulf of Siam. The country is purely agricultural and, owing to the preponderance of celibate priests (*Bonzes*) and the subsequent low birth-rate, entirely self-supporting. It has been troubled by Viet-Minh guerrilla forces, all of which were evacuated following the Geneva Agreements, and various terrorist groups of which the Issaraks, originally in the pay of the Thai government, are the most powerful. The absence of a parliamentary opposition may drive critics of the government into guerrilla activity. Prince Sihanouk hopes to avert this by judicious use of American economic and technical aid.

Cameroons, British. A former trusteeship territory lying (with one short break) along the eastern frontier of Nigeria; area 34,081 sq. m.; population (1960) approximately 1,430,000; capital Buea. The territory is part of the former German protectorate of Kamerun, *q.v.* In 1922 it was placed by the League of Nations under a British mandate, which in 1946 became a trusteeship territory under the United Nations.

The northern area, known as the Northern Cameroons, (area 17,500 sq. m., population 700,000) was for many years attached to three provinces in the Northern Region of Nigeria and administered with them. A plebiscite held on 7 November 1959 showed that a majority wished to delay a decision on the future of the area and not to join Nigeria when it became independent. On 1 July 1960 it became a separate province of the Northern Region known as Trusteeship Province; when Nigeria became independent on 1 October 1960 its administration was taken over by the U.K., but a second plebiscite held in February 1961 resulted in a majority for union with Nigeria, which took place later that year.

The southern area, known as the Southern Cameroons (area 16,581 sq. m., population 830,000) had also for many years been treated in practice as part of Nigeria, but with the status of a separate Region.

A general election in January 1959 resulted in a narrow victory for the Kamerun National Democratic Party, which favoured union with Cameroun. It won 14 out of 26 seats and its leader, John N. Foncha, became Prime Minister, succeeding Dr Emanuel M. L. Endeley, who is married to a Nigerian and whose Kamerun National Congress favoured the retention of the association with Nigeria and the British Commonwealth. In May 1960 the Congress merged with the Kamerun People's Party to form the Cameroons People's National Confederation. A second plebiscite, in February 1961, resulted in a majority for union with Cameroun, *q.v.*, which took place later that year.

The territory as a whole could not balance its budget, although the Nigerian government, before Nigerian independence, spent very considerable sums in the territory. Bananas are the chief cash product, but the weather has often ruined the annual crop. Attempts have been made to develop alternative crops.

Cameroons, French. The name by which the area to the east of Nigeria and the British Cameroons was known during its life as a French mandate (from 1922 to 1946) and a French trusteeship territory (from 1946 to 1960). It achieved independence on 1 January 1960, since when it has been known as the Cameroun Republic, or Cameroun, q.v.

Cameroun. An independent republic on the Gulf of Guinea and to the south-east of Nigeria; area 143,415 sq. m.; population 3,223,000, including 16,382 Europeans; capital Yaoundé. The country is part of the former German protectorate of Kamerun, q.v., and from 1922 until it became independent on 1 January 1960 it was administered by France, first as a mandate under the League of Nations (from 1922 to 1946) and then as a trusteeship territory (from 1946 to 1960). During these periods it was known as the French Cameroons.

The extreme northern part of the country, which is thinly populated, is Moslem, relatively undeveloped, and largely controlled by its cattle-raising chieftains. Its savannah and steppe yield cotton, groundnuts, rice, yams, and other local foods. The southern part of the country is a region of tropical rain forest, producing mainly bananas, cocoa, and coffee, with additional crops of cotton, palm oil, rice, and rubber.

In the area bordering Nigeria the substantial and industrious Bamiléké tribe, which makes up one sixth of the total population, has, with the Bassa and Baoum, organized guerrilla warfare against the government. Its discontent results from the shortage of land and the intense overpopulation, and the Bamiléké tend to support the left-wing Union des Populations Camérounaises (U.P.C.) which was banned from 1955 to 1960. It favoured union with the Southern Cameroons, which took place in 1961.

Government is by a President, a Prime Minister with a cabinet and a legislative assembly of 100 elected by universal suffrage for 5 years. The fact that there are 44 northern and 56 southern seats gives the north an influence out of proportion to its population. By the elections of 10 April 1960 Ahmadu Ahidjo, a northerner and leader of the Union Camérounaise, which obtained a majority, was confirmed as Prime Minister.

Canada. A Dominion and member of the British Commonwealth; area 3,851,809 sq. m.; population (1961) 18,041,000; capital Ottawa. The French took possession of the country in the sixteenth century but by the nineteenth century they had ceded all their conquests to the U.K. The British North America Act, 1867, united into a Federation the Canadian Provinces of New Brunswick, Nova Scotia, Ontario (formerly Upper Canada), and Quebec (formerly Lower Canada); provided that the Constitution should be 'similar in principle to that of the United Kingdom'; that the executive authority should be vested in the Sovereign and carried on in the Sovereign's name by a Governor-General and Privy Council; and that the legislative power should be exercised by a Parliament comprising a Senate and a House of Commons. Later the provinces or territories of Alberta, British Columbia, Manitoba, Newfoundland, q.v., Prince Edward Island, Saskatchewan, the Yukon Territory, and the North-West Territories were added to the Federation. There are 102 Senators, appointed for life by the Governor-General. The House of Commons is elected by the people for five years.

Out of the Canadian population in 1951, which was then 14,009,429, 11,949,518 were Canadian born, 933,049 British born, and 1,126,862 foreign born, 282,010 of the latter having been born in the U.S.A. Immigrants have been arriving at an annual rate of about 166,000 since 1953. Canada has two official languages, English and French. The French Canadians have preserved their French language and civilization to such an extent that some twenty per cent of the population give French as their native language. They live mostly in the Province of Quebec, where there are two separate educational systems, one Roman Catholic, which is of the French tradition, and one Protestant, which is of the English tradition of the other nine Provinces. About eighty-seven per cent of the 4,055,681 (1951 figure) people in Quebec are Roman Catholics, and there are three Catholic universities.

There are three main parties in Canada, the Progressive Conservatives, the Liberals and the Co-operative Commonwealth Federation. As a result of federal elections held in June 1957 the Progressive Conservatives, under John Diefenbaker, q.v., came to power for the first time since 1935. Diefenbaker became Prime Minister but, as he did not have a clear majority in the House of Commons, he went to the country again in April 1958. The Progressive Conservatives then gained an additional 95 seats so that the party representation was: Progressive Conservatives, 208; Liberals, 49; Co-operative Commonwealth Federation, 8. The Liberals had been in power continuously from 1921 to 1957 except for a few weeks in 1926 and from 1930 to 1935. They were led until 1949 by the late W. L. Mackenzie King, from then until 1958 by the French-speaking Louis St Laurent and subsequently by Lester Pearson, q.v. The Co-operative Commonwealth Federation (C.C.F.) is Canada's equivalent of the British Labour Party. It was created in 1932 by a merger of various Socialist and farming interests but has never succeeded in becoming the second largest party. The Social Credit Party (*see* Social Credit) has declined in recent years and in 1958 lost all its 19 seats in the House of Commons.

Canada exports newsprint paper, wood-pulp, wood, fish and fishery products, aluminium, copper, nickel, and grain. It is the world's greatest producer of nickel, platinum. and asbestos, ranks second in aluminium, gold, and zinc, and fourth in copper and lead. Oil wells are being developed. Canada receives over $300,000,000 annually in the form of new capital from abroad for direct investment, of which about ninety per cent comes from the U.S.A.

Canal Waters Dispute. A prolonged dispute between the governments of India and Pakistan concerning their respective rights over the waters of the rivers and canals flowing from Kashmir and the East Punjab into West Pakistan and used for irrigation purposes by both countries. The East Punjab government, supported by the Indian central government, claimed exclusive proprietary rights over the rivers in its territory, whereas the Pakistan government maintained that since its economy was completely dependent on these rivers it was entitled in international law, and in equity, to an equal share in their waters. The rivers in question were the Indus and its five tributaries, the Sutlej, Beas, Ravi, Jhelum, and Chenab. In 1951 the International Bank for Reconstruction and Development began to mediate between the parties, and in 1954 it made certain proposals which were the basis of the settlement reached in September 1960. India is ultimately to have full use of the waters of the three eastern rivers, the Sutlej, Beas, and Ravi, while the Pakistani areas affected will receive water brought from the western rivers, the Indus, Jhelum. and Chenab by new canals.

Capitalism. The economic system under which the ownership of the means of production is concentrated in the hands of a class, consisting of only a minor section of society, and under which there is a propertyless class for whom the sale of their labour-power, as a commodity, is the only source of livelihood. It is not necessarily coincidental with free enterprise; in the nineteenth century, especially in England, the new factory industries repeatedly demanded free access to markets and to labour supplies, but by the beginning of the twentieth century there was a tendency towards monopolies in different industries and a growing demand for state protection against foreign competition. Under capitalism, as above defined, the means of production and the apparatus of distribution are controlled by private owners who run them at their discretion, driven by an urge for profit

Such a system has often been attacked by Socialists, who aim to nationalize the economic apparatus and to plan its development under central management, the driving principle being not individual profit but public welfare. They criticize capitalism as planless anarchy, leading to recurrent crises because of its lack of co-ordination. Defenders of the capitalist system point to its great achievements. They claim that private initiative cannot be replaced by state control and that the interests of capitalism are necessarily identical with public welfare. According to Socialist theories there is an inward tendency in capitalism which leads to ever larger concentrations of capital, the stronger enterprises ousting or absorbing the weaker ones, until a limited number of trusts, combines, and banks virtually controls a nation's economic life. Thus the liberal free-competition capitalism of former times passes into modern monopolist capitalism. The latter foreshadows the state administration desired by Socialists, the enormous combines and groups being necessarily run along bureaucratic lines. They are controlled by their senior executives rather than by their owners, the shareholders, who may have no interest in the businesses other than as reliable sources of dividends. This development is sometimes called the managerial revolution, *q.v.* Free competition, say such critics, is in any case being gradually replaced by large combines and groups, which do a great deal of planning.

Capitol. A building in Washington, D.C., U.S.A., where the Senate, *q.v.*, and the House of Representatives, *q.v.*, meet. Its cornerstone was laid by President Washington on 18 September 1793. The Capitol is on Capitol Hill, where the Senate Office Buildings, the House of Representatives Office Buildings, the Supreme Court, *q.v.*, and the Library of Congress are also to be found. It is one mile from the White House, *q.v.*, because Washington felt that the executive and legislative branches of the government should be separated.

Capitulations. Treaties by which the subjects of one state when entering into the territory of another state remained under the jurisdiction of their own government, which would be exercised by local consuls. These treaties were often made by European states with Asian and African states whose courts and institutions were regarded as incapable of giving proper protection. During the twentieth century capitulations have been gradually discontinued; they came to an end in Japan in 1899, in Turkey in 1923, in Thailand in 1927, in Persia in 1928, in Egypt in 1937, in China in 1943, and apart from some minor exceptions, such as Muscat and Oman, have now ceased to exist.

Caribbean Federation. An association of the British colonies on the

Caribbean Sea. In 1945 the British Colonial Secretary, Oliver Stanley, proposed a federation which would be an economic entity and which could eventually be granted full self-government. The Standing Committee for the Closer Association of the British West Indian Colonies, set up at Montego Bay, Jamaica, in 1947, recommended the unification of public services, a single currency, a plan for inter-island migration and the establishment of a customs union; in 1950 a draft federal constitution was published. Further conferences in 1953 and 1956 resulted in an agreement by Barbados, Jamaica, *q.v.*, Trinidad, the Leeward Islands (except the Virgin Islands), and the Windward Islands to set up a federation. The West Indies Federation, *q.v.*, came into existence on 3 January 1958.

Castro, Fidel. Cuban politician; born in 1926 in Cuba, the son of a Spanish immigrant, and educated at a Roman Catholic boarding school in Santiago, the Jesuit Belén College and, from 1945 to 1950, the University of Havana. In 1947 he took part in an unofficial raid on the Dominican Republic; on 26 July 1953 he organized an attack on an army barracks in Santiago and was subsequently sentenced to fifteen years' imprisonment, his brother Raúl being sentenced to thirteen years' imprisonment. When President Batistá granted an amnesty to political prisoners in 1955 he was released. In 1956 he went to Mexico to organize a Cuban revolutionary movement, and on 2 December 1956 he landed in Oriente province with a small group which then found refuge in the Sierra Maestra. In 1958 the rebels, led by Castro, had many successes, and on 1 January 1959 they occupied Havana. He became Prime Minister on 16 February 1959

Cento. Central Treaty Organization, *q.v.*

Central African Federation. The incorporation under a federal government of the protectorates of Nyasaland and Northern Rhodesia, and the self-governing colony of Southern Rhodesia. In 1938 a commission was appointed under the chairmanship of Lord Bledisloe as a result of which the Central African Council was established in 1945 as a consultative body. With the support of the British Labour government, the possibility of a federation of the three territories was studied; the final proposals for a self-governing federation were accepted by a referendum in Southern Rhodesia in 1953 and approved by the governments of the U.K. and of the three territories. The federation, known as the Federation of Rhodesia and Nyasaland, *q.v.*, was inaugurated on 3 September 1953.

Central African Republic, also known as Centrafrican Republic, an independent republic; area 238,000 sq. m.; population (mostly in the west and south) 1,177,166, comprising Bayas, Mandjas, Badas

Saras, and 5,000 non-Africans; capital Bangui. The country is land-locked, with Cameroun, Chad and Soudan to the west, north, and east respectively, and the Congo Republic (formerly Belgian) and the Congo Republic (formerly French) to the south. The territory was annexed by France in 1888 and later became, as Ubangi-Shari, one of the four territories comprising French Equatorial Africa, *q.v.*; it achieved self-government within the French Community, *q.v.*, on 1 December 1958, and complete independence, still within the Community, on 17 August 1960.

Legislative powers are vested in an assembly of fifty members elected every five years by universal suffrage. As a result of the elections held on 5 and 25 April 1959 the assembly is controlled by the Movement for the Social Emancipation of Africa. Executive power is exercised by the President of the Government (David Dacko) who is elected by the assembly.

The principal product and export is cotton, and coffee, diamonds and lumber are also exported. The southern border with the Congo Republic (formerly French) runs along the river Oubangui, which is a tributary of the river Congo. There is an economic union with Chad, the Congo Republic (formerly French) and Gabon, the three other states which once formed French Equatorial Africa.

Central Treaty Organization. (Cento). Was set up on 21 August 1959 by Pakistan, Persia, Turkey, and the U.K. to succeed the structure established by those countries, with Iraq, under the Baghdad Pact, *q.v.* Iraq ceased to take part in arrangements relating to the Pact after its revolution in July 1958, and formally withdrew in March 1959.

Centralism. A political system under which the whole country is controlled from a central point, as opposed to decentralized systems of administration such as federalism and regionalism, under which local units (states, provinces) enjoy a greater or lesser degree of autonomy.

Cession. The giving up of territory by one state to another state. It may be the result of war, as when Spain ceded the Philippines to the U.S.A. after the Spanish-American War in 1898, or of peaceful negotiations, as when Denmark sold the Danish West Indies to the U.S.A. for $25,000,000 in 1916, or when Austria ceded Venice to France as a gift in 1866. The citizens of the ceding state living in the territory become citizens of the other state, unless some special arrangement is made by which they may keep their old nationality.

Ceylon. An island in the Indian Ocean off the southern coast of India, which is a Dominion and member of the British Commonwealth; area 25,332 sq. m.; capital Colombo; population 8,750,000, of whom 5,621,332 are Sinhalese and another 983,304 Tamils from southern

India. Buddhism is the religion of the majority; there are more than 1,610,000 Hindus. Once a British colony, Ceylon achieved 'fully responsible status' within the British Commonwealth by the Ceylon Independence Act, 1947. The Act incorporated a defence agreement between the U.K. and Ceylon, which provided for mutual protection against aggression and sanctioned the use by the U.K. of naval and air stations in Ceylon in exchange for the training in England of Sinhalese airmen and naval personnel. The stations used were the naval base at Trincomalee and the air base at Katunayake. Under a new arrangement announced in June 1957 the U.K. agreed to hand over the stations to Ceylon and to withdraw its main establishments in three years, although some facilities (such as the right to store ammunition and oil) were to remain for up to five years. Ceylon agreed to pay £1,650,000 for the fixed assets and in settlement of claims, and, on 15 October and 1 November 1957 respectively, took over Trincomalee and Katunayake. As a result of the British withdrawal from Ceylon, a wartime air base was re-established in the Maldive Islands, *q.v.*

In elections held in April 1956 the People's United Front (M.E.P.), led by the late Solomon Bandaranaike, won a majority of the seats in the lower house, thereby displacing the United National Party. A feature of the 1956 elections was the vigorous campaign waged by Buddhist monks against the outgoing government which, they alleged, was dominated by Christians. The subsequent termination of the defence agreement resulted from Bandaranaike's belief that it debarred Ceylon from playing a mediatory role in Asian affairs.

Riots occurred in 1958 among the Tamils following the introduction by the M.E.P. of the Official Language Act, passed in 1956, by which Sinhalese replaced English as the official tongue. The Sinhalese and Tamil languages had previously been on an equal footing. The operation of the Act had the effect of encouraging the separatist tendencies of both the immigrant Tamils from southern India and the 908,705 Ceylon Tamils who are mostly Hindus, and who constitute a minority group in the Sinhalese-speaking Buddhist population.

Bandaranaike was assassinated in September 1959 by a Buddhist monk, and succeeded as Prime Minister by Wijayananda Dahanayake. In the elections of March 1960 the United National Party won only 50 out of 151 seats but was the largest single party, with the result that its leader, Dudley Senanayake, became Prime Minister. Further elections held in July 1960 gave the Sri Lanka Freedom Party 70 seats and reduced the U.N.P. strength to 40. The S.L.F. leader,

Sirimavo Bandaranaike, *q.v.*, the widow of Bandaranaike, thereupon became Prime Minister.

Ceylon's economy is geared to the export trade. Two thirds of the cultivated land is devoted to the production of cash crops such as rubber and tea; in consequence nearly three quarters of the rice needed to feed the island's rapidly increasing population has to be imported. If the world price of rubber or tea should fall Ceylon must import less rice. This dangerous dependence on the price paid in the world market for Ceylon teas, which form the bulk of the exports, has led to a reduction in the rubber acreage in favour of rice-growing, and extensive land reclamation and deforestation. The Ministry of Industries, created in 1947, has encouraged minor developments in the cement industry and leather manufacture.

Chad. An independent republic; area 501,000 sq. m.; population 2,730,000, comprising Arabs, Saras and Peuls, and 3,800 non-Africans; capital Fort Lamy. The country is landlocked, with Niger, Nigeria, and Cameroun to the west and sharing Lake Chad, Libya to the north, Sudan to the east, and the Central African Republic to the south. The territory was annexed by France in 1913 and later became one of the four territories comprising French Equatorial Africa, *q.v.*; it achieved self-government within the French Community, *q.v.*, on 28 November 1958 and complete independence, still within the Community, on 11 August 1960.

Legislative powers are vested in an assembly of 85 members elected every five years by universal suffrage. At the elections held on 31 May 1959 the Chad Progressive Party (the local section of the Rassemblement Démocratique Africain) led by François Tombalbaye, obtained 57 seats, the Chad Democratic and Independent Union, led by Jean Baptiste, 13 seats, Chad Social Action 11 seats, and the Chad Rural Independent Group 4 seats. Executive power is exercised by the Premier (François Tombalbaye) who is designated by a simple majority of the assembly.

The principal exports are livestock, cotton, fish, and groundnuts; rice and millet are also produced and there are deposits of tin. There is an economic union with the Central African Republic, the Congo Republic (formerly French), and Gabon, the three other states which once formed French Equatorial Africa.

Chapultepec, Act of. A declaration made on 3 March 1945 by the Inter-American Conference on War and Peace. It asserted, in terms similar to those of the Declaration of Panama made in 1939 by the Pan American Union, *q.v.*, the determination of American states to assist each other and to prevent any non-American state from violating their political independence. In anticipation of the Charter of the United Nations, the Act stated that the agreement between the American states was a regional arrangement not inconsistent with the principles of the United Nations. The Act was reaffirmed and its provisions extended by the Rio Treaty, *q.v.*, of 2 September 1947.

Chiang Kai-shek. President of Nationalist China; born 31 October 1886. He was sent from China to Japan in 1907 to complete his military training but deserted from the Japanese army in 1911 to take part in the Chinese revolution. As chief of staff to the revolutionary leader Sun Yat Sen, whose sister-in-law he later married, Chiang studied Russian military methods in Moscow in 1923. After his return he opposed the Chinese Communists and in 1928 became the head of the government established at Nanking, the new capital. In the following years his forces fought local war-lords, Japanese invaders, and the Communists (who captured Chiang in 1936 but released him so that he could continue to fight the Japanese). He continued to lead the Chinese government and the Kuomintang, *q.v.*, during the Second World War but in 1948 his forces were defeated by the Communists and he retired to Formosa, *q.v.* He has repeatedly asserted that his forces will one day invade the Chinese mainland and overthrow the Communist government.

Chile. An independent state on the west coast of South America; population 7,364,498, comprising descendants of Spanish settlers, Spanish Indians, natives and Europeans; area 286,397 sq. m.; capital Santiago. Chile was ruled by Spain from the sixteenth century until it achieved independence in 1818. Under the 1925 Constitution laws are passed by a National Congress consisting of a Senate of 45 members elected for eight years, and a Chamber of Deputies with 147 members, elected for four years. The President is elected for six years by direct popular vote.

In recent years the economy has suffered inflation and serious strikes have occurred. A system of subsidies, and a law which tied most wages to the annual price increases, had already caused difficulties when world copper prices fell at the end of the Korean War in 1953. At first the government assisted the inflation by printing paper money and fought the numerous strikes in the mines and elsewhere with such totalitarian powers as the National Congress, which remained influential throughout, would grant. Policy was then altered on the advice of a U.S. firm of economic consultants; the peso was devalued, wage increases were severely limited, taxes on foreign companies were reduced and price ceilings were imposed. Throughout this period the President was Carlos Ibáñez del Campo (born 1878), who was President from 1927 to 1931 and was re-elected in 1952. He was succeeded by a businessman, Jorge Alessandri Rodríguez, in September 1958.

Chile is potentially a rich country; it has large reserves of nitrates and coal, and produces twelve per cent of the world's copper, which is mined by subsidiaries of U.S. companies.

China. Officially the People's Republic of China; area 4,300,000 sq. m.; population (1953) approximately 700,000,000, excluding 10,000,000 in Formosa, *q.v.*; capital Peking. The Imperial Manchu dynasty was overthrown by the 1911 revolution organized by the Kuomintang, *q.v.*, under Sun Yat Sen, who was proclaimed President of the Republic in 1912 in opposition to the reactionary Yuan Shi-kai, who had been declared President in the previous year. Yuan announced his intention of becoming Emperor in 1915, but died soon afterwards. There followed years of strife between Yuan's supporters, with their bases in north China, and Sun Yat Sen's republican followers whose headquarters were at Nanking in the south. When Sun Yat Sen died in 1925 Chiang Kai-shek, *q.v.*, carried on his work and undertook the task of establishing a Republic throughout China. The Kuomintang government became and has remained a military dictatorship, opposed to political democracy, with little concern for the welfare of the Chinese people and indifferent to the popular rights which Sun Yat Sen expounded. Meanwhile the Chinese Communist Party had been founded in 1921 in the north and had developed independently of the Kuomintang, which regarded it as a rebel force. In 1928 Chiang marched north as far as Peking, defeated the war-lord Chang Tso-lin, and massacred the Communists in Shanghai. He then concentrated on restoring peace in the Yangtse valley, driving out Communists who had sovietized two provinces and introduced land reforms. In 1934, led by Mao Tse-tung, *q.v.*, they made their historic 3,000-mile trek to the northern province of Shensi.

Japan had taken advantage of the confusion to invade Manchuria in 1931, and a series of clashes took place culminating in a full-scale invasion of China by Japanese forces in 1937. The Communists had agreed to co-operate with the Kuomintang in resisting Japanese aggression; in return Chiang agreed to reorganize his government at Nanking so as to include all parties, and not merely the Kuomintang. The Japanese succeeded in conquering large areas of China and in driving Chiang's government westwards out of Nanking to a new capital at Chungking. When the war with Japan ended in 1945 the struggle between the Communists and the Kuomintang continued.

In 1946 President Truman's envoy, General Marshall, persuaded the two sides to sign an armistice, but fighting continued; he concluded that the only proper solution would be for the Kuomintang to permit elections to take place and to enforce its plan for constitutional government, which it had postponed seven times since 1936. A similar suggestion had been made in 1942 by the Communist leader Mao Tse-tung, when he was a member of the coalition government. In 1947 Chiang declared that the one-party rule of the Kuomintang was at an end and a National Assembly was elected to serve a term of six years. After a number of military successes the Communists obtained full control in 1949 and the Kuomintang forces retreated to Formosa. A U.S. State Department White Paper, published in 1949, stated that the U.S.A. had given to the Kuomintang government large quantities of military equipment and arms, most of which was either captured by the Communists or handed to them by Kuomintang deserters; the White Paper said that there was no evidence of Russian assistance to the Communists between 1946 and 1948. The new Chinese government has been recognized by the U.K. and by most other countries, but not by the U.S.A.

The constitutional laws of China, as finally approved on 20 September 1954, consist of: (1) a Common Programme of sixty articles chosen by the People's Political Consultative Conference of 636 delegates in 1949; (2) an Organic Law of thirty-one articles; and (3) the Constitution itself of 106 articles. A basic aim of the government is the replacement of capitalist ownership by popular ownership. The National People's Congress is the legislature, and by a two-thirds majority can amend the Constitution. When the Congress is not in session its powers are delegated to a Standing Committee (corresponding to the Presidium of the Supreme Soviet in the U.S.S.R.), a permanent body which has power to interpret the laws passed by Congress, to supervise government departments, to issue decrees and to supervise the courts. The State Council or cabinet has forty-three members, including the Chief of Council (Premier), Chou En-lai, *q.v.* The Chairman of the Standing Committee of the National People's Congress is Chu Te, *q.v.* The Chairman of the Central Committee of the Communist Party is Mao Tse-tung. The Chairman of the Republic is Liu Shao-chi, *q.v.* He is elected by the National People's Congress for four years to the office of Chairman of the Republic, which is similar to that of President of the U.S.A., although China, unlike the U.S.A., also has a Prime Minister.

China has abundant resources of antimony, manganese, tungsten, timber, tin and iron ore; the Second Five-Year Plan, for the years

1958–1962, provided for the doubling of industrial output and an increase in agricultural production of thirty-five per cent by the end of the period. Capital construction, with particular emphasis on machinery and the metallurgical industries, was to receive forty per cent of the government revenue, so that by 1962 seventy per cent of all machinery and equipment needed would be produced at home. The Chairman of the State Planning Commission, Li Fu-chun, anticipated that it would take fifty years fully to develop China's resources. The agricultural programme is frequently interrupted by appalling floods and severe droughts, but its success is vital in a country where the population will exceed 800,000,000 by 1970. In an attempt to end widespread illiteracy, and to enable all Chinese to speak the official national language instead of the numerous dialects, the State Council, in December 1957, approved the use of the Latin alphabet in a thirty-letter version. Eventually this alphabet may supplant the present script with its 30,000 characters.

The foreign policy of China since 1949 has been characterized by a desire to regain control of those areas which, at the height of Chinese power, have been integral parts or vassals of China. The government has accordingly reasserted its authority over Inner Mongolia, *q.v.*, Manchuria, *q.v.*, and Tibet, *q.v.*; it has given support to Chinese Communist elements in Viet-Nam, *q.v.*, and Malaya, *q.v.*, and has sent military forces to Korea, *q.v.* There were some 10,300,000 Chinese living in South-East Asia but outside China in 1958, of whom the majority were in Thailand, Malaya, and Indonesia; the Chinese government policy that overseas Chinese never lose their nationality helps to bind these people more closely to their country of origin.

Chou En-lai. Chief of the State Council (Premier) of the Chinese People's Republic; born 1896. He graduated at Nankai University and went to Paris to continue his studies, where he organized a Communist cell among Chinese expatriates. He returned to China in 1923, became Communist Party Secretary for the Kuangtung Region and then Chief of the Political Section of the Whampoa Military Academy. In 1936 he advocated the unification of the Communist Party and the Kuomintang, *q.v.*, against the Japanese invaders. He became Chief of the State Council in 1949.

Christian Democrats. A term describing the members of moderate Roman Catholic political parties in Belgium (Social Christians, the largest single parliamentary party), France (mostly in the M.R.P.), the German Federal Republic (C.D.U. and C.S.U., which have a majority in the Bundestag; most German Protestants are in East Germany), Italy (the largest single parliamentary party), and the

Netherlands (the Christian Historical Union). After the Second World War the Christian Democratic parties achieved striking successes in these countries on platforms of social reform, particularly where their members had been active in wartime resistance movements against Germany.

Chu Te. Chinese Communist and military leader, born 1886 in Szechuan; son of a prosperous farmer. He graduated from Yunnan Military Academy and took part in revolutionary activities against the Manchu dynasty which was overthrown in 1911 in what has been called the Old Revolution. He joined the Communist Party while in Berlin in 1922. After the 1927 split between the Communists and the Kuomintang, *q.v.*, he led the Nanchang revolt, and later helped Mao Tsetung, *q.v.*, to organize the Red Army. He took part with Mao in the Long March (3,000 miles) from Kiangsi to Yenan. After the Japanese invasion he held a number of high military posts and his soldiers played a very large part in the defeat of the Kuomintang. He is a Vice-Chairman of the People's Revolutionary Military Council, Commander-in-Chief of the Armies of the Chinese People's Republic, and Chairman of the Standing Committee of the National People's Congress.

Churchill, Sir Winston Leonard Spencer. British statesman; born 30 November 1874, son of Lord Randolph Churchill (third son of the seventh Duke of Marlborough) and an American mother; educated at Harrow and Sandhurst. He entered the army in 1895, served with the Spanish forces in Cuba, 1895, and in two colonial campaigns (Malakand 1897, Tirah 1899), and contested the Oldham Parliamentary Division as a Conservative in 1899. He was war correspondent of the *Morning Post* in the South African War, 1899–1900, and taken prisoner by the Boers. On his return to England in 1900 he was elected Conservative M.P. for Oldham; however he opposed Joseph Chamberlain's high tariff plans, and as a free-trader felt compelled to join the Liberals. He became Under-Secretary of State for the Colonies in 1905 and furthered a federation policy in South Africa. He served as Liberal M.P. for North-West Manchester, 1906–8, and for Dundee in 1908, and was President of the Board of Trade, 1908–10, when he carried through important social legislation. In 1910 he became Home Secretary, and in 1911 First Lord of the Admiralty, where he brought about extensive naval reforms, increasing the pay of ratings and raising the educational standard of naval cadets. His preparations for the creation of a naval war staff were cut short by the outbreak of the First World War in which he developed the strategic thesis of the 'Eastern Front', including the Dardanelles expedition, but was not given sufficient forces for its successful realization. In 1915 he resigned from the cabinet, went on active service in France and became Lieutenant-Colonel of the 6th Royal Scots Fusiliers. Recalled by the Prime Minister, Lloyd George, in 1917, he became Minister of Munitions and was then Secretary of State for Air and for War, and later Colonial Secretary from 1921 to 1923. At that time he strongly opposed the Russian Revolution. His views aroused Liberal dislike, and in 1922 he was rejected by his Dundee constituency. He was out of Parliament for two years and began his work on pre-war and war policies, *The World Crisis*. In 1924 he returned to the Conservative Party, was elected M.P. for Epping, and made Chancellor of the Exchequer by Baldwin, a post that he held until 1929. The return to the gold standard in 1925 took place while he was in office.

From 1930 to 1939 Churchill was given no office. He turned his attention to foreign affairs and until 1933 he opposed French disarmament but favoured redress of Germany's grievances. On the advent to power of the Nazis in Germany in 1933 he urged early British rearmament, especially in the air. He did not, however, believe that any attempt should be made to halt the activities of German and Italian forces against the Spanish government, and thought that non-intervention was the correct policy. He strongly opposed German Nazism, partly because it offended his deeply-rooted liberalism and partly because of the growing menace to the U.K. He predicted German expansion in Central Europe, exposed Hitler's intent to dominate the world, attacked the appeasement policy, supported the Eden resignation, rejected the Munich Agreement, *q.v.*, and saw his policies being adopted in 1939 when the U.K. opposed German aggression in Poland. On the outbreak of war he became First Lord of the Admiralty and was later Prime Minister of the coalition government from 1940 to 1945, and of the 'caretaker' Conservative government in 1945. His leadership during the darkest hours of the war, and during the years of preparation for the ultimate victory, earned him the lasting gratitude of the British people and of many millions of people throughout the world.

When the Conservative Party was defeated in the 1945 General Election he became Leader of the Opposition. Since 1945 he has been M.P. for Woodford. While out of office he repeatedly championed a close link between the U.K. and western Europe on the one side and the U.S.A. on the other. He was Minister of Defence, 1951–2, and Prime Minister and First Lord of the Treasury from 1951 until 1955 when he relinquished all ministerial offices. Before he retired he became a Knight of the Garter, refusing the offer of a peerage, and he remained in the House of Commons as the Member for Woodford.

Cold War. A state of tension between countries in which each side adopts policies designed to strengthen itself and weaken the other, but falling short of actual or 'hot' war. The term is frequently used to describe the relationship which has existed between the western powers and the U.S.S.R. since 1947.

Collective Security. A system by which the security and territorial integrity of each country are guaranteed by all countries. The principle was embodied in the Covenant of the League of Nations, *q.v.*, and underlies the Charter of the United Nations, *q.v.* A system of collective security requires the acceptance by individual countries of collective decisions, and their willingness to carry out those decisions, if necessary by military action. Under the United Nations Charter, power to deal with threats to peace is vested in the Security Council, *q.v.*, which cannot act if one of the five major powers (China, France, the U.K., the U.S.A., and the U.S.S.R.) dissents. The principle of collective security has thus not been fully established.

Collectivism. A term covering all economic and political systems based on co-operation and central planning, including not only socialism proper but also looser systems such as co-operativism, corporatism, state control, and the general co-ordination of economic life.

Colombia. An independent state in South America; capital Bogota; area 440,505 sq. m.; population (1959) approximately 13,823,600; Spanish-speaking. Roman Catholicism is the official religion. It was a Spanish colony from 1536 until it achieved independence as part of Greater Colombia (which included Panama, Venezuela, and Ecuador) in 1819, and as a separate republic in 1830. From 1922 to 1953 every President except one completed his four-year term, ruling with a Senate (63 members) and a House of Representatives (131 members). There was civil war from 1949 to 1953, when the army displaced a dictatorship established by President Gomez. The presidency was then seized by General Gustavo Rojas Pinilla, a conservative, and Congress was suspended in favour of a National Constituent Assembly. Pinilla was overthrown in May 1957 by a military junta. Supported by the first vote ever held in Colombia on a basis of universal adult suffrage, the junta amended the Constitution in December 1957 so that Congress would consist of equal numbers of Liberals and Conservatives. Congress then elected as President Alberto Lleras Camargo who took office in August 1958.

The Coffee Growers' Federation of Colombia, the world's second largest producer of coffee, provides eighty-five per cent of the country's exports. There is recurrent difficulty in keeping a stable price level. United States companies have contributed eighty-five per cent and British companies fifteen per cent of the foreign investment in the oil industry. Colombia also produces tobacco, copper, wood, cotton, steel, and bananas.

Colombo Plan. A plan devised at Colombo, Ceylon, in January 1950, by British Commonwealth Foreign Ministers, for the co-operative development of the countries of south and south-east Asia. These countries are Pakistan, Burma, India, Ceylon, Nepal, Thailand, Viet-Nam, Laos, Cambodia, Philippines, Malaya, Singapore, Indonesia and Borneo, containing about 600,000,000 people or one quarter of the world's population. The Plan included a review of possible developments in a six-year period, 1951–7, and was extended in 1959 to cover the period 1961–66. The countries produce almost all the world's jute and natural rubber, more than three quarters of its tea, two thirds of its tin, one third of its oils and fats. The Commonwealth governments (Canada, the U.K., India, Pakistan, Ceylon, Australia, New Zealand) set up a Council for Technical Co-operation with headquarters in Colombo and agreed to help in planning public administration, health services, scientific research, agricultural and industrial activities, and the training and equipment of personnel. Funds come from the assisted areas themselves, other Commonwealth countries, the U.S.A., and the International Bank. The United Nations Technical Assistance Board provides expert advisers but not supplies.

Colonial Development Corporation. Was established by the British government under the Overseas Resources Development Act, 1948, with borrowing powers up to £100,000,000 (increased to £150,000,000 in 1958); its duties are to develop British colonial territories with a view to increasing their general productive capacity and trade. It operates on a commercial basis and in close consultation with colonial governments. In 1959 there was a net trading and investment balance of £2,273,817 and a profit balance of £1,334,286.

Colony. An area of land which, with its inhabitants, is entirely subject to the rule of an independent state, of which it does not form an integral part. It is not itself an independent state, though it may, according to its degree of political maturity, be given some self-government. A grant of self-government and of a representative legislature does not prevent the ruling state from disallowing any legislation of which it may disapprove. Colonies have usually originated in settlements by traders or explorers of territories unoccupied by any other independent states, or in conquests of territories already occupied by other states.

In British colonies the Sovereign is represented by a Governor, who is in most cases assisted by an executive council which he must consult although he is not bound to follow its advice. In many British colonies there is also a legislative council, usually with a minority of elected members, the majority consisting of the chief officials of the colony and a number of unofficial members appointed by the Governor. There is said to be a representative legislative council when at least one half of its members is elected by the inhabitants of the colony. When the Governor is ordered by the British government to select his executive council from members of the legislative council who can command a majority in that body, the colony is said to have attained self-government, although it is still subject to the Acts passed by the British Parliament in London.

Comecon. Council for Mutual Economic Assistance, *q.v.*

Cominform. The Communist Information Bureau, set up in Belgrade on the initiative of the Communist Party of the U.S.S.R. in October 1947 to co-ordinate the activities of the Communist Parties of Bulgaria, Czechoslovakia, France, Hungary, Italy, Poland, Rumania, the U.S.S.R., and Yugoslavia. Its headquarters were moved to Bucharest in 1948 after the expulsion of Yugoslavia from the Cominform and profound disagreements between Yugoslavia and the U.S.S.R., and it was used as an instrument in the Stalinist domination of eastern Europe. In April 1956, after the *rapprochement* of Yugoslavia and the U.S.S.R., the Cominform was dissolved; its winding-up was interpreted as a gesture to disarm western suspicions of Soviet intentions.

Comintern. The Communist International, also known as the Third International in contrast to the First International, founded by Karl Marx in 1864, and the Second International, established in 1889. The Comintern was founded on the initiative of the Russian Communist Party in 1919 in order to rally all extreme left-wing Socialists and Communists who disliked the moderating influence of the Second International. For many years the Comintern encouraged revolution against capitalist governments, but it was dissolved in May 1943, largely as a gesture of goodwill by the U.S.S.R. towards its allies in the Second World War. The Cominform, *q.v.*, 1947–56, took over some of the functions of the Comintern but operated over a smaller area.

Common Market. The scheme for a progressive reduction of tariffs established by the European Economic Community, *q.v.*

Communism. May mean either the type of society in which property is vested in the community, every individual receiving what he needs and working according to his capacity, or the revolutionary movement which seeks to achieve that type of society by overthrowing the capitalist system and establishing a dictatorship of the proletariat. Modern Communism has its basis in Marxism, *q.v.*, as developed by the Russian revolutionary leader Vladimir Ilyitch Lenin (1870–1924), who applied the Marxian analysis to the new forms of capitalism which had developed since the days of Marx. Lenin studied the trusts and combines which, with the inevitable concentration of capital, had superseded the small producers who characterized the earlier stages of capitalism. He concluded that the state and large capital interests were collaborating in imperialist policies leading to recurrent wars, that capitalists would pay higher wages to skilled workers who would then betray the proletariat by adopting moderate policies, and that the poorer classes of workers would continue to adhere to revolutionary Socialism as expounded by Marx. Like Marx, he regarded the state as the instrument of the ruling class and believed that the proletariat must destroy it and replace it by a new state machinery of its own. Communists believe that their first task is the establishment of Socialism, and that the next stage is true Communism. They say that under Socialism they give effect to the principle 'From each according to his ability, to each according to his work', and that there are still distinctions between classes, between mental and manual labour and between state property and co-operative property. Under Communism social life would be guided by the principle 'From each according to his ability, to each according to his needs', and class, labour, and property distinctions would disappear. Eventually the machinery of government would no longer be needed and the state would wither away.

Concentration, Theory of. The Marxian theory that the larger and stronger capitalists gradually oust or absorb the smaller and weaker ones, until all the capital is concentrated in the hands of a few powerful combines, trusts or banks.

Conclave. A secluded assembly of the Cardinals of the Roman Catholic Church for the election of a new Pope. Conclaves are always held in Rome. They must be convoked within three weeks after the death of a Pope. All the Cardinals in the world are summoned to Rome to take part in the Conclave; they are then cut off from communication with the outside world. Each Cardinal may bring into the Conclave a secretary and an attendant. There are, as a rule, about three hundred persons in the Conclave, which must not end until it has elected a Pope.

The Conclave can act if at least half the number of Cardinals is present. The Cardinals are pledged to lifelong secrecy as to the proceedings of the Conclave. The Pope must be elected with a two-thirds majority. If the ballot does not produce this majority the voting papers are wrapped in wet straw and burnt. This produces black smoke which escapes through the chimney and indicates to the crowd waiting outside that no Pope has yet been elected. Ballots are repeated until the prescribed majority is obtained. The voting papers are then burnt without straw so as to produce white smoke. This is the traditional sign for the election of a Pope. The oldest Cardinal-Deacon steps out on the balcony and tells the crowd: 'Habemus papam' (We have a Pope).

Concordat (from the Latin *pactum concordatum*, agreed pact). An agreement between the Pope and a government, providing for mutual rights and duties, the status of the Catholic clergy and religious orders, state subsidies for the Church, the position of Catholic schools, protection of Church property, state influence on the appointment of bishops, etc. It is tantamount to an international convention. Where a Concordat cannot be reached, there is sometimes a *modus vivendi, q.v.*, an informal agreement with similar purposes.

Condominium. The common rule of a territory by two or more countries. There is an Anglo-French condominium in the New Hebrides, in the South Pacific Ocean, and until 1956 there was an Anglo-Egyptian condominium over Sudan, *q.v.*

Confederation. An association of several states which unite for the purpose of mutual co-operation and defence, but which does not have a direct power over the citizens of the associated states, and is not usually entrusted with the conduct of their foreign affairs. It differs from a federation, *q.v.*, which is a much closer association acquiring direct power over its states or provinces and their citizens. From 1778 until 1787, when a federation was created, the U.S.A. was a confederation. There was a Germanic Confederation from 1815 to 1866, and a Confederation of the Netherlands from 1580 to 1795. Switzerland, though in name a confederation, is a federation. The members of a confederation remain separate international persons (while members of a federation usually lose their international personality) but prohibit war between themselves.

Congo Republic. Formerly Belgian Congo, *q.v.*, an independent republic; area 909,000 sq. m.; population 13,540,182 Africans, comprising mostly Hamites and Pygmies (in the east) and Negroes (Bantu, Nilotics, and Sudanese), and approximately 36,000 Europeans, mostly Belgians; capital Leopoldville. There are 150 major tribes, speaking 38 different languages.

The territory became the Congo Free State in 1885 when Leopold II, King of the Belgians, was recognized as its personal sovereign head by the great powers at the Conference of Berlin. It became a Belgian colony when it was officially annexed in 1907, and for many years Belgium practised a policy of paternalism, forbidding political associations and debarring Africans from obtaining professional qualifications. After the Second World War, as industrialization (particularly mining) proceeded and many Africans acquired technical skills, Belgium found it increasingly difficult to arrest the political development of the country. Various plans were advanced in 1958 and 1959 to hold local elections and to grant extensive powers to each of the six provinces, but serious riots in Leopoldville and elsewhere forced Belgium to agree, in January 1960, to complete independence, which was granted on 30 June 1960.

At the election held before independence was achieved, 36 of the 137 seats in the House of Representatives (the lower house) were won by the Congo National Movement (M.N.C.) led by Patrice Lumumba, a member of the Batetela tribe, from Stanleyville in the Eastern Province. One of the M.N.C.'s leading opponents among the 59 other parties was the Abako Party, representing the 800,000 Bakongo tribesmen of south-west Congo, led by Joseph Kasavubu of Leopoldville, who became President after independence, while Lumumba became Prime Minister. Kasavubu had once hoped to revive the fourteenth century unity of the Bakongo, who are now divided between the Congo Republic (formerly Belgian Congo), the Congo Republic (formerly French Congo), and Angola. Many separatist tendencies were evident during the following months, especially among the Baluba of Kasai Province, the Mongo of Equator Province, and the Bakongo of Leopoldville Province, but the most serious was the purported secession of the rich mining province of Katanga, led by the Conakat Party under Moise Tshombe, helped by Belgian interests. In view of the danger of intervention by the major powers the United Nations agreed to give military assistance to the government and a United Nations Emergency Force landed in July 1960. Disturbances continued and in September 1960 Kasavubu dismissed Lumumba, who was seized by Katanga forces in January 1961 and later found dead, having probably been murdered by them.

The country has substantial mineral resources including copper, diamonds, gold, silver, tin, uranium, radium, zinc, and cobalt, of which it is the largest supplier in the world. There are also exports of coffee, palm oil, cotton, and rubber.

Congo Republic. Formerly French Congo, or Middle Congo, an independent republic; area 139,000 sq. m.; population 794,577, comprising Bavilis, Balalis, Batékés, M'Bochis and 10,000 non-Africans; capital Brazzaville, the former capital of French Equatorial Africa, *q.v.* The country has approximately 65 miles of coastline on the Atlantic Ocean, between Gabon to the north and part of Angola to the south; Cameroun and the Central African Republic also lie to the north, and the river Oubangui and the Congo Republic (formerly Belgian) lie to the east. The territory was annexed by France in 1888 and later became one of the four territories comprising French Equatorial Africa; it achieved self-government within the French Community, *q.v.*, on 28 November 1958, and complete independence, still within the Community, on 17 August 1960.

Legislative powers are vested in an assembly of 61 members elected every five years by universal suffrage. At the elections held on 14 June 1959 the Democratic Union for the Defence of African Interests (the local section of the Rassemblement Démocratique Africain), led by Abbé Fulbert Toulou, obtained 51 seats, and the African Socialist Movement obtained 10 seats. Executive power is exercised by the Premier (Abbé Fulbert) who is elected by the assembly.

The principal exports are lumber, palm oil, palm kernels, peanuts, lead ore, and tobacco. It is not fundamentally a rich country and there are few valuable mineral deposits. There is an economic union with the Central African Republic, Chad and Gabon, the three other states which once formed French Equatorial Africa.

Congress. The bicameral federal legislature of the U.S.A., comprising the Senate, *q.v.*, and the House of Representatives, *q.v.* Article One of the U.S. Constitution begins: 'All legislative powers herein granted shall be vested in a Congress of the United States, which shall consist of a Senate and House of Representatives.' Elections take place by popular vote on the first Tuesday after the first Monday in November in the even-numbered years, except in Maine where they are held in September. The Congressional term begins on the following 3 January and continues for two years. A member of the Senate is usually referred to as a senator and a member of the House of Representatives as a congressman.

Congress of Industrial Organizations (C.I.O.). A U.S. and Canadian labour movement with 6,000,000 members when it merged in December 1955 with the American Federation of Labour, *q.v.*, to form the American Federation of Labour and Congress of Industrial Organizations, *q.v.* The C.I.O. arose after the formation of a Committee for Industrial Organization within the A.F. of L. in 1935. This Committee and the unions affiliated to it advocated the formation of general industrial unions comprising all the workers, skilled as well as unskilled, in an industry, in contrast to the craft unions of the A.F. of L. which were limited to skilled workers only. They claimed that the organizing principles of the A.F. of L. were out of date and that the new mass-production industries, such as the automobile, radio, tyre, steel, and aluminium industries, had brought to the fore a new type of worker. After vain demands for a fundamental modification of the structure of the A.F. of L., eight large unions formed the C.I.O. in November 1935, led by the miners' leader, John L. Lewis, who later left the C.I.O. These unions represented mine, textile, clothing, oil, smelting, typographic and millinery workers; they were later joined by steel, glass, automobile, radio, and rubber workers. The C.I.O. started a campaign to recruit the unorganized workers, and its affiliated unions were expelled at the A.F. of L. convention in 1936. During the Democratic administrations of President Roosevelt and President Truman the C.I.O. was, through its political action committee, more willing than the A.F. of L. to declare its support for Democratic candidates. In 1945 it joined the World Federation of Trade Unions, q.v., from which it withdrew in 1949. The President of the C.I.O., Walter Reuther, q.v., signed the agreement for the merger of the C.I.O. with the A.F. of L. in February 1955.

Congress Party (Indian National Congress). The largest political party in India. In the 1957 elections it won 364 out of the 500 seats in the House of the People. It was founded in the late nineteenth century at the instigation of an Englishman, Allan Octavian Hume, who urged Calcutta University graduates to form a party which would encourage national trades, would bridge religious differences, and which would have as its principal aim the improvement of relations between the British Government and India. Originally the party included Moslems, Hindus, and Untouchables; it emerged nevertheless as a Hindu nationalist movement pledged to expel the British, under the domination first of Bal Gengadhar Tilak, who fomented anti-British riots in Bombay in 1903, and then of Mahatma Gandhi, the advocate of Civil Disobedience. British policy in India between 1919 and 1947 consisted largely of attempts to conciliate the Congress Party. In 1935 it obtained control of eight of the eleven state legislatures; it refused to co-operate in the war against Germany in 1939, and in the war against Japan in 1941, and its leaders were imprisoned. Since the death of Gandhi in 1948 the party has been led by Jawaharlal Nehru, q.v. He is no longer its President, but he heads the Congress Party government of India and is a member of the Party's Central Parliamentary Board.

Until 1947 the party concentrated on one political objective; since then it has struggled to formulate a coherent social and economic policy acceptable to its supporters, and in doing so it has lost many former adherents. At the Sixtieth Indian National Congress held at Avadi in January 1955, the party's new objectives were defined as (*a*) social ownership or control of the means of production in the interests of society as a whole, (*b*) equitable distribution of the nation's wealth, resources, and income, and (*c*) equality of opportunity for all sections of society. Congress affirmed that it was not bound to any dogma or doctrine and that it aimed at a socialistic pattern of society rather than Socialism.

The 1957 Party Manifesto emphasized that attainment of these objectives depended on the abandonment of caste, and of provincialism in politics, and a universal effort to improve production in which privately-owned industry would be given encouragement.

Conservative Party. A British political party, also known as the Conservative and Unionist Party; it obtained 13,750,965 out of 27,863,738 votes cast at the 1959 General Election and 365 out of 630 seats in the House of Commons. It is traditionally the right-wing party in Parliament and successor to the Tory Party of the eighteenth and nineteenth centuries, but very different from conservative parties in continental countries. Such parties are often violently reactionary, indifferent or even hostile to democracy, and opposed to social progress. The Conservative Party, particularly after its defeat in 1945 (when it won 213 out of 640 seats in the House of Commons), has adopted a moderately progressive policy and has accepted the principles of the welfare state. It is by no means a liberal party in the economic sense, since it believes in social measures which involve heavy direct and indirect taxation. The influence of the extreme right wing of the party has diminished as the Conservative leaders have realized the importance of obtaining a substantial following in the lower-income groups; however, this influence is often felt in the constituency organizations.

The Conservative Party today has strong support both from the aristocracy and large business interests and from the lower-income groups in the population. It remains to be seen whether a Conservative economic policy can, over a long period, reconcile the interests of these groups, or whether Conservative Chancellors of the Exchequer will be forced to abandon the support of one group to retain the confidence of the other.

The leader of the Conservative Party is the Prime Minister, Harold Macmillan, *q.v.* Other leading figures are Sir Winston

Churchill, *q.v.*, R. A. Butler, *q.v.*, Lord Hailsham, *q.v.*, Edward Heath, *q.v.*, Selwyn Lloyd, *q.v.*, Ian Macleod, *q.v.*, Reginald Maudling, *q.v.*

Contraband (from Latin *contra bandum*, against the ban). Goods forbidden to be supplied by neutrals to belligerents. The Declaration of London, agreed by the International Naval Conference in 1909, distinguished between absolute contraband (arms and ammunition) and conditional contraband (goods normally destined for peaceful purposes but also useful in war). A list of conditional contraband, including certain raw materials, was compiled, but did not come into effect as the Declaration was not ratified. In the First and Second World Wars the contraband list was extended to almost every article of importance to an enemy, including foodstuffs. Neutral merchant ships in wartime can, by international law, be visited and searched, and any contraband may be seized.

Corporate State. A system of government in which trade and professional corporations are the basis of society. The corporations represent the employers and the employed in the various branches of the economic life of a country; parliament is elected not by territorial constituencies but by the corporations. They are supposed to make regulations for industrial production and working conditions. The advocates of the system say that it excludes party politics and makes people conduct public affairs in a realistic manner. The system has attracted those who wish to end the struggle between workers and employers and to concentrate on increasing national production. The corporate states set up hitherto (notably in Portugal and in Fascist Italy) have been in fact dictatorships with a partly corporate structure, so that there has been little opportunity to assess the true value of the system.

Costa Rica. An independent republic in the southern part of Central America between Nicaragua and Panama; area 19,690 sq. m.; population (1959) 1,134,626, and Spanish-speaking, with a high rate of literacy; capital San José. Roman Catholicism is the official and subsidized religion. Spain ruled the area from 1530 until the revolt of 1821; Costa Rica then became part of the United States of Central America until it achieved independence in 1839. In 1948 the army was abolished, the President declaring that a peace-loving country needed no army. In that year the stability of the democratic régime was seriously threatened by a revolt; six years later, in 1954, the same revolutionary elements attempted an unsuccessful invasion, with passive and perhaps active support from Nicaragua. At the request of the Organization of American States, *q.v.*, the U.S.A. provided aircraft which helped to drive back the invaders. Costa Rica and Nicaragua signed a treaty of friendship in January 1956. The government of President José Figueres, in power from 1953 to 1958, supported the principle of government ownership and enforced a capital levy of ten per cent to improve the country's financial position. In February 1958 the Opposition leader, a Conservative lawyer, Mario Echandi, was elected President. His policies included the denationalization of banks and insurance companies and the encouragement of private enterprise. Legislative power is vested in one chamber of 45 members, the Constitutional Congress.

The economy is mainly agricultural, with exports of bananas, nearly all to the United States, coffee, and rice. The United Fruit Company handles nearly all the banana crop and ships it through the Company's two Pacific Ocean ports. Under a 1954 agreement the Costa Rican government received thereafter forty-seven per cent of the Company's profits, and the Company's income-tax was doubled.

Costello, John Aloysius. Irish politician; born 20 June 1891; educated at University College, Dublin; he is a lawyer. He was Assistant to the Law Officer of the Provisional Government of Ireland in 1922, Assistant to the Attorney-General of the Irish Free State from 1922 to 1926, and Attorney-General from 1926 to 1932. He became a member of the Fine Gael group in the Irish Parliament (the Dáil) in 1933. He was the head of government (Taoiseach) from 1948 to 1951 and from 1954 to 1957.

Council for Mutual Economic Assistance (Comecon). Was established in 1949 by a number of eastern European countries to provide an economic structure similar to that set up by the countries of western Europe in 1948, when the Organization for European Economic Co-operation, *q.v.*, was born. Its members are Albania, Bulgaria, Czechoslovakia, the German Democratic Republic, Hungary, Poland, Rumania, and the U.S.S.R. The Council has drawn up plans for the development and co-ordination of the various national economies with a view to specialization in production, adequate provision of raw materials, and co-operation in scientific research and technology.

Council of Europe. Set up on 5 May 1949 by Belgium, Denmark, France, Ireland, Italy, Luxemburg, the Netherlands, Norway, Sweden, and the U.K. It comprises: (1) a Committee of Foreign Ministers or their deputies, and (2) a Consultative Assembly composed of representatives chosen by the governments, meeting at Strasbourg and empowered to discuss all matters of common concern with the exception of national defence. The Assembly can offer recommendations to the Ministers but has no other powers. Any European state accepting the principles of freedom, political liberty and the rule of law is eligible for admission and since 1949 Austria, Cyprus, the German Federal Republic, Greece, Iceland, and Turkey have become members.

Coup d'État. A sudden change of government by force, brought about by those who already hold some governmental or military power. It differs from a revolution in that it is effected from above, while a revolution involves the participation of the masses. Examples of *coups d'état* are the seizures of power by Napoleon III in 1851, by Mussolini in 1925, by Pilsudski (in Poland) in 1928, by the Czechoslovak Communists in 1948, by the anti-Perón movement in Argentina in 1955 and by the republican faction in Iraq in 1958. The usual method employed by organizers of a *coup* is to seize government buildings, railways, broadcasting stations, power plants and waterworks, in order to gain control.

Crossman, Richard Howard Stafford. British Labour Party politician; born 15 December 1907, the son of a High Court Judge, and educated at Winchester and New College, Oxford, where he was a Fellow and Tutor from 1930 to 1937. In 1938 he became Assistant Editor of the *New Statesman and Nation*, and a lecturer for the Oxford University Delegacy for Extra-Mural Studies. During the Second World War he held, in North Africa and Europe, various posts concerned with psychological warfare, and he was elected to the House of Commons in July 1945 as the member for East Coventry.

Crypto-Communist. A secret sympathizer with, or member of, a Communist movement.

Cuba. An independent Central American state which occupies an island in the Caribbean Sea; area 46,736 sq. m.; population (1957) of 6,400,000 Spanish-speaking inhabitants; capital Havana. It was governed by Spain from the sixteenth to the nineteenth centuries; as the Spanish hold weakened there were many revolts and in 1898 the U.S.A. defeated Spain in war and occupied Cuba. Under the 1901 Constitution a republic was proclaimed but there was a U.S. military occupation until 1902 and again from 1906 to 1909. From 1930 to 1959 the effective ruler was, except from 1944 to 1952, General Fulgencio Batistá y Zaldivar. Batistá was military dictator from 1933, when as an army sergeant he seized power, to 1940, when he introduced a Constitution modelled on that of the U.S.A. From 1940 to 1944 he was President, and was then out of office until March 1952, when a *coup d'état* made him provisional President. In 1954 he again became President after his soldiers and police had forced the only challenger at the Presidential election, Dr Grau San Martin, the leader of the Autenticos, to withdraw from the contest. Andres Rivero

Aguero was elected in November 1958 to succeed Batistá, who had supported his candidature, but in January 1959 the military success of the rebel bands of Fidel Castro, *q.v.*, forced Batistá to flee from Cuba, and his régime collapsed.

The radical and nationalist policies of the Castro government have included sweeping land reforms, under which the maximum holding is limited to approximately 1,090 acres for each person or company, except for sugar, rice, and cattle farms, for which the maximum was to be 3,300 acres. The government also set up the National Institute for Agrarian Reform (I.N.R.A.) which administers the 1,400 co-operative holdings established since the revolution and controls approximately sixty per cent of the cultivable land. Previously one per cent of the population had owned more than one third of the land. Factors which have adversely affected relations with the U.S.A. have included the government's seizure of a large number of American-owned firms, its insistence that American refineries in Cuba should refine oil bought from the U.S.S.R., and its resentment at the existence on Cuban territory of the American naval base of Guantánamo.

From January to July 1959 Dr Manuel Urrutia was President; he was succeeded by Dr Osvaldo Dorticós Torredo. The constitution was suspended in January 1959 and government is by decree.

Sugar is grown on fifty-six per cent of the cultivated land and production is the highest in the world, amounting to one eighth of the world total. There is often a surplus and there have been important purchases by the U.S.S.R. Cuba produces one tenth of the world's nickel, and tobacco is also an important export.

Curzon Line. An eastern boundary for Poland, with a racial basis, excluding White Russians and Ukrainians, proposed by Lord Curzon, British Foreign Secretary, after the First World War. After the Russian Revolution Poland had taken the western Ukraine and western White Russia from the U.S.S.R., but lost some of these territories as the result of a Russian counter-attack. Poland would have had to withdraw further if it had accepted the Curzon Line. When Germany invaded Poland from the west in 1939, the U.S.S.R. occupied eastern Poland roughly up to the Curzon Line, and it remained the eastern frontier after the end of the war. Poland was compensated by being awarded German territory as far as the Oder-Neisse Line, *q.v.*

Customs Union. An arrangement whereby two or more states, while retaining their independence and sovereignty, are united into a common tariff area, lifting the tariff frontier between themselves and establishing a common tariff frontier with other countries, as in the

case of Belgium, the Netherlands, and Luxemburg, which formed
Benelux, *q.v.*

Cyprus. A Dominion and member of the British Commonwealth, about
forty miles south of Turkey and sixty miles west of Syria; area
3,572 sq. m.; capital Nicosia; population 549,000, of whom four fifths
are Greek-speaking or belong to the Cypriot branch of the Greek
Orthodox Church, and the rest are Moslems of Turkish origin. The
island was part of the Byzantine Empire until it was captured in 1191
by King Richard I. It was subsequently ruled by the Templars, by
the French Lusignan family, by Venice, and from 1571 to 1878 by
the Turks. Except for part of the fourth century it never belonged to
Greece. In 1878 the British acquired rights in Cyprus, annexing it in
1914 and in 1915 offering it to Greece in return for Greek support to
Serbia; the offer was rejected. Turkey recognized British sovereignty
in 1924; in 1925 Cyprus became a colony. It became independent on
16 August 1960 and joined the British Commonwealth in March 1961.

Under Turkish rule the Ethnarchy, or Church leadership, first
became politically active. It headed the anti-Moslem movement
which, in the nineteenth century, became linked with the idea of
union with a now independent Greece. Enosis (union with Greece)
was for years a rallying-cry for all Cypriots opposed to foreign rule.
An Enosis uprising in 1931 reached such serious proportions that the
legislative council was suspended and two bishops were exiled. Later
the movement, led by the Ethnarch, Archbishop Makarios, *q.v.*,
united two major parties; the right wing which was pledged to support
the Greek monarchy; and the left-wing Reform Party of Working
People, known as A.K.E.L., which was Communist. From 1944 to
1948, while the Communists were engaged in civil war in Greece,
A.K.E.L. advocated independence for Cyprus. In 1948, the political
parties combined to reject British proposals for a new constitution
and to demand a plebiscite; in the absence of any constitutional
channel through which to register their opposition to British policy,
the Enosis parties turned to strike action and rioting, which were
intensified in 1954 when the British transferred the headquarters of
their Middle East Land Forces from the Suez Canal Zone to Cyprus.

At the tripartite talks between the U.K., Greece, and Turkey held
in London in August and September 1955, British proposals for a
new constitution were announced. They endorsed the principle of
self-government but the British Foreign Secretary, Harold Macmillan,
said that British sovereignty over Cyprus was beyond dispute.

After serious riots in Nicosia, following the breakdown of the talks,
the Governor was replaced by Field-Marshal Sir John Harding: by

November 1955 there was one British soldier on the island to every fifty Cypriots. Archbishop Makarios was deported in March 1956 to the Seychelles, in the Indian Ocean, on the ground that he had been 'deeply implicated in the campaign of terrorism' launched by E.O.K.A., the militant right wing of the Enosis movement.

In December 1957 Field-Marshal Sir John Harding was succeeded as Governor by Sir Hugh Foot, till then Governor of Jamaica. The appointment of a civilian Governor was expected to reduce tension, but instead provoked Turkish demands for partition, and armed conflict broke out between the Turkish and Greek Cypriot communities. In February 1959, after discussions in London, an agreement was concluded by Greece, Turkey, and the U.K., and declared acceptable by the Greek and Turkish Cypriots, by which Cyprus was to become an independent republic, although the U.K. was to retain sovereignty over the areas containing its military bases. On 14 December 1959 Archbishop Makarios was proclaimed President, with 144,501 votes, against 71,753 votes for his opponent, John Clerides, who was supported by the left wing.

Under the agreement concluded in July 1960, there were granted to the U.K. certain miliary facilities, comprising: (1) two sovereign base areas at Akrotiri and Dhekelia; (2) (i) 25 scheduled sites to be used 'without restriction or interference', including 13 sites to be returned 'as soon as practicable'; (ii) 15 scheduled leave camps, groups of residential buildings, and other installations; (3) training facilities in 10 areas; (4) the right to use Nicosia airfield. Cyprus undertook 'not to participate, in whole or in part, in any political or economic union with any state whatsoever'.

At the elections to the House of Representatives held on 31 July 1960 the Patriotic Front, supporting Archbishop Makarios, won 30 seats; A.K.E.L. 5 seats; and the Turkish Nationalists, supporting the Vice-President, Dr Fazil Kutchuk, 15 seats.

Czech Arms Deal. A purchase of arms from Czechoslovakia by the Egyptian government in exchange for such Egyptian products as cotton and rice. The purchase was announced on 28 September 1955 by the Egyptian Prime Minister, Colonel Gamal Abdel Nasser, who said that the step had been taken after the repeated failure of Egypt to obtain arms on satisfactory terms from the western powers. The U.K., he said, had been unable to supply arms in sufficient quantities, and France had cut off arms supplies on 2 September 1955 because Radio Cairo had criticized French policy in Algeria and Morocco. The U.S.A. was prepared in principle to sell arms, but unwilling to accept by way of payment the goods offered by Egypt. The arms purchased included fighter aircraft of a Russian design. The agreement was described by Egypt as a necessary measure of self-defence, by the western powers as a sign of increasing Communist influence in the Middle East, and by Israel as an aggressive move.

Czechoslovakia. An independent Central European republic; area 49,381 sq. m.; population 13,581,186, speaking the Czech or Slovak languages; capital Prague. The republic was created in 1918 from the former Austrian provinces of Bohemia, Moravia, and Silesia, and the former Hungarian provinces of Slovakia and Sub-Carpathian Russia. It brought under one government 7,500,000 Czechs, 2,300,000 Slovaks, 3,250,000 Germans, and 690,000 Magyars. The Slovak minority strongly opposed Bohemian centralism and the severance of commercial connexions with Budapest, while the German inhabitants of the Bohemian and Moravian border districts formed the Sudeten-German Party under Henlein in 1933 and demanded autonomy within Czechoslovakia. As soon as this had been granted in 1938 Hitler announced his intention of incorporating the Sudetenland in Germany. By the Munich Agreement, *q.v.*, the Sudetenland was ceded to Germany which guaranteed the new frontier; other parts of Czechoslovakia were ceded to Hungary and Poland. When Germany finally invaded Czechoslovakia in March 1939 Slovakia was separated from the new 'Protectorate of Bohemia and Moravia', which became part of Germany, and was made an 'independent' state under German protection and occupation.

In 1945 the Sudeten-Germans were expelled and, with the exception of the cession of Ruthenia to the U.S.S.R., the pre-1938 frontiers were re-established. The presence of the Germans from 1939 to 1945 had caused a resurgence of nationalism in Czechoslovakia and the first post-war government was a coalition of Czech Socialists, Social Democrats, Communists, and Agrarians, and of Slovak Democrats and Communists; its immediate policy was large-scale nationalization, particularly of former German assets. At elections held in 1946 the Communists emerged as the leading party, obtaining thirty-eight per cent of the votes cast. They formed a National Front government, under Gottwald, with thirteen Social Democrat members (who had polled thirteen per cent of the total vote) and four representatives from each of the other three major parties. Drought and a bad harvest in 1947 were responsible for a shortage of food which, combined with Gottwald's rejection of aid under the Marshall Plan, *q.v.*, made the government, especially the Communists since they were the controlling party, unpopular. The twelve moderates in the government had declared their intention to ask for Marshall Aid if the Communists should ever cease to be the dominant party. Fearing that he would lose ground in the elections which were to be held in June 1948, and foreseeing a repetition in Czechoslovakia of the manoeuvres in the French Assembly which had resulted in 1947 in the exclusion from the French government of the Communists, although they had obtained the highest percentage of votes, Gottwald forced a crisis by 'packing' the police. On 20 February 1948 the twelve moderates resigned in protest, hoping for a dissolution of parliament before the Communists should have time to prevent free elections from being held, but the Social Democrats supported the government and it remained in office. Five days later President Beneš had to accept a new cabinet from which the twelve were excluded, drawn from all parties which, under Communist instructions, had now purged themselves of 'hostile elements'. The Social Democrats' acceptance of the Communist *coup* is explicable only in terms of foreign policy. The west had failed the Czechs at Munich; they still feared Germany and were convinced that only by a military alliance with the U.S.S.R. would they be guaranteed the necessary protection. In a clear choice between Marshall Aid and a Russian alliance the Social Democrats, as Czech nationalists, chose the latter.

At the 1948 elections to the National Assembly the electorate could vote either for or against a single list of National Front candidates. The Front, which now incorporated the Communist Party, the Social Democrats (Socialist), the Popular Party (Roman Catholic), and the Slovak National Reconstruction Party, secured eighty-nine per cent of the total vote and obtained similar majorities in 1954 and 1960. All industry and trade has now been nationalized. The country was highly industrialized before 1939 and the Five-Year Plans for the period 1949–65 have brought about substantial increases in production of machinery, hydro-electric power, steel, and minerals which include iron, coal, silver, lead, copper, and graphite. Over two-thirds of Czechoslovakia's trade is with the U.S.S.R., Eastern Europe and China. The highest executive organ is the Communist Party Politburo; Antonín Novotný (born 1904) was elected President of the Republic in 1957 for a seven-year term, but retained his post as Secretary of the Communist Party.

D

Dahomey. An independent republic; area 44,290 sq. m.; population 1,720,000 comprising Fons and Adjus, Boribas, Yorubas, Mahis, and 3,000 Europeans; capital Porto Novo. It occupies 70 miles of the

Western African coast, between Togo and Nigeria, with the republics of Upper Volta and Niger to the north, and was an independent African kingdom until in 1851 a coastal strip was taken by the French, who annexed the whole territory in 1893. It later became one of the eight territories comprising French West Africa, *q.v.*, and achieved self-government within the French Community, *q.v.*, on 4 December 1958, and complete independence, after breaking with the Community in June 1960, on 1 August 1960.

The economy is almost entirely agricultural, yielding maize (especially in the coastal region), manioc, and yams. There are also extensive forests of oil palms providing palm kernels and palm oil, which constitute 81 per cent of the country's exports.

Legislative powers are vested in an assembly of 70 members elected every five years by universal suffrage. At the elections held on 2 and 23 April 1959 the Republican Party won 28 seats, the Democratic Party 22 seats, and the Democratic Union (the local section of the Rassemblement Démocratique Africain) 20 seats. The leader of the Democratic Party, Hubert Maga, was able to command a majority and became Prime Minister and head of state.

Dáil Éireann. The lower house of the Parliament of Ireland, *q.v.*

Danzig (known as Gdansk). A Polish port on the Baltic Sea and at the mouth of the river Vistula; population 266,100. The city was a Slav foundation, but was conquered in 1310 by the Teutonic Knights who massacred the Slav population. It became a German town but the Poles continually demanded it as their only outlet to the sea. It was a Free City under Polish suzerainty from 1450 until 1793 when it was annexed by Prussia. Apart from the period 1807 to 1815, when it was restored to Poland by Napoleon, it was in German hands until the Versailles Treaty, *q.v.*, which created a Polish corridor separating East Prussia from Germany and ending at Danzig. The major powers took into account the German character of the population and did not award Danzig to Poland, but established it as a Free City within the Polish customs area, entrusting to Poland the conduct of its foreign relations. Its constitution was guaranteed by the League of Nations, *q.v.*, which was represented there by a High Commissioner who had to arbitrate on frequent disputes between Danzig and Poland. In March 1939, after entering Czechoslovakia and demanding the Lithuanian port of Memel, Germany asked Poland for Danzig and the strip of territory connecting East Prussia with the rest of Germany. Disguised German troops occupied the city in August 1939, and on 1 September the local Nazi leader proclaimed the reunion of Danzig with Germany; this was at once confirmed by the German government. Germany invaded Poland on the same day and the U.K. and France declared war on Germany on 3 September in accordance with their previous undertakings to protect Poland. Danzig became part of Poland after the Second World War as a result of the Potsdam Agreement, *q.v.*, of 2 August 1945.

Dardanelles. The southern part of the straits which connect the Mediterranean and the Black Seas. The Bosphorus (the northern part of the straits), the Sea of Marmora (between the two parts) and the Dardanelles belong to Turkey and are of great strategic importance. In the eighteenth and nineteenth centuries Russia pushed towards the straits in order to find an outlet to the Mediterranean Sea. The straits were under the absolute sovereignty of Turkey until 1841 when the major powers and the Sultan pledged themselves not to permit 'vessels of war belonging to foreign powers' to enter the Dardanelles. After the Crimean War France and the U.K. forced the defeated Russia, under the Treaty of Paris, 1856, to declare the Black Sea neutral, and thus to abandon the right to maintain there any military or naval establishment. Russia denounced this provision in 1870. After the First World War the straits were occupied by British, French, and Italian forces, and the peninsula of Gallipoli, forming the European shore of the Dardanelles, was given to Greece. The straits were demilitarized, opened to navigation of every kind, and placed under an international commission. After Turkey had defeated a Greek invasion, Gallipoli was given back to Turkey, and the Treaty of Lausanne, concluded in July 1923, largely restored Turkish sovereignty over the straits whilst still providing for their demilitarization. The Treaty was modified by the Montreux Convention, 1936, *q.v.* Since the Second World War Turkey has rejected several Russian suggestions that a joint Russo-Turkish naval base should be established in the Dardanelles.

De Facto Recognition. An act whereby a new government or state is recognized as being actually independent and wielding effective power in the territory under its control, although not yet willing nor fully able to carry out international obligations. According to British practice, *de facto* recognition does not involve full diplomatic relations or the right of the representatives of the government to diplomatic immunity. The U.S.A. grants diplomatic immunity to such representatives. Strictly speaking, it is not the act of recognition that is *de facto*, but the government or state.

De Gaulle, General Charles André Joseph Marie. French political and military figure, born 22 November 1890 in Lille into a bourgeois

Catholic family. He entered the Military Academy of Saint Cyr in 1911, campaigned in the First World War and in 1920 fought against the Russians in Poland under General Weygand. Between the Wars he gained a reputation as a military theorist and when the German threat to France became apparent he recommended the creation of a highly mechanized core of professional troops to be used in attack. In 1939 he became France's youngest general and was made Under-Secretary at the Ministry of Defence in the Reynaud cabinet. Ten days later France surrendered and de Gaulle flew to London from where he called on French troops to reject the armistice and continue the resistance. He commanded the Fighting French forces until 1944, when he became Head of the Provisional Government of liberated France, and Chief of the Armed Forces. For eighteen months in 1945 and 1946 he was President of France during which period more than one quarter of the national revenue was spent on the armed forces and inflation was allowed to ride unchecked. In response to demands for a reduction in the army estimates he resigned and went into retirement, but re-emerged in 1947 at the head of a right-wing political organization, the Rally of the French People (Rassemblement du Peuple Français) which called for a revision of the Constitution and a stronger executive. It had enormous initial success, but it never secured control of the National Assembly. De Gaulle opposed the formation of any western defence community in which France might play a subordinate role, and was believed to favour a Latin bloc of Spain, Italy, and a predominant France, which would serve as adequate protection for France against Germany. He retired a second time in 1951, and formally dissolved the R.P.F., the members of which formed the Gaullist Social Republican Party (U.A.R.S.). After French army officers seized power in Algeria on 13 May 1958, de Gaulle stated, on 15 May: 'I hold myself in readiness to assume the powers of the Republic'. President Coty then invited him to form a government and he was invested as Prime Minister by the National Assembly on 1 June with a majority of 329 to 224. He gave up this post after being elected, on 21 December 1958, to the office of President.

De Jure Recognition. Unconditional acknowledgement that a new government or state is independent, wields effective power in the territory under its control, and is willing and able to carry out its international obligations. Recognition of a régime as a *de facto* government is provisional, but recognition as a *de jure* government entitles it to full diplomatic relations and its representatives to diplomatic immunity.

De Valera, Eamonn (Edward). Irish politician, born 14 October 1882 in New York, U.S.A., the son of a Spanish musician and his Irish wife. At the age of two he was sent to Ireland to be brought up by relations at Bruree, County Limerick. After graduating in mathematics at Dublin University in 1904 he became a teacher. He joined the Irish Nationalist movement and, as a member of the Gaelic League, learned, and taught, the Irish language. He took part in the Dublin Easter Rising in 1916 and commanded a battalion of the Irish Volunteers. The British captured him and sentenced him to death but he had his sentence commuted and was released from Dartmoor under the general amnesty of June 1917. He was President of the Sinn Fein movement from 1917 to 1926 and was elected Member for County Clare in the British Parliament but, as a Sinn Feiner, refused to take his seat. In May 1918 he was arrested and imprisoned for a further year after which he went to the U.S.A. to raise a loan of six million dollars for the Irish Republican government. On his return he became the Member for County Clare in the Dáil Éireann and President of the Dáil, a post which he resigned in 1922 when the Assembly accepted the treaty by which the six northern counties were excluded from the Irish Free State. He fought with the Irish Republican Army, *q.v.*, against the Free State government in the second Irish civil war and spent another year in gaol from 1923 to 1924, continuing to lead the republicans who would not accept partition. In 1926 he founded a new party, Fianna Fáil (Soldiers of Ireland), with the declared aims of complete independence, union with Northern Ireland and revival of the Irish language and culture. These were to be achieved through parliamentary action and participation in the Free State Parliament. The irreconcilable republicans withdrew their support but Fianna Fáil, in an electoral coalition with the Labour Party, won a majority in the Dáil in 1932 and De Valera became Prime Minister. While he was in office Ireland became a sovereign independent state (Eire) and all ties with the British Commonwealth were dissolved. In 1948, the year in which Ireland became a republic, Fianna Fáil was defeated by the Fine Gael (United Ireland) party. De Valera was Prime Minister (Taoiseach) again in 1951, when his party secured 70 out of the 147 seats in the Dáil, by a coalition of Fianna Fáil members and Independents, but resigned after the elections of May 1954 in which Fianna Fáil lost 5 seats. He continued to lead the party in opposition until the elections of 6 March 1957, when he again became Prime Minister after Fianna Fáil increased its membership in the Dáil to 78. He resigned from the post of Prime Minister in June 1959 on being elected President.

Debré, Michel. French politician; born 1912 in Paris, the son of a leading French doctor, he is a Roman Catholic of partly Jewish ancestry. After studying law and politics he entered the higher civil service, and in 1938 he joined the staff of Paul Reynaud, who was then a minister in the Daladier government. On the outbreak of war in 1939 he became a cavalry officer and after being captured by, and escaping from, the Germans, he served in the French administration in Morocco. In 1942 he returned to France and joined the resistance movement, which entrusted him, towards the end of the war, with preparations for the re-establishment of the French administration. He worked for a time on the staff of General de Gaulle after the latter returned to France, stood unsuccessfully for parliament in 1946, and joined de Gaulle's Rally of the French People when it was founded in 1947. He was elected to the Senate in 1948 by the department of Indre-et-Loire, and as a Senator made many attacks on the parliamentary system of the Fourth Republic. He was appointed Minister of Justice in June 1958 when de Gaulle formed a government, and was largely responsible for drafting the constitution of the Fifth Republic. He became Prime Minister in January 1959 when de Gaulle took office as President.

Deflation. A reduction in money circulation, the opposite of inflation, resulting in lower prices and shortage of credit. This usually follows if interest rates are raised; the rate of addition to real capital slows down, the income and purchasing power of the community are restricted and purchases of foreign goods and securities are reduced. The balance of payments problem is eased, but mere deflation without other measures may involve lower output and more unemployment.

Demagogy. Appeals to the prejudice of the masses, usually by means of lies and half-truths. It is derived from the Greek *demagogoi*, a word used to describe popular leaders who appeared in Athens and other cities of ancient Greece during their period of decay.

Démarche. A diplomatic or political development, proceeding, or step, not to be confused with a *détente q.v.*

Democracy. From the Greek *demos*, people, and *kratos*, power, meaning government by the people. Democracy may be either direct, and exerted by popular assemblies or by plebiscites on all legislation, or indirect, and exerted by representative institutions. Direct democracy was practised in some of the city states of Ancient Greece; indirect democracy, which is better suited to modern nation states with large populations, was developed in England in the seventeenth century and imposed on France and North America, as a result of revolution, in the eighteenth century. By 1850 the majority of civilized nations had adopted democratic institutions.

Democracy, in the sense of the word generally accepted in western Europe, the British Commonwealth, and the U.S.A., is based on the theory of the separation of powers, *q.v.*, legislation being carried out by a freely elected parliament and executive power being vested either in a government responsible to the legislature (as in the U.K.) or in a president responsible to the people (as in the U.S.A.). This implies free choice at regular intervals between two or more parties; an election in which the electorate can only choose or reject a single list of candidates is not democratic in this sense of the word.

In addition to a separation of powers and free elections, other characteristics of western democracy are the rule of law, by which is meant a certainty that one is free from arrest unless charged with some recognized crime and that one will be given a fair trial before an impartial tribunal; freedom of opinion and speech; freedom of association; and protection from arbitrary interference on the part of the authorities.

The expression 'rule of the people' is interpreted in a very different sense in the U.S.S.R., and in parts of Asia and eastern Europe, though it should be noted that the title 'People's Republic' is used of Bulgaria, China, Outer Mongolia, and Yugoslavia. The principles of the separation of powers, free elections, rule of law, freedom of opinion, speech and association are not generally accepted. However, the supporters of these systems regard them as democratic. There is state ownership and central planning to increase the national wealth. The private ownership of the means of production is regarded as undemocratic. In the U.S.S.R. no differences of class prevent people from securing the best education the country can offer. The governments of these Communist countries believe that the subordination of every interest and activity to the state ensures that the common good takes precedence over all private interests. This belief that Communism represents the true interests of the common man underlies their claim to be democracies.

Democratic Party. One of the two great political parties in the U.S.A.; the other is the Republican Party, *q.v.* It emerged about 1787 in opposition to the federalists, and advocated restrictions on the powers of the federal government. It was then also known as the Republican Party. Its leader Thomas Jefferson became President in 1801, and during the so-called 'era of good feeling', from 1817 to 1825, it was the only political party. A group which favoured high tariffs then seceded and became known as the Republican Party, while the remainder, led by Andrew Jackson, was known as the Democratic Party. The Democratic Party split again before the civil war, 1861 to 1865, over the question of slavery, the northern Democrats uniting with the National Republicans to form the Republican Party. In the twentieth century the southern states have for the most part continued to support the Democratic Party, though the Party has gained adherents in the northern industrial states of New York, Michigan, and Illinois. There was a Democratic President from 1933 to 1953, when Dwight D. Eisenhower, the Republican Party candidate, was inaugurated as President after being elected in 1952.

Among the most important members of the Party are: John Kennedy, *q.v.*, and Lyndon Johnson, *q.v.*, who were elected President and Vice-President respectively in 1960, Adlai Stevenson, *q.v.*, the Party's Presidential candidate in 1952 and 1956, Averell Harriman, *q.v.*, and the former President Harry S. Truman, *q.v.* The Party emblem is a donkey.

Denmark. An independent state on the Baltic and North Seas; area 16,608 sq. m.; population (1959) 4,529,000; capital Copenhagen. It has been a separate monarchy since the fifteenth century; Denmark and Norway were one kingdom until, after an unsuccessful war with Sweden, Denmark was forced to relinquish Norway under the Treaty of Kiel, 1814. Denmark kept the Faroes, Greenland, and Iceland. In 1864 it was defeated by Prussia and had to give up Holstein and Schleswig. North Schleswig was recovered after the First World War. In 1940 Denmark was attacked and occupied by Germany, which wanted control of the rich Danish agricultural resources, and needed a base from which to secure Norway. Independence was regained after the war. In 1944 Iceland became an Independent state.

Under the 1953 Constitution legislative power is vested in the King (who acts through the cabinet) and Parliament jointly. Since 1953 parliament has had only one chamber, the Folketing, with 179 members, elected for 4 years by proportional representation. After the 1953 election the Social Democrats, led by Hans Hedtoft, replaced the Farmer-Conservative Coalition which had been in office since 1950. On Hedtoft's death in January 1955, H. C. Hansen became Prime Minister. As a result of the 1957 Election the Social Democrats with their allies, the Social Liberals, found themselves in control of 84 seats, and they were faced with the possibility of an alliance between the Farmers (agrarians, moderate liberals), the Conservatives, and the Radical Liberals (supporting the economic theories of Henry George), who, between them, held an equal number of seats. In order to obtain a majority Hansen, who continued as Prime Minister, formed a coalition comprising Social Democrats, Social Liberals, and three representatives of Dr Starcke's Radical Liberals.

On the death of Hansen in February 1960 Viggo Kampmann, the Finance Minister, became Prime Minister; as a result of the General Election in November 1960 the number of members in the Socialist bloc increased from 84 to 87 (76 Social Democrats and 11 Social Liberals), but its Radical Liberal or Georgist allies lost all their 9 seats. A new, neutralist, left-wing but anti-Communist group, the Socialist People's Party, secured 11, the Farmers 38, the Conservatives 32, and Independents 6 seats. Kampmann formed a new government of Social Democrats and Social Liberals.

Denmark has a high standard of living, a well-developed system of education (including compulsory education since 1814), and extensive social services (including a social security scheme instituted before those of Norway and Sweden). The important exports are dairy produce, bacon, eggs, livestock, machinery, meat, seeds, and ships. The most important trading partners are the U.K. and the German Federal Republic.

Denmark is a member of N.A.T.O. and was a signatory of the 1955 London and Paris Agreements by which the German Federal Republic was rearmed within the Western European Union and admitted to the North Atlantic Treaty Organization. The Faroes, *q.v.*, Greenland, *q.v.*, and Schleswig-Holstein, *q.v.*, are considered separately.

Détente. A diplomatic term meaning the cession of strained relations between states. It represents an earlier stage in the development of good relations than a *rapprochement*, *q.v.* An alternative word, the Italian *distensione*, is sometimes used.

Devaluation. A reduction of the value of the currency.

Development Loan Fund. A U.S. organization established by the Mutual Security Act of 1958 'to assist, on a basis of self-help and mutual co-operation, the efforts of free people abroad to develop their economic resources and to increase their productive capacities'. The Chairman of the Board of Directors is the Under Secretary of State for Economic Affairs and the Fund is subject to the foreign policy guidance of the Secretary of State. The Fund can grant loans for specific projects, if financially sound, whether they are organized by private or government organizations, and loans can, subject to the consent of the Fund, be repaid in local currency or U.S. dollars. The Board of Directors also includes the Director of the International

Co-operation Administration, *q.v.*, the Chairman of the Board of the Export Import Bank, and the Executive Director of the International Bank for Reconstruction and Development, *q.v.*, also known as the World Bank.

Dialectical Materialism. The combination of the dialectical method with a materialistic philosophy. It is politically important because it is the philosophical basis of Marxism, *q.v.* Dialectic, as developed by Greek philosophers, was the art of argument, or the technique of persuasion. It became the name of a method of thinking by the resolution of successive contradictions, as in the philosophical 'dialogue'. Later it was claimed that not only the development of thought, but also actual developments in nature and history, take the course of a dialectical process in which, as in a philosophical discussion, 'thesis' and 'antithesis' follow each other until a solution is found in the form of 'synthesis'. This teaching was particularly developed in the first half of the nineteenth century by Hegel, the German idealistic philosopher, who saw history as the reflection of a dialectical process in the development of certain ideas. Marx and Feuerbach 'reversed' the dialectical principle, denying the dominant role of ideas in history claimed by Hegel, and declaring that material things, while actually developing as dialectical processes, do so in their own right, as it were, and not as reflections of the development of independently existing ideas. On the contrary, it was the ideas which were the reflections of material reality. Marx used dialectical materialism as a method of social criticism and analysis, setting up the theory of 'historical materialism'. Thus every phase of human society, while moved by material forces, develops as a dialectical process, producing within itself its own opposite. Capitalist society creates the proletarian class which is of necessity opposed to it and bound eventually to overthrow it. Marx defined the dialectical method as that of 'including in the positive understanding of existing things also the understanding of the negative implications of their necessary termination'.

Dictatorship. From the Latin *dictator*; the absolute rule of a person or group without the necessity of the consent of the governed. The term dates from Roman republican times; during an emergency, a man could be appointed dictator by the Senate for seven years, and held absolute power for this period. He then had to retire, and constitutional rule was re-established. Modern dictatorship is either personal or that of a group or class (party, army, proletariat), but even in the latter case it is usually embodied in the person of a leader.

Diefenbaker, John George. Canadian Progressive Conservative Party politician; born 18 September 1895 in Normanby, Ontario, and educated at the University of Saskatchewan. He is a Baptist. He practised as a lawyer in Prince Albert, Saskatchewan, and first stood for parliament in 1925, but did not succeed until his fourth attempt in 1940. He was elected leader of his party in December 1956 in succession to George Drew, and became Prime Minister when the Progressive Conservatives came to power in June 1957 for the first time since 1935. He believes in strengthening the bonds between Canada and the rest of the British Commonwealth.

Disarmament. Reduction of armaments. Many unsuccessful attempts were made between 1918 and 1939 to reach international agreement on the limitation of armaments. In 1941 the Atlantic Charter, *q.v.*, looked forward to 'measures which will lighten for peace-loving peoples the crushing burden of armaments'. The Moscow Declaration of October 1943, by the American, British, Chinese, and Russian governments, advocated 'a practical general agreement with respect to the regulation of armaments'. Article 26 of the United Nations Charter provides that the Security Council should draw up plans for the regulation of armaments. The United Nations set up in 1946 the Atomic Energy Commission for the elimination of the use of atomic energy for destructive purposes and in 1947 the Commission for Conventional Armaments, 'for the general regulation and reduction of armaments and armed forces'. These Commissions were separately established as it was thought that the chances of an agreement on atomic control would be lessened if it was made contingent on an agreement on general disarmament.

In the Conventional Armaments Commission the U.S.S.R. argued that nations must first disarm and then evolve a system of control and inspection; the west wanted reduction of armaments accompanied by control and inspection. In 1948 the U.S.S.R. proposed a reduction of armed forces by one third but this was rejected by the west on the ground that it would continue the Russian preponderance in the field of conventional armaments.

In the Atomic Energy Commission the western powers advocated international management and control of all atomic energy plants, believing that inspection alone could not determine whether nuclear material was being diverted to dangerous uses. The U.S.S.R. proposed an immediate convention for the prohibition of atomic weapons and the destruction of existing stocks.

In 1952, in view of the very limited progress made, the two Commissions were merged into the United Nations Disarmament Commission. The U.S.S.R. continued to demand the reduction of armed forces by one third, the immediate prohibition of atomic weapons followed by full exchange of information, and the creation of an international control organization. The west regarded disclosure and verification of information as a first and indispensable step.

In 1953 the U.S.S.R. revealed that it had exploded a hydrogen bomb, though the U.S.A. in 1952 had estimated that it had a four years' lead in thermo-nuclear weapon research. The U.S.S.R. repeated its demand for unconditional prohibition of atomic weapons and a one-third reduction in armed forces, while the U.S.A. proposed an atomic pool in which all nations could develop nuclear energy for peaceful purposes. In May 1954 disarmament talks were held in London by Canada, France, the U.K., the U.S.A., and the U.S.S.R., but no agreement was reached.

In May 1955 the U.S.S.R. fundamentally altered its approach. It agreed that elimination of nuclear arms should not begin until cuts in other arms had been made, and that there should be a reduction of forces to absolute levels rather than proportional cuts. Its agreement, however, was subject to the abolition of 'foreign bases', which would have involved the withdrawal of U.S. ground and air units from western Europe and the Far East. The U.K. demanded further concessions in August 1955, insisting on unlimited rights of inspection over all places where warlike preparations could be carried on. The U.S.A. suggested aerial supervision supplemented by inspectors posted on the ground. At the international discussions held in London in April and May 1956, the U.S.S.R. continued to give priority to the question of reductions in conventional armaments, but was criticized by the western powers for refusing to give the controlling organization power to act in the event of any violations of the proposed disarmament agreements.

After further discussions at the General Assembly in January 1957 the problem was again referred to the sub-committee of the Commission, which met in London from March to September 1957. The U.S.A. proposed exchanges of information on nuclear tests, reductions in armed forces and international inspection of the use of fissionable materials. The U.S.S.R. for the first time suggested reciprocal aerial inspection, though not of the same areas as those suggested by the U.S.A. earlier. The U.K. proposed advanced registration and eventual cessation of nuclear tests. The talks were then abandoned.

The U.S.S.R. withdrew from the Disarmament Commission in November 1957, alleging that it, and the U.N. Political Committee, had 'lost prestige in the eyes of the peoples by the fruitless nature of their work'. The Russians said that this need not prevent international exchanges on disarmament, and in January 1958 Marshal Bulganin proposed a summit conference in Geneva to discuss (1) the ending of nuclear and thermo-nuclear tests for two or three years; (2) the renunciation of the use and manufacture of atomic and hydrogen weapons; (3) a non-aggression pact between N.A.T.O. and the members of the Warsaw Pact, *q.v.*; and (4) the creation of an atomic-free zone in Central Europe, comprising Eastern and Western Germany, Poland and Czechoslovakia, in which atomic and hydrogen weapons would be neither stock-piled nor manufactured. The last proposal was based on the Rapacki Plan, *q.v.* The U.S. State Department, commenting on the proposals in March 1958, said: 'The United States is not prepared to disregard the United Nations in its effort to resume disarmament talks.'

There were no significant developments in disarmament negotiations until March 1960, when the governments of Canada, France, Italy, the U.K., and the U.S.A. proposed the creation of an international disarmament organization to supervise the process of general disarmament, and a separate peace-keeping organization, to be an organ of, or linked to, the United Nations, to prevent aggression and to preserve world peace and security. They also proposed a three-stage programme for nuclear and conventional disarmament. Counter-proposals by the U.S.S.R. proved to be unacceptable by the western powers, who considered that they involved the abandonment of the nuclear deterrent and western bases in Europe at too early a stage.

Displaced Persons. *See* Refugees and Displaced Persons.

Dollar Gap. An adverse balance between a country's receipts from, and its payments to, the group of countries which pay, and can demand settlement of debts, in dollars.

Dominican Republic. An independent Central American state, sharing the Caribbean island of Hispaniola with Haiti; area 18,700 sq. m.; population (1959) 2,843,415, Spanish-speaking and mainly of mixed European, African, and Indian blood; capital Ciudad Trujillo. Roman Catholicism is the state religion; there are about 2,100,000 Catholics. The country was discovered by Columbus in 1492, ruled by Spain until 1795, by France 1795–1808, by Spain 1808–21, by Haitian Negroes 1822–44, and became an independent republic in 1844. Under the 1955 Constitution it is governed by a President and a Congress consisting of a Senate (twenty-three members) and a Chamber of, Deputies (fifty-two members). Rafael Leonidas Trujillo (born 1890) called 'el Benefactor', was dictator from 1930 till his assassination in

May 1961. His brother, Héctor Bienvenido Trujillo, was President from May 1952 to August 1960, when he was replaced by the Vice-President, Joaquín Balaguer; the President has powers to legislate by decree and to suspend the constitutional checks on the executive. Sugar is produced and exported by fifteen main companies of which six are controlled by United States firms; there are exports of cocoa beans, coffee and tobacco. Nearly half of the industrial capital represents investments from U.S. firms.

Dominion. A self-governing member state of the British Commonwealth, *q.v.* At present there are (apart from the U.K.) eleven Dominions: Australia, *q.v.*, Canada, *q.v.*, Ceylon, *q.v.*, Cyprus, *q.v.*, Ghana, *q.v.*, India, *q.v.*, Malaya, *q.v.*, New Zealand, *q.v.*, Nigeria, *q.v.*, Pakistan, *q.v.*, and Sierra Leone. They are independent states.

Downing Street. In Westminster; it contains the residences of the Prime Minister (at No. 10) and the Chancellor of the Exchequer (at No. 11), and the Foreign Office.

Doyen. A French word meaning dean, or senior member of a body, and used in diplomatic parlance to describe the senior member of the diplomatic corps in any capital city.

Dumbarton Oaks Conference. A meeting held in August 1944 at a mansion called Dumbarton Oaks in Washington, D.C., U.S.A., at which representatives of China, the U.K., the U.S.A., and the U.S.S.R. discussed the structure of the proposed United Nations, *q.v.* The conference concluded on 7 October 1944, when the proposals were published. In their main outline they showed a strong resemblance to the Covenant of the League of Nations, *q.v.* They provided that the key body in the United Nations for preserving world peace was to be the Security Council, *q.v.*, on which China, France, the U.K., the U.S.A., and the U.S.S.R. were to be permanently represented, and which was to be given much more power than the League Council. The question of how the Security Council was to vote was left unsettled until February 1945 when the Yalta Conference, *q.v.*, between the U.K., the U.S.A., and the U.S.S.R., established the principle of the veto, *q.v.*

Dunkirk Treaty. Concluded in March 1947 by France and the U.K.; it contained undertakings that the two countries would consult and act together against any aggression or threat of aggression by Germany, and that they would be in constant consultation about their economic relations. It was a symbol of the re-emergence of France as a major European power after its wartime occupation and its non-participation in the Potsdam Agreement, *q.v.*, of 1945.

Dutch New Guinea. *See* Netherlands New Guinea.

Dutch West Indies. *See* Netherlands West Indies.

E

Eastern European Mutual Assistance Treaty. A twenty-year treaty of friendship, co-operation and mutual assistance, signed by the representatives of Albania, Bulgaria, Czechoslovakia, the German Democratic Republic, Hungary, Poland, Rumania, and the U.S.S.R. at Warsaw in May 1955. It established a unified military command for the armed forces of all those countries. Each contracting party undertook to refrain in its international relations from the threat or use of force and to give immediate assistance to any party which was attacked in Europe by all the means it might consider necessary. The conference at which the Treaty was concluded met five days after the date on which the Western European Union, *q.v.*, came into force and the German Federal Republic, *q.v.*, attained full sovereignty.

Eastern Germany. The part of Germany that, under the Berlin Declaration of June 1945 and the Potsdam Agreement, *q.v.*, of August 1945, became the Russian occupation zone at the end of the Second World War. It comprises the former Prussian province of Saxony, the former *Länder* of Saxony, Thuringia, Mecklenburg, and Anhalt, and such parts of the former Prussian provinces of Brandenburg, Pomerania, and Silesia as were situated on the west banks of the rivers Oder and Western Neisse. In 1946 its population was 17,300,000. The U.S.S.R. tried both to eradicate Nazi influence and to reorganize the social and economic structure of Eastern Germany to an extent neither achieved nor attempted in Western Germany, *q.v.* In addition, the industrial equipment of Eastern Germany was largely dismantled and removed to the U.S.S.R., while, until 1956, a substantial proportion of its industrial output was taken by the U.S.S.R. as reparations. Many large estates were broken up and redistributed, and other agricultural properties were run directly by the Russian administration. The international quadripartite control of Germany which had been planned in 1945 was the subject of many disputes, particularly over the Russian demands for reparations, between the four countries concerned. The failure of the Foreign Ministers' Conference held in Moscow in May 1947, the clarification during that conference of the Truman Doctrine, *q.v.*, and the announcement in the following month of the Marshall Plan, *q.v.*, were followed by measures on both sides which made the division between Eastern and Western Germany more pronounced. Under Russian supervision a People's Congress of 1,629 delegates, set up in 1947 and claiming to represent both Eastern Germany and Western Germany, elected in 1948 a People's Council of 400 members; a Presidium of 29 members was then elected, and began to prepare a constitution for a united Germany. The individuals most actively concerned in these developments were all members of the Communist-controlled Socialist Unity Party. After the establishment in May 1949 of the German Federal Republic, *q.v.*, the People's Council was converted into a provisional People's Chamber; elections were held at which voters could accept or reject a single list of candidates, and although the official list was accepted by a majority, 33·9 per cent of voters rejected it. On 7 October 1949 the People's Chamber enacted the constitution of the German Democratic Republic, *q.v.*

Eccles, Sir David McAdam. British Conservative Party politician; born 18 September 1904, son of a surgeon; educated at Winchester and New College, Oxford, where he studied philosophy, politics, and economics. He was successful at an early age as an investor and businessman in the City of London, and on the outbreak of the Second World War he joined the Ministry of Economic Warfare, acting from 1940 to 1942 as economic adviser to the British Ambassadors at Madrid and Lisbon. After joining the Ministry of Production in 1942 to assist Lord Chandos, he was elected to parliament in 1943 to represent Chippenham, and has held this seat since. He was appointed Minister of Works in November 1951, Minister of Education in 1954, President of the Board of Trade in January 1957, and Minister of Education again in October 1959.

E.C.E. Economic Commission for Europe, *q.v.*

Economic Commission for Europe (E.C.E.). Was set up on 28 March 1947 by the Economic and Social Council, *q.v.*, of the United Nations to plan concerted action to raise the level of European economic activity, and to strengthen the economic relations of European countries, both among themselves and with other countries. The members include the European members of the United Nations, and the U.S.A. It has subsidiary committees on coal, electric power, industry and materials, inland transport, manpower, steel, timber, the development of trade, and agricultural problems. The other regional commissions are the Economic Commission for Asia and the Far East (E.C.A.F.E.), set up in 1947, the Economic Commission for Latin America (E.C.L.A.), set up in 1948, and the Economic Commission for Africa, set up in April 1958.

Economic Co-operation Administration. A U.S. organization established by the Economic Co-operation Act of April 1948 as a government agency to administer the European Recovery Programme, *q.v.* It was abolished and its functions were transferred to the Mutual Security Agency, *q.v.*, on 30 December 1951.

Economic and Social Council. One of the six principal organs of the United Nations, *q.v.*, responsible under the authority of the General Assembly for carrying out the functions of the United Nations in economic, social, cultural, educational, health, and related matters, and for promoting the observance of human rights and fundamental freedoms. It comprises eighteen members elected by the General Assembly, six of whom are elected each year for a three-year term.

The United Nations Charter provides for the relating of the various inter-governmental agencies, which have wide responsibilities in economic, social, cultural, educational, health, and other fields, to the United Nations as 'Specialized Agencies'. This is done through the Economic and Social Council, which negotiates with the Agencies subject to approval by the General Assembly. The Council is responsible for co-ordinating the activities of the Specialized Agencies, which are: the Food and Agriculture Organization, *q.v.*, the Inter-Governmental Maritime Consultative Organization, the International Bank for Reconstruction and Development, *q.v.*, the International Labour Organization, *q.v.*, the International Monetary Fund, *q.v.*, the International Telecommunication Union, the United Nations Educational, Scientific, and Cultural Organization, *q.v.*, the Universal Postal Union, the World Health Organization, *q.v.*, the World Meteorological Organization, the International Civil Aviation Organization, the International Atomic Energy Agency, and the International Finance Corporation, *q.v.*

The Council has established the following Commissions to review international problems: Trade, Human Rights, Narcotic Drugs, Population, Social, Statistical, Status of Women, and Transport and Communications. It has set up regional Economic Commissions for Asia and the Far East, Africa, Europe, and Latin America, each consisting of United Nations members in the areas concerned and other United Nations members having special interests there.

Ecosoc. Economic and Social Council of the United Nations, *q.v.*

E.C.S.C. European Coal and Steel Community, *q.v.*

Ecuador. An independent state on the north-west coast of South America; area 276,008 sq. m.; population (1958) 4,119,600, comprising descendants of Spanish settlers, aboriginal Indians, and *mestizos*; capital Quito. Ten per cent of the population are white, thirty-nine per cent Indian, forty-one per cent of mixed blood, and the others are mulatto and Negro. The country was conquered by Peru in the fifteenth century and by Spain in the sixteenth century; complete independence was achieved in 1830. Its unusual features are its political peace and its stable currency. Ecuador exports more bananas than any other country, and also exports cocoa, coffee, and rice. Oil is produced but little is available for export. The U.S.A. buys fifty-eight per cent of all its exports. A long-term plan was instituted in 1953 to improve road and rail communications. After many disputes between Ecuador and Peru the vexed question of the ownership of the upper banks of the Amazon was settled in 1942 by Argentina, Brazil, Chile, and the U.S.A., which awarded them to Peru, but minor frontier clashes continue.

There is a legislature, comprising a Senate and a Chamber of Deputies, elected on a population basis, and a President who is elected for a four-year term by direct popular vote. A sixty-one year old tradition of Liberal Presidents was broken in June 1956 when a Conservative lawyer, Camilo Ponce Enríquez, was returned on a minority vote. In June 1960 he was succeeded by a Liberal, Dr José María Velasco Ibarra, who had been President three times previously, and who promised land reform and substantial government expenditure on housing and roads.

E.D.C. European Defence Community, *q.v.*

Eden, Sir Robert Anthony. Conservative Party politician; born 12 June 1897, son of Sir William Eden, Bt., a Yorkshire squire; educated at Eton and Christ Church, Oxford, where he studied Oriental languages. He went to France in 1915, gained the Military Cross, was a Captain at twenty and later Brigade Major. He contested the Spennymoor Parliamentary Division in 1922. Eden married in 1923 (and divorced in 1950) the daughter of Sir Gervase Beckett, banker and part-owner of the *Yorkshire Post*, and was elected Conservative M.P. for Warwick and Leamington. He became Parliamentary Private Secretary to the Under-Secretary of State for Home Affairs, 1924–6, to the Foreign Secretary, 1926–9, and Parliamentary Under-Secretary of State for Foreign Affairs, 1931–4. In 1934 he became Lord Privy Seal. When at the 'peace ballot' of 1935 eleven million persons had professed their loyalty to the League of Nations, it was decided to set up a Ministry for League Affairs, and Eden was appointed to this post. He urged League of Nations action when Italy attacked Ethiopia, opposed the Anglo-French 'Hoare-Laval plan' to give Italy wide powers in Ethiopia, and at the age of thirty-eight replaced Sir Samuel Hoare (later Lord Templewood) as Foreign Secretary. In February 1938 he resigned in protest against the actions of the Prime Minister, Neville Chamberlain, whom he considered to have negotiated behind his back with the Italian Ambassador. In 1939 he was recalled as Secretary of State for Dominion Affairs; he became Secretary of State for War in 1940, and again

Foreign Secretary from 1940 to 1945. He was Deputy Leader of the Opposition, 1945–51, and Foreign Secretary, 1951–5. In 1952 he married Clarissa Spencer Churchill. On the retirement from ministerial office of Sir Winston Churchill in April 1955 he became Prime Minister and First Lord of the Treasury. He was, however, troubled increasingly by ill-health, and in January 1957 resigned both from government office and from the House of Commons.

E.F.T.A. European Free Trade Association, *q.v.*

Egghead. A derisive term used to describe the more intelligent and thoughtful members of the population. It has been frequently applied in the U.S.A. to Adlai Stevenson, *q.v.*, and his political colleagues.

Egypt. One of the two regions (the other is Syria, *q.v.*) which since 1 February 1958 have comprised the United Arab Republic, *q.v.*; area 386,198 sq. m. only 13,500 sq. m. of which are cultivated; population 25,625,000, comprising Egyptians (*fellahin* or soil-workers), Bedouin nomads, and Nubians of mixed Arab and Negro blood; capital Cairo. The great majority of the population is Moslem. Egypt was a semi-independent state with a hereditary viceroy or Khedive, and under Turkish sovereignty, from 1841 to 1916. From 1882 it was occupied by British troops and under British administration. In 1914 a British protectorate was declared and the pro-German Khedive was deposed; in 1922 the pro-British Sultan Fuad was proclaimed King. The Anglo-Egyptian Treaty of 1936 recognized Egyptian sovereignty but gave to the U.K. the right to maintain a garrison on the Suez Canal, *q.v.*, to use Alexandria and Port Said as naval bases, and to move troops across Egypt in case of war or the threat of war; Sudan, *q.v.*, was to remain an Anglo-Egyptian condominium under joint administration. The 1936 Treaty did not satisfy the growing numbers of Egyptians who resented the presence of foreign troops, and who had since 1918 demanded their departure.

The protests against foreign influence were accompanied after the Second World War by discontent with the economic structure, which permitted a small number of individuals to hold large areas of the fertile land, and with the Egyptian government itself, which failed to develop the industries and natural resources of the country as fully as possible. A *coup d'état* by a group of officers on 23 July 1952 led to the abdication of King Farouk and the eleven-month reign of his infant son, Ahmed Fuad II. Civilian titles such as Pasha were abolished on the grounds that they were undemocratic; taxes were increased to abolish the budget deficit; an agrarian reform was introduced, limiting the area of land which any one person could hold; a Council for the Promotion of National Production was established to develop systematically the production of cotton of a longer staple, more rice, sugar, sugar cane, and maize, and to establish more industries; severe penalties were introduced for corrupt practices; plans were made to build the High Dam, q.v.; social welfare services were extended; and the Moslem Brotherhood, q.v., was dissolved. Negotiations began with the U.K. on the question of the Suez Canal Zone and in 1954 the 1936 Treaty was terminated, it being agreed that all British forces were to leave the zone by June 1956. General Neguib, q.v., declared a republic in June 1953 and was President until 1954, when he was accused of trying to concentrate all power in his own hands and relieved of all his posts. Presidential powers were then vested in the Council of Ministers; Colonel Gamal Abdel Nasser, q.v., became Prime Minister, and in June 1956 became President when the Council was dissolved.

In 1955 and 1956 relations between Egypt and the western powers became strained. Foreign capital was needed for the High Dam; the country found it difficult to sell its cotton and was attracted by Russian offers to buy part of the crop; and, after unsuccessful attempts to buy arms from the west, the government concluded the Czech arms deal, q.v. On 19 July 1956 the U.S.A. informed Egypt that it was not 'feasible in present circumstances' for American aid to be given for the construction of the High Dam. The U.K. made a similar decision and the World Bank's offer lapsed as it had been contingent on American and British assistance. On 26 July President Nasser announced that Egypt would take over the Suez Canal forthwith, and would use the revenue to build the High Dam. Suez Canal Company shareholders were to be paid the Paris Stock Exchange closing prices of their shares as on that day. On 2 August the British government declared its intention of taking 'precautionary measures of a military nature' to strengthen the British position in the eastern Mediterranean. It then requisitioned merchant ships and called up reservists. International discussions, both in London and at the United Nations, produced no general agreement as to the next steps to be taken.

On 29 October 1956 Israel attacked Egypt and on the following day the U.K. told Egypt and Israel that British and French forces would occupy the Suez Canal Zone unless both sides were to 'stop all warlike action by land, sea and air forthwith', and withdraw their forces to a distance of ten miles from the Canal. Egypt rejected the ultimatum as compliance would have involved abandonment of Egyptian control of the Canal. On 31 October Franco-British forces attacked Egypt. In response to appeals from the United Nations the

British and French ceased fire on 6 November when they had occupied only the northern part of the Suez Canal Zone. By 22 December a United Nations Emergency Force had replaced the Franco-British armies, while the Israelis gave up their last foothold in Egypt, the Gaza Strip, *q.v.*, in March 1957.

Egypt has been a leader of the Arab League, *q.v.*, since its formation in 1945, and strongly opposed the conclusion in 1955 of the Baghdad Pact, *q.v.*, which weakened the League by attracting the support of Iraq. The U.A.R. resents the existence of the neighbouring state of Israel, which Egypt failed to defeat in 1948, which defeated the Egyptian army in 1956, and which occupies a larger area of Palestine, *q.v.*, than was originally allotted to it by the United Nations. Egyptian troops have been maintained since 1949 in the Gaza Strip, which the United Nations allotted in 1947 to a proposed new Arab state. The Tripartite Declaration of 1950, *q.v.*, by France, the U.K., and the U.S.A., was made partly with a view to deterring Egypt from aggression against Israel.

Eire. Name by which southern Ireland, now the Republic of Ireland, *q.v.*, was known from 1937 to 1948, during which time it was a Dominion within the British Commonwealth.

Eisenhower, Dwight David. Was President of the U.S.A. from 1953 to 1961; born 14 October 1890 in Denison, Texas. He graduated from West Point Military Academy in 1915, and eleven years later passed out of the General Staff School at Fort Leavenworth, Kansas. For some years afterwards he held Army office and staff appointments. He was with the Battle Monuments Commission in Paris in 1927, was an Assistant Executive in the office of the Assistant Secretary of War from 1929 to 1933, served in the office of the Chief of Staff from 1933 to 1935, and was Assistant Military Adviser in the Philippines from 1935 to 1940. When Japan attacked Pearl Harbour on 7 December 1941 he was a divisional chief of staff, and became assistant chief of staff in charge of the Operations Division in Washington. He was in command of the European theatre of operations in 1942, and was then successively Commander-in-Chief of the Allied Forces in North Africa from 1942 to 1944, Supreme Commander of the Allied Expeditionary Force in Western Europe from 1944 to 1945, Commander of the U.S. Occupation Zone in Germany in 1945, Chief of Staff of the U.S. Army from 1945 to 1948, and Supreme Commander of the North Atlantic Treaty Forces in Europe from 1950 to 1952. In 1952 he retired from the Army, won the Republican Party Presidential nomination against strong opposition from the supporters of Senator Taft, and was elected President of the U.S.A., defeating the Democratic candidate, Adlai Stevenson, *q.v.* He is believed to have been a moderating influence on the right wing of the Republican Party, but his personal political position was obscure. He was baptized as a National Presbyterian after his election; he had formerly been a non-sectarian Christian, having been brought up in a Nonconformist sect, the Brethren of Christ. In September 1955 he suffered a heart attack severe enough to prevent him from resuming his normal duties immediately after his discharge from hospital in November 1955. In June 1956 he underwent an operation for the relief of an intestinal obstruction caused by ileitis, but nevertheless stood again as Presidential candidate in November 1956 and defeated Adlai Stevenson a second time. In a message to Congress in January 1957 he expounded what has become known as the Eisenhower Doctrine, *q.v.* In November 1957 he suffered a mild stroke. His second term of office ended in January 1961, when he was succeeded by John Kennedy.

Eisenhower Doctrine. A term describing proposals for a new Middle East policy made by President Eisenhower to the U.S. Congress on 5 January 1957. He proposed: (1) that U.S. armed forces should be used in the Middle East to secure and protect the territorial integrity and political independence of nations requesting such aid against overt armed aggression from any nation controlled by international Communism; (2) that the U.S.A. should help nations and groups in the Middle East to develop their economic strength; and (3) that the U.S.A. should give military aid to those in the Middle East who desired it. The area to which the Doctrine was to apply lay between (and included) Libya in the west, Pakistan in the east, Turkey in the north, and the Arabian peninsula (with Ethiopia and Sudan) in the south.

El Salvador. *See* Salvador.

Embargo. An order preventing or impeding the movement of ships of a foreign power, either by detaining them in a port or by forbidding them access to a port. Ships are sometimes obstructed in this way in anticipation of a state of war, but this procedure is rare today, and they are usually given liberty to complete their journeys. The term is also used to describe any suspension of trading with a particular state or in particular commodities.

Encirclement. In German *Einkreisung*, a description used by Germans to describe the formation of an alliance between western and eastern powers to prevent German expansion. The term was first used by Reich Chancellor von Bülow in 1906 to recruit popular support for expenditure on the German navy, and it was revived when the U.K. in 1939 (after the annexation of Czechoslovakia by Germany) gave guarantees to Greece, Poland, Rumania, and Turkey, and made a half-hearted attempt to conclude an alliance with the U.S.S.R. The object of encirclement, according to German propaganda at various times, was to deny to Germany its necessary '*Lebensraum*', *q.v.*

Encyclical. From the Latin *bulla encyclica*, a circular letter by the Pope on religious and political questions. The opinions and directions contained in an encyclical have not the power of a dogma but are almost as powerful. Issued only on important occasions and defining papal policies over a length of time, they are significant documents. Famous political encyclicals include Leo XIII's *Rerum Novarum* (against a socialist state), Pius XI's *Quadragesimo Anno* (for a Christian corporate state), *Mit Brennender Sorge* (in German, attacking the extravagances of Nazi doctrines in a way that did not condemn political and social totalitarianism), and on Atheistic Communism (describing Communism as intrinsically wrong).

Enosis. *See* Cyprus.

Entente Cordiale. From the French, 'cordial understanding'; the understanding reached in 1904 between the U.K. and France. The friendship between the two countries has continued ever since, but there has not always been agreement on foreign policy. Between the two World Wars and after 1945 there was much greater opposition in France than in the U.K. to the resurgence of Germany and a correspondingly greater reluctance on the part of France to join an anti-Soviet coalition. The friendship was reaffirmed in 1947 by the Dunkirk Treaty, *q.v.*

Entente, Council of. An association set up by the independent republics of Dahomey, *q.v.*, Ivory Coast, *q.v.*, Niger, *q.v.*, and Upper Volta, *q.v.* Before independence these countries were, with four other territories which have now become independent, part of French West Africa, *q.v.* This loose grouping may be compared with the Union of Central African Republics, an economic union of the four states which once formed part of French Equatorial Africa, *q.v.*

Entrenched Provisions. Those sections of the South Africa Act, 1909, which can be altered or repealed only by a Bill passed by both Houses of Parliament sitting together, and agreed to at the third reading by not less than two thirds of the total number of members of both Houses. The 1909 Act gives to South Africa full powers of constitutional amendment, but states, in Section 152, that Sections 33 and 34 (regulating the proportionate representation of the original four colonies), Section 35 (safeguarding the Coloured franchise in Cape Province), and Section 137 (guaranteeing the equality of the English and Dutch languages), can only be altered or repealed in the way described. Section 152 was also made subject to this rule, so that it should itself be safeguarded from a mere majority vote in separate sessions. Nationalists in South Africa considered that the Statute of Westminster, *q.v.*, passed in the U.K. in 1931, gave their Parliament power to repeal the entrenched provisions, because it empowered it to repeal any Act which was part of the law of South Africa. In 1951 the Nationalist government passed a law to remove Cape Coloured voters from the common roll, thus altering Section 35, an entrenched provision. The law was passed by the two Houses sitting separately. The Appellate Division of the South African Supreme Court, in a decision of great constitutional importance, decided that, although South Africa was a sovereign independent state, its Parliament must pass, repeal, and alter laws, including the entrenched provisions, in the manner laid down by Section 152 of the 1909 Act; if it wanted to alter Section 152, it must do so in the prescribed manner. The Nationalist Party administration thereupon introduced laws to increase the membership of the Senate from forty-eight to eighty-nine, and to change the method of electing Senators, so that it could obtain the two-thirds majority in a joint session necessary to alter an entrenched provision and place the Cape Coloured voters on a separate electoral roll. The 1951 law was then re-introduced, and passed in the prescribed manner in May 1956.

E.P.U. European Payments Union, *q.v.*

Erhard, Professor Ludwig. West German Christian Democratic leader; born 4 February 1897 in Fürth, near Nürnberg, the son of a shopkeeper. After being badly wounded in the First World War, he was educated at a Commercial College in Nürnberg and at Frankfurt University, where he studied economics. From 1928 onwards he worked in the Institute of Industrial Research in Nürnberg, of which he later became chairman. After the Second World War he became the Bavarian economics minister, and in 1947 he moved to Frankfurt, where he became Minister of Economics for the German Federal Republic, under Dr Adenauer, and supervised the currency reform of June 1948. Since then he has been particularly concerned with the related problems of German industrial expansion, western European economic unity, and western aid to the underdeveloped countries.

Eritrea. An area of 45,000 sq. m. on the Red Sea, formerly an Italian colony and now federated with Ethiopia; population approximately 1,000,000; capital Asmara. Eritrea was occupied by British forces in the spring of 1941 and from then on was administered by the U.K. On 2 December 1950 the U.N. General Assembly adopted a resolution whereby Eritrea was to constitute an autonomous unit federated with

Ethiopia under the sovereignty of the Ethiopian Crown. An Eritrean government was organized under the supervision of a U.N. Commissioner, and the British administration ended on 15 September 1952. In May 1960 Eritrea was brought more firmly under the control of the central government at Addís Ababa, which announced that the Eritrean government would no longer be known as such, but would be described only as the Eritrean administration.

E.R.P. European Recovery Programme, *q.v.*

Estonia. Since 1940 one of the fifteen constituent Republics of the Union of Soviet Socialist Republics; area 18,353 sq. m.; population (1959) 1,197,000; capital Tallinn. The language is related to Finnish, having nothing in common with that of the Latvians to the south. The Republic, which is on the Baltic Sea, was ruled by foreigners (including Danes, Swedes, Germans, and Russians) for seven hundred years and was a Russian province when it achieved independence, with Finnish and British assistance, at the end of the First World War as a result of the simultaneous collapse of Russia and Germany. The people are mostly Lutherans, the Tsarist Russians having failed in their efforts to convert the country to the Russian Orthodox faith. The existence of a literate peasantry and of a substantial class of bourgeois and intelligentsia facilitated the establishment of a peaceful and democratic society in the nineteen-twenties. An Agrarian Law transformed a semi-feudal system of land-holding, in which nearly half of Estonia had belonged to six hundred families of the Germanic Balt nobility, into a society in which the redistributed land was owned by individuals (each allowed as much as could be worked by his family and two horses), educational, co-operative, and industrial institutions, and workers' collective associations. The world-wide economic crisis of 1929 was largely responsible for the emergence of an authoritarian régime under Konstantin Päts, under whose leadership the land was more intensively cultivated and the valuable oil shale deposits were more efficiently exploited. By 1939 there had been a material improvement in the economic position, there was no unemployment, and the Constitution of 1938 had marked the beginning of a return to normal parliamentary government. The government found itself unable to reject a Russian demand for the use of Estonian naval bases, and concluded a treaty with the U.S.S.R. on 28 September 1939, which was followed by the Russian occupation of the country with German consent in June 1940, and the establishment of Estonia as a constituent Republic on 6 August 1940. Approximately 60,000 Estonians, or five per cent of the population, including many of the country's leading figures, were deported to the U.S.S.R. within a year of the occupation.

From 1941 to 1944 Estonia was occupied by German troops; after their withdrawal some Estonians tried to re-establish an independent government but were prevented from doing so by the U.S.S.R. The U.K. and the U.S.A. do not recognize Estonia as being in law a constituent Republic of the U.S.S.R. Agriculture, dairy farming, and cattle breeding are the mainstays of the economy. Mining of shale has been developed to supply Leningrad with gas. There are highly developed textile industries, valuable peat deposits, and good timber supplies from the forests which cover twenty-two per cent of the total area.

Ethiopia. Also known as Abyssinia; an independent empire in north-east Africa; area 395,000 sq. m.; population about 18,000,000, comprising Amharas, the ruling race, of Semitic and Hamitic origin, Gallas, Guraghi, and Negro tribes, in the west and south, Danakil and Somalis in the east; capital Addis Ababa. It was originally a group of kingdoms and later twelve land-locked provinces; as a result of a United Nations resolution in 1950, the provinces were federated in 1952 with the former Italian colony of Eritrea on the Red Sea. Since 1930 it has been ruled by Emperor Haile Selassie, *q.v.*, who, with his Minister of the Pen, exercises almost absolute power in spite of the limitations imposed on him by the 1955 Constitution, which provided for universal suffrage and a two-chamber assembly, comprising an upper chamber of nobles (partly elected and partly nominated by the Emperor) and a lower chamber (nominated by the nobles and local chiefs). Ethiopia was invaded by Italy in 1935 and with Eritrea, *q.v.*, and Somalia, *q.v.*, became part of the Italian East African Empire until the Italian forces were defeated in 1941.

The country is almost entirely agricultural. Its exports of coffee, which doubled in volume between 1945 and 1959, make up fifty-two per cent of the value of exports. The fertile central province of Shoa, in which a subsistence agriculture is still practised, remains undeveloped owing to insufficient investment (about seventeen per cent of the annual expenditure) and the government's failure to attract foreign capital into Ethiopia. Gold is mined in the south. There was an unsuccessful revolt by young members of the ruling classes in December 1960; demands for land and administrative reforms probably lay behind their discontent.

Ethnographical Principle. The principle that all persons of the same race or language should be united in a common state.

Euratom. European Atomic Energy Community, *q.v.*

European Assembly. The parliamentary body of the European Atomic Energy Community, *q.v.*, the European Coal and Steel Community, *q.v.*, and the European Economic Community, *q.v.* It was inaugurated at Strasbourg on 19 March 1958, its 142 members being drawn from the parliaments of the participating countries. France, Italy, and the German Federal Republic have 36 members each, Belgium and the Netherlands 14 each, and Luxemburg 6.

European Atomic Energy Community (Euratom). An organization established with effect from 1 January 1958 by Belgium, France, the German Federal Republic, Italy, Luxemburg and the Netherlands, to create the technical and industrial conditions necessary to utilize nuclear discoveries, and to produce nuclear energy on a large scale. On the same day the European Economic Community, *q.v.*, also known as the Common Market, with the same member countries, came into existence. Both Communities were established as a result of the Rome Treaties, *q.v.*, which were concluded on 25 March 1957.

Executive powers are vested in a Council of Ministers, of six members appointed for four years, which reaches decisions unanimously or by a weighted or non-weighted majority, depending upon the issue. In the case of a weighted vote France, Germany and Italy each have four votes, Belgium and the Netherlands two each and Luxemburg one. A Consultative Assembly of 142 members exercises a general control over the Community, and over the European Economic Community and the European Coal and Steel Community, *q.v.* Legal problems concerning the interpretation of the Treaty and the legality of decisions of the Council of Ministers are submitted to the Court of Justice of seven judges nominated by agreement; the Court performs a similar function for the other two Communities.

The Community established, on 1 January 1959, a common market for nuclear products. It has also undertaken a comprehensive research programme.

European Coal and Steel Community. A body set up in 1952 by Belgium, France, the German Federal Republic, Italy, Luxemburg, and the Netherlands, to control the production and marketing of coal and steel in those countries. It was intended to be a counterpart of the European Defence Community, *q.v.* Executive powers are vested in the High Authority, comprising the President and eight others. Originally the Community had its own Consultative Assembly but this was replaced on 1 January 1958 by the European Assembly, *q.v.*, which also supervises the work of the European Atomic Energy Community, *q.v.*, and the European Economic Community, *q.v.* The legal validity of acts of the High Authority may be tested by argument before the Court of Justice, which also serves all three Communities and replaced an earlier Court. The treaty establishing the Community authorizes the High Authority to set maximum prices for coal and steel in certain carefully defined situations in the different coal and steel producing regions. It also forbids certain trade activities, such as 'double-pricing', and all private agreements, the effect of which is to restrict or to control production, such as cartels.

The High Authority is trying to modernize coal mines and methods of steel production, and has succeeded in abolishing many laws and regulations as to customs and quotas. The Community established a common market with no customs duties for coal and iron ore on 10 February 1953, and for steel on 1 May 1953. The coal and steel industries concerned involve about fifteen per cent of the industrial output of the six member nations.

European Defence Community (E.D.C.). A supra-national community, defensive in its objectives, with common institutions, common armed forces, and a common budget, which was to assure the security of its member states against aggression; an attack on one member state was to be considered as an attack against all. The aim was to produce a defensive community, which would be a more coherent group than the North Atlantic Treaty Organization, with an international army. The member states were to be the same as those of N.A.T.O., with the exception of the U.K. and the U.S.A. and the addition of Italy and Western Germany. The E.D.C. never came into existence. Negotiations to establish it began in Paris in February 1951 and on 8 May 1952 a draft treaty setting it up was initialled by the experts of the six participating countries – Belgium, France, Italy, Luxemburg, the Netherlands, and the German Federal Republic. The E.D.C. treaty was formally signed by the six foreign ministers on 27 May 1952, the day after the signature in Bonn of the new contractual agreements between the German Federal Republic and the western powers, which restored West German sovereignty and formally terminated the occupation of the Republic. The structure of the E.D.C. was to resemble that of the European Coal and Steel Community, *q.v.*,

The E.D.C. treaty provided that it was not to come into force until it had been ratified by the parliaments of the six parties. It was ratified by the parliaments of Belgium, Italy, Luxemburg, the Netherlands, and the German Federal Republic, but was rejected by the French National Assembly. The project was abandoned and there was instituted instead the Western European Union, *q.v.*, with effect from 5 May 1955; the six parties to the proposed European Defence Community, with the addition of the U.K., all became members of the W.E.U.

European Economic Community (Common Market). An organization which came into existence on 1 January 1958, with Belgium, France, the German Federal Republic, Italy, Luxemburg, and the Netherlands as member countries, to establish a common market and a common external tariff or customs union for all their goods, to devise common policies for agriculture, the movement of labour and transport, and to set up common institutions for economic development. On the same day the European Atomic Energy Community, *q.v.*, also known as Euratom, with the same member countries, came into existence. Both Communities were established as a result of the Rome Treaties, *q.v.*, which were concluded on 25 March 1957.

Executive powers are vested in a Council of Ministers, of nine members appointed for four years, which reaches decisions either unanimously or by a weighted or a non-weighted majority, depending upon the issue. In the case of a weighted vote France, Germany, and Italy each have four votes, Belgium and the Netherlands two each and Luxemburg one. A Consultative Assembly of 142 members exercises a general control over the Community, and over the European Atomic Energy Community and the European Coal and Steel Community, *q.v.* Legal problems concerning the interpretation of the Treaty and the legality of decisions of the Council of Ministers are submitted to the Court of Justice of seven judges nominated by agreement; the Court performs a similar function for the other two Communities.

The member countries agreed to reduce all tariffs, both on industrial and agricultural goods, by an average of ten per cent on 1 January 1959, by a further ten per cent on 1 January 1960 and by a further ten per cent on 1 January 1962, making a thirty per cent reduction over the four years. Complete abolition of tariffs should be achieved after a period of twelve to fifteen years, i.e. between 1970 and 1973. The U.K., which did not want to bind itself to discriminate against imports from the British Commonwealth, did not join the Community but entered the European Free Trade Association, *q.v.*

European Free Trade Association (E.F.T.A.). An association of western European states (Austria, Denmark, Norway, Portugal, Sweden, Switzerland, and the U.K.) which have agreed to eliminate, over a period, tariffs and restrictions on trade with each other without the necessity of bringing into alignment their individual tariff and trade policies with countries outside the area. Proposals for such an area were made in July 1956 at the Council of Ministers of the Organization for European Economic Co-operation, *q.v.*, and an O.E.E.C. committee reported in January 1957 that such an Association was technically feasible. Meanwhile six members of O.E.E.C. (Belgium, France, the German Federal Republic, Italy, Luxemburg, and the Netherlands) where themselves conducting negotiations which led in March 1957 to the Rome Treaties, *q.v.*, and to the establishment on 1 January 1958 of the European Atomic Energy Community, *q.v.*, and the European Economic Community, *q.v.*

The U.K., itself a member of O.E.E.C., supported the proposals for this Association with the proviso that foodstuffs should be excluded from their scope; the reasons given for this exception were that many areas in the British Commonwealth relied on the preferential treatment which their exports of foodstuffs received in the U.K., and that several European countries, including the U.K. and Denmark, protected their home agriculture and would wish to continue to do so. The convention establishing the Association was initialled at Stockholm on 20 November 1959, and the first tariff cut, of 20 per cent on industrial goods, was made on 1 July 1960. It is intended to remove all import duties and quantitative restrictions by 1 January 1970. Agricultural products are not affected by the cuts, but members may negotiate agreements relating to such products. Finland is linked with E.F.T.A. by an agreement signed on 27 March 1961.

The seven members of the Association are sometimes known as 'the Outer Seven', whereas the members of the European Economic Community (the Common Market) are known as 'the Six'.

European Monetary Agreement. Was concluded on 5 August 1955 by the members of the Organization for European Economic Co-operation to provide for a return to convertibility of their currencies. The Agreement provided facilities for monthly dollar settlements and established a European Fund of $600,000,000 to assist in these settlements between the various central banks and to grant short-term credits (up to two years) to members. The machinery envisaged by the Agreement came into operation on 27 December 1958, upon the termination of the European Payments Union, *q.v.*

European Payments Union. Set up as from 1 July 1950 by the Organization for European Economic Co-operation to encourage European trade by removing some of the impediments that had prevented payments from one European country to another. European currencies were to be freely convertible into each other but not into dollars. The Managing Board said in its third annual report in 1953: 'the Union is intended only as a temporary system designed to assist European countries until they are able once again fully to take their place in a world-wide system'. With the movement towards the re-introduction of convertibility of sterling and of the other main European currencies, it was agreed that E.P.U. should be continued temporarily and that a European Fund and Multilateral Clearing System should be set up to provide short-term credits for any member country adversely affected by the convertibility of the currency of one or more of its neighbours. On 27 December 1958 a majority of the voting strength notified the Secretary-General of O.E.E.C. of its wish to terminate E.P.U. and bring into force the European Monetary Agreement, *q.v.* The Union accordingly came to an end.

European Recovery Programme. Proposals for economic development and co-operation presented to the U.S.A. on 22 September 1947 by sixteen European states (Austria, Belgium, Denmark, France, Greece, Iceland, Ireland, Italy, Luxemburg, the Netherlands, Norway, Portugal, Sweden, Switzerland, Turkey, and the U.K.) which founded the Organization for European Economic Co-operation, *q.v.*, in response to the Marshall Plan, *q.v.* The Programme covered the four years 1948–51 and was based on (1) a strong production effort by each participating country, (2) internal financial stability, (3) economic co-operation, and (4) a solution of the problem of the deficit with the American continent, particularly by increased exports.

President Truman proposed that U.S. aid (often called Marshall Aid) should be given over the period 1948–51, and the U.S. Congress appropriated $522,000,000 of interim aid to Austria, France, and Italy in 1947, and by the Economic Co-operation Act in April 1948 authorized expenditure on the Programme. It also set up the Economic Co-operation Administration, *q.v.*, to supervise the Programme and the distribution of U.S. aid. The following annual amounts were appropriated by Congress under the Programme: 1948–9 $5,000,000,000; 1949–50 $5,430,000,000; 1950–1 $2,850,000,000.

Exchange Control. A system under which the government or the central bank controls all transactions in foreign exchange in order to conserve the country's supply of foreign currency. The government or central bank buys all foreign currency accruing to exporters and others with credit abroad, and then allocates it, usually on special application, to importers and others owing foreign debts. In the U.K. the Exchange Control Act, 1947, contains the fundamental provisions of the British exchange control system.

Extradition. The removal of a person, by the state where he happens to be, to the state on the territory of which he is alleged to have committed or been convicted of a crime. As there is no rule of international law by which states must hand over people in this way many extradition treaties have been concluded specifying the cases in which extradition shall take place. The treaties generally provide that individuals charged or convicted of the more important crimes, with the exception of political crimes, shall be surrendered.

F

Fair Deal. A policy proclaimed by President Truman in January 1949, and designed, like President Roosevelt's New Deal, *q.v.*, to improve the U.S. standard of living, especially among lower-income groups, and to extend social justice by fair labour legislation and civil rights measures. It denied the need for a planned economy but looked to Presidential influence to prevent undue inflation or deflation so that programmes for housing, health, education, and the development of national resources could be undertaken. It also involved programmes of foreign economic and military aid.

Falangists. Spanish Fascists. The falange española, or falangists, were created on 29 October 1933 by José Antonio Primo de Rivera, son of Primo de Rivera, the dictator of Spain from 1923 to 1930. Their founder was shot by the Republicans. On 19 April 1937 the right-wing political groups, including the falange española (which had shown unwelcome signs of social radicalism), were merged to form the Falange Española Tradicionalista y de las Juntas de Ofensiva Nacional Sindicalistas. This body replaced the Cortes (Assembly) from June 1939 until the Cortes was reinstituted in July 1942. It is the only political organization allowed in Spain.

Falkland Islands. A British colony in the South Atlantic, 300 miles east of the Magellan Straits; the island group has a total area of 4,618 sq. m.; population 1,271; capital Stanley. The colony, which has been occupied continuously by the U.K. for over a hundred years, is claimed by Argentina, which includes the population of the islands in its official census. The Falkland Islands Dependencies in the Antarctic Continent, *q.v.*, are the subject of both Argentinian and Chilean claims.

F.A.O. Food and Agriculture Organization, *q.v.*

Faroes. A group of islands under Danish sovereignty, in the Atlantic Ocean, north of the U.K.; area 540 sq. m.; population about 32,400, descended from Norsemen; capital Thorshavn. More than half of the population is engaged in fishing activities or agriculture or both. There are eighteen inhabited islands, twelve uninhabited islands on which sheep graze, and other almost inaccessible small islands and rocks. The islands were Norwegian dependencies from 1030 to 1814, when they passed to Denmark. The Danes suspended the ancient Lagting (parliament) for many years and forbade teaching and preaching in Faroese, a mixture of Icelandic and Norwegian. In 1816 the islands became a Danish county. They were occupied by British forces in the Second World War, and in 1946 the Lagting held a plebiscite by which a narrow majority favoured separation from Denmark and the creation of an independent state. In 1948 a Danish law, supported by four out of the five parties in the Lagting, made the islands a self-governing community, without conceding independence. The Faroes return two members to the Danish Parliament in Copenhagen. There were serious disputes between the Landsstyre (provincial government), representing the Copenhagen government, and some elements in the Faroes from 1953 onwards. These differences arose from a Copenhagen decision to appoint a permanent head of a Faroes hospital (at Klaksvig) in succession to a temporary holder of that post, who had been sent there after being found guilty by the Danish Medical Association of 'national misconduct' and wartime associations with Danish traitors. Danish Communists, Faroese separatists, and some others with whom the temporary head was very popular, opposed by force the landing of the new doctor.

Further differences between the Faroese and the Danes arose in June 1958 when the Lagting passed a Bill purporting to abrogate the Anglo-Danish Fishery Convention of June 1901. The Convention, as modified by a later agreement in April 1955, provided for a four-mile limit for territorial waters as far as fishing rights were concerned. The Bill followed a decision of the Iceland government to extend its fishing limits to twelve miles from 1 September 1958. The Danish government rejected the Bill on the ground that it related to foreign affairs which were outside the competence of the Lagting. In April 1959 a temporary Anglo-Danish agreement was signed, permitting British vessels to fish up to six miles within the twelve-mile limit, as they were regarded as having historic rights in the waters.

Fascism. A nationalist, anti-Communist, and authoritarian political creed founded by Benito Mussolini in Italy in 1919. The Italian Fascist movement adopted as its emblem the fasces, a bundle of rods with an axe in the middle, which was the symbol of state power carried in front of the consuls by the lictors in ancient Rome. The movement claimed to be neither capitalistic nor socialistic, and advocated the founding of a corporate state, *q.v.* After Mussolini came to power in 1922 the Fascist Party became the only authorized political organization in Italy; its members wore black shirts, used the Roman greeting of the outstretched arm, were organized as a military formation, and adopted the slogan 'Mussolini ha sempre ragione' (Mussolini is always right). Italian Fascism served as a model to a number of similar movements in other countries, and in particular to National Socialism in Germany. In the U.K. a Fascist movement called the British Union, which was active between 1931 and 1939, advocated the abolition of free speech and greater interest in the British Commonwealth, and preached anti-semitic propaganda. Its leader, Sir Oswald Mosley, a former Labour M.P. and Minister, was interned during the Second World War.

F.B.I. Federal Bureau of Investigation, *q.v.*

Federal Bureau of Investigation. A branch of the U.S. Department of Justice. Its Director has responsibility for investigating all alleged violations of federal laws except those which, by federal enactment or otherwise, have been assigned to some other body. It is especially concerned with internal security, espionage, and sabotage.

Federal Reserve System. The U.S. central bank system, organized in 1915 under the Federal Reserve Act, 1913. There are twelve Federal Reserve Banks located in the most important regions of the U.S., and the member banks of the Federal Reserve System are normally indebted to the Federal Reserve Banks, which re-discount trade bills on their behalf. The Federal Reserve Banks jointly constitute the central banking system and correspond to the Bank of England. The system is controlled by the Federal Reserve Board, a Board consisting of government nominees, created in 1936 under the Banking Act, 1935. The Reserve Banks have the power to influence the member banks in the matter of loans to customers.

Federation. A political unit on which a number of smaller political units devolve certain power over themselves and their citizens, and to which they usually entrust the conduct of their foreign affairs. The individual provinces or states, as they are often called, retain some control over their internal affairs, and in order that their rights should be clearly defined there is usually a federal constitution which allocates powers between them and the federal government. As disputes often arise as to the constitutional legality of executive decisions or laws made by the federal government, a supreme court is generally created to interpret the constitution. It is frequently provided that amendments to the constitution can be made only with the consent of a fixed number of the provinces or states.

Examples of federations, or federal unions, may be found in the United States of America, the United States of Argentina, the United States of Brazil, the United States of Mexico, the Union of Soviet Socialist Republics, Canada, Australia, Venezuela, and the Federation of Rhodesia and Nyasaland. The U.S. Constitution forbids the individual states to make treaties with foreign governments, but the Russian Constitution permits such treaties and even allows the constituent Republics of the U.S.S.R. to have separate military forces, though this right is not exercised. The Ukraine and Byelorussia, however, which are constituent Republics, have separate representation at the United Nations Assembly.

A federal constitution can be contrasted with a unitary constitution where a supreme legislature may enact any law, and with the constitution of a confederation, *q.v.*, which is a looser association than a federation. The essential difference between a federation and a confederation is that the organs of a federation have a direct power over the citizens of its component provinces or states. Thus Switzerland is officially called a confederation but is really a federation.

Federation of Rhodesia and Nyasaland. A largely self-governing British territory in Central Africa, created as a Federation on 1 August 1953; area 486,722 sq. m.; population (1958) 7,886,400, including 291,600 Europeans; capital Salisbury. It comprises the self-governing territory of Southern Rhodesia, *q.v.*, and the protectorates of Northern Rhodesia, *q.v.*, and Nyasaland, *q.v.*; the union is often called the Central African Federation, *q.v.* The economic argument for federation was strong; Nyasaland is almost entirely agricultural, with insufficient work for its inhabitants, Northern Rhodesia is almost wholly dependent on the wealth to be derived from its copper belt, and therefore on the world price of copper, and would benefit from development of secondary industries, while Southern Rhodesia has the most balanced economy of the three units but anticipates a shortage of labour. In spite of this many Africans in the two protectorates regarded federation, and the end of Colonial Office supervision, as a setback to their hopes for self-government. Under the 1953 Constitution an African Affairs Board was empowered to draw attention to any Bill disadvantageous to Africans by asking that the Bill should be reserved for the approval of the British government. The Board comprises the three European members appointed to the Assembly to represent African interests, and one of the elected African members from each territory.

Its objections, in 1957, to the Federal Franchise Bill and the bill to amend the composition of the federal legislature, were overruled by the British government and the bills were thereupon passed by the British parliament. The possibility of introducing amendments to the 1953 Constitution has been considered by a British government advisory commission under the chairmanship of Viscount Monckton; in 1960 this commission issued its report, which became known as the Monckton Report, *q.v.*

The Federal Assembly elected on 12 November 1958 consisted of 59 members, including 29 representing Southern Rhodesia, 19 from

Northern Rhodesia, and 11 from Nyasaland. Of the 59, 12 were Africans and 3 Europeans specially elected to represent African interests. The United Federal Party, led by Sir Roy Welensky, *q.v.*, won 46 seats; it favoured the elevation of the Federation to full membership of the British Commonwealth as soon as possible and opposed any rapid transfer of power to Africans. The Federal Dominion Party, led by Winston Field, won 8 seats; it sympathized with some of the South African Nationalist Party views on apartheid.

There have been disputes between the European Mineworkers' Union and the employers over the advancement of African workers in the Northern Rhodesian copper belt, caused fundamentally by jealousy on the part of the European workers, who are reluctant to agree to the extension of equal opportunities for promotion to African workers. The Dalgleish Commission recommended in 1947 that African workers should be given increased opportunities for promotion, but its findings were rejected by the employers and the European workers. In 1949, however, the African Mineworkers' Union was created and recognized by the employers who are anxious to use all available labour to develop the mines. The two most important groups of employers, the Rhodesian Selection Trust group (which has a parent organization in the U.S.A.) and the Anglo-American Corporation (controlled from South Africa) made new agreements with the European Mineworkers' Union in 1955, by which the employers were given greater freedom of action in the advancement and training of Africans. The Anglo-American Corporation, however, granted to the European workers a right to prevent African advancement beyond certain agreed categories of jobs, although the whole question of promoting Africans further was to be reviewed at regular intervals.

Fellow Traveller. One who accepts most Communist conclusions but is not, or denies he is, a Communist. The term usually has a derogatory meaning. It is a useful expression when applied to people who, favouring a particular Communist policy, falsely claim that they, as independents, have come to the same conclusion. It is a malicious and unilluminating expression when used by politicians of persons whose honest left-wing deviations from their own views they wish to attack.

Fertile Crescent. The area between the Mediterranean Sea and the Persian Gulf, now occupied by Jordan, Syria, and Iraq, which was once a fertile region, particularly in the valleys of the Euphrates and the Tigris, but which is now largely an arid desert region.

Fifth Amendment Communist. A term of abuse or reproach, current in the United States. It is used loosely to describe certain witnesses, suspected of being Communists or Communist sympathizers, who plead the Fifth Amendment to the Constitution of the United States to justify their refusal to answer questions before a civil court or Congressional committee.

The Amendment says: 'No person . . . shall be compelled in any criminal case to be a witness against himself.' The classic interpretation of the Amendment was given by Chief Justice Marshall (1755–1835) in the treason trial of Aaron Burr. He said that two principles, that the United States was entitled to the testimony of every citizen, and that every witness was entitled not to accuse himself, had to be reconciled. It would be virtually a perjury, he said, to use the Fifth Amendment to protect oneself against social disgrace or other embarrassments, for it should only be used where one might be accused of a crime. In law, therefore, his disapproval of the activities of a court or committee would not entitle a man to plead the Fifth Amendment in order to avoid answering questions. The Amendment was criticized by the late Senator McCarthy and his supporters, as enabling Communist sympathizers to conceal information. It was similarly attacked in the early years of the twentieth century by writers in American liberal periodicals on the grounds that it was being improperly pleaded by politicians and business men in anti-trust cases.

Fifth Column. A term originating from the Spanish Civil War, 1936–9 when the rebels under Franco attacked Madrid in four columns, while their adherents organized uprisings, espionage, and sabotage within the government ranks. These secret fighters behind the front were called the 'fifth column'.

Fifth Republic. The system of government established in France in 1958. The First Republic lasted from 1793 until 1804 when Napoleon Bonaparte set up the First Empire. The Second Republic, which was created in 1848, became the Second Empire in 1852, and the Third Republic was set up in 1870 following the deposition of the Emperor Napoleon III. France was governed by the Constitution of the Third Republic until the German occupation of 1940. After the liberation of Paris in 1944 a provisional government under General de Gaulle, *q.v.*, was set up with a single-chamber legislature (the National Constituent Assembly). By a referendum held in October 1945 the Constitution of the Third Republic was abandoned. In May 1946 a draft constitution was rejected by the Assembly: a second draft constitution was eventually accepted by the Assembly on 29 September 1946, and adopted by a referendum, held on 13 October, in which 9,297,470 voted in favour, 8,165,459 against, and 8,519,635 abstained. The Fourth Republic lasted from 24 December 1946 to 5 October, 1958, when it was replaced by the Fifth Republic. The Constitution of the Fifth Republic was approved by a referendum, held in France and the overseas departments and territories on 28 September 1958, in which 31,066,502 voted in favour and 5,419,749 against.

Filibustering (U.S.A.). Holding up Bills in the Senate by organizing a continuous succession of interminable opposition speeches. If more than one third of the Senators present and voting are opposed to a cosure, it is impossible to end a filibuster.

Finland. An independent state on the Baltic Sea; area 130,127 sq. m.; population (1958) 4,394,700. It was part of Sweden from 1154 to 1809, when it became an autonomous Grand Duchy within Russia. After the Russian Revolution its independence was declared; the new Russian government tried to retain it, but with the help of German troops the Finns prevailed. Defeated in 1939–40 after a Russian invasion, and forced to cede 16,170 sq. m. (including the Karelian Isthmus and the western shore of Lake Ladoga), the Finns helped Germany to invade the U.S.S.R. in 1941 but concluded an armistice in 1944.

The President is appointed for six years by an electoral college elected by popular vote. The legislature is a single chamber of two hundred members elected for four years by universal suffrage and proportional representation. Elections were held in July 1958. The results were: Social Democrats, a left-wing but strong anti-Communist group representing the poorer townspeople, 48 seats, Popular Democrats or Democratic Union, an extreme left-wing group which includes the Communists 50, Agrarians 48, National Union (Consensatives) 29, Swedish People's Party 14, Finnish People's Party, an organization based on the amalgamation of the Liberal Party and certain right-wing groups, 8, and Independent Socialists, 3.

Between 1951 and 1954 there was a series of cabinet crises which were mainly due to differences as to economic policy, particularly over measures to check the rise in the cost of living. From 1951 to 1953 there was a coalition of Social Democrats and Agrarians, with Dr Urho Kekkonen, then the Social Democrat leader, as Premier. In 1953 Kekkonen's proposals to cut wages by ten per cent were rejected by his Social Democrat colleagues, and for four months he governed with a coalition of Agrarians and members of the Swedish People's Party. When this government fell, Dr Sakari Tuomioja, Governor of the Bank of Finland, led a coalition of all parties except the Social Democrats and Popular Democrats. This right-wing alliance was replaced by a coalition under the leader of the Swedish People's Party, Ralf Törngren, after the election of March 1954; it comprised all parties except the Finnish People's Party and the Popular Democrats, and remained in office until October 1954 when Dr Kekkonen, as an Agrarian, formed a new coalition government of Agrarians and Social Democrats. After Dr Kekkonen was elected President in February 1956, Karl-August Fagerholm (a Social Democrat) became Premier of a government based on the coalition of Agrarians and Social Democrats, with one member each from the Swedish People's Party and the Finnish People's Party. The withdrawal of its six Agrarian ministers in March 1957, after a disagreement over butter and milk prices, weakened the government, and Fagerholm resigned in May 1957. He was succeeded by the leader of the Agrarian Party, Dr Veino Johannes Sukselainen, who included members of the Swedish People's and Finnish People's Parties in his cabinet. The devaluation of the Finnmark in September 1957 was followed by the fall of Sukselainen, and a prolonged government crisis occurred when the President found it difficult to persuade any politician to accept the premiership. A non-political business government which was eventually formed in November 1957 was defeated in April 1958. After the July elections Fagerholm formed a government supported by all parties except the Communists and 13 left-wing Social Democrats. He was succeeded in January 1959 by Sukselainen, whose government consisted almost entirely of Agrarians.

Finland lies in an important strategic position between east and west as one of the two democracies in the world (the other is Turkey) which share major land frontiers with Russia. It concluded a Treaty of Friendship and Mutual Assistance with the U.S.S.R. in April 1948, and in 1959 renewed its long-term agreement between the two states. Finland, however, resisted invitations by the U.S.S.R. to be the first non-Communist state to join the Eastern European Mutual Assistance Treaty, q.v. A Russo-Finnish military alliance would give the U.S.S.R. the use of radar bases and fighter stations on Finland's north-western coast. After the Second World War the U.S.S.R. occupied the important Finnish base of Porkkala on the coast, west of Helsinki, but gave it up in 1955 in return for a twenty-year prolongation of the 1948 Russo-Finnish Treaty. The Åland Islands, q.v., are under Finnish sovereignty and have potential strategic importance. The U.K. and U.S.S.R. are the largest trading partners of Finland.

F.L.N. Front de Libération Nationale, q.v.

Food and Agriculture Organization (F.A.O.). Came into being on 16 October 1945 as a result of the United Nations Conference on Food and Agriculture at Hot Springs, Virginia, in May 1943. It has numerous functions: (1) it continually reviews world food and agricultural conditions, and supplies member governments with facts and figures relating to nutrition, agriculture, forestry, and fisheries, and appraisals and forecasts of the production, distribution, and consumption of agricultural products; (2) it promotes and recommends national and international action to improve processing, marketing, and distribution, to conserve resources and to provide agricultural credit; (3) it gives technical assistance to enable members to cultivate new land, to improve yields, to reduce production costs, to improve the efficiency of distribution, to raise levels of consumption, and to improve rural living conditions. The Conference, on which each member has a representative, and which meets every two years, is the policy-making body. A Council of twenty-five members elected by the Conference supervises the work of the F.A.O. between sessions of the Conference, reviews the world food and agricultural situation, and makes recommendations to members and other international bodies on measures to improve the situation. There is a Director-General and a permanent staff at the headquarters in Rome. F.A.O. is one of the specialized agencies of the United Nations.

Foreign Operations Administration. A U.S. organization set up on 1 August 1953 by the new Republican government to co-ordinate all the programmes by which the U.S.A. gave assistance to foreign countries and to conduct all mutual security programmes with the exception of military assistance. All the functions of the Mutual Security Agency, *q.v.*, the Technical Co-operation Administration, the Institute of Inter-American Affairs, and of several other foreign assistance organizations were transferred to the F.O.A. Its Director, Harold Stassen, was supervised in policy matters by the Secretary of State, the Secretary for Defence, and the Secretary to the Treasury; he was therefore more restricted than when he was Director of the M.S.A., in which post he had been responsible only to the President. The F.O.A. was abolished with effect from 30 June 1955 and replaced by the International Co-operation Administration, *q.v.*

Formosa. A large island approximately a hundred miles off the south-eastern coast of China; area 13,890 sq. m.; population 9,409,886; capital Taipei. It was part of the old Chinese Empire for many years until it was ceded to Japan in 1895. In the Cairo Declaration, *q.v.*, the U.K. and the U.S.A. promised that Formosa and all other territories taken by Japan from China (such as Manchuria, *q.v.*, and the Pescadores) should be restored to China. In 1945 China, then led by Chiang Kai-shek, *q.v.*, was allowed to occupy and administer the island. By the end of 1949 the Chinese Communists had become so powerful that Chiang's forces, which included most of the scanty Chinese navy, occupied only Formosa, Hainan, and some parts of western China. At one time the U.S. State Department decided to give no further support to Chiang, regarding his government as inefficient and corrupt. Both the U.S. and British governments regarded Formosa as still forming part of Japan until a Japanese peace treaty was signed, and in 1950 (at the outset of the war in Korea) President Truman ordered the U.S. navy to protect Formosa from the Chinese Communists, but in the Japanese peace treaty of 1951 the issue of Formosa was not dealt with. The Chinese government stated repeatedly that Formosa should be brought into the Chinese People's Republic, but President Eisenhower said that any invasion of the island or of the nearby Pescadores would have to get past the U.S. Seventh Fleet, with its powerful carrier-based air arm and the possibility of land-based air support from Okinawa. The U.K. has given *de jure* recognition to the Chinese People's Republic, but the U.S. recognizes only the government of General Chiang Kai-shek. The latter agreed not to invade the mainland without U.S. consent. Between 1951 and 1957 the Chinese Nationalist government received $550,000,000 from the U.S.A. in economic aid.

France. An independent republic; area 212,895 sq. m.; population (1960) 45,730,000; capital Paris. Under the Constitution of the Fifth Republic, *q.v.*, which came into force on 5 October 1958, the President to whose powers considerable importance is attached, is elected for seven years by a special body of electors, numbering about 81,000, including members of parliament, of local councils, and of overseas territorial assemblies. Article 5 provides that: 'The President of the Republic ensures that the Constitution is observed. He intervenes in order to ensure the proper working of the public authorities and the continuity of the State. He is the guardian of national independence, territorial integrity, and respect for Community [the French Community, *q.v.*] agreements and for treaties.' Under Article 16 he may assume emergency powers 'if there is a serious and immediate threat to the institutions of the Republic, the Nation's independence, its territorial integrity, or the fulfilment of its international undertakings, and the constitutional machinery breaks down.' He nominates the Prime Minister and appoints Ministers on his recommendation; he is empowered to dissolve parliament, but not more than once a year, after consulting the Prime Minister and the presidents of the two houses of parliament. He negotiates and ratifies international treaties, and if called on to do so by the government or by both houses jointly, he can submit certain legislation to a referendum. On 21 December 1958, General de Gaulle, *q.v.*, was elected President by a substantial majority.

Parliament consists of: an upper house, the Senate, of 255 members representing metropolitan France and 52 members representing Algeria (32), Sahara (2), overseas departments (7) and territories (5), and Frenchmen abroad (6); and a lower house, the National Assembly, of 465 members representing metropolitan France and 89 members representing Algeria (66), Sahara (4), and overseas departments and territories. The National Assembly, elected by popular ballot on 23 and 30 November 1958 for five years on the basis of single-member constituencies in France and multi-member constituencies in Algeria, included: 10 Communists (145 in 1956; the Party, led by Maurice Thorez and Jacques Duclos, obtained the largest number of seats in the 1945 election and was in a left-wing coalition until May 1947 since when it has been excluded from all governments); 40 Socialists and their supporters (88 in 1956; led by Guy Mollet, *q.v.*, they believe in a planned economy); 13 Radicals (56 in 1956; a middle-class and small farmers' party, the traditional centre party, opposing Communism and Fascism); 57 Mouvement Républicain Populaire or M.R.P. (71 in 1956; a progressive Catholic party); 189 Union pour la Nouvelle République or U.N.R. (16 in 1956; led by Michel Debré, *q.v.*, Jacques Soustelle, *q.v.*, and others, it comprised several former Gaullist movements which supported the return to power of de Gaulle in May 1958); 132 right-wing independents (94 in 1956; led by Antoine Pinay, Paul Reynaud, and others, they are an amorphous group of orthodox Catholic conservatives, mostly supporting the theory of l'Algerie Française).

The Senate, elected in April and May 1959 by 108,200 deputies, mayors, municipal councillors, and special delegates, included: 14 Communists, 48 Socialists, 51 Radicals, 29 M.R.P., 27 U.N.R., and 85 right-wing independents.

There were twenty-five cabinets from 1944 to May 1958, and more than one quarter of the non-Communist deputies held cabinet office. The apparent inability of French governments to enact legislation, which brought the charge of *immobilisme*, and their instability, were due in part to the constitution of the Fourth Republic, which had been framed in fear of a Communist-dominated government. It specified two thirds and three fifths, rather than simple, majorities on most legislation thereby weakening the executive and creating a strong legislature. The absence of party discipline in the Assembly and the vulnerability of ministers to lobbying (the Présence Française, q.v., lobbied successfully to delay constitutional reform in Algeria) also contributed to political instability.

The coup by French army officers in Algeria, q.v., on 13 May 1958, precipitated a crisis in France, and for a time it was thought probable that the French army would seize key points in France itself. On 15 May General de Gaulle, during negotiations with President Coty, announced that he was ready to assume power. On 1 June, by 329 votes to 224 (147 Communists and Progressistes, 49 Socialists, 18 Radicals, including Mendès-France and Daladier, 4 U.D.S.R., 3 M.R.P., and 3 others) de Gaulle was invested as Premier by the Assembly, giving up this post for that of President in December 1958. The new Constitution was adopted by a referendum held on 28 September 1958.

Government inaction has enfeebled the economy. It is common practice to meet budget deficits by Exchequer loans rather than by retrenchment or increased taxation. Industrial production made slow recovery after 1945, inflation has not been controlled, aid under the Marshall Plan, q.v., was used initially to reduce tariffs on luxury goods and profits made since 1945 have largely been invested abroad. A crisis has been averted only because France is self-supporting in basic foodstuffs and produces enough coal and steel for domestic needs. However, without drastic economic reform, the standard of living, which has been achieved mainly by a systematic exploitation of the resources of the overseas dependencies and by orientating French trade almost exclusively towards them, is likely to fall. The collapse of the French colonial empire, the loss of Syria, q.v., and Lebanon q.v., in 1941, Indo-China, q.v., in 1945, Morocco, q.v., and Tunisia, q.v., in 1956, and the prospective secession of Algeria, have already closed sources of potential French investment and markets for surplus wheat and dairy produce.

Franco, Francisco. Prime Minister, Chief of State and Generalissimo of the armed forces of Spain; born 4 December 1892 in Galicia. He was commissioned in the army in 1910 after spending three years at the Toledo Infantry Academy, and served in Spanish Morocco before and after the First World War. He commanded the Spanish Foreign Legion from 1923 to 1927, and while in Morocco helped to defeat the Rif chieftain, Abd-el-Krim. From 1927 to 1931 he directed the Saragossa Military Academy, which was dissolved by the new republican government in 1931 as a result of its monarchist tendencies. In 1935 he became Chief of the Army General Staff, and in 1936 led a

Fascist revolt and formed a government which was at once recognized and supplied with arms by Germany and Italy. In 1937 Franco proclaimed himself El Caudillo (the leader); in 1939 his government was recognized by France and the U.K., his forces took Madrid, and he became Prime Minister. At the outset of the Second World War he declared his sympathy for Germany and Italy and made plans to enter Gibraltar and French Morocco. He later professed neutrality and in 1943 urged Anglo-German unity against the U.S.S.R. In 1947 he was declared Chief of State for life, with the right to choose his successor.

Free Economy. A school of economists wishing to cure economic evils by a new monetary system. The basic idea is that the value of money should be automatically reduced every month by a certain percentage, and replaced by new money. This would enforce steady circulation of money, as people would try to pass it on by buying goods before its value went down. A steady flow of money would ensure steady employment, and there would be no economic crises. Free economists wish to maintain freedom of enterprise and to avoid socialism. Silvio Gesell (1862–1930) developed the theory in Germany, and its English and Commonwealth variant is Social Credit, *q.v.*

Free Port. Also Free Harbour; a port in one state which other states are allowed to use freely, loading and unloading goods and conveying them to and from the harbour without interference and without customs duties.

Free Trade. An economic policy which does not discriminate between foreign goods and goods produced at home and thus gives no protection against foreign competitors. It may involve a complete absence of tariffs in respect of all goods or of a class of goods; alternatively, any tariffs are matched by an excise duty on goods produced at home. The doctrine of free trade arose in the seventeenth and eighteenth centuries as a reaction to mercantilism (a policy involving the closing of frontiers to foreign goods and producing everything at home). The U.K. became the leading exponent of free trade after the repeal of the Corn Laws in 1846 and Peel's low tariff Acts. (Towards the end of the nineteenth century industrialization in many countries, especially Germany and the U.S.A., was followed by the erection of high tariff barriers.) A high tariff movement in the U.K., which was concerned to protect Empire industry and trade, was defeated in the 1906 General Election by the Liberals who professed free trade. After the First World War protection policies prevailed nearly everywhere, and with the passing of the Import Duties Act in 1932 the U.K. adopted a protective tariff as a permanent institution. Adherents to the doctrine of free trade claim that free international exchange of goods is most economical and encourages specialization and international collaboration. Advocates of high tariffs claim that their system protects domestic industries and the workers employed in them from foreign competition.

Free Trade Area. *See* European Free Trade Association.

French Cameroons. *See* Cameroons, French.

French Community. Established by the Constitution of the Fifth Republic, *q.v.*, which came into force on 5 October 1958 as the result of a referendum on 28 September 1958. As a result of voting against the proposed Constitution, the territory of Guinea had become independent on 2 October 1958, but the remaining departments and territories were then offered a choice between (*a*) retaining their respective statuses (article 76 of the Constitution) and (*b*) becoming member states of the Community with full internal autonomy (article 77) but leaving the control of many matters, including currency, defence, foreign affairs, and higher education, with the Community (article 78). The four existing overseas departments (Martinique, Guadeloupe, Réunion, and Guiana) chose to retain their status, but twelve of the nineteen overseas territories (Central African Republic, Chad, Congo, Dahomey, Gabon, Ivory Coast, Madagascar, Mauritania, Niger, Senegal, Soudan, and Upper Volta) agreed, in October and November 1958, to become members.

The restrictions on sovereignty became irksome, and although the Constitution (article 86) specifically prohibited complete independence within the Community (by stating that upon achieving independence a member state 'then ceases to belong to the Community'), it proved impossible to resist the demand for greater liberty of action. On 3 June 1960 the Community Senate (abolished in March 1961) amended the Constitution to allow member states to remain in the Community after attaining full independence. Between April and November 1960 all the members made declarations by which they attained complete independence but the so-called Entente states (Dahomey, Ivory Coast, Niger, and Upper Volta) left the Community in June 1960.

The organs of the Community are: (1) the President, who is the President of France; (2) the Executive Council, consisting of the Prime Minister of France, the heads of government of the member states, and the Ministers responsible to the Community for common affairs; (3) the Senate, comprising delegates from the parliaments of France and the member states; (4) the Court of Arbitration.

French Congo. *See* Congo Republic (formerly French).

French Equatorial Africa. The name formerly given to the group of four French overseas territories which are now independent states under the names of the Central African Republic, *q.v.*, Chad, *q.v.*, the Congo Republic, *q.v.*, and Gabon, *q.v.* In January 1959 the four states established an economic and technical union.

French Morocco. The name formerly given to the southern portion of Morocco, *q.v.*, which from 1912 to 1956 was recognized as a French sphere of influence; area approximately 164,065 sq. m; capital Rabat; population 8,000,000 of whom all but 562,000 are Sunni Moslems of Arab or Berber stock; there are 150,000 French citizens among the mixed European and Jewish community. France acquired the area as a protectorate as a result of the Treaty of Fez with the Sultan of Morocco signed on 30 March 1912, and by agreement with Italy, Spain, and the U.K. The first Resident-General, Hubert Lyautey, created favourable conditions for French settlement, and immigration and investment gave France a valuable stake in the country's mineral wealth – manganese, cobalt, oil, and one sixth of the world's supply of phosphates – and in its agriculture.

In principle Morocco continued throughout the protectorate to be an Empire ruled by a Sultan, reigning through a government consisting of a Grand Vizier and his deputies. Effective authority, until October 1955, was exercised by the French Resident-General who acted as the Sultan's Minister of Foreign Affairs. The French encouraged Arab–Berber hostility, which had its origins in the opposing interests of town-dwellers (Arabs) and nomad tribesmen (mainly Berbers), and did not scruple to use the Pasha of Marrakesh, El Glaoui (1874–1956), to maintain their authority against the Nationalists. An Arab rising was imminent in 1953 when they enrolled El Glaoui's support to depose the Sultan, Sidi Mohammed Ben Youssef, the eighteenth of his dynasty, who was exiled to Madagascar, and to enthrone his uncle, Sidi Mohammed Ben Arafa, whom the Istiqlal, *q.v.*, immediately denounced as a usurper. Between 1954 and 1955 anti-French riots occurred on an ever-increasing scale.

At a conference with Moroccan nationalist leaders, held at Aix-les-Bains in August 1955, the French government sanctioned the creation of a Regency Council in Morocco and the recall of the former Sultan from exile in Madagascar. Attempts were then made by the Présence Française, *q.v.*, the settlers' organization with a powerful lobby in the National Assembly, to obstruct further reform, but in October 1955 the government agreed to legalize the return of Sidi Mohammed Ben Youssef, to arrange the abdication of Sidi Mohammed Ben Arafa, and to permit the formation of a Moroccan government which would represent all parties, including the outlawed Istiqlal. The French capitulation was confirmed when El Glaoui announced his support for Ben Youssef; practically all the former opponents of Ben Youssef made similar declarations.

Following the return of Ben Youssef to Rabat in November 1955, the Moroccan and French governments announced, on 2 March 1956, the abrogation of the Treaty of Fez and the emergence of Morocco as an independent sovereign state.

French Somaliland. A French overseas territory in the Gulf of Aden between Eritrea and that part of Somalia which was until 1960 British Somaliland; area 9,000 sq. m.; population (1959) 67,300, including 27,000 Danakils, 25,000 Somalis, 4,000 Europeans, and 3,000 Arabs; capital Djibouti, which represents the only rail link between Addis Ababa, capital of Ethiopia, and a sea port. The French government in Paris reserves to itself control of external affairs and defence, but since 1957 local ministers have been responsible for all internal affairs. Administrative powers are vested in an executive council of 8 members, of which the Governor is president, and the council is elected by a territorial assembly of 32 members elected by universal suffrage. The main political party is the Union Républicaine, which is composed of the Arab, Danakil, and Somali elements in the population. Many of the Somalis favour integration with Somalia.

The economy has to be subsidized by France, and also relies considerably on the transit trade with Ethiopia. The port of Djibouti is used principally by French vessels trading to the East.

French Togoland. A former trusteeship territory which became independent on 27 April 1960 under the name of Togo, *q.v.*

French Union. An association of all French overseas possessions and metropolitan France, established under the Constitution of the Fourth Republic in 1946. It had a President who was also the President of the Republic, a High Council which was to include a delegation of the French government and representatives of the Associate States, and an Assembly of representatives of the entire Union. The function of the High Council was to advise and assist the French government in the management of the Union; its powers were almost negligible. In 1954 the Associate States (Viet-Nam, Laos, and Cambodia) withdrew from the Union. The overseas departments and territories which remained as members were: Algeria, Martinique, Guadeloupe, Réunion, Guiana, the eight territories of French West Africa, the four territories of French Equatorial Africa, Madagascar, Comoro Archipelago, French Somaliland, New Caledonia, French settlements in Oceania, Saint-Pierre and Miquelon, the trusteeship territories of Togoland and the Cameroons, and the Anglo-French condominium of the New Hebrides. The former French settlements in India retained their membership until they formally acceded to India in 1954. On the inception of the Fifth Republic, *q.v.*, in 1958, the Union was succeeded by the French Community, *q.v.*

French West Africa. The name formerly given to the group of eight French overseas territories which are now independent states under the names of Dahomey, *q.v.*, Guinea, *q.v.*, Ivory Coast, *q.v.*, Mali, *q.v.*, Mauritania, *q.v.*, Niger, *q.v.*, Senegal, *q.v.*, and Upper Volta, *q.v.*

Front De Libération Nationale (F.L.N.). The principal nationalist organization in Algeria, *q.v.* The nationalist movement developed through two main groups; the moderate Democratic Union of the Algerian Manifesto (U.D.M.A.), which originally supported federation within the French Union, *q.v.*, and the Movement for the Triumph of Democratic Liberties (M.T.L.D.), which demanded complete independence of France. Leaders of the M.T.L.D., including Mohammed ben Bella, a former French army sergeant-major, fled to Cairo where they founded a military organization (C.R.U.A.) to foment rebellion against the French in 1954. Ben Bella then launched the National Liberation Front (F.L.N.) with the aim of expelling the French from North Africa. It was supported by the majority of members of the M.T.L.D., but the leader of U.D.M.A., Messali Hadj, formed a rival Algerian National Movement (M.N.A.) because he disagreed with the ultimate objectives of the F.L.N. and was prepared to co-operate with the French should they prove ready to make concessions.

On 1 November 1954 the F.L.N. formally declared war on France, and fighting began in earnest. However, bitterness between the two factions was dividing the rebel forces to such an extent that urgent efforts were made during 1956 to fuse the movement into one fighting force. Negotiations between the leaders at Berne broke down because the F.L.N. demanded the dissolution of the M.N.A., but there was subsequent co-operation between the guerrilla bands of the M.N.A. and the National Liberation Army, the fighting wing of the F.L.N., and the two parties restrained their rivalry to France itself where some 600 Algerians were murdered in 1956–57.

The F.L.N. operates an administrative system in Algeria independently of the French. It has its own tax-collectors, hospitals, schools, courts and public officials. The fighting strength of the F.L.N. has been estimated by the French at 25,000. Equipment comes from three sources: weapons and supplies captured from the French; arms bought from Israel, Czechoslovakia and elsewhere, which are smuggled over the Moroccan frontier; and other equipment from Cairo which is brought in through Tripoli and across Libya. The F.L.N. has a representative at the United Nations and enjoys official recognition as the government of Algeria by a number of governments, including those of Morocco and Tunisia. However, the F.L.N., which since the capture of ben Bella by the French in 1956 has been led by Ferhat Abbas and Krim Belkacem, is determined not to negotiate except on the basis of Algerian independence, which no French government has yet been prepared to concede.

Führer. A German word meaning 'leader'. This was the title assumed by the German dictator and Nazi leader, Adolf Hitler (born 1889), who came to power in 1933 and is believed to have committed suicide in Berlin in 1945.

Full Employment. Defined by Lord Beveridge, in his *Full Employment in a Free Society*, as a state of affairs in which there are 'more vacant jobs than unemployed men'. There can therefore be unemployment and full employment at the same time, but Beveridge further defined the expression by saying that in the U.K. an unemployment rate of over three per cent would be incompatible with full employment. This rate was to be taken as a percentage of those who were capable of work and willing to work. The incapable and the unwilling were not, in his definition, to be included among the unemployed.

G

Gabon, an independent republic; area 102,290 sq. m.; population 420,709 comprising Pahouins, Pongwés, Adounas, Chiras, Punu, and Lumbu, and 4,000 non-Africans; capital Libreville. The country is on the west coast of Africa, between Spanish Guinea (Rio Muni) to the north and the Congo Republic (formerly French) to the south and east. The territory was annexed by France in 1888 and later became one of the four territories comprising French Equatorial Africa, *q.v.*; it achieved self-government within the French Community, *q.v.*, on 28 November 1958, and complete independence, still within the Community, on 17 August 1960.

Legislative powers are vested in an assembly of 40 members elected every five years by universal suffrage. As a result of the elections held in 1957 control of the assembly is exercised by the Gabon Democratic Bloc, led by Léon M'Ba; the other main party is the Gabon Democratic and Social Union. Executive power is exercised by the Premier (Léon M'Ba) who is elected by the assembly.

The principal exports are lumber, petroleum, cocoa, and gold; there are deposits of iron and manganese. There is an economic union with the Central African Republic, Chad, and the Congo Republic, the three other states which once formed French Equatorial Africa. Gabon is the wealthiest of these states.

Gaitskell, Hugh Todd Naylor. British Labour Party politician; born 9 April 1906, educated Winchester and New College, Oxford. He was a London University Reader and Lecturer, 1928–39, and contested unsuccessfully the Chatham Parliamentary Division in 1935. He was Principal Private Secretary to the Minister of Economic Warfare, 1940–2, Principal Assistant Secretary, Board of Trade, 1942–5, and has been M.P. for Leeds South since 1945. In the Labour government of 1945 he held the offices of Parliamentary Secretary at the Ministry of Fuel and Power, 1946–7, and Minister of Fuel and Power, 1947–50. In 1950 he succeeded Sir Stafford Cripps as Chancellor of the Exchequer. As Treasurer of the Labour Party he reorganized Party finances after the Conservative victory in 1951. He succeeded Clement Attlee (now Earl Attlee) as leader of the Parliamentary Labour Party on 14 December 1955, having obtained 157 votes in a contest with Aneurin Bevan and Herbert Morrison, who obtained 70 votes and 40 votes respectively.

Gallup Poll. A method devised by an American, Dr Gallup, of assessing public opinion. Questions are asked of a representative cross-section of the population. The method has been used in the U.S.A. and by the British Institute of Public Opinion in the U.K. to forecast election results, which it has done with only a narrow margin of error.

G.A.T.T. General Agreement on Tariffs and Trade, *q.v.*

Gaza Strip. An area of approximately 100 sq. m. in south-western Palestine on the Mediterranean Sea and adjacent to the Egyptian border. The United Nations, proposing the partition of Palestine in 1947, decided that the Strip should be part of a new Arab state. It includes the town of Gaza, six miles from the Israeli border, and the railway junction of Rafa. Armed forces from Egypt, Iraq, Jordan, Lebanon, and Syria invaded Palestine when the British mandate ended in May 1948, and hostilities ceased in January 1949. At that date Egyptian forces occupied the Gaza Strip, and remained there after the armistice concluded on 24 February 1949. Thereafter there were frequent raids by Israelis on the Egyptian forces (whose headquarters were at Khan Yunis, between Gaza and Rafa) and by Egyptian-led forces on Israeli villages. The Egyptian raiders have often been recruited from the 200,000 Arab refugees from other parts of Palestine who live in the Gaza Strip. The Israeli government does not accept the line held by the Egyptians as a permanent frontier, and maintains that the frontiers of Israel in this area should be those of the old mandated territory of Palestine. A United Nations Truce Supervisory Organization was made responsible for supervising this and other areas on the borders of Israel, and for preventing, as far as possible, breaches of the armistice agreement. In the Gaza Strip it collaborates with the Egyptian-Israeli Mixed Armistice Commission. The Tripartite Declaration of 1950, *q.v.*, made it unlikely that either the Egyptian or the Israeli governments would launch a full-scale attack with regular forces unless it was confident of a speedy victory. In October 1956 Israeli forces, hopeful of such a victory, overran the Strip in their successful attempt to defeat the Egyptian army and reach the Suez Canal, *q.v.* While British and French troops withdrew from Egypt by 22 December 1956, and were replaced by the United Nations Emergency Force (U.N.E.F.), Israeli troops remained in the Strip until 7 March 1957. The border between the Strip and Israel was then taken over by U.N.E.F. and an Egyptian civil governor was re-appointed. In February and March 1958 Egypt established an executive council and a legislative council with 30 members to assist the governor.

Gdansk. *See* Danzig.

General Agreement on Tariffs and Trade (G.A.T.T.). An international trade agreement on tariffs, which resulted from negotiations at Geneva between 10 April and 30 October 1947, arranged by the Preparatory Committee of the International Trade Organization, *q.v.*, while the Havana Charter, *q.v.*, was in the course of preparation. Many individual tariff bargains between pairs of countries have been concluded and the reductions in tariffs have been extended to all through the operation of the principle of the most favoured nation. The Agreement came into force on 1 January 1948.

At one time further progress was made difficult as a result of: (1) British reluctance to abandon Imperial Preference, *q.v.*; the 1953 session of the contracting parties gave the U.K. the right to raise import duties on certain goods from outside the Commonwealth without applying the increase to the same goods from Commonwealth countries; (2) high U.S. tariff barriers; (3) the weak bargaining position of low tariff states; (4) the many exceptions in the Agreement, which permitted certain discriminatory measures if they were in operation when a state became a party to the Agreement or if a state's balance of payments position could not otherwise be safeguarded.

After 1951 the emphasis therefore moved from tariff bargaining to the prevention of restrictive and discriminatory controls over imports. It was agreed that the organization of the Agreement should be strengthened, and in 1955 the ninth session of the contracting parties decided to set up the Organization for Trade Co-operation, *q.v.*

The Agreement contains provisions which protect the tariff concessions from being nullified by other methods of protection, e.g., by quantitative import and export restrictions, internal taxes, customs administration, as well as arrangements for consultation and for settlement of differences arising out of the administration of the Agreement. The countries adhering to G.A.T.T. account for over four fifths of world trade.

General Assembly of the United Nations. Comprises all the members of the U.N., of whom there were ninety-nine in 1961: Afghanistan, Albania, Argentina, Australia, Austria, Belgium, Bolivia, Brazil, Bulgaria, Burma, Byelorussia, Cambodia, Cameroun, Canada, Central African Republic, Ceylon, Chad, Chile, China (Formosa), Colombia, Congo Republic (formerly Belgian) Congo Republic (formerly French), Costa Rica, Cuba, Cyprus, Czechoslovakia, Dahomey, Denmark, Dominican Republic, Ecuador, Ethiopia, Finland, France, Gabon, Ghana, Greece, Guatemala, Guinea, Haiti, Honduras, Hungary, Iceland, India, Indonesia, Iraq, Ireland, Israel, Italy, Ivory Coast, Japan, Jordan, Laos, Lebanon, Liberia, Libya, Luxemburg, Malagasy, Malaya, Mali, Mexico, Morocco, Nepal, Netherlands, New Zealand, Nicaragua, Niger, Nigeria, Norway, Pakistan, Panama, Paraguay, Persia, Peru, Philippines, Poland, Portugal, Rumania, Salvador, Saudi Arabia, Senegal, Somalia, South Africa, Spain, Sudan, Sweden, Thailand, Togo, Tunisia, Turkey, Ukraine, United Arab Republic, U.K., U.S.A., Upper Volta, Uruguay, U.S.S.R., Venezuela, Yemen, and Yugoslavia.

It is one of the principal organs of the United Nations; each member can be represented at its annual meetings by five delegates and five alternate delegates, but has only one vote. Its meetings begin on the third Tuesday in September, but special sessions can be convoked by the Secretary-General if so requested by the Security Council, *q.v.*, by a majority of members of the United Nations, or by one member with the concurrence of the majority of members. Decisions on 'important questions' (defined in the Charter as including recommendations concerning international peace and security; election of members of the Councils; admission, expulsion, and suspension of members; questions relating to the trusteeship system; and budgetary matters) are made by a two-thirds majority of members present and voting.

The General Assembly is the only organ of the United Nations in which all members are represented. It elects by itself, or with the Security Council, some or all members of the other organs, and it has the right to discuss all matters within the scope of the Charter. The Security Council, the Economic and Social Council, *q.v.*, the Trusteeship Council, and the Secretary-General submit annual and special reports to the Assembly, which discusses them and makes recommendations thereon, thus reviewing and guiding the work of the entire organization. It also controls the budget of the organization and the contributions of members. It elects its President for each session.

The General Assembly does most of its work in committees, of which there are four types: main committees, procedural committees, standing committees, and *ad hoc* committees. Main committees consider agenda items referred to them by the Assembly and prepare recommendations for submission to the plenary meetings; they are the Political and Security; Economic and Financial; Social, Humanitarian and Cultural; Trusteeship; Administrative and Budgetary; Special Political; and Legal Committees. Procedural committees deal with the organization and conduct of the Assembly's business; they are the General and the Credentials Committees. Standing committees deal with continuing problems; an example is the Advisory Committee on Administrative and Budgetary Questions. *Ad hoc* committees are committees appointed by the Assembly or any of its committees for a special purpose; examples are the United Nations Relief and Works Agency and the Collective Measures Committee.

Gentlemen's Agreement. An informal agreement based on verbal assurances or the exchange of mere letters without a formal treaty being signed.

German Democratic Republic. A state not recognized by the western powers; area 41,380 sq. m.; population (1958) 16,221,354 excluding Berlin, *q.v.* It is sometimes known as Eastern Germany; its constitution was enacted on 7 October 1949 by a provisional People's Chamber which had been set up in the Russian Zone of Germany under the supervision of the U.S.S.R. In July 1950 the Republic defined its eastern boundary by an agreement with Poland by which the Oder-Neisse Line, *q.v.*, was declared to be a permanent frontier. Under the constitution there is a more centralized form of government than in the German Federal Republic, *q.v.*; the abolition in

July 1952 of the *Land* governments and diets of Brandenburg, Mecklenburg, Saxony, Saxony-Anhalt, and Thuringia, and their replacement by fourteen regions (*Bezirke*) increased the degree of centralization. In 1953 the Russian Commander-in-Chief was replaced by a High Commissioner who was also to hold the post of Ambassador. At elections held in November 1958 the candidates of the Communist-controlled National Front, which comprises the Socialist Unity, the Liberal Democratic, the Christian Democratic, the Democratic Peasant, and the National Democratic Parties, obtained ninety-nine per cent of the votes. Electors voted publicly for the single list of candidates by placing it, unmarked, in a ballot box.

Under a treaty between the German Democratic Republic and the U.S.S.R., which came into force on 6 October 1955, the Republic became a sovereign state and was given complete freedom to decide all questions concerning its internal and foreign policy, including its relations with the German Federal Republic. Russian forces stationed there under Four-Power agreements continued to be stationed there temporarily with the approval of the government. Under previous arrangements, however, which remained unchanged, the Republic had to pay reparations to the U.S.S.R. from current production until 1956.

The Seven Year Plan (1958–1965) has provisions for substantial increases in production. The Republic contains in its area a large part of the mechanical engineering, chemical, optical, and electrical industries of pre-war Germany, and their products have found ready buyers in eastern Europe. The area yielded only a small proportion of pre-war Germany's iron and steel, but these are now manufactured by a process which dispenses with hard coal, which is scarce in the east, and employs brown coal, of which the Republic is the world's largest producer.

German Federal Republic. A federation which was established by France, the U.K., and the U.S.A. in May 1949, and which became completely independent on 5 May 1955; area 95,725 sq. m.; population (1958) 54,493,200, some twenty-five per cent higher than that of the same area before 1939, largely owing to immigration from the East; capital Bonn. Approximately forty-five per cent of the population are Roman Catholics. It is sometimes known as Western Germany; a constitution (known as the Basic Law), enacted by a Constituent Assembly, came into force on 23 May 1949. The Republic was given full legislative, executive, and judicial powers, but not in respect of such matters as armaments, reparations, decartelization, foreign affairs, the admission of refugees, and other matters mentioned in the Occupation Statute, a proclamation by France, the

U.K., and the U.S.A. which became effective on 21 September 1949. On the same day all authority vested in the three commanders-in-chief was transferred to three High Commissioners.

The Occupation Statute was superseded by the London and Paris Agreements of October 1954, which came into force on 5 May 1955 after they had been ratified by the three occupying powers and the Republic. Under the Agreements the Republic attained full sovereignty and independence and American, British, and French forces were given permission to remain on German territory. The High Commission came to an end and the Republic became a member of the North Atlantic Treaty Organization, *q.v.*, and the Western European Union, *q.v.*

Under the constitution contained in the Basic Law, a Federal Diet (Bundestag) is elected by universal suffrage for a term of four years and a Federal Council (Bundesrat), consisting of members of the governments of the *Länder*, is elected by the ten *Länder* of Baden-Württemberg, Bavaria, Bremen, Hamburg, Hessen, Lower Saxony, North Rhine-Westphalia, Rhineland-Palatinate, Saarland, *q.v.*, and Schleswig-Holstein. Federal laws are passed by the Diet and, after their adoption, submitted to the Council which has a limited veto. At the Diet elections held on 15 September 1957 the conservative Christian Democratic Union (C.D.U.), led by Konrad Adenauer, *q.v.*, and acting in Bavaria through the Christian Social Union, won 270 of the 497 seats. The Social Democratic Party (S.P.D.), a left-wing party led by Erich Ollenhauer and supported by the German Trade Union Congress (D.G.B.), won 169 seats. The Free Democratic Party (F.D.P.), a right-wing anti-Catholic party now led by Dr Erich Mende, won 41 seats. The extreme right-wing German Party (D.P.) won 17 seats. The Refugee Party, which in the 1953 election won 27 seats, failed to obtain any representation as it did not secure the five per cent of the votes required under a law introduced in 1956. Adenauer formed a coalition government comprising representatives of the Christian Democratic Union, the Christian Social Union and the German Party.

Since the currency reform of 1948 the Republic has expanded industrial production to such an extent that in 1960 it was one hundred and seventy-four per cent higher than in 1936, the most important products being iron and steel, electric power, agricultural and industrial chemicals, textiles, passenger cars, and commercial vehicles. The principal buyers of German goods are the Netherlands, the U.S.A., Italy, Belgium and Luxemburg, Sweden, France, and Switzerland.

Germany. An area in central and northern Europe which consists of the German Federal Republic, *q.v.*, and the German Democratic Republic, *q.v.* Modern Germany was created in 1871 by Bismarck, who established the Germanic Federation, consisting of the North Germanic Confederation, led by Prussia, and Bavaria, Württemberg, and Baden. The King of Prussia took the title of German Emperor. The Federation was thought by Germans to be the lawful successor of the Holy Roman Empire, which was created by Otto the Great of Saxony in 962 and came to an end in 1806. When Germany was defeated in the First World War the emperor, Wilhelm II, abdicated and the Weimar Republic, *q.v.*, was established. At the elections held in 1933 the Nazis (the National Socialist German Workers' Party) won a majority in the legislature (the Reichstag) and their leader, Adolf Hitler, became Chancellor or Prime Minister. On the death in 1934 of President von Hindenburg the offices of President and Chancellor were fused and Hitler became a dictator. Between 1934 and 1939 the Germans rearmed in defiance of the Versailles Treaty, *q.v.*, built many roads for the speedy carriage of troops and supplies, persecuted Jews and liberals and tortured them in concentration camps, won the sympathy of British and French right-wing politicians by denouncing the U.S.S.R., and occupied Saarland, *q.v.*, the Rhineland, Austria, and Czechoslovakia. In 1939 Germany concluded a non-aggression treaty with the U.S.S.R. and invaded Poland on 1 September, thus precipitating a war with France and the U.K., which had promised to defend Poland. During the subsequent war Germany occupied most of the European continent west of the U.S.S.R., and joined forces with Italy in 1940, and Japan in 1941, against the U.K., the U.S.A., the U.S.S.R., China, and many other countries. Germany was defeated and occupied by British, French, Russian, and U.S. forces in 1945, and the unconditional surrender of all German forces was accepted on 8 May 1945. Under the Berlin Declaration of June 1945 and the Potsdam Agreement, *q.v.*, of August 1945, the country was divided into four Zones and occupied by the forces of France, the U.K., the U.S.A., and the U.S.S.R., respectively. Special arrangements were made for Berlin, *q.v.* The four powers were unable to agree upon common policies for Germany as a whole, and there were differing political and economic developments in the Russian Zone, or Eastern Germany, *q.v.*, on the one hand, and in the British, French, and U.S. Zones, or Western Germany, *q.v.*, on the other hand. As power was gradually transferred to the Germans by the occupying forces, two rival governments emerged. In 1949 the German Democratic Republic in the east, and the German Federal Republic in the west, were established. In 1955 the two Republics became sovereign and independent.

Gerrymandering. A reorganization of electoral districts to gain some advantage in a forthcoming election. When Elbridge Gerry was Governor of Massachusetts in 1812, the state legislature divided Essex County into two districts with borders so drawn as to give the maximum advantage to the Republican Party. On a map one of the districts, with pencilled additions, looked like a salamander, and the expression 'to gerrymander' was coined. It should be distinguished from the reorganization of electoral districts which is sometimes essential to ensure that every parliamentary representative speaks for approximately the same number of voters, and which is known as redistribution, *q.v.*

Gestapo. The Geheime Staatspolizei, or German secret police, which became an official body immediately after Adolf Hitler and the Nazis came to power in 1933. Its task was to discover and punish the opponents of Nazism; its agents became members of many illegal anti-Nazi organizations which were subsequently dissolved. Although the Gestapo came to an end with the collapse of the Nazi régime in 1945, the term is often used to describe secret police forces or methods which are characteristic of the Gestapo.

Ghana. A Dominion and member of the British Commonwealth; area 92,100 sq. m.; population (1959 estimate) 4,911,000 including 2,000,000 in the Eastern and Western Regions (formerly the Gold Coast Colony), more than 1,000,000 in the Northern Region (formerly the Northern Territories), nearly 1,000,000 in the Ashanti Region (formerly Ashanti) and 500,000 in the Volta Region, formerly the British-administered Trusteeship Territory of Togoland, *q.v.*; nearly 500,000 in the Brong–Ahafo Region; capital Accra.

Ghana was a West African empire which existed from the third to the thirteenth century, though it never included the area now known by that name. The U.K. finally assumed control of the trading settlements in the region from the Danes and the Dutch in 1820, and the coastal strip was constituted as a Colony in 1874. Ashanti and the Northern Territories were brought into the administrative area of the Governor of the Colony in 1901. As a result of a plebiscite in May 1956 authorized by the United Nations, the British-administered part of the Trusteeship Territory of Togoland became a Region of the Dominion of Ghana which came into existence on 6 March 1957.

Legislative power is vested in the President and the National Assembly consisting of a Speaker and 104 members elected for a maximum of five years. Each Region has a House of Chiefs which chooses a Head, except in Ashanti where the Asantehene is the Head. The country became a republic within the British Commonwealth on 1 July 1960.

At the elections held in July 1956 the Convention People's Party (C.P.P.), which came to power in 1950, won 71 seats. It is a party of the left, but is not Communist; its leader, the President, Kwame Nkrumah, *q.v.*, has in the past suspended members who engaged in pro-Communist activities. The United Party was set up in October 1957 when the main opposition parties and three regional groups joined forces. The parties were the Northern People's Party (15 seats in 1956) with considerable strength in the north, which is poorer in resources and less advanced educationally than the south; the Ashanti National Liberation Movement (12 seats) with support from Ashanti tribal elements who are opposed to westernization; and the Moslem Association (1 seat).

Ghana has valuable exports of cocoa, gold, manganese, timber and diamonds, and is economically self-sufficient, with favourable dollar and sterling balances. There has been considerable foreign investment, especially by the U.K., in capital development. Such investment, both generally and in particular for the Volta River aluminium and power project, is regarded as essential by Nkrumah and his followers, despite objections from politicians on the extreme left.

Gibraltar. A British colony on the southern tip of the Iberian peninsula at the entrance to the Mediterranean Sea; area two sq. m.; population 25,637. Its usefulness as a port of call for the British Levant Company, and those doing business with the Company, was one of the motives for its capture by British troops in 1704 during the war of the Spanish Succession. Spain formally ceded Gibraltar to Britain under the Treaty of Utrecht in 1713; by the Treaty of Versailles in 1783 Spain renounced all claims to the area and received, in return, Minorca and Florida. The Spanish government which came to power in 1939 has frequently demanded its return, and during the Second World War planned with Germany an operation (called 'Isabella-Felix') to seize Gibraltar. This was abandoned when Germany decided in 1941 to invade the U.S.S.R. rather than the U.K. The port is an important British naval base and obtains considerable revenue from dues paid by ships in transit.

Goa. Portuguese settlement on the west coast of India: population of approximately 600,000 of whom all but 1,438 are of Hindu origin. Thirty-seven per cent are Roman Catholic converts; the rest are

147

Hindu. Goa is economically dependent upon India from which it imports most of its rice. More than 40 per cent of the total export trade is with India and 0·5 per cent with Portugal. The iron and manganese mines, which provide most of its exports, are largely run by Indian industrialists and worked by Indian labour. The trade deficit is met by income from shipping, tourists, and emigrants' remittances. After 1953, encouraged by the support of 200,000 Goans who work in Bombay, the Indian government accelerated its attempts to exclude Portuguese sovereignty from the Indian mainland and to bring Goa into the Indian Union. Congress declared its policy to be one of non-violence and relied on an economic blockade. Air and rail communications were severed, money-order services were suspended and the Bombay Transport and Dock Workers' Union boycotted foreign ships bound for Goa. Throughout 1955 tacit approval was given to the Goa Liberation Aid Committee, which organized strikes in Bombay, and to the Satyagrahis (exponents of 'soul-force', or non-violent resisters) who attempted several 'invasions' of Goa without using arms. On each occasion they were forced back by Portuguese troops.

New legislation, permitting the inclusion of elected members in the Legislative Council and extending the electoral roll to 50,000, was introduced on 1 August 1955. However, in the first elections, held on 22 August, all but one of the candidates were returned unopposed. It is illegal to criticize the legislature or the Portuguese government: Portuguese threats to invoke the Anglo-Portuguese Treaty of 1642 or Article IV of the North Atlantic Treaty, which guarantees the territorial integrity of the signatories, were ignored in India, as were the protests of various European and South American Roman Catholic states. In 1951 Portugal altered its status from 'colony' to 'overseas territory'.

Gold Coast. The name given to the British territory in West Africa, comprising the Gold Coast colony, Ashanti, and the Northern Territories, until it became, on 6 March 1957, together with the British administered Trusteeship Territory of Togoland, *q.v.*, a Dominion within the British Commonwealth. It then took the name of Ghana, *q.v.*

Gold Standard. A currency system under which money is either unconditionally, or subject to certain conditions, exchangeable for a fixed weight of gold. To say that a country is on the gold standard may mean one of three things: (1) that its central bank is in a position to redeem its currency in gold and is bound by law to buy and sell gold at a fixed price (this is the full gold standard, as it existed in the U.K.

before 1914); (2) that the central bank is merely bound to buy and sell gold at a fixed price (the gold bullion standard, as it existed in the U.K. from 1925 to 1931); (3) that the central bank is bound to buy and sell at a fixed price, not gold, but merely the currencies of countries that are on the full gold or the gold bullion standard (the gold exchange standard).

The system was practised in Europe and America from the middle of the nineteenth century until 1914. It was an internationally convenient system, for each country valued its own currency in terms of gold and arranged for its central bank to convert gold into currency and currency into gold whenever it was asked to do so. A debtor could therefore settle a debt abroad almost as easily as in his own country. As all debts could be taken as representing a definite amount of gold, gold did not often have to be sent from place to place, and debts could be set off against each other in a free market. Difficulties arose whenever it was not possible simply to balance debts against each other, and where a country had actually to pay in gold. As its currency was based on gold, internal restriction of credit and falling prices would follow.

If many countries are on the gold standard international trade is facilitated because the rates of exchange between their different currencies are fixed and certain and because, as a result, their price levels tend to become equal. However, since the effect of a country being on the gold standard is that its internal purchasing power and price level are dependent upon its balance of payments, *q.v.*, the gold standard has now been generally abandoned in favour of the greater degree of autonomy given by fluctuating exchange rates.

Great Britain and Northern Ireland. The Kingdoms of England and Scotland, the Principality of Wales, and Northern Ireland, which are officially called the United Kingdom of Great Britain and Northern Ireland, *q.v.*

Greece. An independent south European state; area (including the Dodecanese Islands) 51,180 sq. m.; population (1958) 8,555,000, of whom more than 7,000,000 belong to the established Greek Orthodox Church. After gaining independence from Turkey, Greece was declared a kingdom in 1830 and Prince Otto of Bavaria was offered the crown. Since 1862, when Otto was expelled, Greek kings have all been members of the Glucksburg branch of the Danish royal family: George I of Greece was assassinated, his second son, Constantine, was twice deposed, in 1917 and in 1921, and his eldest son, George II, was exiled between 1923 and 1935, during which time a republic was declared, and again from 1941–6. The present King, Paul I (born

1901), ascended the throne in 1947. Although the Constitution of 1911 allowed for parliamentary government most administrations have been authoritarian. There was a dictatorship before 1935, and from 1936 to 1941 General Metaxas introduced a 'Third Civilization', a semi-Fascist régime, to which no opposition was permitted. The Communist Party went underground.

In 1940 the Italians invaded Greece from Albania. They met with unexpected resistance and were decisively defeated until Germany entered the war in April 1941, overran Greece, and forced the evacuation of British troops by way of Crete. King George and the Greek government went into exile. Early in 1942 a central committee of the Greek Resistance (E.A.M.) was formed. It was built on the Communist underground network but it embraced all parties of the left. Its guerrilla army, E.L.A.S., achieved such success that by the summer of 1943 one third of the mainland had been liberated. The U.K., however, supported a second partisan movement, the 'X-Bands' of the pro-monarchist General Zervas. There were clashes between the two resistance groups which led to the expulsion of Zervas in 1943, and the landing of fresh British troops in Greece in 1944 to prevent civil war. A truce was declared and the Patriarch of Athens, Archbishop Damaskinos, was appointed Regent until the burning question of the monarchy could be settled by a plebiscite. In 1946 King George II returned, and the United Nations Security Council rejected a complaint by the U.S.S.R. that British troops in Greece were endangering the peace of the world. At the request of the U.S.A. they remained in Greece until 1950. The militant remnants of E.L.A.S., under the command of General Markos Vafiades, began a new offensive in the autumn of 1946. They received arms and supplies from Yugoslavia, Bulgaria, and Albania, and in 1948 had 25,000 men and women under arms. Vafiades was murdered by his own Communist supporters on instructions from Moscow. Yugoslavia's expulsion from the Cominform, *q.v.*, in 1948 closed the supply lines, and the war ended in 1949.

From 1946, when a Liberal–Social Democrat coalition replaced the right-wing government of Papandreou, Greece was governed by the parties of the centre. Between 1947 and 1951 thirteen cabinets held office and the repeated government changes hindered the country's economic recovery. In July 1951 Field-Marshal Papagos launched his right-wing Greek Rally 'to rescue Greece from political bankruptcy and give her the strong government she needs'; it secured a majority in the General Election in 1952 and became the governing party. The Constitution of 1911 was amended in 1951–2 to include provision for land expropriation and redistribution, and for the dismissal of civil servants and public employees suspected of Communist sympathies. In May 1952, women over twenty-one were given the vote, and those over twenty-five allowed to stand for parliament. On the death of Papagos in October 1955, Constantine Karamanlis, previously Minister of Works, became Prime Minister. A new electoral law substituted the simple majority system for proportional representation; it was introduced in order to exclude Communists from the legislature. In the elections of 1956 held under the new system the National Radical Union, a new party founded by Karamanlis as the successor to the Greek Rally, became the largest single party. In May 1958, following an internal disagreement in the Karamanlis government over proposed electoral reforms, further elections were held. The National Radical Union, improving its position, obtained 173 seats; the extreme left-wing United Democratic Left (E.D.A.) emerged as the second strongest party with 78 seats; and the Liberals secured 34 seats.

Greece faces serious economic problems. Only fifteen per cent of the land is productive and soil erosion and the depredations of goats are diminishing the area. Tobacco, olives, and currants are exported, but the merchant navy lost its pre-war dominance in the Mediterranean carrying-trade as a result of wartime losses: there is an annual deficit on the balance of payments which is met by U.S. aid.

Greece was admitted to the Council of Europe in 1949, to N.A.T.O. in 1951, and is a party to the Balkan Pact, *q.v.*, with Turkey and Yugoslavia.

Greenland. A strategically important island in the Atlantic Ocean, most of which lies north of the Arctic Circle; it has been an integral part of Denmark since 1953; area 840,000 sq. m., of which eighty-five per cent is under an ice-cap; population (1955) 27,101; administrative centre Godthaab. It began to be colonized by the Danes in 1721; it now returns two members to the Danish parliament.

The people, who are mostly of mixed Eskimo and Scandinavian blood, live in some 185 settlements, mainly on the south-western coastal fringe. Meteorological stations and air bases were established in the Second World War, and in 1951 the U.S.A. was permitted by Denmark to use, rent-free, bases at Narssarsuak, Søndre Strømfjord and Thule. A radar network was established and supply depots and runways were built. Greenland is also an important air base for civil flights between Europe and the Pacific Ocean.

The economy was once dependent on the hunting of seal, but now relies on the fishing and processing of cod, shrimps, and prawns; there are deposits of coal, copper, graphite, lead, wolframite, uranium, zinc, and cryolite, which is essential in the manufacture of aluminium. Oil has been discovered in the west. The ice-cap, which is two miles deep in places, is retreating and this will make development of these resources less difficult.

Griffiths, James. British Labour Party politician; born September 1890; educated at an elementary school and at the National Labour College, London. He worked in the Welsh coal mines and was from 1925 to 1936 a miners' agent in the South Wales Miners' Federation. He became the Member of Parliament for Llanelly in 1936. He was Minister of National Insurance from 1945 to 1950 and Secretary of State for the Colonies from 1950 to 1951. In February 1956 he was elected Deputy Leader of the Parliamentary Labour Party, defeating Aneurin Bevan by 141 to 111 votes, but he resigned from this position in October 1959.

Grimond, Joseph. British Liberal Party politician, born 29 July 1913, the son of a Dundee jute manufacturer; educated at Eton and Balliol College, Oxford, and married (in 1938) Laura, youngest daughter of Lady Violet Bonham-Carter and granddaughter of Asquith, the Liberal leader. He was called to the Bar in 1937 and on the outbreak of war joined the army, in which he became a Major. In the 1945 elections he unsuccessfully contested the Orkney and Shetland constituency, but after a period as Secretary of the Scottish National Trust in Edinburgh (from 1947 to 1949) won the seat in 1950. Upon the retirement of Clement Davies in 1956 he became the leader of the Parliamentary Liberal Party.

Gromyko, Andrei Andreyevich. Russian politician; born 1909 in the Gomel region of Byelorussia and educated at the Minsk agricultural institute and at the Lenin Institute of Economics in Moscow, where he took a degree in economics. From 1936 to 1939 he was the senior scientific worker at the institute of economics of the Academy of Science, and simultaneously edited *Problems of Economics*, an official economic review. In 1939 he became head of the American section in the Foreign Ministry, and soon afterwards was appointed Counsellor at the Russian Embassy in Washington, becoming Ambassador there in 1943. He was the Russian representative to the United Nations from 1946 to 1949, when he became deputy Foreign Minister, and in February 1957 he succeeded Dimitri Shepilov as Foreign Minister.

Grotewohl, Otto. Communist politician in the German Democratic Republic; born 11 March 1894 in Brunswick; a printer by trade. He was active in local government in Brunswick from 1920 onwards, and was a Socialist member of the German parliament (Reichstag) from 1925 to 1933 when the Nazis imprisoned him in a concentration camp. After the Second World War he joined the Communist-dominated Socialist Unity Party in East Germany and in 1949 was appointed Prime Minister of the German Democratic Republic.

Guatemala. An independent Central American state, area 42,042 sq. m.; population 3,545,212 of whom over half are illiterate and extremely poor Indians, about thirty-eight per cent are of mixed Indian and white ancestry (Ladinos), and the rest white; capital Guatemala City. Guatemala was conquered by Spain in 1536, became independent in 1823 and has at most times been a dictatorship. Its most important products are coffee (the world's fourth largest crop) and bananas. Seventy-one per cent of its exports go to the U.S.A. After a revolution in 1944 Jacob Arbenz became President and during his rule enacted social health schemes in the cities, schemes to protect many coffee and banana workers, and, in 1952, a measure of land redistribution. He prohibited the entry of foreign oil prospectors and expropriated about 408,000 acres of land owned by the U.S.-controlled United Fruit Company on the Pacific and Atlantic coasts for redistribution among the peasants. The Arbenz government offered compensation which was rejected as inadequate by the United Fruit Company; this bitter dispute was resolved in July 1954 by a revolt by the exiled right-wing opposition under Colonel Carlos Castillo Armas, who became President, repealed the land confiscation laws, and admitted U.S. oil companies. In the overthrow of the Arbenz government he was aided by Honduras and Nicaragua, and advised by the U.S. Ambassador to Guatemala. He restored all the expropriated estates and in return the Company undertook to pay income and profits taxes in conformity with Guatemalan legislation, with an upper limit of thirty per cent of any profits made.

Following the assassination of Armas in July 1957, General Miguel Ydígoras Fuentes was elected President for a six-year term which began in March 1958. Only ten per cent of Guatemala's land is cultivated; seventy per cent of the cultivated land is held by two per cent of the population. Guatemala has repeatedly claimed the adjacent territory of British Honduras, with its Caribbean port of Belize which would be convenient as an outlet for Guatemalan oil.

Guild Socialism. A British variant of syndicalism, *q.v.* The movement emerged in 1906 and advocated a restoration of the mediaeval guild system along modern lines. Guild Socialists believed that value was created corporately by society rather than by individuals singly, and that capitalist economists had defended the acquisition of wealth without reference to the responsibilities and the opportunities for rendering service to the community which it entailed. The trade unions were to be organized as guilds to take over and run their respective industries after nationalization. This policy was also opposed to that of state Socialism, which provided that the state should assume control of industry. No Guild Socialist movement has existed in the U.K. since the dissolution of the National Guilds League (founded in 1915) in 1925, but the theories of Guild Socialism are frequently referred to by British Labour Party theorists.

Guilt by Association. The responsibility of a person for the alleged faults of those with whom he associates or has associated in the past. In the U.S.A. persons testifying before Congressional committees, or being considered for employment, have often been blamed in this way for present or past association with Communists or Communist sympathizers. This does not mean that they have been regarded as guilty of a legal offence, but their evidence has been regarded as unreliable, and they have sometimes been considered unfit for particular posts.

Guinea. An independent state on the west coast of Africa with Portuguese Guinea to the north and Sierra Leone to the south; area 96,865 sq. m.; population (mostly Moslem) 2,500,000 of whom about 10 per cent speak French, and among whom the leading tribes are the Fullah (866,400) the Malinké (492,800), and the Soussou (243,900); capital Conakry. The country was formerly one of the eight territories comprising French West Africa, *q.v.*, but at the referendum held on 29 September 1958 Guinea, by an overwhelming vote, rejected the proposed constitution of the Fifth Republic, *q.v.*, and thus chose immediate independence, which became effective by proclamation on 2 October 1958.

The country is controlled by its only effective political party, the Democratic Party or Parti Démocratique de Guinée (P.D.G.), which is inclined to be Marxist in outlook, and there is no articulate opposition. The ministers are appointed by the President, Sekou Touré, in his capacity as head of the P.D.G. and party policy is decided by a bureau of 17 members, elected every five years by delegates from regional committees. The efficiency of the party organization did much to overcome the problems which arose after independence, when French subsidies were withdrawn and the majority of the French administrators left, and when there were very few educated persons in the public service.

There are bauxite deposits, exploited by an international consortium, in the Los Islands, and the revenue therefrom provides approximately one quarter of the annual budget. Other minerals found include diamonds and iron ore. There are also exports of citrus fruits, palm kernels, bananas, and coffee.

H

Haile Selassie I, Emperor of Ethiopia. Born 24 July 1891. His dynasty claims descent from Menelik I, the son of King Solomon and the Queen of Sheba; he is the son of Ras Makonnen, cousin of MenelikII and one of his generals. Menelik's daughter became Empress, and he became heir, in 1916 when the British organized a revolt which deposed the Emperor Lidj Yassu, his cousin, who had shown sympathy towards Germany and Turkey. He became King or Negus in October 1928 and was proclaimed Emperor after the death of Empress Zauditu in April 1930. He introduced a new constitution in July 1931, and was forced to flee from Ethiopia after the Italian invaders had captured Addis Ababa in May 1936. He went to the Anglo-Egyptian Sudan in July 1940, where he organized the Ethiopian forces which marched from Khartoum into Ethiopia and defeated the Italians. He was reinstated in Addis Ababa in June 1941. In 1954 he made an extensive tour of North America and Europe during which he paid state visits to fourteen countries; this tour was the first of its kind ever undertaken by an Ethiopian sovereign.

Hailsham, 2nd Viscount, Quintin McGarel Hogg. British Conservative Party politician; born 9 October 1907 and educated at Eton and Christ Church, Oxford, where he was President of the Union Society; after being elected to a Fellowship at All Souls College, Oxford, he practised at the Bar. He entered the House of Commons in 1938 as the member for Oxford, having fought a by-election as an ardent supporter of the Munich Agreement, *q.v.* After serving in the army in the Second World War, he was Parliamentary Under-Secretary of State for Air in the Conservative 'caretaker' government from April to July 1945. He entered the House of Lords reluctantly on the death of his father in 1950, and returned to office as First Lord of the Admiralty in 1956. He became Minister of Education in 1957, but in September of the same year gave up that post to become Lord President of the Council and Chairman of the Conservative Party. After the General Election of October 1959 he was replaced as Lord President by Lord Home and as Chairman by R. A. Butler, and became instead Lord Privy Seal and Minister of Science. In a further reshuffle in July 1960 he was restored to the office of Lord President, while remaining Minister of Science, and became also Leader of the House of Lords.

Haiti. Independent state sharing the Caribbean island of Hispaniola with the Dominican Republic; area 10,500 sq. m., largely mountainous; population about 3,500,000, mostly Negroes speaking a French dialect, and eighty-five per cent illiterate; capital Port-au-Prince. Haiti was once ruled by France and provided one half of the revenues of Louis XIV; it became independent in 1840. It is now one of the world's poorest and most primitive countries, virtually without industry, although it has important sugar exports. There are U.N. and U.S. plans to provide hydro-electric power, to irrigate the land, to develop the tourist industry, to spread literacy and to improve agricultural techniques. Progress has been slow, and is hindered by a traditional rivalry between the aristocracy of mulattos (of mixed European and Negro blood) and the Negro masses. Ancient feuds with Dominica abated when an agreement was signed in 1951 to promote commerce, to lower tariff barriers and to fight Communism. Paul Eugène Magloire (born 1907) was the first popularly elected President of Haiti, having been returned in 1950 with ninety-nine per cent of the votes cast. Under army pressure, and after a general strike, he resigned in December 1956. There followed four Presidents in rapid succession until, in September 1957, François Duvalier, a liberal, was elected by a substantial majority. He was re-elected in May 1961 for a further six years.

Hammarskjöld, Dag Hjalmar Agne Carl. Secretary-General of the United Nations since 1953; born 29 July 1905 in Jönköping, Sweden, and educated at the universities of Uppsala and Stockholm. A financial expert, he was Secretary to the Unemployment Commission from 1930 to 1934 and to the Bank of Sweden in 1935; from 1936 to 1946 he was Under-Secretary of Finance, during which period he became Chairman of the Bank of Sweden. After entering the Swedish foreign ministry as a financial adviser he rose to become Deputy Foreign Minister, a post he held until he was appointed Secretary-General of the United Nations.

Harriman, William Averell. U.S. Democratic politician; born 15 November 1891 and educated at Yale University. By inheritance a millionaire, he helped to manage some of his family's railway, shipping, and banking interests between 1915 and 1930, since when he has been a partner in the family banking firm, Brown Brothers Harriman and Co. He was attracted by the progressive policies of the New Deal, *q.v.*, and after the inauguration of President Franklin D. Roosevelt in 1933 he held a number of posts in the government agencies which were established to carry out these policies. During the Second World War he was Roosevelt's special representative in the U.K. and then in the U.S.S.R., where he was Ambassador from 1943 to 1946. After a short period as Ambassador to the U.K. he returned home to become Secretary for Commerce, and was from 1948 to 1950 the special U.S. representative in Europe for the Economic Co-operation Administration, *q.v.* He then became special assistant to President Truman for a year and from 1951 to 1953 was Mutual Security Director. In 1955 he became Governor of New York, his first elective post.

Haud. A disputed territory on the borders of Ethiopia, *q.v.*, and British Somaliland, *q.v.*

Havana Charter. A document summarizing the agreements reached at the United Nations Conference on Trade and Employment, held at Havana, Cuba, from 21 November 1947 to 24 March 1948. The Charter provided for an International Trade Organization, *q.v.*, which would expand world trade and remove trade barriers. Though fifty-four states agreed to the Charter at Havana, the U.S. Congress did not ratify it and the I.T.O. never came into existence. Before the meeting at Havana the General Agreement on Tariffs and Trade, *q.v.*, had been concluded at Geneva between April and October 1947, and the Havana Charter stated that if the Charter had not entered into force by 30 September 1949, the contracting parties should meet before 31 December 1949 to decide whether G.A.T.T. should be amended, supplemented, or maintained. It was thus recognized that the rules of the Charter were stiffer and more comprehensive than the terms of G.A.T.T.

Heath, Edward Richard George. British Conservative Party politician; born 9 July 1916; educated at Chatham House School, Ramsgate, and Balliol College, Oxford, where he was President of the Oxford Union in 1939. After serving in the army in the Second World War, and becoming a Lieutenant-Colonel, he entered the civil service in 1946 but left in 1947 to become the Conservative candidate for Bexley, a seat which he won in 1950. He became a Lord Commissioner of the Treasury and an Assistant Whip in 1951, Joint Deputy Government Chief Whip in 1952, Deputy Government Chief Whip in 1953, Chief Whip in December 1955, and Minister of Labour, with a seat in the Cabinet, immediately after the General Election of October 1959. In July 1960 he became Lord Privy Seal, with special responsibility for foreign affairs, as the new Foreign Secretary (the Earl of Home) was in the House of Lords.

Hegemony. Leadership; the word is often used to describe the powerful influence exercised by one state over other states.

High Commission Territories. The Territory of Basutoland, the Bechuanaland Protectorate and the Swaziland Protectorate, all in southern Africa. The U.K. High Commissioner in South Africa holds the office of High Commissioner for these areas, and administers them under the general direction of the British Commonwealth Relations Office. (1) Basutoland, which is surrounded by South African territory, came under the protection of the U.K. in 1868 as a result of appeals from the Basuto, who wanted to avoid annexation by the Boers; area 11,716 sq. m.; population (1960 census) 638,857 Africans and 1,926 Europeans; capital Maseru. (2) Bechuanaland, between South Africa, South-West Africa, and the Federation of Rhodesia and Nyasaland, became a Protectorate in 1885 when the U.K. wanted to prevent an extension of German territory eastward from South-West Africa; area 275,000 sq. m.; population (1946 census) 292,755 Africans and 3,173 Europeans; headquarters of the administration Mafeking. (3) Swaziland, between Portuguese East Africa and South Africa, came under the protection of the U.K. in 1903 after the conquest of the Transvaal; area 6,705 sq. m.; population (1956 census) 229,744 Africans and 5,919 Europeans; headquarters of the administration Mbabane. South Africa has on several occasions demanded that these three areas be ceded by the U.K.

High Dam, also called the Aswan Dam. A Dam which the Egyptian government proposes to complete on the river Nile, to provide for Egypt: (1) a steady supply of water, so that there need be no shortage in a dry year; (2) electric power; (3) irrigation of approximately 2,000,000 acres of land, as a result of which Egypt's cultivated area would be increased by one third. The Dam, which will be in southern Egypt, will be 300 miles farther up the river than the existing Aswan Dam, *q.v.*, and will hold twenty times as much water. The population of Egypt doubled between 1907 and 1958, but Egypt's capacity to feed its population did not increase to the same extent, and the High Dam is planned as a partial answer to this problem. The Egyptian government anticipates that the Dam will be completed in 1970.

Ho Chi-Minh (He Who Enlightens). Founder of the Viet-Minh, *q.v.*, in Indo-China and President of the Viet-Minh controlled state of North Viet-Nam. He was born about 1892, the son of a local official who lost his job for opposing the French; self-educated and multi-lingual, he went to sea from 1911 to 1914, then worked in London, cleaning silver at the Carlton Hotel Restaurant, and in Paris, where he preached revolution to the Viet-Namese community. He attended the 1922 Congress of the French Communist Party, spent the next three years in Moscow, then worked under Borodin in Canton from where he organized the South-East Asia Comintern and encouraged nationalist revolts in Indo-China. In 1941, when Vichy France agreed to co-operate with the Japanese, he formed a resistance movement of Communists and Nationalists called the Viet-Minh. Four years later its guerrilla army received the Japanese surrender in Tonkin and Annam and defied British, French, and Nationalist-Chinese Liberation forces while Ho declared a Democratic Republic of Viet-Nam. In the negotiations of 1945–6 to determine the future status of Indo-China, the French recognized him as the effective political leader of the Viet-Namese but denounced him as a rebel when the negotiations broke down and Viet-Minh troops launched an attack on Hanoi in December 1946. The U.S.S.R. and China formally recognized him as Head of State of the Democratic Republic of Viet-Nam in 1950, while the western powers acknowledged the French-sponsored Bao Dai, *q.v.*; since the Geneva Agreements of 1954, however, he has been universally recognized as President of North Viet-Nam. In September 1955 he was succeeded as Premier, and leader of the government, by Pham Van Dong. He is believed to be directing the Viet-Minh attempts to raise revolution in Laos, Cambodia, and Thailand.

Holland. Comprises two of the provinces of the Netherlands, *q.v.*, and is an alternative name for that country.

Home Rule. The aim of those who sought self-government for Ireland when that country was still part of the U.K., and who expressed their goal in the words 'Home Rule for Ireland'. The term is used to describe the aims of many movements towards autonomy by national or minority groups.

Honduras. An independent Central American state on the Atlantic and Pacific Oceans; population (1958) 1,828,183, of mixed Spanish and Indian blood; area 43,227 square miles; capital Tegucigalpa. Honduras was ruled by Spain from the sixteenth century until independence was proclaimed in 1821; the Federation of Central America was then formed, out of which Honduras emerged as an independent state in 1838.

The chief commercial activity is the cultivation of bananas and coconuts on the Atlantic coast. The banana industry is dominated by the United and Standard Fruit Companies; bananas constitute about sixty per cent of the total value of the exports. Other products are beans, coconuts, coffee, and tobacco, while cattle-raising is becoming increasingly important. In May, June, and July 1954 there was a well-organized strike of banana-workers, supported by most sections of the community. The workers demanded higher wages and the confiscation of the lands owned by the United Fruit Company, and asked the Company to improve their working conditions as it had improved those of the Guatemalan banana-workers. The strike was settled by the intervention of the President, on terms which for the first time gave the country a functioning trade union movement.

Under the 1957 Constitution the legislature is a single chamber of fifty-eight members elected for six years by universal adult suffrage. The executive authority is vested in the President, elected by popular vote for six years, who is assisted by a Council of nine ministers. From 1939 to 1949, however, Honduras was ruled by General Tiburcio Carías Andino who led the Nationalist Party and had dictatorial powers. In 1949 Juan Manuel Galvez, a former Minister of War, and once a lawyer employed by the United Fruit Company, was elected President; in his five years of office he granted Honduras more civil freedom than it had known in most of its history, re-established freedom of the press, allowed the principal opposition party, the Liberals, to criticize his government, built roads, established a National Bank, and promoted agricultural and industrial development

At the presidential election in October 1954 the Liberal leader, Dr Ramon Villeda Morales, polled the largest number of votes, but not a majority. Julio Lozano, who had been Vice-President under Galvez, staged a successful coup in December 1954. A military junta, which seized power from Lozano in October 1956, permitted popular elections in September 1957; these resulted in another victory for Dr Villeda's party, which had campaigned for improved social conditions. Villeda was appointed President for a six-year term in December 1957.

Hong Kong. A British colony claimed by China and comprising part of the Chinese mainland and some islands; total area 391 sq. m.; population approximately 2,806,000, including 1,010,500 refugees from China; capital Victoria, on Hong Kong Island. The island was seized by British forces in 1841 after the Chinese government had prohibited the import of opium, which was a valuable source of income for British business men exporting to China. Kowloon was acquired in 1860; in 1898 the U.K. was granted a lease of the New Territories, comprising a peninsula in the mainland province of Kuangtung and some adjacent islands, which expires in 1997. Hong Kong declined in importance as an entrepôt port during and after the Korean War, when it was prevented by the United Nations resolution of 18 May

1951 from re-exporting tin, rubber, and other strategic materials to China. It has since concentrated on developing its manufacturing industries, which provided ten per cent of the value of its exports in 1947 and about sixty-five per cent in 1959. Two thirds of the manufactured exports are cotton goods, most of which are sent to Indonesia.

House of Commons. The lower house of the United Kingdom Houses of Parliament, and virtually the ruling one since the reduction of the powers of the House of Lords by the Parliament Acts, 1911 and 1949, *q.v.* The House of Commons has 630 members elected by adult male and female suffrage. England has 511 members, Wales 36, Scotland 71, and Northern Ireland 12. These members were returned at the General Election of October 1959 by 27,862,738 votes, representing 78·7 per cent of the electorate, as against 26,760,754 (76·8 per cent) in 1955, and 28,596,695 (82·6 per cent) in 1951. Lunatics, felons, traitors, members of the House of Lords, clergymen of the Church of England, and ministers of the Church of Scotland and the Roman Catholic Church are ineligible as candidates, as are certain government officials, Sheriffs, government contractors, and others regarded in law as holding an 'office of profit under the Crown'. The House of Commons is elected for a maximum period of five years but earlier dissolution is possible. Members of the House (who can add the initials M.P. to their names) receive a salary of £1,000 a year and (since 1957) a further annual expense allowance of £750. The House usually sits for not less than 150 days each year. The Leader of the Opposition receives an annual salary of £3,000 from the government.

House of Lords. The upper house of the United Kingdom Houses of Parliament, comprising the Lords Spiritual and the Lords Temporal. The Archbishops and 24 Church of England bishops constitute the Lords Spiritual, while the majority of the Lords Temporal consist of the Royal Dukes, other Dukes, and all Lords (whether Earl, Marquis, Viscount or Baron) who are peers of the United Kingdom. Their right to sit is hereditary. The other Lords Temporal are the 16 Scottish peers elected by their fellow Scottish peers for the duration of each Parliament, 9 Lords of Appeal (who hold life peerages), Irish peers who were elected for life before the establishment of the Irish Free State in 1922 (only one remained alive in 1961), and life peers and peeresses under the Life Peerages Act, 1958. Members are unpaid but may draw a daily expense allowance of not more than three guineas. An ordinary meeting of the House of Lords is seldom attended by more than 50 members, although the full membership is about 900. In earlier days the House had the right to veto Bills passed by the House of Commons. This right has been greatly restricted by the Parliament Acts of 1911 and 1949, *q.v.* The Lord Chancellor presides over the House of Lords and is also a member of the government. The 9 Lords of Appeal and certain other peers sit as the highest court of appeal in the United Kingdom.

House of Representatives. The lower house of the U.S. Congress, *q.v.* Under the Constitution each state is entitled to at least one representative, but beyond that minimum number representatives are apportioned among states according to population as shown by the decennial census. Under the law now in force the membership is fixed at 437 indefinitely. A new House is elected every two years, towards the end of the Congressional term. A member must reside within the state, but not necessarily within the district, for which he is elected; he must be at least twenty-five years of age and must have been a U.S. citizen for at least seven years. The House appoints one of its members as Speaker, to preside over its meetings and to appoint chairmen of committees, and to appoint special committees. The Constitution (Article One) provides, as an adaptation of British practice, that all Bills for raising revenue shall originate in the House, although the Senate has power to amend revenue legislation. The origin of this rule lies in an old practice by which members of the Senate were chosen by the state legislatures, and were thus not directly responsible to the people. Although Senators are now chosen by direct vote, this rule remains. To some extent the House is the more representative of popular opinion, as its members submit to elections every two rather than every six years, and representation depends upon the size of the population, whereas in the Senate an under-populated state has the same representation as a densely-populated state.

Hungary. An independent eastern European state; area 35,912 sq. m.; population (January 1960) 9,977,870; capital Budapest. The country was declared an independent republic upon the collapse of the Empire of Austria-Hungary in 1918, but was reconstituted as a kingdom in 1920; Admiral Nicholas Horthy de Nagybana, who had served in the Austro-Hungarian navy, against the U.K., in the First World War, became Regent and left the throne vacant, refusing to let the Habsburg claimants return.

Between the two world wars Hungary wanted to recover the areas that had passed to other nations when the Austro-Hungarian Empire broke up. These included Slovakia, which was taken by Czechoslovakia, Transylvania (by Rumania), Croatia and other areas (by Yugoslavia), and Burgenland (by Austria). Hungary allied itself with Germany and obtained a large part of Slovakia at the first partition of Czechoslovakia in September 1938 and the province of Sub-Carpathian Ruthenia at the second partition in March 1939. The government passed anti-semitic laws under which many of the landowners were enabled to take over the businesses, the lands, and the houses of the Jews. Hungary joined the Anti-Comintern Pact on 24 February 1939 and from 1941 supported Germany in the Second World War. A Provisional Government of Liberation signed an armistice with the United Nations on 20 January 1945, under which the frontiers of 1 January 1938 were restored.

Until 1944, when the Provisional Government of Liberation was set up, the landed aristocracy had been the ruling class. In free elections in 1945 the Small Farmers' Party won fifty-seven per cent, and the Communists and Social Democrats seventeen per cent each of the votes. Before 1945, about 2,000 Hungarians owned one half of the arable land; under the Land Reform Act of 1945, 5,599,645 acres of large estates were confiscated and appropriated for the creation of smallholdings. Heavy industry and the mines were nationalized in 1946 and the banks were taken over in 1947. In the 1947 election the Communists became the largest single party with 22·7 per cent of the vote, the Smallholders' vote dropping to 15·4 per cent; by skilful political manoeuvring they obtained the most important government posts and secured absolute power.

On 1 February 1949 the People's Independence Front, comprising the Communists, the Smallholders, the National Peasant Party, the Trade Union Federation, the Association of Working Peasants, the Democratic Women's Association, and the Federation of Working Youth, was set up. In the May election the Front, with no opponents, obtained 95·6 per cent of the votes, and a predominantly Communist government was then appointed. In the following year, 1950, fifty-nine Roman Catholic orders with more than 10,000 monks and nuns were dissolved and their monasteries taken over by the state. An election result similar to that of 1949 was achieved in May 1953. In spite of great efforts to improve agricultural output, it was announced in 1953 that the grain yield barely exceeded 'the pre-liberation level', that is, the 1940–6 average.

Matyas Rakosi, q.v., was replaced as Prime Minister by Imre Nagy, in July 1953, but remained First Secretary of the Communist Party until July 1956, when he was replaced by Ernö Gerö, a Deputy Premier. The government confessed to serious economic and political errors; it placed less emphasis on the development of heavy industry and collective farming. In 1954 the Patriotic People's Front was formed with the professed aim of enabling everyone to work with the Communists. It is not a coalition of political parties but an alliance of writers, artists, scientists, churchmen, and industrial and agricultural workers. Thousands of deportees were allowed to return, and many people were released from internment camps, including some who had held important posts under Horthy. Restrictions were eased and the supply of consumer goods was increased.

Under Nagy industrial and agricultural production did not greatly improve and in April 1955 he was dismissed. He was accused of impeding industrial development and co-operative farming and of belittling the importance of the Communist Party. Andras Hegedüs, a Deputy Premier, succeeded Nagy, and announced plans to develop heavy industry and to increase the socialist sector of agriculture. The dismissal of Rakosi from his Party post in July 1956 was followed by the replacement of Hegedüs as Premier by Nagy on 23 October 1957 in the course of an anti-Russian revolution. On 1 November it was announced that Hungary had withdrawn from the Eastern European Mutual Assistance Treaty, *q.v.* Russian forces in Hungary and from outside attacked Budapest on 4 November and set up a new government under Janos Kadar, who had succeeded Gerö as First Secretary of the Communist Party in October. This government gave Nagy a guarantee of safety, as a result of which he left the sanctuary of the Yugoslav Embassy in Budapest on 22 November; it announced on 17 June 1958 that he had been executed for treason, but no date of execution was given. In January 1958 Kadar resigned the premiership in order to concentrate on his duties as First Secretary of the Socialist Workers' Party, as the Communist Party had been re-named. He was replaced by Ferenc Münnich, a lawyer who, as Minister of Public Security, had played a leading part in executing and imprisoning the supporters of Nagy.

Under the Constitution supreme power is vested in a National Assembly of 338 deputies elected for four years. At the elections held in November 1958 the Patriotic People's Front, with no opponents, obtained over 99 per cent of the votes cast. A Presidium of twenty-one members exercises the functions of parliament between Parliamentary sessions.

I

Iceland. An independent island state in the North Atlantic Ocean, near the Arctic Circle; area 40,500 sq. m., population (1958) 170,156;

capital Reykjavik. An independent republic was set up in 930, but Iceland came under the rule of Norway from 1263 to 1381 and of Denmark from 1381 to 1918. It then recovered its independence, acknowledging, with Denmark, the Danish king as a common sovereign; on 24 May 1944 the people of Iceland decided, by an overwhelming majority in a referendum, to establish a republic, and this was done on 17 June 1944 when the present Constitution came into force.

Iceland is a member of the North Atlantic Treaty Organization, *q.v.*, but possesses no armed forces except for her fishery protection vessels. Under the Treaty and a 1951 agreement the U.S.A. maintains on the island army, navy, and air forces, known as the Iceland Defence Force.

The Icelandic parliament (the Althing, founded in 930) elects one third of its 60 members to form an upper house. The remaining two thirds of the members form the lower house. Executive power is vested in the cabinet, under the President, who is elected by popular vote for a four-year term. At the elections held in October 1959 the results were: Independence Party 24; Progressives 17; Communists 10; Labour 9. The government is a coalition of the Labour and Independence (Conservative) Parties, under the Premiership of Ólafur Thors (Independence Party).

Iceland exports fish, fish meal, herring oil, and sheepskins. There have been serious disputes as a result of heavy fishing by British trawlers off the coast. In 1952 the International Court of Justice found in favour of Norway's claim to extend the limits of its territorial waters to four miles, and to measure them from headland to headland instead of following the coastline, and Iceland accordingly made a similar claim. The British trawler owners retaliated by refusing the use of their landing gear for Icelandic fish. This put a total stop to imports of Icelandic fish into the U.K. The Icelanders tried to circumvent this by using their own gear, but as British trawler skippers and mates then threatened to refuse to go to sea if English distributors handled Icelandic fish, the trade would not distribute such fish, and the attempt was abandoned. In 1956 the British trawler owners accepted the four-mile limit, and in June 1958 the territorial waters were, for the purpose of fishery limits only, extended to twelve miles with effect from 1 September 1958. The U.K. accepted this in February 1961 when Iceland granted British trawlers a three-year period of grace to fish at certain times and places between the six- and twelve-mile lines.

I.C.F.T.U. International Confederation of Free Trade Unions, *q.v.*

I.F.C. International Finance Corporation, *q.v.*

Ifni. A Spanish province on the Atlantic coast of Africa, surrounded on the north, east, and south by the independent state of Morocco, *q.v.;* area 741 sq. m.; population about 38,000, the majority being of Moorish origin. In the late fifteenth century there was, in the area of Ifni, a Spanish settlement known as Santa Cruz di Mar Pequeña. The exact site of the settlement became a matter of dispute in succeeding centuries, but it was named in the Treaty of Tetuan in 1860 between the Queen of Spain and the Sultan of Morocco who admitted Spanish sovereignty over it. Under the Madrid Convention of 1912 it was agreed that the term 'Santa Cruz di Mar Pequeña' referred to Ifni, over which the Spanish flag was eventually hoisted in 1934. After Morocco became independent in 1956, sporadic raids were made from Moroccan territory on Ifni, which was elevated to the status of a Spanish province in January 1958; the Moroccan government disclaimed responsibility for the raids. The port of Ifni is used by Spanish fishing vessels but the area has no known economic resources. The refusal of Spain to yield the province to Morocco has been determined largely by Spanish fears for the province of Spanish Sahara, *q.v.*

Ikeda, Hayato. Japanese Liberal Democratic Party politician; born in 1899 in Hiroshima, of a family of brewers whose fortunes were founded on the sale of the Japanese drink, *sake*; he is a Buddhist. He graduated in law at Kyoto University and worked for many years in the income tax service; during the U.S. occupation of Japan after the Second World War he assisted the American economic experts in their control of the Japanese economy. He was Minister of Finance from 1951 to 1952, and again in 1956; he then became successively Minister Without Portfolio and Minister for Trade and Industry, and in July 1960 became Prime Minister after the resignation of his colleague and leader, Nobusuke Kishi. His tendency to make caustic remarks at the expense of others was exemplified by his comment in 1951, when he was Minister of Finance, at a time when there was severe rationing and a shortage of food, that poor people should eat barley instead of rice; in fact, the poorer Japanese have always eaten barley.

I.L.O. International Labour Organization, *q.v.*

Imperial Preference. The traditional system of preferential arrangements by which the U.K. accords duty-free entry to most imports from the British Commonwealth. The General Agreement on Tariffs and Trade, *q.v.*, concluded in 1947, recognized existing preferential arrangements in respect of import duties but did not permit the 'margin of preference' (the difference between the most favoured nation rate and the preferential rate) to be increased. A waiver was granted by the parties to the General Agreement which enabled the U.K. to increase the protective tariff on goods not bound under the Agreement, while maintaining duty-free entry for these same goods when imported from the Commonwealth, if they were traditionally imported duty-free, and thereby allowing the margin of preference to be increased. The existence of imperial preference made it difficult for the U.K. to devise a satisfactory method of joining the European Free Trade Association, *q.v.*, or the European Economic Community, *q.v.*

Imperialism. The practice, by a country, of acquiring and administering colonies and dependencies after it has achieved national unity and embarked upon commercial or industrial expansion. Belgium, the Netherlands, France, Spain, Portugal, and the U.K. acquired overseas territories before and during the nineteenth century, whereas Germany, Italy, and Japan, which did not achieve unity and industrial and military power until the late nineteenth century, made their efforts to acquire such territories, usually by war, during the twentieth century. The U.S.S.R. has also been described as an imperialist power, since it has continued the Tsarist policy of trying to dominate the countries (such as Finland, Poland, Hungary, Rumania, Czechoslovakia, Bulgaria, Persia, Afghanistan, and China) which are on, or near, its borders, and has actually absorbed three formerly independent countries (Estonia, Latvia, and Lithuania). The economic dependence of many states (particularly in Latin America) upon the U.S.A. is often regarded as yet another expression of imperialism.

India. An independent republic, with Dominion status, within the British Commonwealth; area 1,259,765 sq. m.; population (1961 census) 438,000,000, of whom 303,186,000 are Hindus, 35,400,000 Moslems, 8,000,000 Christians and 6,200,000 Sikhs; seat of government New Delhi. By the terms of the India Independence Act, 1947, India comprises the former provinces of British India which had Hindu majorities, and those among the 507 States which chose to join India rather than Pakistan, *q.v.* Under the Constitution of the Republic of India, which came into force on 26 January 1950, India is a Union of States, each with its own Governor and legislative assembly. As a result of the States Reorganization Act, 1956, and legislation passed in 1960, India now comprises sixteen States (including Jammu and Kashmir, *q.v.*), and six centrally administered Territories. The State legislatures are subordinate to the President of the Union, who appoints the Governors and is himself elected by an electoral college consisting of all the elected members of

Parliament and of the various State legislative assemblies, and to the Parliament of the Union; the division of authority between Union and State is carefully defined in the Constitution. Parliament consists of the President of the Republic (elected for a five-year term, and then eligible for re-election) in whom all executive power is vested, the Council of States ('Rajya Sabha') of not more than 250 representatives of the States elected, indirectly, through the State legislatures, and the House of the People ('Lok Sabha') of not more than 500 members directly elected by the voters of the States on the basis of adult suffrage. The Council of States is a permanent assembly, but one third of its members retire every second year; the House of the People is dissolved after five years. An Election Commission supervises all elections.

The Congress Party, *q.v.*, dominates Indian politics. It retains the prestige it acquired before 1947 as the principal nationalist movement opposing the British and as the chosen political instrument of Mahatma Gandhi. In the biggest democratic elections ever organized, from February to March 1957, in which 121,500,000 votes were cast, the Congress Party won 369 out of 500 seats in the House of the People; Independents won 23 seats; Communists 29; Socialists 19; Jansangh (democratic nationalists) 4; Scheduled Castes Federation 7, other parties 49. The Congress Party therefore forms the Council of Ministers (government), which is headed by Jawaharlal Nehru, *q.v.* There is no unified opposition; some left-wing parties on the fringe of Congress are periodically expelled and readmitted, as are extremist right-wing Hindu organizations. The Socialists form the main parliamentary opposition, but the strongest organization is that of the Communists whose general secretary, Ajoy Ghosh, gradually rebuilt the party after the complete failure of its armed revolt in Telangana between 1948 and 1950. The Communist 'All-India' Trades Union Congress is the best organized of the four major union groups; its leaders exert better control and have gained a reputation for keeping agreements with managements so that many firms prefer to deal with Communist unions.

India is almost entirely agricultural; seventy per cent of the population depend on the land for their livelihood. There are two systems of landholding; the *ryotwari* system, by which each peasant becomes a freeholder, is gradually superseding the *zamindari* system of tenant-farming and absentee landlords. Although socially desirable, the *ryotwari* system is uneconomic since the peasant farmer employs primitive methods and is too poor to buy equipment and fertilizers; it results in an inadequate food supply for the family. Irrigation projects on the upper Ganges and in the East Punjab have reduced flooding and have increased rice and maize yields. The country is being gradually industrialized. Iron and steel, coal-mining, cotton textiles, sugar, cement, and matches provide employment for ten per cent of the working population and small-scale industries for another ten per cent. But the population (increasing by 7,900,000 a year) continues to grow at a greater rate than India's capacity to produce food and work, and the Hindu is faced with the dilemma of countenancing birth control, which his religion forbids, or mass starvation, which would inevitably encourage Communism. Nehru launched a Five-Year Plan to increase food production and simultaneously decrease births by government instruction in contraception, but religious opposition and illiteracy have hindered progress, and in January 1955 Dr Radhakamal Mukerjee predicted that the entire Five-Year Plan would be nullified unless each married Indian couple assumed responsibility for bearing not more than three children. The Plan covered the period from 1951 to 1956, when the Second Five-Year Plan (1956–1961) was begun. During the two Plans national income rose by thirty-eight per cent but, as a result of the rise in population and the need for investment, income for consumption rose by only sixteen per cent. The principal aims of the Third Five-Year Plan (1961–1966) are a thirty per cent increase in the national income, self-sufficiency in food, and a rapid expansion of basic industry. The estimated population for 1966 is 478,000,000, and it is expected to reach 568,000,000 by 1976.

India, which has frontiers with Nepal, China, and Pakistan, maintains an independent, neutralist foreign policy and frequently acts as an arbiter between east and west in the United Nations. It has withheld support from any Asian military alliance involving non-Asian powers, for example the South-East Asia Collective Defence Treaty, q.v., and has refused U.S. military aid. In 1960–1 nearly half of the central government revenue was spent on defence. The government has experienced many difficulties with Portugal which maintains its sovereignty over Goa, q.v., a territory which India wants to incorporate in the Union on the same basis as the former French settlements of Chandernagore, Pondicherry, Karikal, Mahé, and Yanaon. Agreement has not yet been reached with Pakistan over Jammu and Kashmir where more than 30,000 Indian troups are permanently garrisoned.

Indo-China. A former French dependency in South-East Asia created in 1887 and comprising the colony of Cochin China and the four protectorates of Annam, Tonkin, Laos, q.v., and Cambodia, q.v. In

1949 Annam, Tonkin, and Cochin China were merged into the single independent state of Viet-Nam, *q.v.*, which, with Cambodia and Laos, became an Associate State of the French Union until all three achieved independent status under the Geneva Agreements of 1954.

Indonesia. Formerly the Netherlands East Indies, now an independent republic comprising the four large islands of Java, Sumatra, most of Borneo and Celebes, fifteen minor islands including Madura, the Moluccas, and Bali, and thousands of small ones; area 735,865 sq. m.; population (1958) 86,900,000 of whom ninety per cent are Moslems; capital Djakarta in Java. The islands were controlled by the Dutch from the seventeenth century until 1941 when they were occupied by the Japanese who encouraged a nationalist movement and set up a nationalist Indonesian government. Two days after the surrender of the Japanese in 1945 Dr Sukarno and Dr Hatta declared an independent republic and formed a government the authority of which was recognized by the British and U.S. liberation forces. However, the Dutch attempted to oust the new administration and in some instances employed surrendered Japanese forces against the Indonesians. In 1948 troops landed in Java to suppress a Communist rising in Madium, and civil war broke out. The U.N. intervened; two Good Offices Missions were sent to Indonesia, and on 28 December 1949 power was officially transferred to the Indonesian government. Excluded from this agreement was Netherlands New Guinea, *q.v.* (West Irian), the status of which was to be determined later.

Under the provisional Constitution adopted in August 1950 the legislature consisted of a President (Dr Ahmed Sukarno, *q.v.*, who is Supreme Commander of the Armed Forces), a Vice-President (Dr Hatta until 1956), a Senate and a House of Representatives. The original plan for a federation of the United States of Indonesia was abandoned in favour of a centralized state administered from Djakarta, a decision which has produced innumerable difficulties. Lack of experience in administration and mass illiteracy (fifty-one per cent of the population in 1956) have impeded co-operation between the scattered islands with their different peoples and traditions. The Dutch discouraged higher education among the natives and the Indonesians have had to struggle to set up their own educational institutions as well as a system of government. On 5 July 1959 Sukarno decreed a return to the 1945 Constitution, and the dissolution of the elected Constituent Assembly.

Communist risings, led by the now legendary Tan Malakka, and guerilla activity on the part of Dar-ul-Islam, a militant and fanatical sect which opposes the religious toleration extended to 3,000,000

Christians and 1,000,000 Buddhists and aims to establish a Moslem theocracy, have weakened the authority of the central government. There is continual unrest in west Java, north-eastern Sumatra, Borneo, and in the Moluccas where, with help from the remnants of the former Netherlands East Indies Army (K.N.I.L.) an independent Republic of the South Moluccas was proclaimed in 1950. The army has become an essential instrument of government policy and exercises considerable political influence. In August 1955 it forced the resignation of the government of Dr Sastroamidjojo whose Minister of Defence, Iwa Kusumasumantri, it claimed, had promoted only Communist officers. Sastroamidjojo, whose nationalist government had pursued a foreign policy sympathetic to China, was replaced by Dr Burhanuddin Harahap, a member of the Masjumi (Moslem) Party executive, and, at thirty-eight, the youngest Prime Minister yet to be appointed. He formed an administration (the thirteenth in ten years) of twelve parties which excluded the Nationalists (P.N.I.), the party of Sastroamidjojo, and the Communists (P.K.I.), and promised to re-establish the confidence of the army in particular, and the people in general, in the government. In his first three months in office he secured the appointment of an anti-Communist, General Nasution, as commander-in-chief of the army, acted ruthlessly against corruption in the civil service, reduced the budget deficit and checked inflation by an intelligent use of import controls.

In the first national elections to the House of Representatives held on 29 September 1955 the Communist Party (P.K.I.), the National Party (P.N.I.), the Masjumi (Council of Indonesian Moslem Associations) and the Nahdatul Ulama (a breakaway Moslem group) obtained the largest numbers of seats. After the final results of the elections were announced in March 1956 Harahap resigned; Sastroamidjojo then formed a coalition government which included representatives of all the major parties except the Communists, and of several minor parties. After military revolts in Sumatra in December 1956, and the withdrawal of the Masjumi from the government, the coalition broke down. Sastroamidjojo resigned in March 1957 and Sukarno proclaimed a state of martial law. On 8 April 1957 he set up what he described as an 'emergency extra-parliamentary cabinet of experts' under Dr Djuanda. The cabinet contained a number of members recommended by army leaders. Sukarno also established a National Advisory Council in June 1957 with himself as chairman; its declared aims included the restoration of normal conditions and the planning of the economy.

In July 1959, after issuing his decree ordering a return to the 1945

Constitution, Sukarno formed a cabinet with himself as Prime Minister and Dr Djuanda as Chief Minister, with General Nasution as Minister of Defence. In March 1960 he decreed the dismissal of the House of Representatives, after it had criticized his budget.

Participation in the government by the Communists is unlikely, but they control the largest trade union group, S.O.B.S.I., which has nearly 1,000,000 members, and have infiltrated most government departments and voluntary organizations. However, in foreign affairs, Indonesia, which was the sponsor of the Afro-Asian Conference, *q.v.*, at Bandung, inclines to a general pro-Asian, anti-colonial, policy rather than to a specific alliance with the Chinese who are not popular in this predominantly Moslem republic.

Given stable and honest government Indonesia could prosper. Its mineral resources are among the most valuable in the world; it is the principal producer of petroleum in the Far East and rivals Malaya in its output of rubber and tin. It also exports coffee, tea, sugar, copra, and rice. It lacks capital for investment and has so far pursued a policy of discrimination against foreign, and particularly Dutch, firms that has forced many of them out of business. In 1954 General Motors closed its assembly plant at Tandjong Priok after twenty-seven years of operation. Nevertheless the Netherlands and the U.S.A. remain Indonesia's foremost trading partners, although an export trade to China and Viet-Nam through Singapore has been developed since 1951.

Indus Waters Dispute. *See* Canal Waters Dispute.

Inflation. A rise in the level of prices due not to a rise in import or production costs but to a relative increase in purchasing power as compared with the volume of goods available for purchase. A rise in the level of prices means a fall in the value of money. If the value of money falls greatly people try to exchange it for goods, and so increase still further the rise in the level of prices. A moderate inflation appears in practice to be necessary for full employment since this depends on purchasing power being always maintained at a high level.

Initiative. An instruction by the electorate to parliament to proceed with a measure. In Switzerland, for example, any 50,000 citizens may propose a total or a partial revision of the federal Constitution. The device is usually found as a supplement to the referendum, *q.v.* It is not used in the U.K.

Inner Mongolia. *See* Mongolia, Inner.

Insurgent (derived from the Latin *surgere*, to arise). One who rises in revolt. This is one of several terms, such as bandit, loyalist, partisan resistance-worker, revolutionary, and terrorist, *q.v.*, which may be used to describe a person who employs force to attack the established order. Unlike these other terms, however, it does not in itself suggest either praise or blame.

International Atomic Energy Agency. Came into existence on 29 July 1957 and is one of the United Nations specialized agencies, although also an independent international organization. Its aims are to ensure that atomic energy contributes to world peace, health, and prosperity, and to prevent its own activities from contributing in any way to military purposes. There is an annual general conference, and the board of governors (of 23 members) and staff have their headquarters in Vienna, where the Agency has a research laboratory. Requests for technical assistance, which the Agency has tried to meet, have concerned such activities as agricultural research, uranium mining, and prospecting for and analysing nuclear material.

International Bank for Reconstruction and Development. Often known as the World Bank, it was set up, with the International Monetary Fund, *q.v.*, by the United Nations Monetary and Financial Conference of forty-four nations which met at Bretton Woods, New Hampshire, U.S.A., in July 1944. The Articles of Agreement of the Bank came into force in December 1945. It is a specialized agency of the United Nations, but is also an independent international organization.

The aims of the Bank are to help to develop member countries by facilitating the investment of capital for productive purposes, to promote the long-range growth of international trade, to encourage private foreign investment by guaranteeing and participating in such investment, and to arrange loans for productive purposes where private capital is not available on reasonable terms. Lord Keynes, on behalf of the U.K., and Harry Dexter White, on behalf of the U.S.A., had once hoped to persuade the Bretton Woods Conference to accept far-reaching proposals for a central bank which would be able to eliminate world-wide financial crises.

From 1946 to 1959 the Bank made 249 loans amounting to $4,871,000,000. These loans were for such purposes as flood control, communications, mining, irrigation, transport, agriculture, forestry, electric power, and industrial development generally. Political conditions in a member country are considered only in so far as they are likely to affect economic conditions and the prospects of repayment. Loans are usually made only to a member country, or to a private enterprise within a member country, if the loan is guaranteed by the country's government or central bank. The Bank also gives technical assistance, where required, by sending missions to survey the econo--

mies of member countries which can then be helped to draw up investment programmes and to improve their productive efficiency. It will also advise on particular development programmes or recommend outside consultants for this purpose.

Each member has a right to appoint persons to the Board of Governors, which meets annually. Most of the Board's powers are delegated to sixteen Executive Directors, who meet monthly in Washington, D.C., U.S.A. Five Directors are appointed by the five members having the largest share of capital stock. Eleven Directors are elected by the Governors representing the remaining members. In board meetings each Director can cast as a unit the number of votes of the member or members by which he was appointed or elected. A President is appointed by the Directors. The Bank has an authorized capital of $21,000,000,000, of which about $18,400,000,000 is subscribed. Ten per cent of this subscribed capital is paid up and is used for loans. The remaining ninety per cent constitutes a reserve fund which can be called upon only to meet the obligations of the Bank. In 1955 the Bank decided to set up the International Finance Corporation, *q.v.*, to supervise private investment in under-developed countries. The International Development Association, *q.v.*, was established as an affiliate of the Bank in 1960.

International Confederation of Free Trade Unions. An international organization established in 1949 by the American Federation of Labour, *q.v.*, the Congress of Industrial Organizations, *q.v.*, the Trades Union Congress, *q.v.*, and other national unions, to represent those labour movements which wished to have no connexion with the World Federation of Trade Unions, *q.v.* The I.C.F.T.U. represents about 56,000,000 workers in ninety-seven countries outside the Communist influence.

International Co-operation Administration. A semi-autonomous organization within the U.S. State Department, set up on 30 June 1955 to supersede the Foreign Operations Administration, *q.v.* It supervises all U.S. foreign aid programmes, including economic and military assistance, and technical aid (which includes the former Point Four projects, *q.v.*). An increasing percentage of the money allocated under these programmes is being directed to Asia.

International Court of Justice. The principal judicial organ of the United Nations; it held its inaugural meeting at The Hague on 18 April 1946; its Statute is an integral part of the U.N. Charter. Its predecessor, in the days of the League of Nations, *q.v.*, was the Permanent Court of International Justice, established in 1921 to decide disputes between states. States had in previous centuries arranged arbitral tribunals, with chosen arbitrators, to settle their disputes, but the principles of a standing court and compulsory jurisdiction were only generally accepted in 1921, although the Central American Court of Justice, 1908–18, had introduced compulsory jurisdiction on a regional scale.

The fifteen judges of the Court are, indirectly, elected jointly by the General Assembly and the Security Council, five places falling vacant every three years. The Statute of the Court states that it shall be comprised of 'a body of independent Judges, elected regardless of their nationality'. This clause was intended to ensure that it was understood that the major powers had no special right to be represented. In practice there has always been a judge corresponding to the nationality of each permanent member of the Security Council, and a judge retiring or dying is usually replaced by one of the same nationality. Where there is not a judge who is a national of one party to a dispute, an *ad hoc* appointment is made of such a national for the duration of the hearing.

By accepting the 'optional clause' of the Statute of the Court a state agrees that the jurisdiction of the Court is compulsory in all legal disputes concerning: (1) the interpretation of a treaty; (2) any question of international law; (3) the existence of any fact which, if established, would constitute a breach of an international obligation; and (4) the nature or extent of the reparation to be made for the breach of an international obligation. About forty states have accepted the optional clause, though in some cases for limited periods and with reservations. The U.K., for example, excludes disputes with members of the Commonwealth from the compulsory jurisdiction of the International Court. The U.S.A. excludes 'disputes which are essentially within the jurisdiction of the U.S.A., as determined by the U.S.A.'. This reservation conflicts with the clause in the Court's Statute that entitles the Court itself to decide whether a dispute is within a state's own jurisdiction; serious disputes could arise over problems such as tariffs if the U.S.A. and another country quarrelled over a tariff treaty.

International Development Association. An affiliate of the International Bank for Reconstruction and Development, used to finance economic growth in the less developed countries, it came into being on 26 September 1960 and began operations on 8 November 1960. Membership is open to all members of the International Bank. A proposal that there should be such a body was made by Senator A. S. Mike Monroney in the U.S. Senate on 24 February 1958, and the suggestion was eventually adopted by the Governors of the International

Bank, after the U.S. government had endorsed it, on 1 October 1959. The aims of the Association are stated to be: 'to promote economic development, increase productivity, and thus raise standards of living in the less developed areas of the world included within the Association membership, in particular by providing finance to meet their important developmental requirements on terms which are more flexible and bear less heavily on the balance of payments than those of conventional loans, thereby furthering the developmental objectives of the International Bank for Reconstruction and Development and supplementing its activities'. The Association has considerable latitude as to the manner in which loans are repaid. The President of the International Bank is, ex-officio, President of the Association.

International Finance Corporation (I.F.C.). Set up by the International Bank for Reconstruction and Development, *q.v.*, to encourage the growth of productive private enterprises, particularly in the less developed areas of the world, by investing in undertakings where sufficient private capital is not available on reasonable terms; by seeking to recruit private capital and to find experienced management; and by generally creating conditions which will stimulate the flow of investment. There is an authorized capital of $100,000,000, paid in gold or U.S. dollars and subscribed by members in amounts proportionate to their capital in the International Bank. The I.F.C. came into existence in July 1956.

International Labour Organization (I.L.O.). Came into being in 1919 as an autonomous institution, associated with the League of Nations, seeking through international action to improve labour conditions, raise living standards, and promote economic and social stability. In 1946 the I.L.O. and the United Nations signed an agreement which recognized the responsibility of I.L.O. in these fields, and established I.L.O. as one of the United Nations specialized agencies. Its tripartite structure, representing governments, employers, and workers, is unique. It is especially concerned with: the regulation of hours of work; the regulation of the supply of labour and the prevention of unemployment; the provision of an adequate living wage; the protection of the worker against sickness and injury arising out of his employment; the protection of children, young persons, and women; provision for old age and injury; protection of the interests of workers when employed in countries other than their own; recognition of the principles of equal pay for equal work and of freedom of association; the organization of vocational and technical education.

Policy is decided by the annual International Labour Conference, at which each member state is represented by two government delegates, one employer and one employee. A Governing Body, comprising twenty government delegates, ten employers and ten employees, appoints the Director-General and supervises the work of the International Labour Office (the permanent secretariat of I.L.O.) at the I.L.O. headquarters at Geneva. Western employer delegates have tried to exclude employer delegates from Communist countries on the ground that they merely echo their governments' policies and represent no separate interest. Ten governments (Canada, China, France, German Federal Republic, India, Italy, Japan, U.K., U.S.A., U.S.S.R.) hold seats on the Governing Body because of their industrial importance. Each of the three groups represented at the Conference elects its own representatives to the remaining thirty places on the Governing Body.

International Monetary Fund. Was set up, with the International Bank for Reconstruction and Development, *q.v.*, by the United Nations Monetary and Financial Conference of forty-four nations which met at Bretton Woods, New Hampshire, U.S.A., in July 1944. The Articles of Agreement of the Fund came into force in December 1945. It is a specialized agency of the United Nations, but is also an independent international organization.

The aims of the Fund are to expand international trade, and thus to establish a high level of employment, real income, and production, to make exchange rates stable, and to make its own funds available to members. To achieve its aims it discusses with member countries their balance of payments problems, currency par values, exchange restrictions, and the use of their resources. It has pointed out that currency exchange restrictions may be a restraining factor on exports, and has stressed the need for deflationary measures to prevent payment deficits. It arranges with members a pattern of exchange rates fixed in proportion to the value of gold and the U.S. dollar. A member is not allowed to change this rate by more than ten per cent without obtaining the approval of the Fund's Board of Executive Directors. The staff of the Fund gives advice to members about fiscal, monetary, and credit policy, so far as this bears on the problem of international payments, and about the establishment of central banking systems.

The Fund has a Board of Governors, a Board of Executive Directors, a Managing Director and a staff. Each member government is represented on the Board of Governors, which meets annually and delegates most of its powers to the Directors. The Board of Executive Directors conducts the general operation of the Fund. Each of the five nations which subscribe the largest quotas appoints a Director; there must be at least seven other Directors, who are elected by the Governors representing the remaining members. Voting in this election and by the appointed Directors is in proportion to each member's quota. Voting by the elected Directors is in proportion to the votes they received.

Quotas are fixed on joining; a member must pay either twenty-five per cent of its quota in gold or, as part of its quota, ten per cent of its net official gold and dollar holdings, whichever is the less. The balance of the quota is payable in the member's national currency. In 1959, the total subscription in gold and national currencies from the sixty-eight member nations was $13,800,000,000.

International Refugee Organization (I.R.O.). Was responsible from 20 August 1948 to 31 December 1951, when it was brought to an end, for the care and repatriation of refugees and displaced persons, for their identification and classification, for their legal and political protection and for their resettlement and establishment in countries able and willing to receive them. Its constitution was approved by the United Nations General Assembly on 15 December 1946; its Preparatory Commission took over many functions of the United Nations Relief and Rehabilitation Administration, *q.v.*, on 30 June 1947, including the direct care of 719,600 refugees and displaced persons throughout the world, and responsibility for the protection of the interests of 900,000 other refugees and displaced persons eligible for I.R.O. assistance. Between 1947 and 1951 the Preparatory Commission and I.R.O. resettled more than one million persons in new homes throughout the world, repatriated approximately 73,000 to their former homelands, and gave some form of assistance to more than 1,600,000. I.R.O. became a migration organization because only a small minority of those under its care were willing to be repatriated. It was in origin a temporary organization, designed to deal with the problems raised by the cessation of U.N.R.R.A.; when it was abolished at the end of 1951 its responsibilities passed to the United Nations High Commissioner for Refugees, *q.v.*

International Trade Organization (I.T.O.). Was to have come into existence when the Havana Charter, *q.v.*, was ratified by the fifty-four states which met at Havana in 1947–8 to make plans for the removal of trade barriers. An interim commission (I.C.I.T.O.) was created to prepare for the first conference of I.T.O., but the organization has never been set up as the result of the U.S. refusal to ratify the Havana Charter. I.C.I.T.O. concerned itself instead with liaison duties for the contracting parties to the General Agreement on Tariffs and Trade, *q.v.*, which was concluded in 1947 as an interim measure. In 1955 the parties to G.A.T.T. agreed to set up the Organization for Trade Co-operation, *q.v.*, to administer the General Agreement.

Interstate Commerce Commission. Is responsible for federal, as opposed to state, transport in the U.S.A. It has jurisdiction over passenger and cargo rates and can make regulations concerning facilities for passengers. In 1955 it ruled that there should be no segregation of Negro interstate railway and bus passengers; Negroes were to have the same accommodation as whites, and must be permitted to use the same railway waiting-rooms as whites. The Commission's decision reflected the views of the Supreme Court, which has condemned the belief that it is possible to give Negroes facilities that are separate but equal.

Intervention. Interference in the domestic or external affairs of another state which violates that state's independence. A state may justify an act of intervention where it has a treaty right to interfere in the external affairs of one of its protected states; where it interferes to protect one of its citizens; where it invades in self-defence; where it joins with other members of the United Nations to restrain a state which disturbs world peace by resorting to war; and in certain other cases. Unless there is some such justification any intervention is a breach of international law.

Invisible Exports. That part of a country's income from overseas which is derived otherwise than by exports of goods which are visible exports. They include insurance premiums, tourist expenditure, interest on debts and on capital invested abroad, and payments for banking and shipping services.

I.R.A. Irish Republican Army, *q.v.*

Iran. *See* Persia.

Iraq. An independent state between the rivers Tigris and Euphrates, covering the territory once known as Mesopotamia; area 172,000 sq. m.; population (1957) 6,538,109, nearly all Moslems, mostly of Shiite but some of Sunni sects; capital Baghdad. Most of the population speak Arabic. Formerly a Turkish province, Iraq was prepared for independence under a British Mandate after the First World War and Emir Faisal (son of King Hussein of Mecca) who had just been driven out of Syria by the French, was made King in 1921. Under the Treaty of Lausanne, 1923, Turkey gave up its claims to rule the area. In accordance with the terms of the Mandate, the U.K. recognized Iraq's independence in 1927, and in 1932 the Mandate ended, Iraq becoming a sovereign state with a seat in the League of Nations.

From 1932 to 1958 Iraq was a constitutional monarchy with a

two-chamber legislature. On 14 February 1958 King Faisal II (who was born in 1935 and became King in 1939) proclaimed the establishment of the Arab Federation, *q.v.*, with Jordan. He became head of state of the Arab Union, *q.v.*, as the two countries then were known, on 13 May. On 14 July there was a *coup d'état* in the course of which King Faisal, the Prime Minister of the Arab Union, General Nuri-es-Said, and Faisal's uncle, Crown Prince Abdul Illah, were murdered. The new government, led by Najib al Rubaii (President of the Council of State) and Brigadier Abdul Karim Kassem (Prime Minister), then announced the withdrawal of Iraq from the Arab Union, and declared a republic.

Oil production increased rapidly from 4,066,782 tons in 1949 to 40,000,000 tons in 1959. Most of the oil comes from the Kirkuk oilfield, established in 1927, which has pipelines to the Mediterranean Sea and is owned by the Iraq Petroleum Co., *q.v.* Other firms with oil concessions include Mosul Petroleum Co. and Basra Petroleum Co., both with the same ownership as I.P.C., and Khanaqin Oil Co., working near the Persian border, which is a subsidiary of the British Petroleum Co. Under an agreement between the government and the Iraq, Basra, and Mosul Companies, the government receives fifty per cent of the profits after deduction of foreign taxes. Oil revenues represent more than one third of the national income. Other products are wheat, barley, beans, rice, and eighty per cent of the world's dates. Extensive irrigation is badly needed in this area, which was once able to support 30,000,000 people.

In foreign policy the 1955 mutual assistance treaty with Turkey, later joined by Pakistan, Persia, and the U.K., and known as the Baghdad Pact, *q.v.*, was Iraq's most important action in recent years. By supporting the Pact, Iraq was the first Arab state to join the western chain of alliances. This weakened the Arab League, *q.v.*, which Iraq took an important part in founding in 1945, but the country withdrew from the Pact in March 1959, as a result of the revolution.

Iraq Petroleum Company. An oil company holding concessions in many states throughout the Middle East. It has interests, directly or indirectly, in Cyprus, Israel, Iraq, Jordan, Lebanon, Muscat and Oman, the Trucial Coast, Qatar, Syria, and elsewhere. The controlling interests in the Company are: British Petroleum 23·75 per cent; the Shell Group 23·75 per cent; Compagnie Française des Pétroles 23·75 per cent; Standard Oil of New Jersey 11·875 per cent; Socony Mobil Oil 11·875 per cent; and the Gulbenkian group (Participations and Explorations Corporation) 5 per cent.

Ireland. An independent state, area 26,600 sq. m.; population (1956) 2,898,264, of whom some 2,800,000 are Roman Catholics; capital Dublin. Ireland was divided into a number of Celtic kingdoms until 1152, when one king invoked the aid of the Anglo-Normans. This led to the first English landings; the Irish, however, constantly opposed English rule, especially after the reformation of the English Church, when Ireland remained Roman Catholic. Cromwell ordered the evacuation of the northern counties, now known as Northern Ireland, *q.v.*, and settled Protestant Englishmen and Scots there. An Irish Parliament existed till 1800 when the United Kingdom of Great Britain and Ireland was created. In the nineteenth century there was mass emigration to the U.S.A. by peasants who could not obtain a living from the land or had been driven from their tenancies by English landowners to whom they owed rent. One half of Ireland's total income went to absentee English landlords.

The Liberal Gladstone government increased the security of tenure of the Irish peasant and in 1886 and 1893 made unsuccessful attempts to introduce Home Rule. A Home Rule Act was eventually passed, against Conservative opposition, in 1914, but its operation was delayed until after the war. A group of Southern Irish Nationalists (Sinn Feiners) co-operated with Germany in organizing the Easter Rising in Dublin in 1916. The execution and repressions which followed hardened the division between loyal Irishmen (mainly in Ulster) and the nationalists, who dominated the south. After the First World War the Government of Ireland Act provided for a Northern Irish Parliament at Belfast and a Southern Irish one at Dublin. This was resisted forcibly by the Sinn Feiners, who were opposed by a special British police force known as the Black-and-Tans. Outrages were committed on both sides, the Irish nationalists attacking not only the British but that section of the Irish population which did not sympathize with them. The Irish Free State Act, 1922, repealed the Government of Ireland Act of 1920 and set up the Dominion of the Irish Free State.

In 1937 a new constitution, adopted by plebiscite, renamed the country Eire and declared the national territory to be the whole of Ireland, although the laws of the Irish Parliament were to apply only to Eire. The country was neutral in the Second World War, and in 1948 the Republic of Ireland Act removed the last constitutional link with the U.K. The official name is now the Republic of Ireland.

Ireland comprises the provinces of Leinster, Munster, Connacht, and part of Ulster, *q.v.*, or 26 of the 32 Irish counties. The President (since June 1959 Eamonn de Valera, *q.v.*) is appointed for seven years by direct popular vote. The Prime Minister, or Taoiseach, is appointed by the President on the nomination of the House of Representatives. Legislation is by the President and Parliament, which consists of a Senate (Seanad Éireann) of 60 who represent the universities, labour, the public services, and the arts, and a House of Representatives (Dáil Éireann) of 147 elected for five years by adult suffrage.

In the 1957 elections to the Dáil, Fianna Fáil (which maintains the Sinn Fein tradition, has been the largest single party for over twenty years, and is led by Séan Lemass, *q.v.*,) obtained 78 seats, winning 10 seats thus returning to power. Fine Gael, the moderate nationalist party led by John Costello, *q.v.*, and James Dillon, obtained 40 seats, having lost 10 seats. The Irish Labour Party's representation fell, by 7 from 19 to 12, and Clann na Poblachta's (led by Séan MacBride) from 3 to 1. Clann na Talmhan (the Farmers' Party) and Independents won 3 seats and 9 seats respectively. De Valera then became Prime Minister of a government drawn entirely from the Fianna Fáil, but on being elected to the office of President in June 1959 he was succeeded by Séan Lemass.

Irish Republican Army. An association of radical Irish nationalists claiming to be a continuation of the Irish Republican Volunteers (Sinn Feiners) who seceded from the Southern Irish Volunteers in 1914 over the question of participation in the First World War, received German co-operation in their Easter Rising at Dublin in 1916, proclaimed an Irish Republic, and fought the Irish Free State government in the Civil War of 1922. They regard themselves as the Army of an Irish Republic which includes the six northern counties ruled by the U.K. They were outlawed in 1931 by President Cosgrave, and in 1939 conducted a series of attacks in London and Manchester by means of bomb explosions. Several hundred members were imprisoned in the U.K. and in Ireland. In 1954 and 1955 the I.R.A. carried out raids on barracks in Northern Ireland and the U.K. to obtain arms. At the 1955 General Election to the British Parliament two members of the I.R.A., standing as Anti-Partitionists, obtained a majority of votes in two Northern Ireland constituencies although they were at the time serving jail sentences; they were eventually held to be ineligible as convicted felons, and their Conservative opponents were declared to have been elected. At the 1959 General Election none of the Anti-Partitionists secured a majority, and all the seats were won by Conservatives.

I.R.O. International Refugee Organization, *q.v.*

Iron Curtain. The frontiers dividing the U.S.S.R. and the pro-Russian Communist states of eastern Europe (Albania, Bulgaria, Czechoslovakia, Hungary, Poland, and Rumania) from the rest of Europe. The term is used to indicate the lack of freedom of ideas and movement into and out of these seven countries.

Isolationists. A group in the U.S.A., particularly active before the Second World War, which opposed any involvement of the U.S.A. in European affairs. The result of the Japanese attack on the U.S. base at Pearl Harbour on 7 December 1941 was a state of war between the U.S.A. and the Japanese-Italian-German alliance. This entry by the U.S.A. into a war with European powers, combined with a close post-war economic relationship between the U.S.A. and Europe, brought about a decline in the number of isolationists. They were succeeded by those who felt that the prime object of American economic and military commitments should be Asia, but admitted the necessity for European commitments.

Israel. An independent state at the eastern end of the Mediterranean Sea; area 7,993 sq. m.; population (1960) 2,089,000, of whom 1,859,000 are Jews and 153,000 are Moslems; capital Jerusalem. The state was established by proclamation on 14 May 1948 when the British Mandate in Palestine, *q.v.*, came to an end. According to a recommendation by the United Nations General Assembly, a Jewish state and an Arab state were to be set up in Palestine and their boundaries were defined. After the establishment of Israel as the Jewish state its territory was invaded by Egypt, Iraq, Jordan, Lebanon, and Syria; during the fighting Israel acquired some of the land allotted to the Arab state but lost an area west of the river Jordan to Jordan, and the Gaza Strip, *q.v.*, to Egypt. Hostilities ceased in January 1949 and the Tripartite Declaration of 1950, *q.v.*, helped to stabilize the situation although raids by both Israelis and Arabs continued to take place. On 29 October 1956 Israeli forces invaded Egypt and soon occupied most of the Sinai peninsula to the east of the Suez Canal. On the next day the U.K. demanded that Egypt and Israel should each withdraw to a distance of ten miles from the Canal. At the United Nations Security Council, however, the U.S.A. asked that Israel should withdraw to its own borders, and did not suggest that Egypt should give up its own territory. The U.S.A. also moved a resolution urging United Nations members to withhold help from Israel until Israeli forces had left Egypt. This resolution, which was supported by the U.S.S.R., was vetoed by the U.K. and France. On 31 October Franco-British forces attacked Egypt, but, after the arrival of a United Nations Emergency force, both they and the Israeli forces withdrew from Egypt. The last Israelis left the Gaza Strip in March 1957.

Of the total population 916,200 came to Israel between 1948 and 1957; by the Law of the Return, enacted on 5 July 1950, every Jew has the right to immigrate to Israel. While the working population thus increased the government attempted to expand production so that the state could be self-supporting. An adverse trade balance has been partly bridged by German reparations, which cease in 1965, of about £14,000,000 each year, U.S. aid (£14,800,000 in 1959-60) of a gradually decreasing amount, and gifts and loans from Jews in other parts of the world. In spite of increased agricultural and industrial production the sum earned from exports (which include citrus fruits, textiles, and polished diamonds) is only one third of the sum required to pay for Israel's essential imports of foodstuffs, crude oil, machinery, iron and steel, and chemicals. This may be compared, however, with a proportion of just over one ninth in 1949. The discovery of oil near Beersheba has lessened slightly the dependence of the country on imported petroleum. Approximately one half of the total area of Israel is taken up by the Negev, an infertile desert region with an increasing number of farms. A pipeline sixty-six inches wide, which was completed in 1955, carries water from the river Yarkon by Tel Aviv to irrigate 50,000 acres of the western plateau of the Negev. Extensive irrigation of the Negev would necessitate the diversion of the waters of the river Jordan. (*See* Jordan Valley Plan.)

The legislature (the Knesset) comprises a single chamber of 120 members elected for four years by universal suffrage and proportional representation. At the elections held in 1959 the Mapai (Labour Party) led by David Ben-Gurion, *q.v.*, and Moshe Sharett, *q.v.*, obtained 47 seats. Two other left-wing parties, the Mapam, a radical party which believes in a planned economy and close ties with the U.S.S.R., and the Ahdut Avoda, a Socialist group which seceded from the Mapam in criticism of its sympathy with Communism, obtained 9 seats and 7 seats respectively. The other parties which won seats were: Hapoel Hamizrachi, an orthodox religious group which wants to ban the use of public transport on the Sabbath and the sale of pork, 12; General Zionists, a right-wing middle-class party which believes in private enterprise, 8; Progressives, who are moderate liberals, 6; Freedom Movement or Heruth, an extreme right-wing party, formerly the Irgun Zvai Leumi, 17; Agudat Israel and Poalei Agudat Israel, a religious association, 6; Communists 3; and the Arab Democrats, who usually support the Mapai, 5. A government coalition was formed, comprising the Mapai, the Mapam, Ahdut Avoda, Hapoel Hamizrachi, and the Progressives.

Istiqlal. The Moroccan Independence Party, founded in 1943. For most of its existence until Morocco became independent in 1956 it was banned by the French; it held its first National Congress in Rabat in November 1955. It defied the French administration by acknowledging only Sidi Mohammed Ben Youssef, the Sultan of Morocco, as head of state and in 1955 it combined with the Algerian National Liberation Front (F.L.N., *q.v.*) to form the Liberation Army of North Africa, pledged to expel the French by military action if necessary. The Party, which contains both conservatives and radical elements, draws its support from the townspeople, intellectuals, the trade union movement and the Communist Party which is nominally banned. It held a majority of seats in the governments of Si Bekkai (November 1955 to April 1958) and of Ahmed Balafrej (May to November 1958), but in January 1960 the Party split, a rival organization being formed and claiming to be the true Istiqlal. The political crisis which resulted was one of the factors affecting the decision in May 1960 of King Mohammed V (who died in February 1961), to become Premier.

Italian Somaliland. The name of an area in East Africa which was an Italian colony from 1925 to 1947, when it became the trusteeship territory (now independent) of Somalia, *q.v.*

Italy. An independent European state; area 131,000 sq. m.; population (1960) 49,230,000; capital Rome. After years of struggle, in which Mazzini and Garibaldi played important roles, Italy achieved unity in 1870 under the House of Savoy. From 1925 to 1943 Italy was effectively ruled by the dictator Benito Mussolini, who was called Il Duce. A former Socialist, he was appointed Prime Minister in 1922 after he and 40,000 other Fascists had marched on Rome; he secured a Fascist majority in the legislature by passing a law that two thirds of the seats should be allotted to any party which obtained one quarter of the votes at an election. In 1935, prompted by the rapid increase in population and a lack of raw materials, Italy conquered Ethiopia; it then helped Franco with his Fascist revolution in Spain, and supported Germany in the Second World War, which it entered in 1940. As the allied powers invaded Italy the Fascist régime came to an end; Mussolini was killed by partisans in 1945 and King Victor Emmanuel III abdicated in 1946, being succeeded by his son, Umberto II, who was rejected by a popular referendum which, by a narrow majority, established a republic.

Under the 1947 Constitution there is a bicameral legislature with a Senate of 246 members elected for six years on a regional basis and a Chamber of Deputies of 596 members elected for five years by universal suffrage. The President is elected for a seven-year term by a two-thirds majority of a joint session of the legislature, sitting with delegates from each of the nineteen Regions of Italy. Giovanni Gronchi, a Christian Democrat, was inaugurated as President on 11 May 1955. At the elections for the Chamber of Deputies held in May 1958 the results were: Christian Democrats (a Roman Catholic party, with some extreme right-wing members and some land-reforming members, led by Antonio Segni, *q.v.*, Mario Scelba, coalition Premier till 1955, Giuseppe Pella, a former Premier, and Amintore Fanfani, a former Premier and leader of Democratic Initiative, a militant Christian and land-reforming group) 273 seats; Communists (the largest Communist Party in Western Europe, with 2,000,000 members) 140 seats; Italian Socialist Party (left-wing Socialists, led by Pietro Nenni, *q.v.*, favourable to the Communists and boycotted by the British Labour Party) 84 seats; Popular and National Monarchists 23 seats; the neo-Fascist Italian Social Movement 25 seats; Italian Socialist-Democratic Party (right-wing Socialists, anti-Communist, supported by the British Labour Party, led by Giuseppe Saragat) 23 seats; Liberals (fundamentally opposed to land reform) 16 seats; the Republicans 7 seats; and the South Tirol Popular Party 3 seats. Elections for the Senate were also held in May 1958 and the results were: Christian Democrats 122, Communists 60, Italian Socialist Party 35, Monarchists 7, Italian Social Movement 8, Italian Socialist-Democratic Party 5, Liberals 4, and others 5 seats.

In July 1958 Amintore Fanfani became Prime Minister of a coalition government of sixteen Christian Democrats and four Social Democrats. He lost his narrow majority in January 1959 and was succeeded by Antonio Segni, who formed a government composed entirely of Christian Democrats but supported by the Monarchists and the Liberals. When the Liberals withdraw their support in February 1960 the government fell, but a new ministry, again consisting entirely of Christian Democrats (though they were in a minority in the Chamber of Deputies), was formed by Fernando Tambroni, a lawyer.

Nearly half of the working population is employed on the land, producing grapes, olives, wheat, and silkworms. Italy is poor in mineral resources, although there are valuable deposits of iron pyrites and sulphur, and supplies of natural methane. Large oil reserves have been discovered in the southern part of central Italy. Exports include cotton and woollen goods, fibres, and machinery, but are normally exceeded in value by imports; this adverse balance is a permanent feature of Italian trade, and is made up as far as possible by foreign aid, tourist traffic, shipping, and remittances from Italians overseas. After the Second World War Italian heavy industry proved uncompetitive and considerable unemployment resulted. There are many depressed agricultural areas, particularly in southern Italy. Extensive unemployment (nearly 1,700,000 in 1960) and under-employment have strengthened the Communist Party, and there has not been sufficient foreign investment to solve these problems, and the related problem of under-development in southern Italy. The government's ten-year economic development programme (the Vanoni Plan) aims to provide 4,000,000 new jobs in Italy by 1965, to balance the Italian economy, and to raise the standard of living in southern Italy.

I.T.O. International Trade Organization, *q.v.*

Ivory Coast. An independent republic; area 127,520 sq. m; population 3,214,100, comprising Agnis, Baoulés, Senoufos, Kroumen, Mandes, Dan-fouros, and 20,000 Europeans; capital Abidjan. It occupies approximately 330 miles of the West African coast, between Liberia and Ghana, with the republics of Guinea, Mali, and Upper Volta to the north-west and north. The French took a coastal strip in 1842 and annexed the territory in 1893. It later became one of the eight territories comprising French West Africa, *q.v.*, and achieved self-government within the French Community, *q.v.*, on 4 December 1958, and complete independence, after breaking with the Community in June 1960, on 7 August 1960.

Agriculture occupies 95 per cent of the population, who produce groundnuts, rice, manioc, yams, and rubber, and (for export) coffee, cocoa, bananas, and timber. There are forests of mahogany and palm oil trees, and deposits of manganese, gold, and diamonds. Abidjan is the port not only for the Ivory Coast but also for Upper Volta, which is connected by railway to the coast.

Legislative powers are vested in an assembly of 100 members elected every five years by universal suffrage. At the elections held on 12 April 1959 every seat was won by the Union for the Economic and Social Development of the Ivory Coast (the local section of the Rassemblement Démocratique Africain) led by the Prime Minister Félix Houphouët-Boigny, a supporter of a close relationship with France.

Izvestia. A newspaper which is the official organ of the Supreme Soviet, *q.v.*, the legislature of the U.S.S.R. It devotes much of its space to the laws passed by the Supreme Soviet and to the administrative orders of the Russian government, on which it also comments. However, it is not so reliable an exponent of the Communist Party line as *Pravda*, *q.v.* The word *izvestia* means news; the newspaper was founded in 1916.

J

Jamaica. A British colony in the West Indies, comprising the island of Jamaica, with an area of 4,411 sq. m., and other islands, including the Turks and Caicos Islands, with an area of 202 sq. m.; population (1960) 1,606,546; capital Kingston. The main island was seized from the Spaniards in 1655. Of its exports, the majority of which goes to the U.K., the most valuable are sugar, bananas, bauxite, and rum.

At the elections to the House of Representatives held on 28 July 1959 the People's National Party (P.N.P.) won 29 seats and the Jamaica Labour Party 16 seats. The P.N.P., led by Norman Manley, *q.v.*, was originally modelled on the British Labour Party; it believes in moderate socialism and is supported both by the middle class and by the organized urban workers. The Jamaica Labour Party, which was in power from 1945 to 1955 under the leadership of W. A. Bustamante, *q.v.*, is anti-socialist and is supported by most of the business community and many of the illiterate poor. The standard of living is low and both parties agree that more agricultural and industrial development is needed. There is considerable emigration to the U.K., which has no restrictions on the entry of people who are, as a result of the British Nationality Act of 1948, 'citizens of the United Kingdom and Colonies'.

On 11 November 1957 a cabinet system was introduced and the colony was made virtually self-governing. Norman Manley remained Chief Minister but the Governor ceased to preside over meetings of the Executive Council, which became known as the Council of Ministers, or Cabinet. The Cabinet may include members of both the Houses of Representatives and the Legislative Council, which is the upper house of the legislature and consists of members appointed by the Governor after consultation with the party leaders. On 3 January 1958 Jamaica became a member of the West Indies Federation, *q.v.* On 4 July 1959 full self-government was granted, all the powers of the British Colonial Office coming to an end except in a few limited cases.

The sugar and banana industries, which export chiefly to the U.K., have suffered in recent years from the British decision to abandon colonial preference in favour of buying in the cheapest possible markets. The existence of the citrus fruit industry has been threatened by Israeli competition and by subsidized American exports to the U.K. Foreign investors have been encouraged to establish industrial firms and efforts have been made to diversify the economy by setting up factories to produce boots and shoes, leather goods, metal and plastic containers, and textiles. The national income more than doubled between 1955 and 1959. Jamaica is the world's largest exporter of bauxite.

Jammu and Kashmir. The name by which the state of Kashmir, *q.v.*, is known in India, and under which it was integrated with the Republic of India on 26 January 1957.

Japan. An independent empire in the Pacific Ocean; area 142,748 sq. m., comprising the four large islands of Honshu, Kyushyu, Hokkaido, and Shikoku, and many smaller islands; population (1959) 93,100,000, most of whom profess Buddhism or Shintoism; capital Tokyo. The Emperors are said to be descended from a dynasty founded in 660 B.C., but from 1186 until 1867 their powers were largely ceremonial. Japan resisted contact with the west until 1853 when Commodore Perry from a gun-boat in Tokyo Bay forced an exchange of goods with U.S. merchants. In 1859 a commercial treaty was signed with the U.S.A. and a rapid process of westernization was begun, during which Japan became a dominant power in Asia. Its first war with China in 1894, in which it acquired Formosa, was followed by war with Russia in 1905, and the acquisition of Karafuto, Korea, and leased territory, including the port of Dairen, in the Kuangtung peninsula; by participation in the First World War on the allied side, which resulted in a Japanese Mandate over the former German South Sea Islands – Bismarck, Marshall, and the Carolines; by intervention in the U.S.S.R. in 1918, seizure of Manchuria in 1931; by a second war with China in 1937; and by its attack on the U.S.A. in 1941. When U.S. aircraft dropped the first atomic bomb upon Hiroshima on 6 August 1945, and a second atomic bomb upon Nagasaki on 9 August 1945, the Emperor broadcast an appeal for terms of surrender and the war ended. The large population of Japan and the shortage of raw materials were partly responsible for its expansionist policies and the accession to power of a military caste, the Gunbatsu, supported by the leading industrial combines, known as the Zaibatsu.

After the 1945 surrender Japan was occupied by the allied forces under General Douglas MacArthur. A new constitution was enacted in 1946; it established a Supreme Court, renounced war, and abandoned the doctrine of the divinity of the Emperor. Legislative authority is vested in a Diet comprising a House of Representatives of 467 members elected for four years and a House of Councillors for which elections are held every three years to elect half of the House's 250 members, whose terms run for six years. Executive authority is vested in a Cabinet responsible to the Diet. The functions of the Emperor are purely ceremonial. The Allied Supreme Command broke up the Zaibatsu and removed 1,200 firms from the control of eleven huge concerns, although by 1952 the pre-war position had been largely restored by Japanese business interests in defiance of allied policy. The Constitution provided that Japan should never have any land, sea, or air forces, but at the request of General MacArthur a constabulary of 75,000 men was recruited in 1950. This National Police Reserve, equipped with tanks, later became the National Safety Force and then the Self-Defence Force; Japan had 231,000 men in the armed services, which were largely supplied with U.S. equipment, by 1959.

At the 1955 election the largest number of votes was secured by the Democratic Party, which was formed in November 1954 by dissident Liberals and by the Progressives (the principal opposition party). The Liberals had been in power since 1948, and had been attacked as being too closely tied to the U.S.A. In November 1955 the Democrats and the Liberals merged themselves into the Liberal-Democratic Party. At the elections held on 22 May 1958 the ruling Liberal Democrats were returned to power, and the new House comprised 298 Liberal Democrats, 167 Socialists, 1 Communist and 1 Independent. Both the major parties advocated the immediate ending of nuclear tests, but they again disagreed over the proposal that the Constitution should be revised, and the Liberal Democrats did not obtain the two-thirds majority needed to make constitutional amendments. Nobusuke Kishi, a lawyer, who had become Premier in February 1957, continued in office until July 1960, when he was succeeded by Hayato Ikeda, *q.v.* At the elections held on 20 November 1960 the recent signature of a security treaty with the U.S.A. was a leading issue; the results were: Liberal Democrats 296, Socialists 145, Democratic Socialists 17, Communists 3, and Independents and minor parties 6 seats.

Japan is the most highly industrialized power in Asia, with a wide range of heavy and light industries and important exports of cotton and rayon fabrics, cotton yarn, raw silk, and knitted goods. Although there is still a strong antipathy towards China, the success of Japan's export drive before the Second World War was largely due to the China trade, which took forty-three per cent of Japanese exports as compared with four per cent in 1954. A U.S. economic advisory group, appointed by President Eisenhower, recommended in 1954 that this trade should be developed in order to improve Japan's balance of payments position. Many of Japan's pre-war economic problems remain unsolved; the population is still increasing rapidly, and there is a dearth of natural resources. Some right-wing elements have already demanded the return of southern Sakhalin and some of the Kurile Islands, which became part of the U.S.S.R. after the Second World War. Others seek to reach agreement with the Asian Communist powers and so improve the prospects for Japanese trade in China.

Jewish Agency. An organization which links the state of Israel with Jews in the rest of the world. It was established under the terms of the Mandate for Palestine, *q.v.*, given by the League of Nations to the U.K., which said that 'an appropriate Jewish Agency shall be recognized as a public body for the purpose of advising and co-operating with the administration of Palestine in such economic, social, and other matters as may affect the establishment of the Jewish national home'. The Jewish Agency today is, for all practical purposes, a world organization. A law passed in the Israeli parliament gave the Agency extra-territorial rights and made it responsible for the absorption of immigrants, land development, and co-operation with Jewry outside Israel, including Jewish institutions and organizations willing to participate in the building up of the state. Its activities include all problems concerned with the cultural and economic progress of Israel as far as they interest or affect Jewry outside the state.

John XXIII. Angelo Giuseppe Roncalli, 263rd Pope; born 25 November 1881 at Sotto il Monte, near Bergamo, Lombardy, the son of a peasant; educated at the episcopal seminary in Bergamo and at the pontifical seminary in Rome, where he was ordained on 10 August 1904, thereupon becoming private secretary to the Bishop of Bergamo, a leading figure in the Catholic Social movement. In the First World War he served in the army, and then returned to Bergamo until 1921, when he was called to Rome by Benedict XV to reorganize the missionary work of the Sacred Congregation for the Propagation of the Faith. In 1925 Pius XI made him Titular Archbishop of Areopoli and Apostolic Visitor to Bulgaria; he later became Nuncio to Bulgaria and (in 1935) Apostolic Delegate to Greece, and then to Turkey, where he stayed until the end of the Second World War. In January 1945 he was appointed Papal Nuncio to France, where he successfully resisted French requests for the withdrawal of a large number of Bishops who were alleged to have collaborated with the Germans, and where he also concerned himself with the activities of worker priests. He was created a Cardinal and Patriarch of Venice in January 1953, and was elected by conclave to succeed Pius XII as Pope on 28 October 1958.

Johnson, Lyndon Baines. U.S. Democratic Party politician; born

27 August 1908 in Gillespie County, Texas, the son of a member of the Texas state legislature. His first appearance in Washington, D.C., was in 1931 as assistant to a Texas member of the House of Representatives, and in 1935 he became Texas director of the National Youth Administration. He was elected to the House of Representatives as a supporter of the New Deal in 1938 and to the Senate in 1948, becoming Democratic leader of the Senate in 1953. He held that post, despite a severe heart attack in 1955, until, after the elections of November 1960, he took office as Vice-President of the U.S.A. in January 1961.

Jordan. An independent kingdom, capital Amman, with an area of 37,700 sq. m. The language is Arabic and Islam is the state religion. Formerly an Amirate under Turkish rule, the area was put under British Mandate after the First World War and became independent as the Hashemite Kingdom of Jordan in 1946, although the name of Transjordan was in general use until 1949. There is a population of about 1,072,000 with an additional 535,000 Arab refugees from the part of Palestine which became Israel in 1948. Jordan formerly consisted of territory to the east of the river Jordan but, on the establishment of Israel, it extended its frontiers to include part of Palestine west of the river, which it formally incorporated on 24 April 1950.

Government is by an Executive Council of 12 Ministers and a legislature comprising a Council of Notables (25 nominated by the King) and a Council of Representatives (50 members, 25 from each side of the river Jordan, elected by manhood suffrage). Under the 1951 Constitution the Executive Council is responsible to the legislature. King Hussein (born 1935) ascended the throne in 1952 on the deposition, by the legislature, of his father, King Talal, who was mentally ill. Elections in 1956 resulted in the return of Independents to 13 out of the 40 places in the Council of Representatives, no organized party or group gaining a significant number of seats. In June 1957 parliamentary activities were suspended following the discovery of a series of plots against the monarchy some of which were said by the Jordanian government to have been organized by Egypt.

On 14 February 1958 Jordan agreed to join Iraq in the Arab Federation, *q.v.*, which became known as the Arab Union, *q.v.*, when the two countries were united on 13 May 1958. After the overthrow of the monarchy in Iraq on 14 July, King Hussein claimed to have succeeded King Faisal as head of state of the Union, but he later agreed that, as from 1 August, the Union had ceased to exist. The Anglo-Jordanian Treaty of March 1948 had been ended by mutual consent in March 1957 so that the last British troops had left in

July of that year. However, in July 1958, King Hussein called for, and was given, the support of British forces to maintain his régime against subversive attempts by the United Arab Republic, and by some Jordanians; these forces left in October 1958.

West Jordan is potentially fertile but eroded; East Jordan, the former Amirate of Transjordan, is a fertile mountainous area. The Jordanian development plans cover such projects as irrigation, food production, exploitation of mineral resources, improvement of communications by the construction of roads, railways, and development of the new port at Akaba, and canalization of the Yarmuk river, a Jordan tributary on the Syria-Jordan frontier. There are also plans to develop the resources of the river Jordan.

Jordan Valley Plan. A scheme proposed in 1953 by the adviser to President Eisenhower on schemes for international development, Eric Johnston, for the unified development of the water resources of the Jordan Valley region. For its execution it would require the co-operation of Israel, Jordan, and the United Arab Republic, but the differences between these states make progress difficult. As a first stage the scheme proposed the digging of a canal from the Yarmuk river (a tributary of the Jordan river on the Syria–Jordan frontier) along the east bank of the Jordan, which would irrigate the five- to eight-mile wide plateau between the foot of the mountainous escarpment and the Jordan river. This area is irrigated only by small streams from the side valleys and by pumping water up from the bed of the Jordan river. If the first stage of the Jordan Valley Plan were carried out this area could support three times as many people. This stage could be executed entirely inside Jordan and would assist in settling the 535,000 Arab refugees there. A second stage would involve the building of a Yarmuk dam partly in Israel and partly in Jordan. A third stage, which the Israeli government is particularly anxious to undertake, would be a diversion of the waters of the river Jordan to facilitate the irrigation of the desert region known as the Negev.

K

Kamerun. The name of a German protectorate on the Gulf of Guinea, south-east of Nigeria, which was conquered by British and French forces during the First World War and divided, by the Milner-Simon Agreement of 1919, into a British sphere (*see* Cameroons, British), and a French sphere (*see* Cameroons, French) which in 1960 became the independent republic of Cameroun, *q.v.*

Kardelj, Edward. Vice-Premier of the Yugoslavian Executive Council since 1948; born in Ljubljana, Slovenia, on 27 January 1910. After qualifying as a teacher in 1928 at the Ljubljana Teachers' College, he studied economics and political science and worked in the then illegal Yugoslav Communist Party, being imprisoned from 1930 to 1932 for his political activities. He was the author of many hundreds of Communist pamphlets. From 1934 to 1937 he lived abroad and visited among other places Moscow and Odessa, where he underwent a training course in the organization of underground movements; on his return to Yugoslavia he spent several years in prison.

After the German invasion in 1941 he helped to organize the Partisan movement in Yugoslavia, and became a member of the headquarters staff of the National Army of Liberation. In November 1943 Kardelj, representing Slovenia, was elected as the first Vice-President of the new National Liberation Committee, and on 2 March 1945 became Vice-Premier of Yugoslavia, Minister for the Constitution (which he largely drafted), and President of the Control Commission, holding the two latter posts till 31 August 1948, when he became Foreign Minister. He had already represented his country many times at United Nations and other international conferences. He is a leading Communist theorist, having written a number of books on Yugoslavian international and domestic policy, and has been described as the chief political architect of the new Yugoslavia. He was in frequent touch with Russian Communist leaders until Yugoslavia's secession from the Cominform, *q.v.*, in 1948, and is one of the few non-Russians ever to be honoured with the Order of Lenin. Kardelj has often been mentioned as a likely successor to Marshal Tito, who is twenty years his senior.

Kashmir. The most northerly state of British India, area 84,471 sq. m.; population (1941 census) 4,021,616, of whom all except 880,000 are Moslems; capital Srinagar. Most of the 807,000 Hindus live in the Jammu district, and in deference to them the state is known throughout India as Jammu and Kashmir. After the partition of India in 1947 the Maharajah, Sir Hari Singh, who was himself a Hindu, announced the accession of Kashmir to the Republic of India, a decision unacceptable to Pakistan in view of the large numbers of Moslems in the state. Fighting broke out between Hindus and Moslem tribesmen, and both India and Pakistan moved in troops. In December 1947 the Indian government, alleging armed intervention in the state by Pakistan, referred the dispute to the Security Council. A Peace Commission was set up and on 26 July 1949 a cease-fire line was agreed, but the Indian government rejected the

Commission's suggestion to appoint an arbitrator whose decision would be binding on both sides, lest this should involve a plebiscite the result of which would undoubtedly favour Pakistan. On five occasions between 1948 and 1957 the Security Council passed resolutions urging that a plebiscite should be held in Kashmir to determine its future status; India's refusal to agree has so far rendered them unenforceable.

The government of Kashmir, headed by Sheikh Abdullah, the leader of the National Conference from 1947 until 1953 when he was imprisoned and replaced by Bakshi Ghulam Mohammed, resisted integration with the Indian Union until 26 January 1957 when the state was incorporated, in spite of U.N. protests, into the Republic of India. In 1951 the Maharajah left Kashmir, a republic was proclaimed and the Maharajah's son, Karan Singh, was elected as Sadar-i-Ryasat, or head of state. In spite of the Kashmiri demand for autonomy India has spent considerable sums on the development of its communications with the south-east part of the state. Roads and schools have been built, hydro-electric projects begun and land redistribution carried out. This is in sharp contrast to the policy pursued in Azad Kashmir, the north-west area occupied by Pakistan, in which there is increasing poverty and economic stagnation as well as political repression. Indian intransigence over Kashmir is now a matter of prestige aggravated by the fact that Jawaharlal Nehru, *q.v.*, the Indian Prime Minister, is himself a Kashmiri. For Pakistan the issue is of far greater importance; Indian control of Kashmir would put the entire economy of West Pakistan at India's mercy since the three rivers allocated to Pakistan in 1960 under the agreed settlement of the canal waters dispute, *q.v.*, flow through, or rise in, Kashmir.

Kellogg Pact. Officially called a General Pact for the Renunciation of War, it was a treaty concluded by nine powers on 27 August 1928 on the initiative of Frank B. Kellogg, then U.S. Secretary of State, and by 1930 adopted by nearly all the nations in the world, by which war was condemned as an instrument for settling international disputes. The nine original signatories were Belgium, Czechoslovakia, France, Germany, Italy, Japan, Poland, the U.K., and the U.S.A. Although the signatories agreed that settlement of disputes should be achieved only by pacific means, there was no provision for the enforcement of this obligation or for consultation among the signatories in the event of a breach of the pact.

Kennedy, John Fitzgerald. Inaugurated as President of the U.S.A. in January 1961; born 29 May 1917 in Boston, Massachusetts, son of

John Kennedy, a former Ambassador to the U.K. and highly successful business man of Irish extraction; he is a Roman Catholic. He graduated from Harvard University in 1940 and in the Second World War served in the U.S. Navy, earning renown in 1943 when he saved the lives of his crew members after his motor torpedo vessel had been run down and sunk by a Japanese destroyer. He was then invalided out of the Navy, and after working as a journalist for the International News Service he was elected as a Democrat to the House of Representatives in 1946, being re-elected in 1948 and 1950. In 1952 he defeated Henry Cabot Lodge in a contest for a seat in the Senate, and in November 1960 he defeated Richard Nixon in the Presidential election by a narrow margin.

Kenya. A colony and protectorate in British East Africa; area 224,960 sq. m.; population (1959) 6,450,000, including 6,170,000 Africans, 207,000 Asians and 66,400 Europeans; capital Nairobi. Kenya is economically dependent on its agricultural products (especially coffee, tea, sisal, maize, hides, and skins); the Royal Commission on East Africa reported in 1955 that increased agricultural productivity was essential and could be achieved by substituting private ownership for the customary African system of tribal ownership, by the use of fertilizers, crop specialization, and mechanization, and by the construction of more roads and railways. The Commission said that the fear of over-population might prove to be unjustified, and that the anticipated economic development might require an even larger population. There are scarcely any minerals, and the basic problem of the government has been described by Lord Howick, a former Governor, as being the maintenance of the fertility of the land, and the attraction of capital, so as to develop work for an expanding population in manufacturing industry, in both African and European farming, and in forestry.

For some time the structure of government was influenced by the need for strong measures against the Mau Mau, *q.v.* In 1954 a multi-racial Council of Ministers was set up at the instigation of the British Colonial Secretary who persuaded all concerned to enter into a 'standstill agreement' by which the Council should deal with the emergency and not occupy itself with the common electoral roll, multi-racial schools, and the policy for land owned by Europeans, until 1960. The success of the operations against the Mau Mau was followed by strong pressure for reform from the African leaders, and the British government decided that it was impracticable to postpone all change until 1960. In November 1957, after discussions in Nairobi with all parties, the British Colonial Secretary proposed (1) the establishment of a Council of State, with defined powers of delay, revision and reference; (2) an increase in the number of elected African members on the Legislative Council from 8 to 14 (the same number as that held by the elected European members); and (3) 12 new elective non-government seats, divided equally between Europeans, Africans and Asians, the members to be elected by the Legislative Council. The 8 African members opposed the scheme on the ground that the Europeans would continue to be dominant, but the proposals were adopted by the Legislative Council in January 1958. However, the electoral law was eventually amended, the Legislative Council elected in January and February 1961 comprising 65 elected members, i.e. 53 elected on a common roll and 12 national members elected by the other 53.

The Kenya African National Union (K.A.N.U.) (16 seats at the 1961 elections) was the first nation-wide African party to arise since the Kenya African Union, led by Jomo Kenyatta, *q.v.*, was proscribed in 1953, when a ban was imposed on national parties. Its leaders include James Samuel Gichuru and Tom Mboya, *q.v.*, and it has widespread support among Africans, especially those of the Kikuyu tribe. The Kenya African Democratic Union (K.A.D.U.) (10 seats), another African party, has much less influence, while the New Kenya Party (4 seats), led by Michael Blundell, *q.v.*, invites the support of all races, and the United Party has a membership restricted to Europeans who favour continued British control of Kenya.

Kenyatta, Jomo. A Kikuyu born in 1893 near Nairobi and educated at a Scottish Presbyterian Mission School. He worked for some years as a clerk in Nairobi and later for the Kikuyu Independent Schools Association. In 1922 he became General Secretary of the Kenya Central Association, which wanted to recover the lands lost by the Africans under a law, passed in 1921, which made them tenants-at-will and permitted only whites to hold leases. He represented the Kikuyu on several government committees and Royal Commissions and travelled widely, studying at the London School of Economics and Moscow University. In 1938 his book, *Facing Mount Kenya*, one of the first reliable contributions to African ethnography by an African, was published. When he returned to Kenya in 1946 he continued his work for the Kikuyu Independent Schools Association, and stressed the family unity of Africans and the value of their way of life when compared with that of the whites. In 1947 he became President of the Kenya African Union, which was banned during the emergency in Kenya when it was used as a screen for the activities of the Mau Mau, *q.v.*; as President he demanded for Africans the removal of the colour bar, equal representation in government, higher wages, and a redistribution of land. He was arrested in 1952 and sentenced in 1953 to seven years' imprisonment for assisting in the management of Mau Mau and three years' imprisonment for being a member of a proscribed cult.

Khrushchev, Nikita Sergeyevich. Chairman of the Council of Ministers of the U.S.S.R.; born 17 April 1894 on the Ukrainian border, the son of a mine-worker. After working as a shepherd, and as a locksmith in a Ukrainian factory, he served with the Russian Army in the First World War, then joined the Communist Party and fought with the Red Army during the Russian civil war. After 1921 he worked in the Ukrainian mines and at the same time went to a high school. For a time he directed party work at Kiev and Stalino, and after studying at the Moscow Industrial Academy from 1929 to 1931 he became a district party secretary in Moscow, and later held several other senior posts. In 1935 he became first secretary of the Moscow Regional Committee with responsibility for industrialization which included the building of the Moscow underground railway, for which he received the Order of Lenin. In 1937 he became a member of the Supreme Soviet and in 1938 he was appointed First Secretary of the Communist Party in the Ukraine. From 1941 onwards he organized guerilla warfare in the Ukraine; after the war he supervised the execution of many Ukrainians who were believed to have assisted the Germans, and he helped in the reconstruction of the area. In 1949 he assumed responsibility for Russian agriculture. On the death of Stalin in 1953 he became increasingly important and was appointed First Secretary of the Communist Party (a post held by Stalin for thirty years) in September 1953. At a secret session of the Russian Communist Party Congress in February 1956 he said that Stalin had abused his powers, had permitted loyal Communists to be falsely accused and punished, had failed to prepare for the German invasion, had made blunders in strategy, and had been responsible for the rupture with Yugoslavia in 1948. In March 1958 he replaced Marshal Bulganin as Chairman of the Council of Ministers, while retaining his post as First Secretary of the Communist Party.

Korea. A former kingdom in north-east Asia, for five hundred years a vassal of China. In 1905 it was occupied, and in 1910 annexed, by the Japanese. It has always been of strategic importance to Russia, China, and Japan because its ports are never ice-bound, and coveted for its fertile soil and its mineral wealth – gold, copper, coal, iron, graphite, and tungsten are found in abundance in northern Korea. In 1896, in 1903, and in 1910 Russia entered into secret negotiations with

Japan to divide Korea along the 38th parallel. Russian troops eventually entered Korea on 8 August 1945, immediately after the Russian declaration of war on Japan, and the country was temporarily partitioned, along the 38th parallel, between the U.S.S.R. and the U.S.A. who established zones of occupation. It remains divided into the two states of North Korea, *q.v.*, and South Korea, *q.v.*

Kozlov, Frol Romanovich. Member of the Secretariat of the Central Committee of the Communist Party of the U.S.S.R.; born in 1908 in the village of Loshchinino in the province of Ryazan, the son of a farmer. He went to work in a textile plant at the age of 15 and on becoming a member of the Communist Party in 1926 he went to a workers' school and thereafter to the Leningrad Polytechnic Institute. He worked as an engineer for some years, becoming foreman in a steel factory and in 1939 Communist Party secretary in his factory. In 1944 he moved to Moscow, where he was a full-time Party official, and in 1953 he became head of the Party in the Leningrad area. In June 1957 he was elected to the Presidium of the Central Committee of the Party, and he was a First Vice-Chairman of the Council of Ministers (the other Vice-Chairman being Anastas Mikoyan) from March 1958 to May 1960, when he became one of the ten members of the Secretariat of the Central Committee of the Party.

Kremlin. Russian term meaning citadel, but applied especially to the Moscow citadel occupied by the former Imperial Palace and now the administrative headquarters of the government of the U.S.S.R.

Kuomintang. A Chinese nationalist party founded in 1891 by Sun Yat Sen. It was active in the first Chinese revolution of 1911 and led the second revolution in 1912 against Marshal Yuan Shi-kai; it dominated south China by 1930 and conducted China's defence against the Japanese invasion from 1937 until 1945. Under the leadership of Chiang Kai-shek, *q.v.*, who succeeded Sun Yat Sen in 1925, the party subordinated its political and social ideals to the achievement of military victory. In 1946 Sun Fo, the son of Sun Yat Sen, deplored its departure from the principles of political democracy and the welfare of the people on which his father had founded the Kuomintang. In 1948 the Communist Party replaced the Kuomintang as the governing party of China. Chiang Kai-shek and his followers were driven from the mainland to Formosa, *q.v.*

Kuwait. Sheikhdom at the north-western end of the Persian Gulf; area 5,800 sq. m., mostly desert; population (1957 census) 206,177; capital Kuwait. It is an independent state but under a treaty of 1899 (concluded by the Sheikh to obtain protection from Turkey) the U.K. is responsible for foreign relations. The source of four fifths of its revenues is oil, found in southern Kuwait and also in the Neutral Zone farther south, an area delineated by treaty in 1922 and in which the Sheikh shares an undivided half-interest with Saudi Arabia both as to sovereignty and as to oil. In Kuwait itself the oil concession (granted in 1934 for seventy-five years) is held by the Kuwait Oil Co., in which the British Petroleum and Gulf Exploration Companies hold equal shares. Production, which began in 1946, reached 37 million tons in 1952 and 60 million tons in 1956. By a 1951 agreement the Sheikh receives personally one half of the profits. A very large oilfield was discovered in northern Kuwait, near the Iraq border, in 1956. Much of the profits have been used to provide social services, a development scheme, power stations, the world's largest sea-water distillation plant, roads in and around Kuwait town, free education and a number of excellently built schools, and a hospital and sanatorium. In the Neutral Zone, where oil was discovered in 1953, the oil concession is held, as to the Kuwaiti share, by the American Independent Oil Company. The Saudi Arabian share was held by the Arabian American Oil Company till 1948 but given up by them to the Saudi Arabian government in exchange for undersea rights. It is now held by the Pacific Western Oil Corporation. Oil goes by pipe from the Neutral Zone to Kuwait proper, but production is expanding and a pipe is planned to the coast of the Neutral Zone itself. The Kuwaiti concession to the American Independent Oil Company does not include offshore rights in the Neutral Zone. These were the subject of an agreement in May 1958 with a Japanese consortium which promised to pay Kuwait fifty-seven per cent of the profits. The increasing importance of the Neutral Zone may produce tension between Kuwait and Saudi Arabia on problems such as policing, taxation, and general responsibility for the area. The ruler since 1950 has been Sheikh Abdulla al Salim al Sabah (born 1895), a member of the dynasty which has been in power since 1756.

L

Labour Management Relations Act, 1947. *See* Taft-Hartley Act.

Labour Party. A British political party; it obtained 12,216,166 out of 27,863,738 votes cast at the 1959 General Election and 258 out of 630 seats in the House of Commons. In 1892 the first Labour members, John Burns and Keir Hardie, were elected to the House of Commons, with 13 Liberal-Labour members. In 1900 the Trades Union Congress, *q.v.*, the Independent Labour Party, the Fabian Society and the Social Democratic Federation formed the Labour

Representation Committee, comprising 7 trade unionists, 2 members of the I.L.P., 1 member of the Fabian Society, and 2 members of the S.D.F., to establish a Labour group in Parliament. In 1906 the L.R.C. became known as the Labour Party, and in 1922 it replaced the Liberal Party as one of the two major British parties. In 1924 and in 1929 it formed a government, but on each occasion it was in a minority in the House of Commons and was unable to introduce radical legislation. In 1945 it obtained an overwhelming majority; it nationalized the coal, electricity, gas, steel, and transport industries, introduced a national health service and a comprehensive scheme of national insurance and national industrial injuries insurance, and encouraged the emergence as independent countries of India, Pakistan, Ceylon, and Burma. After losing 81 seats but retaining its majority in 1950, the Labour Party was defeated at the General Elections of 1951 and 1955.

After the defeat of the Labour Party at the 1955 General Election its National Executive appointed a sub-committee under the chairmanship of Harold Wilson 'to enquire into the general organization of the party'. The sub-committee reported a progressive deterioration of the organization of the party, particularly at constituency level. It said that the organization had been getting worse at a time when the Conservative Party had been becoming more efficient. Apathy, disputes in the party, the absence of sufficient clearly defined differences between the parties and disillusionment with nationalization had all, according to the report, played a part in the defeat and in reducing the numbers and enthusiasm of the party workers available.

The administrative organ of the British Labour Party is the National Executive, which is elected annually by the annual conference. The conference is composed of delegates from the constituency parties, the trade unions, and Socialist, co-operative, and professional organizations. The National Executive consists of the leader and the deputy leader of the Parliamentary Labour Party, the party treasurer, seven constituency members, one representative of the socialist, co-operative and professional organizations, five women members and twelve trade union representatives. The trade unions provide over seventy-five per cent of the Labour Party's income. The conference can decide the Labour Party's election policy. The leader of the Parliamentary Labour Party, who is the the effective leader of the Labour Party as a whole, the Chairmanship of the National Executive being only a courtesy appointment for one year, is Hugh Gaitskell, *q.v.*, who was elected in December 1955; he replaced Earl Attlee, *q.v.*, who had been the leader since 1935. Other leading figures in the Labour Party are George Brown, *q.v.*, James Callaghan, *q.v.*, Richard Crossman, *q.v.*, James Griffiths, *q.v.*, and Harold Wilson, *q.v.*

Land Reform. A redistribution of land among, or a reduction of the rent of land to, those who farm it. Since 1945 all the progressive parties of Asia have included land reform in their social policy and several Asian governments have undertaken programmes of land reform. In China it has taken the form of expropriation and free redistribution; in Kashmir all who farm more than $22\frac{1}{2}$ acres have had to yield the excess to the man who tills it: the Indian State governments have acquired land, compulsorily but with compensation, from the *zamindars* (landlords) and have rented out plots to peasants under a *ryotwari* system which enables the farmer to hold his land directly from the state. In South Korea the peasants have been encouraged to become freeholders and to purchase land previously owned by the Japanese in grain, the total price being three times the annual yield. Land reform has been possible only in countries from which foreign landowners have been recently expelled, as in Korea, or in which the landowning class has been overthrown by the workers or by the army, as in China. Where the landowner retains powerful domestic influence, as in the case of the Roman Catholic Church in Italy, land reform, in the sense here described, has not taken place. Latin American countries which have undertaken land reform include Mexico (1910), Bolivia (1952), and Cuba (1959).

Laos. An independent state, formerly of the French Union, *q.v.*, predominantly Buddhist, situated in north-west Indo-China; area 90,000 sq. m.; royal capital Luang Prabang; old French administrative capital Vientiane; population approximately 2,000,000 of whom more than two thirds are of Laotian origin. The country is unproductive and mountainous and has poor communications with the rest of Indo-China, and the peasantry are among the most primitive in Asia. It became a French protectorate in 1893 and an Associate State of the French Union in 1949. The Geneva Agreements of 1954 recognized Laos' freedom to enlist foreign military aid (other than French) for its own protection.

From 1904 to 1954 the French governed through King Somdet Prachao Sisavong Vong (1885–1959) who maintained a strong private army of 10,000 men. A Free Laotian movement, the Lao Issarak, was founded in 1940 to end French rule. Three of its members, the Princes Petsarath, Souvanna Phouma, and Souphanou Vong, formed a government early in 1945 under Japanese protection.

This was dissolved as soon as the French returned in 1946 and Petsarath and Souvanna Phouma fled to Thailand while Souphanou Vong rejoined the underground Lao Issarak. With the declaration of independence in 1949 Souvanna Phouma returned to lead a new government. The Lao Issarak then split; several of its older members supported the government and the rump, led by Souphanou Vong, was renamed Pathet Lao. At the end of 1950 it established contact with the Viet-Minh, with whom it collaborated in the invasion of Laos in 1953. At Geneva the authority of the Pathet Lao over the northern provinces of Phong Saly and Sam Neua was recognized until such times as elections could be held for the whole country. After July 1954 these two permitted enclaves became extended by more than 13,000 sq. m. of territory seized in violation of the Agreements, but in 1956 they were yielded to the government. In October 1957 Souvanna Phouma and Souphanou Vong (his half-brother) agreed that there should be: (1) immediate cessation of hostilities; (2) restoration of the government's authority over the two northern provinces; and (3) the granting of civil rights to Pathet Lao followers. In November 1957 two Pathet Lao representatives joined the cabinet.

The situation deteriorated in 1959 as armed forces from North Viet-Nam gave their support to dissident elements in the frontier areas. In August 1960 Souvanna Phouma formed a neutralist government and thereupon made further attempts to come to terms with the Pathet Lao, which continued to be led by his half-brother, Souphanou Vong. Souvanna Phouma took refuge in Cambodia in December 1960 and was succeeded as Prime Minister by the right-wing Prince Boun Oum, who received strong support from the U.S.A.

The King is the head of state and the supreme religious authority. Tiao Savang Vatthana became King on 29 October 1959, upon the death of his father. The legislature is the National Assembly, elected every four years by indirect universal suffrage. The results of the General Election held on 25 December 1955, as supplemented by elections held on 5 May 1958, were: Laotian People's Rally 36; Neo Lao Hak Sat 9; Unionists 2; Peace Party 7; Democrats 3; unaffiliated 2.

Latvia. One of the fifteen constituent Republics of the Union of Soviet Socialist Republics since 1940; area 25,200 sq. m.; population (1959) 2,094,000; capital Riga. The Republic, which is situated between Estonia and Lithuania on the Baltic Sea, was ruled by foreigners, including Germans, Poles, Danes, Swedes, and Russians for hundreds of years, and was a province of the Russian Empire when it proclaimed independence in April 1918. The large estates of the German 'Baltic Barons' were broken up and redistributed to the peasants. As an independent state Latvia had highly developed chemical, engineering, shipbuilding, textile, and wood-working industries, but there were also many cattle-breeders and dairy-farmers. The democratic constitution was suspended in May 1934 largely as a result of the world economic crisis which damaged the Latvian economy; all political parties were dissolved and government passed into the hands of a conservative, agrarian, and nationalist group. Under an agreement between the U.S.S.R. and Germany, made on 23 August 1939, Latvia was occupied by the U.S.S.R. in June 1940, and became a constituent Republic on 5 August 1940. Many Latvians were deported to camps east of the Ural Mountains. The U.S.S.R. ordered the redistribution of land to those with no land or only very small holdings, and nationalized most of the industrial enterprises. There are valuable deposits of gypsum, peat, and soft coal. Forests occupy twenty per cent of the whole area. There are two strategically important ice-free ports, Liepāja (Libau), which is used by the U.S.S.R. as a naval base and from which commercial shipping has been excluded, and Ventspils (Windau).

League of Nations. An international organization established in 1920 under a Covenant of twenty-six articles forming part of the Versailles Treaty, *q.v.*, which was concluded after the First World War. It came to an end in 1946 when the United Nations, *q.v.*, was founded. The formation of the League was Point 14 of President Wilson's Fourteen Points, but the U.S. Congress refused to ratify the Versailles Treaty and to join the League. The League Covenant bound the members to respect and to preserve against aggression their independence and territorial integrity and not to employ force for the settlement of a dispute until they had first submitted it to the League or to arbitrators; if the League or the arbitrators failed to reach a unanimous decision within six months, the disputing nations could go to war only after an additional delay of three months. Sanctions could be applied against any country committing aggression in breach of the Covenant. The League Assembly met annually and the League Council (of fifteen members, including France, the U.K., and the U.S.S.R. as permanent members) three times a year. Decisions had to be by a unanimous vote.

The objects of the League of Nations were fundamentally the same as those expressed in the Covenant and Charter of the United Nations, although the Charter avoids the use of League of Nations terms which might have unfortunate associations. The expressions Security

Council, General Assembly, and Trusteeship were all new. Under the League one power (the U.S.A.) refused to join, one (the U.S.S.R.) was ostracized by the others, two (France and the U.K.) gave half-hearted support, and three (Germany, Italy, and Japan) ignored their responsibilities. So far all these faults have been absent from the United Nations, although the exclusion of Germany clearly makes it impossible to say whether it would discharge its duties as a member.

A fundamental difference between the two organizations lies in the methods of dealing with threats to security. In spite of the unanimity rule in the Covenant, the effectiveness of the League depended not on the ability of its organs to reach decisions, but on the individual members' observance of their obligations under the Covenant. No decision or lack of a decision could alter these obligations. Under the United Nations Charter the Security Council has the primary responsibility of maintaining peace, and a decision is necessary if the machinery is to be put into operation at all. To enable the organization to reach decisions the principle of majority voting has been accepted, but the price of that advance, demanded by the major powers, has been the veto, *q.v.*

Lebanon. An independent state on the eastern Mediterranean; area 3,400 sq. m.; population about 1,450,000, half of whom are Christians, the rest being Moslems and Druses. About eleven per cent of the population are Arab refugees from Palestine. The capital is Beirut. Lebanon was part of the Ottoman Empire until its capture in 1918 by the U.K. with French and Arab help; France became the mandatory power under the League of Nations in 1920. As the French in Syria favoured Vichy France, *q.v.*, and could not be trusted to resist German penetration, British troops fought and removed the French garrison in 1941. The independence of Lebanon was declared on 26 November 1941, both the U.K. and the Free French forces agreeing to this step, and the first President of the independent republic was elected in 1943. All foreign troops departed by December 1946.

Fruit, tobacco, silk and cotton are produced, and gold and precious metals are mined. Only twenty-six per cent of the area is cultivated. The country is not wealthy, and about 500,000 have emigrated to the U.S.A., 250,000 to Brazil, and 150,000 to Argentina. There is a transit trade in crude oil, Lebanon being the terminal for the pipe-lines of the Iraq Petroleum Company which has refineries at Tripoli and Sidon, and the Trans-Arabian Pipeline Company, also with a refinery at Sidon. A 1943 customs union with Syria came to an end in 1950.

The Constitution creates a delicate balance of power between the Christians and the Moslems, who may now comprise a majority of the population. There is a President who appoints a Prime Minister and a Cabinet; there is also a unicameral legislature elected by universal adult suffrage. Conventionally, the President is a Maronite Christian, the Prime Minister a Sunni Moslem, and the Speaker a Shia Moslem. The electoral law is designed to produce a legislature representing the sects in proportion to their strengths. The 99 deputies elected in June and July 1960 consisted of: Maronite Christians (a sect in communion with Rome, and to which approximately 424,000 people belong) 30 seats, Sunni Moslems 20, Shia Moslems 19, Greek Orthodox 11, Uniate Greek 6, Druses 6, Armenian Orthodox 4, Uniate Armenian 1, others 2. Attempts to create national, rather than religious, parties have been largely unsuccessful, although in 1947 the Druse leader, Kemal Jumblatt, formed the Progressive Socialist Party. There are political as well as religious divisions in the legislature; thus the 99 members include 11 members of the moderate Moslem group, Rashid Karami; 7 members of the Christian, Pan-Arabic, Constitutional Party; 7 members of the Ahmed El-Assaad group (southern Moslems); 6 Falangists; 6 National Bloc members; 5 Progressive Socialists; and 5 National Liberals (led by Chamoun).

Camille Chamoun was elected President on 23 September 1952 for a six-year term. The President, by the Constitution, is not eligible for immediate re-election. Moslem and Druse discontent, already considerable because they felt themselves to be dominated by the Christians and because they were receiving moral, financial and military support from the United Arab Republic, increased when it was understood that Chamoun wanted a second term as President. Moreover, not only the Moslems and Druses, but also a number of Christians of various sects (including the Maronite Patriarch) had for some time been opposed to the pro-western orientation of the government's foreign policy, and its association with the Eisenhower Doctrine, *q.v.* Attempts in April 1958 to amend the Constitution to permit Chamoun's re-election were followed by clashes between government and Druse forces.

A United Nations observation group reported in July that the extent of the infiltration of men and arms from Syria (one of the two regions of the United Arab Republic) could not be easily determined because both countries had for many years ignored the frontier. Chamoun then announced his intention not to seek a second term, but he also appealed for military aid as a result of which U.S. forces were in Lebanon from July to October 1958. With the active help of

U.S. diplomats, who sought to bring the various sects together, General Fuad Chehab (born 1902), a Maronite Christian who had been educated at the French Academy of St Cyr, was elected President by the legislature with the necessary two-thirds majority.

Lebensraum. A German word meaning 'living-space', and a slogan adopted by German nationalists, particularly between 1933 and 1945. The word was used with reference to: (1) Germany's alleged over-population and its consequent need to acquire more territory, so that it could produce all its own food; (2) Germany's claim to bring certain neighbouring zones, particularly in eastern Europe, within its sphere of influence.

Legitimists. Monarchists who advocate the return of the head of a deposed dynasty whose claim is based on direct descent. The term is used especially with reference to the Habsburg followers of Archduke Otto, son of the last Emperor of Austria-Hungary.

Lemass, Séan F. Irish politician; born 26 December 1890; he took part in the rising against the British in 1916 and was for many years a member of the Irish Republican Army. He was Minister for Industry and Commerce from 1932 to 1939 and 1941 to 1948, Minister for Supplies from 1939 to 1945, and became Minister for Industry and Commerce again in 1951. As a leading member of the Fianna Fáil party, he was a natural choice as successor to de Valera, who retired from the post of Prime Minister, or Taoiseach, in June 1959.

Liberal Party. A British political party; it obtained 1,640,761 out of 27,863,738 votes cast at the 1959 General Election and 6 out of 630 seats in the House of Commons. It is the successor to the Whig Party of the eighteenth and nineteenth centuries and was one of the two major British political parties until it was supplanted by the Labour Party at the 1922 General Election. It is a moderately progressive party. It advocates co-ownership in industry to end the conflict between capital and labour, protection of individual liberties, a reform of the electoral system, separate Parliamentary Assemblies for Scotland and Wales, more school building, an international agreement on atomic energy, and strict measures to prevent the growth of monopolies. In 1956 Joseph Grimond, *q.v.*, M.P. for Orkney and Shetland, became the leader of the Parliamentary Liberal Party.

Liberia. An independent West African state between Sierra Leone and the Ivory Coast; area 43,000 sq. m.; population approximately 2,500,000 Africans of whom over 12,000 are Negroes of U.S. origin; capital Monrovia, a free port; official language English. Liberia was founded in 1820 by the philanthropic American Colonization Society as a country for freed slaves from the U.S.A., and became an independent republic in 1847. Executive power is vested in a President elected for eight years and eligible for further periods of four years, and his cabinet. The constitution, modelled on that of the U.S.A., provides for a legislature comprising a Senate of ten elected for six years, and a House of Representatives of thirty-one elected for four years. The political parties are the Independent True Whigs and the True Whigs. Electors must be of Negro blood and landowners; women can also vote if so qualified. Liberia exports crude rubber, high-grade ores, gold, palm kernels, and palm oil. In the Second World War it allowed the U.S.A. to construct airports, but all U.S. forces left the country after the war. Under the Point Four programme $30,000,000 was spent by a joint U.S.-Liberian Commission on development in the years 1950–5. There has also been technical help, a loan from the Export-Import Bank for road construction, and U.N.E.S.C.O. aid for scientific education.

Libya. An independent state in North Africa, comprising the provinces of Cyrenaica, the Fezzan, and Tripolitania; area 679,358 sq. m., mostly consisting of barren deserts; population (1954 census) 1,091,830, mostly Arabs, with some Berbers in the west, African Negroes in the Fezzan, some Jews, and an Italian minority in Tripolitania; official religion Islam and official language Arabic; capitals Tripoli and Benghazi. From the sixteenth century the land was ruled by the Turks; in a secret agreement of 1900 the French, who already controlled Tunisia, undertook not to oppose Italian claims in Libya, while Italy promised France a free hand in Morocco. Accordingly, in 1912, France established its protectorate over Morocco, and Italy annexed Libya after the Turco-Italian War of 1911–12. Under Italian rule there was considerable migration from Italy to Libya, road construction and agricultural improvement, all of which met with strong local resistance, particularly among the Senussi tribesmen of Cyrenaica.

In 1942 the U.K. gave a pledge that the Senussi would never again be subjected to Italian rule, but after the defeat of Italy in the Second World War there was considerable disagreement among the victorious powers as to the fate of Libya. France advocated Italian trusteeship, feeling the need of a companion in its own position. The U.S.S.R. also advocated Italian trusteeship, hoping in this way to win support for the Communists in the Italian elections. On 21 November 1949 the United Nations General Assembly resolved that Libya should become independent, and this was achieved on 24 December 1951. Mohammed Idris el Mahdi el Senussi, Emir of Cyrenaica, leader of the Senussi religious sect since 1916 and exiled since 1922, became King Idris I.

Libya is a constitutional monarchy with a Council of Ministers and a bicameral legislature comprising a Senate (24 members, 8 from each Province, serving a term of eight years, half nominated by the King and half by the Provincial Legislative Councils), and a House of Representatives (55 members, 35 from Tripolitania, 15 from Cyrenaica, 5 from the Fezzan, with elections every four years).

Technical and financial help has been essential to prevent Libya from reverting to its former primitive pastoral economy, and by a treaty of alliance and friendship signed on 30 July 1953 the U.K. promised financial aid for twenty years, including £5,000,000 for economic development and £13,750,000 for balancing the budget over the first five years of that period. At the end of the five-year period the U.K. increased the annual sum for balancing the budget from £2,750,000 to £3,250,000. The responsibility for assistance in economic development was taken over by the U.S.A., which agreed to pay $5,500,000 annually, quite apart from any other aid provided under special agreements. In return Libya permits the U.S.A. and the U.K. to maintain military bases.

An additional problem for the Libyan government is the difference of outlook between Tripolitania, which traditionally looks westwards and was not reluctant to accept Italian rule, and Cyrenaica, which feels itself to be part of the Middle East, and where the Italians were bitterly disliked. Although concerned to unite his kingdom, Idris I is, at heart, a Cyrenaican.

Liechtenstein. An independent state on the Upper Rhine between Austria and Switzerland; area 62 sq. m.; population (1955) 14,757; language German; capital Vaduz. The principality, which has one town and ten villages, was formerly part of the Holy Roman Empire, achieving complete independence in 1806. It has a customs union with Switzerland, and the currency is Swiss. Under the 1921 Constitution the legislature is a Diet of fifteen members elected for four years by universal suffrage and proportional representation. Prince Franz Josef II (born 1906) became head of state in 1938. There is no army.

Liquidation. Literally the winding up of the affairs of a company and its termination as a legal entity. The term is used also to describe the removal of people for political reasons, usually by execution but sometimes by imprisonment in an unknown place. In recent years the Communists in China and the French authorities in North Africa have been euphemistically described as having 'liquidated' many who opposed their régimes.

Lithuania. One of the fifteen constituent Republics of the Union of
Soviet Socialist Republics since 1940; area about 25,500 sq. m.;
population (1959) approximately 2,700,000 of whom about 2,000,000
are Roman Catholics; capital Vilnius (Vilna). The Republic, which is
on the Baltic Sea, was a great power in the fourteenth and fifteenth
centuries with territories stretching to the Black Sea, but was a
province of the Russian Empire when it recovered its independence
in 1918. Poland seized the capital, then called Vilna, in 1920. Quarrels
with Poland over Vilna and with Germany over Memel (a seaport
detached from Germany in 1919 and made a free city to give
Lithuania a port on the Baltic Sea but seized by the Lithuanians
in 1923) were the main preoccupation of Lithuanian foreign ministers between the two World Wars. A benevolent dictatorship was
overthrown in 1926 and the parliamentary constitution ignored by
the conservative and agrarian Nationalist Union Party which allowed
no opposition at all. In March 1939 Germany re-annexed Memel after
local elections in which the German Party had secured eighty-seven
per cent of the vote, but Lithuania was granted a free zone in the
port. The U.S.S.R. restored Vilna to Lithuania in 1939 after it had
invaded Poland, but manned the town with a Russian garrison. Under
an agreement between the U.S.S.R. and Germany made on 23 August
1939, Lithuania was occupied by the U.S.S.R. in June 1940, and
became a constituent Republic on 3 August 1940. Large numbers of
Lithuanians and Poles were deported to the east. The chief industries
are agriculture and forestry; forests occupy sixteen per cent of the
whole area. There were distributions of land to the landless and to
smallholders in 1940 and 1944.

Little Ruhr. A term used to describe an area in eastern Europe similar
to the concentration of industry around the river Ruhr in western
Europe. It is an area which produces coal and steel, comprising the
Moravská Ostrava coalfield of Czechoslovakia, Upper Silesia (for-
merly part of Germany but awarded to Poland under the Potsdam
and Yalta agreements) and the district between Krakow and
Czestochowa, in Poland. It is exploited not by the two nations
separately but as an economic unit, thus resembling the European
Coal and Steel Community, *q.v.*, and its development is linked to the
Russian industrial plan.

Liu Shao-chi. A leading Chinese Communist; the Chairman since
27 April 1959 of the People's Republic of China; born 1905. In 1921
he joined the Socialist Youth Group; in 1922 he became a member of
the Secretariat of the China Labour Union, and he has led the Chinese
Revolutionary Trade Union Movement since 1927. He worked under-

ground as a trade union leader from 1927 to 1932 and led the Workers' Movement in Kiangsi (where Mao Tse-tung, *q.v.*, had set up a soviet government) from 1932 to 1935. At the age of thirty he led a students' movement against Japanese aggression, and he was Secretary of the North China and Central China Bureaux of the Communist Central Committee from 1936 to 1942, becoming a member of the Secretariat of the Central Committee and a Vice-Chairman of the People's Revolutionary Military Council in 1943. He is also Chairman of the International Labour Federation, and has been Vice-Chairman of the People's Political Consultative Council. As his record shows, he is an important figure in Chinese trade union affairs; he is also considered to be one of the Chinese Communist Party's leading theorists and among its most influential members.

Lloyd, John Selwyn Brooke. British Conservative Party politician; born 28 July 1904 in Liverpool and educated at Magdalene College, Cambridge. He was a Liberal until the age of twenty-seven, when he joined the Conservative Party. He practised law in Liverpool and was active in local government until the outbreak of the Second World War, during which he became a Brigadier. He was elected to the House of Commons to represent a Cheshire constituency in 1945 and helped R. A. Butler to plan the policy of the Conservative Party which was then in opposition. After becoming Minister of State in 1951 he represented the U.K. for three years at the United Nations. Sir Anthony Eden appointed him successively as Minister of Defence in April 1955 and Foreign Secretary in December 1955; he became Chancellor of the Exchequer in July 1960.

Lobbying (originally a U.S. expression). Persuading members of a legislature to support or oppose a Bill by means of personal contacts, especially in the 'lobbies' or parts of a legislative building to which the public has access. Reference is frequently made in the U.S.A. to the China Lobby (advocating support of Chiang Kai-shek), and to the Farmers' Lobby (advocating higher federal subsidies for agricultural interests).

Locarno Treaty. An agreement concluded between Belgium, France, Germany, Italy, and the U.K. on 16 November 1925, by which Belgium, France, and Germany undertook to maintain their frontiers as they then were and to abstain from the use of force against each other. Germany recognized the status of the Rhineland, which had been demilitarized in perpetuity by the peace treaties after the First World War. Italy and the U.K. guaranteed the Treaty, and there were provisions for mutual assistance in the event of its breach. The Treaty was brought to an end by Germany in 1936 when Adolf Hitler sent German troops into the Rhineland. In 1953 Sir Winston Churchill, then Prime Minister of the U.K., proposed a new agreement between the German Federal Republic, Poland, the U.K., the U.S.S.R., and others, by which the eastern European frontiers established after the Second World War could be guaranteed in a manner similar to that adopted in the Treaty of Locarno.

Lodge, Henry Cabot. U.S. Republican politician; born 5 July 1902 in Massachusetts, the grandson of a Senator of the same name who opposed U.S. ratification of the Covenant of the League of Nations, *q.v.* After graduating from Harvard University he became a reporter on the *Boston Transcript* in 1923, and on the *New York Herald Tribune* in 1924, specializing in international affairs. From 1923 to 1936 he was a Republican district representative in the lower house of the Massachusetts State legislature, and represented Massachusetts in the U.S. Senate from 1936 to 1944. His election in 1936 represented the only Republican gain in that year's Senatorial elections; he supported parts of President Roosevelt's New Deal, *q.v.*, but agreed with the Isolationists, *q.v.*, in foreign policy. In 1942 he served with British Eighth Army tank units in Libya; on being refused further permission to serve while still a Senator, he resigned from the Senate in 1944 and saw active service in France, Germany, and Italy. In 1946 he supported the establishment of the United Nations, was re-elected to the Senate and became a member of the Senate Foreign Relations Committee. He was sent by President Truman as an alternate delegate to the United Nations General Assembly in 1950 and was manager of the 'Draft Eisenhower for President' Movement in 1952, in which year he was defeated when submitting himself for re-election to the Senate. President Eisenhower appointed him Chief Liaison Officer on all government matters (except the Budget) in November 1952. In January 1953 he became U.S. representative to the United Nations, carrying the rank of Ambassador. In November 1960 he was the unsuccessful Republican Vice-Presidential candidate.

Low Countries. A collective name for Belgium, Luxemburg, and the Netherlands.

Luxemburg. An independent state, and a Grand Duchy, situated between Germany, Belgium, and France; area 1,000 sq. m.: population (1958) 317,853, nearly all Roman Catholics; capital Luxemburg. Most people speak German or Letzeburgesch but the official language is French; they are a Germanic people with a French outlook.

Luxemburg was given to the Orange family (rulers of the Netherlands) in 1815 in compensation for their estates in Nassau, which were handed over to Prussia. In 1890 the King of the Netherlands died and it passed to the Duke of Nassau. It was occupied by Germany in the First World War and in 1921 entered a customs union with Belgium. After being again occupied by Germany in the Second World War it was freed and, with Belgium, entered the customs union of Benelux, q.v., on 29 October 1947. On 28 April 1948 Luxemburg amended its constitution so as to abandon its former neutrality (which had prevailed since 1867) and then joined the Brussels Treaty Organization, q.v., and the North Atlantic Treaty Organization, q.v.

The ruler since 1919 has been Grand Duchess Charlotte (born 1896) and there is a Chamber of 52 Deputies, elected by universal suffrage, general elections for the whole Chamber being held once every five years. In the 1959 elections there were returned 20 Social Christians, and 17 Socialists, 12 Liberals, and 3 Communists. In April 1959 Pierre Werner (Social Christian) became Prime Minister, heading a coalition of Social Christians and Liberals. There is an important steel industry with an annual productive capacity of 3,300,000 tons, giving the country the world's highest output per head; the headquarters of the European Coal and Steel Community, q.v., are in Luxemburg. Since May 1961 the powers of the ruler have been delegated to her son, Prince Jean.

M

McCarthyism. Intolerance of liberalism. Joseph McCarthy (1909–1957), was elected to the U.S. Senate to represent Wisconsin in 1946; in February 1950 he said that there were 205 Communists in the State Department (a figure which he later reduced to 57 and then increased to 81) and subsequently made a number of other attacks on the political and moral integrity of individual government employees. In a large majority of cases his accusations, which were often made at public sessions of Senate sub-committees so that he was protected by the rule of Congressional privilege, were found to have no substance. In December 1954 his colleagues, by a majority of 67 to 22, censured him for bringing the Senate into dishonour and disrepute. His activities, which probably hampered the government in its task of seeking out Russian spies, won the approval of a body of American opinion which suspected most liberals, and even those who tried to be impartial politically, of being sympathetic to the Communist cause.

Macedonia. A region in the centre of the Balkan peninsula which gives its name both to a Greek prefecture and to one of the Federal Republics of Yugoslavia; it has never been a racial, linguistic, or political unit. It was for many years under Turkish rule and, in the latter half of the nineteenth and the early years of the twentieth century, was coveted by Austria-Hungary, Bulgaria, Greece, Russia, and Serbia. The population is a mixture of Serbs, Bulgars, Greeks, Turks, Arnauts, Gipsies, Spanish Jews, and a people called Kutso-Vlakhs.

After the Second Balkan War of 1912–13 Macedonia was partitioned, mainly between Serbia and Greece, although Bulgaria obtained a small area in the east near Strumitza. Thereafter the parts were called South Serbia and North Greece respectively. After the First World War Bulgaria retained a still smaller area, the Petritch district. Approximately 209,000 Macedonians fled to Bulgaria, where they formed an influential political group. A secret organization in Macedonia, the Internal Macedonian Revolutionary Organization (I.M.R.O.), which had been created to fight the Turks, carried on subversive activities against the Yugoslavian government in Macedonia, with support from Bulgaria and at times from Italy. In 1941 Bulgaria occupied Yugoslavian Macedonia and the eastern part of Greek Macedonia, but the Paris Peace Treaty of January 1947 restored the frontier to its pre-1941 limits. The Greek prefecture of Macedonia has a population of approximately 1,800,000, the Yugoslavian Republic of Macedonia has approximately 1,300,000 people, while there are also nearly 300,000 Macedonians across the border in Bulgaria.

Macleod, Iain Norman. British Conservative Party politician; born 11 November 1913; educated at Fettes College and at Gonville and Caius College, Cambridge, where he studied history and captained the University bridge team. After working in the City of London for three years he began to read for the bar in 1938, but with the advent of the Second World War he joined the army, attaining the rank of Major. In 1945 he contested, unsuccessfully, the Scottish parliamentary constituency of Western Isles. He joined the Conservative parliamentary secretariat in 1946 and was head of the Home Affairs Research Department of the Conservative Party from 1948 to 1950. He was elected to the House of Commons as member for Enfield West in 1950, in which year he also became Bridge Editor of a London newspaper, *The Sunday Times*. He then became, successively, Minister of Health in 1952, Minister of Labour in December 1955, and Colonial Secretary in October 1959.

McMahon Correspondence. Eight letters, written between Emir Hussein, Sherif of Mecca, and Sir Henry McMahon, the High Commissioner for Egypt, in 1915 and 1916, which the Arabs regarded as involving a British promise to include at least part of Palestine, *q.v.*, in an Arab state. In the correspondence McMahon agreed that an Arab state should be established as payment to the Arabs for their help to the allied powers in the war against the Turks. Hussein had in July 1915 demanded Arab independence in Arabia, Syria, and Mesopotamia, in an area bounded on the south and east by the Indian Ocean, the Persian Gulf, and the Persian frontier, on the west by the Red Sea and the Mediterranean, and on the north by latitude thirty-seven from Mersina to Persia. McMahon, realizing the urgent need for Arab help, wrote to Hussein on 24 October 1915, stating that the U.K. was prepared 'to recognize and uphold the independence of the Arabs in all the regions lying within the frontiers proposed by the Sherif of Mecca', with the exception of certain areas 'lying to the west of the districts of Damascus, Homs, Hama, and Aleppo', on the ground that they were not purely Arab. The U.K. later claimed that Palestine, which in 1919 was still almost entirely Arab, had been included in this exemption as lying west of Damascus. There was considerable argument as to whether the McMahon undertaking contradicted the Balfour Declaration, q.v. After the First World War only Saudi Arabia, in Arabia proper, became independent; farther north, Iraq, Palestine, and Transjordan were established as British Mandates, and Lebanon and Syria as French Mandates.

Macmillan, Harold. British Prime Minister (since 1957) and Conservative Party politician; born 10 February 1894, educated at Eton. He served during the First World War in the Grenadier Guards, being wounded three times, and was at Balliol College, Oxford, from 1918 to 1919; when he left he became A.D.C. to the Governor-General of Canada, a post which he held until 1920. He contested unsuccessfully the Stockton-on-Tees Parliamentary Division in 1923, but later served as M.P. for the Division from 1924 to 1929 and from 1931 to 1945. He was for some time a Director in the family publishing firm of Macmillan and Co. In the years between his election as an M.P. and the outbreak of the Second World War, Macmillan repeatedly attacked the leaders and the doctrines of the Conservative Party. He criticized the party for its foreign as well as for its domestic policy, and temporarily withdrew from the Conservative Parliamentary Party in 1936 in protest against the government's acceptance of the Italian invasion of Ethiopia. He became Parliamentary Secretary to the Ministry of Supply, his first office, when the Churchill government was formed in 1940, and Parliamentary Under-Secretary of State for the Colonies in 1942. From 1942 to 1945 he was Minister Resident at Allied H.Q. in North-West Africa, and helped to negotiate the settlement between the French Generals de Gaulle and Giraud. He became Secretary of State for Air in 1945. At the General Election of that year he lost his parliamentary seat, but won a by-election at Bromley in November 1945. In opposition he did much, with R. A. Butler, to modernize Conservative policy. On the return to power of the Conservatives in 1951, he became Minister of Housing and Local Government. The number of houses built in the United Kingdom in 1950 was 205,000. A resolution passed by the Conservative Party Conference, against the advice of the leadership, set an annual target of 300,000 houses, which was attained during Macmillan's Ministry, and in 1954 354,000 houses were built. He was Minister of Defence from 1954 to 1955, and Foreign Secretary from May to December 1955 when he succeeded R. A. Butler as Chancellor of the Exchequer. He became Prime Minister in January 1957 after the resignation of Sir Anthony Eden.

Madagascar. An island, off the east coast of southern Africa, which in 1958 became an independent republic known as the Malagasy Republic, *q.v.*, and one of the member states of the French Community, *q.v.*

Makarios, Archbishop. Ethnarch (church leader) of the Orthodox Church in Cyprus, *q.v.*; born 1913 at Panayia in Cyprus; educated at a village school, at Kykko Monastery, at the Pancyprian gymnasium in Nicosia and at the Athens School of Theology, from which he graduated in 1943. He was ordained as a priest of the Greek Orthodox Church in 1946; with a scholarship awarded by the World Council of Churches he studied at Boston University. He returned to Cyprus when he was elected Bishop of Kitiou and after two years was elected Archbishop. He advocated Enosis (union with Greece) but opinions varied as to the extent of his responsibility for the acts of violence that took place in Cyprus. In March 1956 he was deported to the Seychelles Islands by order of the Governor of Cyprus, who said that Makarios was 'deeply implicated in the campaign of terrorism'. He was released in March 1957, and after the Cyprus settlement had been concluded was elected President, being proclaimed on 14 December 1959. Cyprus became independent on 16 August 1960.

Malagasy Republic. An independent republic; area 227,800 sq. m.; population 5,071,000, nearly all of Asian origin, comprising Merina (or Hova) (1,188,000), Betsimisaraka (728,000), Betsileo (576,000), Tsimihety (350,000), Antaisaka (300,000), Antandroy (280,000), with Arabs, Chinese, French, and Hindus; capital Tananarive. The country is an island 240 miles off the east coast of southern Africa and was originally called Madagascar after being discovered by the Portuguese Diaz in 1500, owing to a confusion with the Kingdom of Mogadishu on the north-eastern coast of Africa. France controlled the island from 1885 until it achieved self-government within the French Community, *q.v.*, on 14 October 1958, followed by complete independence, still within the Community, on 4 April 1960.

Legislative powers are vested in two bodies: the National Assembly of 90 members elected by universal suffrage every five years, and the Senate of 37 members who serve for six years and are appointed partly by representatives of local authorities and partly by the government itself. The principal political parties are the Social Democratic Party, led by Philibert Tsiranana (the President of the Republic), and the Malagasy Democratic and Social Union. Executive powers are exercised by the President who is also leader of the government; he is elected for seven years by an electoral college consisting of the National Assembly, the Senate, and representatives of local authorities.

The principal exports are rice, coffee, sugar, groundnuts, sisal, raffia, cloves, vanilla, meat, graphite, and mica; there are also deposits of beryl, columbium, and quartz. Most of the trade is with France.

Malawi. An alternative term, often used by Africans, for Nyasaland, *q.v.*, It is derived from the African Maravi, the old name for the lake area covered now by Nyasaland.

Malaya. A Dominion within the British Commonwealth; area 50,690 sq. m.; population 6,363,853 of whom 2,431,325 are Chinese, about 3,126,000 are Malays, and the rest Indians, Eurasians, and Malayan aboriginal natives; capital Kuala Lumpur. In 1948 it became a federation of the nine states of the Malay peninsula and the two British straits settlements of Penang and Malacca. On 31 August 1957 it became a sovereign and independent member of the British Commonwealth. Under the constitution, the nine rulers of the states elect a Paramount Ruler who holds office as Head of State for five years. The Head elected for 1960–5 was H. M. Syed Sir Putra ibni Almarhum Syed Hassan Jamalullail, Raja of Perlis. Parliament comprises the Head of State, a Senate (of 38 members, some elected and some appointed by the Head of State) and a House of Representatives of 100 members, elected by popular vote. The first Prime Minister was Tunku Abdul Rahman, *q.v.*, who was the first Chief Minister to be appointed under the 1955 Constitution, when a ministerial system of government replaced the old wholly-nominated Executive Council. He leads the Triple Alliance, formed by the United Malays' National Organization (U.M.N.O.), the Malayan Chinese Association (President, Sir Cheng Lock Tan) and the Malayan Indian Congress, which in July 1955 won 51 out of the 52 elective seats on a programme of self-government by 1959; the remaining seat was won by the Pan-Malayan Moslem Party. At elections to the House of Representatives held on 19 August 1959 the Alliance won 70 seats, the Pan-Malayan Islamic Party 13, the Socialist Front 8, the People's Progressive Party 4, Independents 3, and Malayan Party and Party Negara 1 each.

The country was a centre of Communist guerilla warfare after 1948; British armed forces were engaged in putting down a small jungle army, recruited from members of the Malayan Communist Party (banned since 1926) who had resisted the Japanese occupation, and supplied with arms smuggled across the Thai frontier from China. General Templer, the High Commissioner from 1952 to 1954, employed punitive measures against jungle villagers who gave food to the guerillas and against members of the Min Yuen, the civilian wing of the Communist army which provided it with information and equipment; at the same time he introduced constitutional and social reforms and arranged the first municipal elections. In 1955 several areas were declared free of Communist troops, and the Chief Minister met Ching Peng, Secretary-General of the Malayan Communist Party, but rejected his demands for the legalization of the Communist Party and its participation in Malayan politics. On 31 July 1960 the state of emergency was declared to be at an end, the last Communist-occupied areas having been cleared.

The situation is complicated by the racial divisions in the population and by the economic dependence of the colony on rubber and tin. A slump in the price of rubber, of which Malaya is the world's largest producer, caused wage reductions and unemployment on the rubber plantations and discontent which was reflected throughout the colony. World prices recovered in 1955 and the Dunlop Rubber Company decided to expand its plant in Malaya. An era of economic prosperity, in which the 2,000,000 Chinese who are engaged mainly in trade and distribution would undoubtedly benefit, would ease racial tensions.

Maldive Islands. A British protected state 400 miles south-west of Ceylon, comprising over 7,000 islands in 17 groups; area 115 sq. m.; population (living on approximately 215 of the islands) 81,950 in 1956; capital Malé, on King's Island. The people are of Sinhalese extraction and were once Buddhists, but they were converted to Islam in the twelfth century. In 1887 the Sultan recognized British suzerainty and agreed not to enter into treaty relations with other states, except through the U.K., in its capacity as ruler of Ceylon. When Ceylon became independent in 1948 this obligation continued, but was transferred to the U.K. High Commissioner in Ceylon. During the Second World War there was a British air base on Gan Island in the Addu Atoll of the Maldive Islands. In January 1957 the Maldivian government agreed that the U.K. should have facilities for re-establishing the air base. This step was necessitated by the agreement between Ceylon and the U.K. by which, towards the end of 1957, Ceylon took over the British bases of Trincomalee and Katunayake. On 1 February 1960 the Maldivian government leased Gan Island to the U.K. for 30 years.

The Maldive Islands, which have complete independence in the management of their internal affairs, are ruled by a Sultan, H.M. Sultan Al Amir Mohamed Farid Didi.

Malenkov, Georgy Maximilianovich. A former Chairman of the Council of Ministers of the U.S.S.R.; born 8 January 1902. He fought in the Red Army during the civil war which followed the 1917 Revolution, joined the Communist Party in 1920, and then attended a Moscow higher technical school, where he was secretary of the Communist students' group. From 1925 onwards he worked at the offices of the Central Committee of the Communist Party and on Stalin's personal staff. During the Second World War he was appointed to the war cabinet, the only other members of which were Stalin, Molotov, Beria, and Zhdanov, and was in charge of aircraft and tank production. When Stalin died in 1953 Malenkov succeeded him as Chairman of the Council of Ministers, but resigned in February 1955, saying publicly that he was not competent to hold the post; he was then appointed to be Minister of Electric Power Stations and a Vice-Chairman of the Council of Ministers, and succeeded as Chairman by Nikolai Bulganin, *q.v.* In July 1957 it was announced that Malenkov had been dismissed from both these posts and expelled from the Presidium and the Central Committee of the Communist Party for assisting in the creation of an 'anti-party group'.

Mali. An independent republic; area 463,500 sq. m.; population (of whom 92 per cent are illiterate) 3,708,000 comprising Bambara, Peuls, Markas, Songhais, Malinkes, Touareg, Miniunkas, Senoufos, Dogons, and 8,000 Europeans; capital Bamako. The country is land-locked, with Mauritania and the Sahara departments of Algeria to the north, Senegal to the west, Guinea, Ivory Coast, and Upper Volta to the south, and Niger to the east. For twelve centuries it was ruled successively by the Ghana, Mali, and Songhai empires and by local Bambara chiefs; the French took it over in 1904 and, as French Soudan, it later became one of the eight territories of French West

Africa, *q.v.*; as the Soudanese Republic, it achieved self-government within the French Community, *q.v.*, on 24 November 1958. On 4 April 1959 it entered into a federal union with Senegal, known as the Mali Federation, which itself achieved complete independence, still within the Community, on 20 June 1960. Senegal seceded from the Federation in August 1960, and on 22 September 1960 the Soudanese Republic declared that it would thenceforth be known as the Republic of Mali.

Legislative powers are vested in an assembly of 80 members elected every five years by universal suffrage. At the elections held on 8 March 1959 all the seats were won by the Sudanese Union. The other main party, which obtained 24 per cent of the votes but no seats, was the Soudanese Regroupment Party, led by Hamadou Dicko. Executive power is exercised by the Prime Minister or President of the Council (Mobido Keita, leader of the African Federation Party, who held office in the French government in Paris from 1957 to 1958) who is invested by an absolute majority of the assembly.

The principal exports are groundnuts, cotton, kapok, rice, livestock, and dried fish. Millet, maize, and sorghum are also produced, and the most favourable area for crops is in the south, along the Niger. Most of the country's trade has to pass through the port of Dakar, in Senegal. There are economic aid agreements with France and the U.S.A.

Mali Federation. Created on 4 April 1959 by Senegal and the Soudanese Republic, it came to an end in the autumn of 1960, with the secession of Senegal in August of that year and a proclamation by the Soudanese Republic on 22 September that it would thenceforth be known as the Republic of Mali. Political and personal differences between the Senegalese, who are more prosperous, and whose population is smaller, but includes 47,000 Europeans, and the Soudanese, who were hoping for a federal policy of planning and controls, brought about the dissolution of the Federation.

Malta. An island between Sicily and Africa, seized by the British from the French in 1800, and, with Maltese consent, made a British colony in 1814; area, with two adjacent islands, 121·8 sq. m.; population (1958) 323,667, mostly Roman Catholics; capital Valletta. It has one of the highest population densities in the world, and there has been large-scale emigration. Malta was frequently attacked from the air in the Second World War and was awarded the George Cross by King George VI in 1942. Under the Constitution of September 1947, there was a Legislative Assembly of 40 members, elected by universal suffrage and proportional representation, but powers relating to defence, immigration, currency, and external relations were reserved to the Governor. At the elections held in February 1955 the results were: Malta Labour Party, led by Dominic Mintoff, 23 seats in the Legislative Assembly; Nationalists, led by Dr G. Borg Olivier, 17 seats. The conservartive Progressive Constitutional Party, led by Mabel Strickland, won no seats. Mintoff was appointed Prime Minister in succession to Borg Olivier. The Malta Labour Party demanded a status for Malta similar to that of Northern Ireland, *q.v.*, seats for Malta in the British House of Commons, and the extension of British social services to Malta in return for the payment by Maltese of British taxes. The Nationalists opposed integration, and want dominion status within the British Commonwealth. The Maltese government is particularly anxious to attract new industries to Malta, where capital investment is badly needed. A round table conference to discuss the status of Malta was held by British and Maltese Members of Parliament in 1955; the British representatives recommended that Malta should have parliamentary representation in London. In a referendum held in February 1956, 75 per cent of those voting favoured integration with the U.K.; just over 60 per cent of the total electorate voted, Borg Olivier having called upon his supporters to boycott the referendum. Discussions as to the method of integrating Malta with the U.K. broke down in April 1958 when Mintoff rejected a British proposal that there should be a five-year trial period during which the financial and constitutional provisions of the integration scheme would be put into effect, except that Malta would not during that period become part of the U.K. or be represented in the British House of Commons. Mintoff then resigned and the Governor declared a state of emergency and took over the administration. Most of Malta's products are bought by the U.K., by British forces in Malta and by ships calling at Valletta. The colony's budget is balanced by a British grant.

Managerial Revolution. The passing of control from capitalists into the hands of the administrators in business and government. James Burnham (a New York University lecturer) in his book, *The Managerial Revolution*, published 1941, said that this process is taking place at the present day. He said that the future governing class would be the possessors not of wealth but of technical or administrative skill. They would control the instruments of production and receive preferential treatment in the distribution of the product of those instruments. The capitalists once had the benefits because they held property rights in the instruments of production. The managers would gain these benefits indirectly by control of the state which in turn would own and control the instruments of production. The state would, in effect, be the 'property' of the managers, and that would be enough to place them in the position of a ruling class.

Manchukuo. The name given by Japan to Manchuria, *q.v.*, when, after expelling the Chinese, it proclaimed a new independent state on 18 February 1932. The last Chinese Emperor of the Manchu dynasty, Pu Yi, deposed as a boy in 1911 and brought up in Japan, was made President of Manchukuo. On 1 March 1934 he took the title of Emperor under the name of Kang Teh. The Empire of Manchukuo was at all times a puppet state under Japanese control. The country was occupied by a large Japanese army and there were Japanese advisers at all government offices. Japan did much to develop the agriculture and the rich mineral resources of Manchuria, established a number of industries, and in March 1935 forced the government to buy the Russian share in the East Chinese Railway (running through Manchuria to Vladivostok) for £10,000,000. The state was not recognized by China, the U.S.S.R., or any other powers except Germany, Italy, and Japan. When the Japanese armies were defeated it reverted to China, to which it had never ceased, in law, to belong.

Manchuria. Part of north-east China, covering Heilungkiang, Liaoning, and Kirin provinces and the former Jehol province; area 825,700 sq. m.; population approximately 42,000,000; three main cities Shenyang (Mukden) Changchun, and Dairen. Japan has often tried to gain control of Manchuria's valuable mineral resources. After defeating Russia, whose forces had occupied much of Manchuria, the Japanese were granted special privileges under the Treaty of Peking, 1905, including the right to maintain some 15,000 soldiers in Manchuria to protect the South Manchurian Railway, the line running south from the Trans-Siberian Railway to the naval base of Port Arthur. Russia continued to control the Trans-Siberian Railway through its own territory and the East Chinese Railway through Manchuria, both of which lines ran to Vladivostok. In September 1931 Japan accused the Chinese of having blown up part of the South Manchurian line at Mukden, north of Port Arthur, and at once took military action, occupying the whole of Manchuria by the end of 1932. The Japanese proclaimed a new state called Manchukuo, *q.v.*

In the Cairo Declaration, *q.v.*, in 1943, it was stated that Manchuria was part of China, and it was reincorporated in China on the withdrawal of the Japanese forces. The U.S.S.R. occupied Port Arthur towards the end of the Second World War, and after protracted negotiations finally withdrew its forces in May 1955.

Largely as a result of the recent Japanese exploitation of its fuel and mineral resources Manchuria has become China's most important area of industrial development. It provides approximately one half of the total Chinese output of coal, and one half of the oil and two thirds of the iron reserves.

Manila, Treaty of. Concluded in September 1954, and also known as the South-East Asia Collective Defence Treaty, *q.v.*

Manley, Norman Washington. Jamaican politician and Chief Minister; born 4 July 1893; educated at elementary schools, Jamaica College (1906–12), and Oxford University, in 1914 and 1919–21, his studies there being interrupted by the First World War. He practised at the Jamaica bar for many years with great success and became a King's Counsel in 1932. In 1937 he persuaded the United Fruit and Standard Fruit and Steamship Companies to contribute towards the development of local industries and culture. He founded the People's National Party in 1938 and also served on a number of official bodies, including the Central Board of Health, the Agricultural Produce Advisory Board, the Agricultural Policy Committee, and the Social Security Committee. In 1949 he was elected to the Jamaican House of Representatives as member for East St Andrew and led the opposition of the left-wing People's National Party to the Jamaica Labour Party led by his cousin Bustamante, *q.v.* When the P.N.P. won a majority of seats in the election of January 1955 he became Chief Minister.

Mao Tse-tung. Chairman of the Central Committee of the Chinese Communist Party and Chairman (1949–1959) of the People's Republic of China; born 1893 in Hunan. He took part in the assembly which founded the Chinese Communist Party in 1921, and in 1927 he organized the Hunan Autumn Revolt. In the same year there was a split between the Communists and the Kuomintang, *q.v.*, and Mao thereupon organized the Kiangsi Red Army with Chu Te, *q.v.*, set up a soviet government and instituted land reforms in the province of Kiangsi. In 1934 he led the trek of 3,000 miles from Kiangsi to Yenan, during which his first wife died. For some years he advocated a common front with the Kuomintang against Japan, and reorganized the Red Army in 1937 so that it could fight as part of the Chinese national army. In 1945 he took part with the U.S. Ambassador to China in an unsuccessful attempt to reach agreement with the Kuomintang leader Chiang Kai-shek, *q.v.* In 1949 he visited Moscow, where he signed a treaty of mutual alliance with the U.S.S.R. His second wife died at a Kuomintang strangling-post; he is now married to a Shanghai actress.

Marshall Plan. A proposal outlined by George Marshall, U.S. Secretary of State, in a speech at Harvard on 5 June 1947: 'It is logical that the

United States should do whatever it is able to do to assist in the return of normal economic health in the world without which there can be no political stability and no assured peace. Our policy is directed not against any country or doctrine but against hunger, poverty, desperation, and chaos. . . . It would be neither fitting nor efficacious for this government to draw up unilaterally a programme designed to place Europe on its feet economically. That is the business of the Europeans. The initiative, I think, must come from Europe. The role of this country should consist of friendly aid in the drafting of a European programme and of later support of such a programme so far as it may be practical for us to do so. The programme should be a joint one, agreed to by a number of, if not all, European nations.'

The proposal was welcomed by the British Foreign Secretary, Ernest Bevin, in the House of Commons on 13 June 1947. The Foreign Ministers of France, the U.K., and the U.S.S.R. met on 27 June to discuss the offer, which the U.S.S.R. later rejected. No Communist countries accepted the offer; Czechoslovakia accepted and then withdrew its acceptance. Finland and Spain did not participate. Sixteen nations (Austria, Belgium, Denmark, France, Greece, Iceland, Ireland, Italy, Luxemburg, the Netherlands, Norway, Portugal, Sweden, Switzerland, Turkey, and the U.K.) met for a Conference on European Economic Co-operation in Paris on 12 July 1947.

These nations then drew up a report which described the destruction caused by the Second World War and the resulting upset of the balance of trade with the western hemisphere, and outlined a plan for 1947–51 which came to be known as the European Recovery Programme, *q.v.* The report and plan were handed to Mr Marshall on 22 September 1947. The Organization for European Economic Co-operation, *q.v.*, was set up to administer the European Recovery Programme.

Marxism. The philosophy of history and the programme of revolutionary reform expounded by Karl Marx (1818–83), a German Jew. The underlying basis of Marxism as a philosophy of history is dialectical materialism, *q.v.*, by which Marx sought to prove that capitalism, *q.v.*, carried within itself the seeds of its own decay and that revolution was inevitable. During the revolutionary upheavals of 1848 he issued the Communist Manifesto, in which he advocated: (1) the expropriation of landed property and the use of rent from land to cover state expenditure; (2) a high and progressively graded income tax; (3) the abolition of the right of inheritance; (4) the centralization of credit by the establishment of a state bank; (5) the nationalization of transport; (6) an increase in the state ownership of factories and the redistribution of land; (7) the duty of all to work; (8) state education of all children and abolition of factory labour for children. The Manifesto stated that Communists believed that their aims could only be achieved by the violent overthrow of the whole contemporary social order, and concluded with the words: 'Let the governing classes tremble before the Communist revolution. The proletarians have nothing to lose in it but their chains. They have the whole world to gain. Proletarians of all countries, unite!' Marx and his colleague, Friedrich Engels, are today regarded as the first exponents of Communism as a coherent body of doctrine. Marxian Socialists are those who accept the Marxist analysis of history but do not wish to plan the violent overthrow of governments.

Matsu. A group of five islands, with a combined area of less than 10 sq. m., approximately 10 miles from the Chinese mainland, and 130 miles north-west of Formosa, *q.v.*, to the government of which the Chinese forces occupying Matsu are loyal.

Mau Mau. A militant African secret society, active among the Kikuyu, Meru, and Embu tribes in Kenya. Its aim is to expel the white settlers, and to achieve this end it terrorized the Kikuyu in particular so that they became divided into loyalists, Mau Mau supporters, and others who gave passive support to the society. Members of Mau Mau are bound by secret oaths to mutilate and kill their enemies, African and European. Reluctant Africans were sometimes forced to take oaths, which involved rituals of a barbarous nature, and which they were then terrified to disobey. The Kenya government forces found it difficult to eradicate the influence of Mau Mau; the thick forests provided shelter for the gangs, while many Africans in the over-crowded Kikuyu reserves sympathized with the uncompromising opposition of Mau Mau to the white way of life. In October 1957 the Governor of Kenya said that the task of capturing the 150 terrorists still at large would a long one. A secret society similar to Mau Mau, the Kiama Kia Muingi (K.K.M.), was outlawed in January 1958. A proclamation was issued on 10 November 1959, announcing the end, after seven years, of the state of emergency resulting from the activities of Mau Mau.

Maudling, Reginald. British Conservative Party politician; born 7 March 1917 and educated at Merchant Taylors' School and Merton College, Oxford. After qualifying as a barrister in 1940 he served in the Royal Air Force until 1945, when he unsuccessfully contested a parliamentary seat. He then concerned himself with economic research in the Conservative parliamentary secretariat, and was elected to the House of Commons to represent Barnet in 1950. He became Parliamentary Secretary to the Minister of Civil Aviation in 1952, and then successively Economic Secretary to the Treasury, Minister of Supply, and Paymaster-General. In this last capacity he was entrusted with negotiations between the U.K. and the European Economic Community, and with the task of working out the place of the U.K. in the Free Trade Area. In October 1959 he became President of the Board of Trade.

Mauritania. An independent republic; area 418,120 sq. m.; population 624,000, comprising nomad white Moors (approximately 462,000), Toucouleurs (49,200), Sarakollés (24,000), Peuls (24,000), Bambaras, Ouolofs, and 1,600 Europeans; capital Nouakchott. The country is on the west coast of Africa, with Rio de Oro (part of Spanish Sahara) to the north, Senegal to the south, and Sahara and Mali to the east. It became a French protectorate in 1903 and later was one of the eight territories comprising French West Africa, *q.v.*; it achieved self-government within the French Community, *q.v.*, on 28 November 1958, and complete independence, still within the Community, on 28 November 1960. It is known officially as the Islamic Republic of Mauritania, since the official religion is the Moslem religion, the white Moors being descendants of an ancient Moslem civilization.

Legislative powers are vested in an assembly of 40 members elected every five years by universal suffrage. At the elections held on 17 May 1959 the Mauritanian Regroupment Party (P.R.M.) obtained control. Executive power is exercised by the Prime Minister (Mocktar Ould Daddah, leader of the P.R.M.), who is elected by the assembly.

Millet, dates, maize, cattle, dried and salted fish, gum, and salt, are the main products; there are deposits of copper, and there are very considerable iron ore deposits in the region of Fort Gouraud, in the hills 400 miles inland to the east of Spanish Sahara. Most of the trade is with Senegal, Mali, and Gambia, but there are also links with the north, and Morocco has advanced historical claims to the country.

Mboya, Tom. Kenyan politician, born in 1931, the son of a sisal-plantation worker and a member of the Luo tribe, which is the second largest tribe in Kenya; he was educated at the Roman Catholic mission at Kabaa, St Mary's School near Lake Victoria, and the Holy Ghost College at Mangu. After a three-year training course he became a sanitary inspector in Nairobi, where he became interested in politics and joined the Kenya African Union, of which he became successively public relations officer and, in March 1953, treasurer.

After the K.A.U. was banned, later in 1953, he became general secretary of the Kenya Federation of Labour. In 1954 he attended a course in Calcutta organized by the International Confederation of Free Trade Unions, and from 1955 to 1956 he held a scholarship at Ruskin College, Oxford. He was later elected as a Nairobi representative to the Legislative Council and in August 1959 helped to form the Kenya Independence Party, which was based upon most of the existing African political groups; he was later, in March 1960, one of the founders of the Kenya African National Union.

Meany, William George. President of the American Federation of Labour and Congress of Industrial Organizations, *q.v.*, the combined trade union organization formed in 1955; born in 1894 in Harlem, the son of a plumber; he is a Roman Catholic. He became a journeyman plumber at the age of sixteen, and soon became active in trade union affairs. In 1923 he became Secretary and Treasurer of the New York Building Trades Council, and from 1934 to 1939 was President of the New York branch of the American Federation of Labour, *q.v.*, during which period he persuaded the State to pass many laws improving the status of organized labour. He became Secretary and Treasurer of the A.F. of L. headquarters in Washington and was a member of the government War Labour Board from 1941 to 1945. He successfully opposed participation by the A.F. of L. in the World Federation of Trade Unions, *q.v.* He believes that the U.S. labour movement can gain far more from collective bargaining than by forming a political party. Unlike his colleague, Walter Reuther, *q.v.*, he has never taken part in a strike.

Mendès-France, Pierre. French politician, born 1907 and educated at the law faculty and the school of political science at Paris University. He joined the Radical Socialist Party when he was sixteen and took his doctorate of laws in 1925, having won first place out of eight hundred students. He also obtained a diploma in political science and wrote a study of the financial policy of the government of Poincaré, who was then Prime Minister, and books on cartels and the function of an international bank. In 1932 he became the youngest member of the Chamber of Deputies, and in 1938 he was Under-Secretary of State to the Treasury in the Popular Front government of Léon Blum. In 1939 he joined the Air Force, and later served with the Free French forces in England, from where he took part in air raids over France and Germany. In 1943 he became Commissioner of Finance in the Committee of National Liberation at Algiers under General de Gaulle, and in 1944 represented France at Bretton Woods, *q.v.*, becoming a Governor of the International Monetary Fund and an

Alternate Governor of the International Bank for Reconstruction and Development. He was Minister of National Economy under de Gaulle from 1944 to 1945 but resigned when his plans for wage and price limitations, capital levies on profits, rationing, abolition of the black market, and other anti-inflationary measures, were rejected by the cabinet. He tried unsuccessfully to form a cabinet in June 1953, but succeeded in doing so in June 1954 without the aid of Communist votes in the Chamber of Deputies. He brought new and young men into his cabinet, stopped cabinet leakages to the press, advocated French withdrawal from Indo-China, wanted to renovate the French economy, and strove for peace in French North Africa, setting up a Ministry for Moroccan and Tunisian Affairs. He obtained wide economic powers for his government. He wanted to co-operate with the U.K. and suggested that France and the U.K. should together join the European Defence Community or create an alternative organization, but this plan was rejected by Sir Winston Churchill. In February 1955 his government was defeated in the National Assembly on a vote of confidence in connexion with his North African policy. He was Minister of State in the Mollet government from January to May 1956, resigning because he disagreed with the government's Algerian policy. He was one of the 77 non-Communist Deputies who voted against the investiture of de Gaulle as Prime Minister on 1 June 1958. He lost his parliamentary seat in the general election held in November 1958.

Mensheviks. The moderate Russian Socialists who opposed Bolshevism, after the split in the Russian Socialist Party in 1903, and particularly in the Russian Revolution in 1917. They had been in a minority (Russian: *menshinstvo*) at the Party congress preceding the split; hence the name.

Menzies, Robert Gordon. Politician and Australian Liberal Party leader; born 20 December 1894 and educated at Melbourne University; he is a barrister. From 1928 to 1934 he was active in local government, and in 1934 he became a member of the Federal House of Representatives and was appointed Attorney-General. He became deputy leader of the United Australian Party in 1935 and Opposition leader in 1943. He was Prime Minister from 1939 to 1941 and was reappointed as Prime Minister in 1949.

Mexico, United States of. An independent republic; area 760,375 sq. m.; population (1959) 33,304,253; capital Mexico City. It was ruled by Spain from the sixteenth century until the revolutionary war of 1810–21; a series of wars then occurred in which the U.S.A., France, and Austria were all concerned at various times, and the present republic was inaugurated after the execution of the Emperor Ferdinand Maximilian of Austria in 1867. Under the 1917 Constitution, amended frequently between 1929 and 1953, Mexico is a federative republic of 29 states, 2 territories, and the federal district of Mexico City. Congress consists of a Senate of 60 members, elected for six years, and a Chamber of Deputies of 177 members, elected for three years. The President is elected by direct popular vote in a general election, and holds office for six years; Adolfo López Mateos became President on 1 December 1958. He was the candidate of the dominant party, Partido Revolucionario Institucional (P.R.I.).

The country is fertile but is obliged to import food. The principal crops are maize, beans, wheat, and barley. About fifty per cent of the world's supply of sisal is produced in the Yucatán peninsula, although since 1938 there has been a decline in production. This is due partly to competition from Kenya, Haiti, Indonesia, and Tanganyika, and partly to mistaken efforts to merge all the sisal areas into one enormous co-operative estate. Recently the government has improved matters by permitting peasants to sell their fibre direct to the consumer. Mexico is one of the world's largest producers of sulphur, which is mined by three large American firms, the Texas Gulf, Panamerican Sulphur, and Mexican Gulf Sulphur Companies. There are large oil reserves; most of the oil properties were expropriated in March 1938 and placed under a government organization called Petroleos Mexicanos ('Pemex') with a board comprising five government and four workers' representatives. The oilfields had belonged to U.K., U.S., and Dutch companies, the largest being the Mexican Eagle Oil Co. of the Royal Dutch-Shell group. There are also exports of uranium ore, lead, silver, gold, copper, zinc and antimony, and coffee. During the last ten years successful attempts have been made to encourage private investment in railways, fertilizer production, and the development of ports. A public works programme has been launched and there is a plan to treble power production which is expected to cost about $500,000,000. Industrial production more than doubled between 1951 and 1960.

Mirza, Major-General Iskander. First President of Pakistan. He was born in 1900 in West Bengal, was educated at Sandhurst and gazetted to the Indian army in 1919. He transferred to the political service in 1926 and in 1947 became Defence Secretary in the first Pakistan government. From May until October 1954 he served as Governor of East Bengal where he reorganized the provincial administration and suppressed Communist agitation after the dismissal of the United Front ministry headed by Fazlal Huq. He entered

Mohammed Ali's government in November 1954 as Minister for the Interior, States, and Frontier Regions although he was not an elected member of the Constituent Assembly, and after deputizing for two months for the ailing Governor-General, Ghulam Mohammad, he succeeded him on 6 October 1955. He has expressed the view that Pakistan needs 'controlled democracy' under the rule of 'one good strong man', rather than government by the immature and irresponsible politicians who, in his opinion, have dominated the political scene since 1947. He is a fervent Moslem and wants Pakistan's development to resemble that of Turkey under Kemal Ataturk. He was President from 5 March 1956 until his replacement by General Ayub Khan on 28 October 1958.

Modus Vivendi. Latin term meaning 'way of living'; used to describe provisional and informal arrangements in political affairs, whether international or internal. It is employed especially in relation to an agreement between the Pope and a government for the regulation of Roman Catholic affairs within a country, when it is a substitute for a Concordat, *q.v.*

Mollet, Guy. French Socialist politician; born 31 December 1905 in Normandy. He became a teacher at the age of seventeen, when he also joined the Socialist Party, and in 1932 he became secretary of the teachers' union. In the Second World War he was a prisoner of war from 1940 to 1942, after which he was repatriated and worked for the resistance movement. After his election as a deputy from Pas-de-Calais to the Constituent Assembly in 1946, he became General Secretary of the Socialist Party. He was Minister of State in the all-Socialist cabinet of Léon Blum from 1946 to 1947, and Deputy Premier in the Pleven government in 1951. In January 1956 he became Prime Minister of a coalition government which did not fall until May 1957, and which thus had the longest life of any post-war French cabinet. He was one of the 44 (out of 93) Socialist Deputies who on 1 June 1958 voted for the investiture of de Gaulle as Prime Minister. He then took office as Minister of State under de Gaulle, but in December 1958 the Socialist Party decided not to serve in the government which was to be formed when de Gaulle became President, and Mollet was therefore not included in the Debré ministry chosen in January 1959.

Molotov, Vyacheslav Mikhailovich; A former Vice-Chairman of the Council of Ministers of the U.S.S.R.; born 9 March 1890 with the surname of Scriabin and educated at a polytechnic in St Petersburg (now Leningrad). He became a Bolshevik when he was sixteen, took the name of Molotov ('the hammer'), helped Stalin to found *Pravda,* *q.v.*, and when the revolution broke out in 1917 he had been in jail six times and in exile twice. By 1921 he was the Second Secretary of the Communist Party, the First Secretary being Stalin. From 1930 to 1941 he was Chairman of the Council of People's Commissars, a post then roughly equivalent to that of Prime Minister, in which capacity he supervised the completion of the first two Five-Year Plans for agriculture and industry. In 1939 he succeeded Maxim Litvinov as Foreign Minister and negotiated the Russo-German Pact. He was active in international affairs until 1949, when Vyshinsky took over his post, but he was Foreign Minister again from 1953 until his resignation in June 1956 in favour of Shepilov. In July 1957 it was announced that Molotov, with Malenkov and Kaganovich, had been expelled from the Presidium and the Central Committee of the Communist Party for establishing an 'anti-party group'. He then became Russian Ambassador to the Mongolian Peoples Republic, until 1960 when he was appointed to be the Russian representative to the International Atomic Energy Agency.

Monaco, Principality of. An independent state on the French Riviera, ruled since 1949 by Prince Rainier III (Louis Henri Maxence Bertrand, born 1923), and by his family, the Genoese Grimaldi dynasty, since 1297; area (which includes Monte Carlo) about two miles by half a mile, or 368 acres; population about 20,000 of whom 2,245 are citizens of Monaco (Monégasques). Under the 1911 Constitution legislative powers are vested in the Prince and a National Council of eighteen members elected every four years. A Council of Government has executive powers. In January 1959 Prince Rainier suspended the Constitution after a number of disputes with the National Council which, in his view, had been trying to extend its powers at his expense. Monaco has a customs union with France, but Monégasques do not pay French taxes. Under a 1918 treaty Monaco would have become a protectorate of France, although an autonomous state (and Monégasques would pay French taxes), if the Prince had died without an heir. A son, Prince Albert Alexander Louis Peter, was born in March 1958.

Monckton Report. The report, published in October 1960, of the Commission headed by Viscount Monckton, the purpose of which was to study the problems of the Federation of Rhodesia and Nyasaland, *q.v.*, and to advise the British government as to 'the constitutional programme and framework best suited to the achievement of the objects contained in the Constitution of 1953'. It stated: (1) that the British government should declare its willingness to consider any request for secession from the Federation and should insert such a declaration in the preamble to the new constitution; (2) that certain discriminatory laws and practices, including the Southern Rhodesian pass laws, discrimination in local government, the public services, and industry, and the Southern Rhodesian Land Apportionment Act, should be removed or amended; (3) that the franchise should be broadened to include Africans with experience and judgement even if they did not possess minimum education or income qualifications; (4) that the greater part of the taxing powers and responsibility for health, roads, and prisons, and non-African education and agriculture, should be transferred to the constituent territories of the Federation, the federal government being left only with enough financial power to exert broad economic control; (5) that federal powers should be confined to economic policy, and a limited range of external relations and defence functions.

Mongolia, Inner. An autonomous region of north-western China which, like Tibet, is outside the Chinese system of provinces; population (1953) 6,100,104; capital Huhehot. For some years after 1932 it was under the influence of the Japanese, who set up an autonomous Mongol administration and tried to turn the Mongols against China. An Inner Mongolian autonomous government set up by the Chinese in 1947 was an amalgamation of Inner Mongolian with some Manchurian elements. The government, most of the members of which are Chinese and not Mongols, has launched a programme designed to remove the special privileges of the Mongol princes and aristocracy, and has redistributed land and animals.

Mongolian People's Republic. An independent state to the north-west of China; area about 1,750,000 sq. m.; population 1,000,000; capital Ulan Bator, formerly known as Urga. The country was under Chinese suzerainty until 1915 when it declared its independence. A provisional People's Government was later established which appealed to Moscow for help. By the Russo-Chinese Treaty of 1924 the U.S.S.R. formally acknowledged Chinese suzerainty, but the Mongolian People's Republic proclaimed in that year was almost entirely dependent on the U.S.S.R. After 1930 several Japanese attacks were repulsed by joint forces of Mongolian and Russian troops. By the second Russo-Chinese Treaty of 1945 China recognized the complete independence of Outer Mongolia. Under the 1940 Constitution, as amended in 1944, 1949, 1952, and 1955, there is a Great People's Khural (Parliament) elected for three years by universal suffrage, which elects a Little People's Khural, or Presidium, which acts as a cabinet. The population is largely nomad and is dependent on cattle-breeding, although two Five-Year Plans

(1948–52, 1953–7) and a Three-Year Plan (1958–60) have begun to develop meat-packing and engineering industries, and established tractor stations.

Monroe Doctrine. A principle of U.S. policy, opposing any European intervention in the political affairs of the American continent. In 1821 the Russian government, then still in possession of Alaska (which it later sold to the U.S.A.), attempted to exclude all but Russian ships from the north-western coast of America; at the same time the reactionary Holy Alliance of Prussia, Austria, and Russia, having just quelled the Spanish revolution, contemplated intervention to help Spain against the newly-created South American republics. President Monroe declared in a message to Congress on 2 December 1823, 'that the American continents, by the free and independent condition which they have assumed and maintained, are henceforth not to be considered as subjects for future colonization by any European Powers. . . . With the movements in this hemisphere we are of necessity more immediately concerned. The political system of the Allied Powers is essentially different from that of America. . . . We should consider any attempt on their part to extend their system to any part of this hemisphere as dangerous to our peace and safety.' The British Foreign Secretary, George Canning, had suggested, unsuccessfully, a joint Anglo-American declaration against intervention in South America. The Monroe Doctrine grew in popularity in the U.S.A. in the mid-nineteenth century, but the French intervention in Mexico in 1860 challenged it seriously. The American Civil War hampered the application of the Doctrine for some time, but in 1865 the U.S.A. insisted on it, and the French had to withdraw.

Once firmly established, the Doctrine was applied to the building of the Panama Canal, and the Clayton-Bulmer Treaty of 1850, which had provided for joint Anglo-American control of the Canal, was replaced by the Hay-Pauncefote Treaty of 1901, recognizing complete U.S. control. In 1896 President Cleveland said that it gave to the U.S.A. the right to decide the frontier dispute between British Guiana and Venezuela, and his Secretary of State declared that the U.S.A. was 'practically sovereign' and 'her fiat law'. In 1902 the Anglo-German-Italian blockade of Venezuela (to enforce payment of debts) angered Americans and President Theodore Roosevelt extended the theory so that the U.S.A. could act preventively to forestall European intervention. U.S. control of customs in San Domingo was the first result, and the Doctrine has since been repeatedly invoked in connexion with U.S. actions in the Caribbean Sea.

The Doctrine has become a common principle of all the American republics instead of a unilateral U.S. policy. By the Declaration o Lima, 1942, the members of the Pan American Union, *q.v.*, declared their determination to defend themselves against all foreign intervention. In the Rio Treaty, *q.v.*, in 1947, they reaffirmed this attitude and agreed that an attack against one of them should be considered to be an attack against them all.

The U.S. Secretary of State, John Foster Dulles, said in 1954 that among the most fundamental of U.S. foreign policies was an objection to the existence of Communist or pro-Communist governments in the American continent. If a pro-Communist government were freely elected in a Latin American state, the U.S. objection to it would in fact be inconsistent with that part of the Monroe Doctrine which encouraged Latin American self-determination; the U.S. attitude would presumably be that such a government must of its nature be subject to a foreign influence and that this was directly contrary to the Doctrine. President Eisenhower said in February 1960 that the U.S.A. would consider it an intervention in the internal affairs of an American state if any power, 'whether by invasion, coercion or subversion' succeeded in denying freedom of choice to the people of that state.

Montreux Convention, 1936. An international agreement permitting Turkey to fortify the Dardanelles, *q.v.*, and laying down rules for the passage of warships between the Mediterranean and Black Seas in time of peace and war. It modified the Treaty of Lausanne, concluded in 1923, which had provided that Turkey, defeated in the First World War, should demilitarize the Dardanelles. In peacetime commercial shipping must be allowed to use the straits freely; warships of more than 10,000 tons, submarines, and aircraft carriers are excluded, and other naval vessels may pass only by day. In any war in which Turkey is neutral, warships of the belligerent powers are banned from the straits, except where they are proceeding by order of the United Nations, or in fulfilment of a pact of assistance to which Turkey is a party. If Turkey is a belligerent, commercial navigation is forbidden to countries at war with Turkey, and to neutral ships carrying men or material to support the enemy. The passage of warships in such a case is left to the discretion of Turkey.

Morocco. An independent state in north-west Africa, on the Mediterranean Sea in the north and the Atlantic Ocean in the west; area approximately 173,150 square miles; population approximately 9,252,000, of whom 8,472,000 are Moslems; main capital Rabat. Although Morocco has in theory been an independent sultanate since the Middle Ages, the country was in effect partitioned and subjected to foreign rule from 1912 to 1956. As a result of a Protectorate Treaty between France and the Sultan at Fez on 30 March 1912 and a Convention between France and Spain at Madrid on 27 November 1912, the country was divided into French and Spanish spheres of influence, known respectively as French Morocco, *q.v.*, and Spanish Morocco, *q.v.* In 1923 the city of Tangier, *q.v.*, with a small enclave in Spanish Morocco, was neutralized and demilitarized. After a lengthy period of unrest (*see* French Morocco) the French government was forced, on 2 March 1956, to recognize Morocco as an independent sovereign state; the Spanish government agreed on 7 April 1956 that Spanish Morocco was an integral part of the Morocco state; and on 18 May 1956 the Tangier International Control Committee agreed to the integration of Tangier with the rest of Morocco. Spanish Morocco was transferred to Moroccan jurisdiction on 10 April 1958, but there remained a dispute as to sovereignty over the two Spanish provinces of Spanish Sahara, *q.v.* (Rio de Oro and Saguia el-Hamra), and Ifni, *q.v.* Both these provinces and the neighbouring state of Mauritania, in what was formerly French West Africa, have been claimed by Morocco.

When independence was achieved in March 1956 the Prime Minister, Si Bekkai, who had formed Morocco's first cabinet in December 1955, was leader of a coalition between the Istiqlal, *q.v.*, and the Democratic Independence Party (P.D.I.). A new cabinet formed in October 1956 was drawn entirely from the Istiqlal, except for three Independents, including Si Bekkai. In April 1958 a crisis occurred when the Prime Minister and others publicly criticized Istiqlal policies, accusing it of attacking freedom of the press, freedom of assembly, and freedom of organization. King Mohammed V (who had abandoned his earlier title of Sultan in August 1957) then asked Ahmed Belafrej, the Secretary-General of Istiqlal, to form a government, and promised that eventually a National Assembly would be elected by universal suffrage. Belafrej, a moderate, resigned in November 1958, and was succeeded by Abdullah Ibrahim, who received the support of the left wing and the labour unions but was dismissed by the King in May 1960. The King became Premier, but died in March 1961, being succeeded by his son who became Hassan II.

Morrison, Lord, Herbert Stanley Morrison, British politician; born 3 January 1888 and educated at elementary schools. In his youth he worked as an errand boy, a shop assistant, a telephone operator, and a newspaper deputy circulation manager. Most of his political career was spent in local government activities, in which he achieved great success; he was Secretary of the London Labour Party from 1915 to 1947 and for twenty-three years a member of the London County Council, of which he was Leader from 1934 to 1940. He became a Member of Parliament in 1923 and was Minister of Transport from 1929 to 1931, Minister of Supply in 1940, Home Secretary from 1940 to 1945, Lord President of the Council and Leader of the House of Commons from 1945 to 1951, and Foreign Secretary in 1951. During the Labour Party's term of office from 1945 to 1951, he was one of the first to suggest that the Party should consolidate the reforms that it had introduced, and place less emphasis on nationalization. On the retirement of Earl Attlee, *q.v.*, from the leadership of the Parliamentary Labour Party in December 1955, Morrison stood for election but was defeated by Hugh Gaitskell, *q.v.*, obtaining 40 votes out of 267 votes cast. He then retired from the post of deputy leader but remained a member of the House of Commons until 1959, when he was appointed a Life Peer.

Moslem Brotherhood (Ikhwan al Muslimin). A movement, founded in Egypt in 1929 by Hasan al-Banna, favouring a return to strict Islamic faith, as practised in the eighth century, as a guide to political and social action. It attracted much support among fervent Moslems of all classes and by the end of the Second World War had nearly 2,000,000 members and considerable influence on Arab governments, particularly in Egypt, where more than one quarter of its members lived. It arranged the murder of the Egyptian Prime Minister who suppressed it in 1948; as a result Banna himself was killed, but the Wafd government allowed the Brotherhood to resume its activities. It at first supported the revolution of July 1952, but it opposed the attempts of Neguib and Nasser to establish better relations with the west, and demanded that the government's policies for Egypt be submitted to the Brotherhood for approval. In 1954 it made an attempt on the life of Nasser, who dissolved it and ordered the confiscation of its Egyptian properties. Its leader, Hasan al-Hodaibi, then moved its headquarters from Cairo to Damascus.

Moslem League. The first political party of Pakistan. It was founded as an orthodox religious organization to protect the interests of Moslems in British India. Its politically active members supported the Indian National Congress until 1935 when Hindu aspirations predominated in the Congress Party, *q.v.*, and prominent Moslems left it to mould the League into a political organization representative of Moslems of all classes. Under the leadership of Mohammed Ali Jinnah the League opposed the Congress Party and demanded the partition of India and the creation of an autonomous Moslem state.

It automatically secured control in 1947 of Pakistan's first Constituent Assembly. Immediately after partition Jinnah realized that the League needed to be thoroughly reorganized to undertake its new rôle as a responsible political party. He died, however, in 1948, and the League lapsed into lethargic complacency until it suffered a resounding defeat in the East Pakistan provincial elections of April 1954 in which it won only 6 out of 71 seats. In the 1955 elections for the Constituent Assembly the League won 25 out of 72 contested seats and retained its control of the government, although it found it necessary to form a coalition with the United Front, *q.v.*; but in 1956 its parliamentary supporters seceded to the new Republican Party of Dr Khan Sahib, which formed a government in coalition with the new Awami League. In October 1957 the Republican Party withdrew its support from the Awami League Prime Minister, Suhrawardy; a new coalition was then formed, comprising seven Republicans, four members of the Moslem League and five others. The Moslem League left the government, and was replaced by the Republican Party, in December 1957. Its two principal aims are the defence of Islam, to achieve which it is prepared to insist on the national observance of the tenets of Islam and the universal recognition of Urdu as the sole state language, and the development of a prosperous and peaceful Pakistan.

Most Favoured Nation Clause. A common clause in trade treaties whereby each signatory undertakes to extend to the other signatory automatically any tariff reduction, or other favour, granted in the future to any third country. The aim is to exclude preferences for any particular country.

Munich Agreement. The agreement between France, Germany, Italy, and the U.K., signed at Munich on 29 September 1938, and providing for the immediate cession to Germany of certain Sudeten-German districts in Czechoslovakia, for plebiscites under international supervision to be taken in other districts, and for the frontiers finally to be settled by an International Commission.

After an assurance to Czechoslovakia in March 1938 that Germany had no designs upon Czech territory, Adolf Hitler had moved some ten divisions towards the frontier. The Czech government ordered a partial mobilization as a defensive measure on 20 May. France and the U.S.S.R. were pledged to defend the Czech frontiers against aggression but seemed unlikely to do so. The British Prime Minister, Neville Chamberlain, had stated that he would not guarantee Czechoslovakia, but that there might be circumstances under which the U.K. would intervene to defend the country. Early in August

Lord Runciman was sent from London to see whether a compromise could be reached. Runciman proposed a solution which in his opinion embodied almost all the requirements of the Sudeten-German minority, and could with some clarifications and extensions have been made to cover them in their entirety. The Czech President, Edward Beneš, accepted this solution, but on the 7 September the Sudeten-Germans made a border incident the pretext for breaking off the talks. Negotiations were resumed but Hitler, in a speech on 12 September, incited the minority to acts of disorder. Runciman returned to London and on 15 September Chamberlain went to Berchtesgaden to see Hitler and the French representative Edouard Daladier. The U.K. and France then recommended the Czechs to agree to cede to Germany all districts containing more than fifty per cent of Germans, without any plebiscite. On 23 September Hitler demanded larger concessions still, asking Chamberlain at Godesberg for the immediate cession of a much greater zone, and a plebiscite in another area.

France and the U.K. then mobilized and war seemed likely when Hitler suggested a four-power conference at Munich, having been told by Chamberlain that he could get what he wanted without war and without delay. Chamberlain, Daladier, Hitler, and Mussolini met at Munich on 28 September. Hitler made insignificant modifications to his Godesberg demands, which were now accepted by Chamberlain and Daladier. German troops crossed the border on 1 October. No representative of Czechoslovakia was present at the Munich discussions.

Muscat and Oman. An independent state on the eastern corner of Arabia; area approximately 82,000 sq. m.; population 550,000, mostly Arab, but with a strong infusion of Negro blood. It is a Sultanate ruled since 1932 by Said bin Taimur (born 1910). It has had a close relationship with the U.K. for about 150 years; on 20 December 1951 a new fifteen-year treaty of commerce and friendship was signed by the Sultan and by British representatives. In July 1957 the former Imam of Oman, Ghalib bin Ali (who for some time had exercised a *de facto* control in the interior) led a revolt against the Sultan. British land and air forces helped the Sultan to suppress the rising. Relations between the Imam and the Sultan are governed by the Treaty of Sib, *q.v.*, concluded in 1920. In addition to useful exports of dates, fish, limes, and pomegranates, the possible presence of oil in the interior near Buraimi, *q.v.*, makes the area one of considerable economic significance.

Mutual Security Agency. A U.S. organization established by the Mutual

Security Act of 1951 with the declared object of providing for the general welfare of the U.S.A. by furnishing military, economic, and technical assistance to friendly nations in the interest of international peace. It provided assistance to friendly nations throughout the world and so was wider in scope than the Economic Co-operation Administration, *q.v.*, which it replaced with effect from 30 December 1951. Its Director, Harold Stassen, was responsible only to the President; he became Director of the Foreign Operations Administration, *q.v.*, with which the new Republican administration replaced the Mutual Security Agency on 1 August 1953.

N

Nasser, Gamal Abdel. Egyptian political leader; born 15 January 1918 and educated at Cairo Military Academy. From 1942 onwards, while an officer in the Egyptian Army, he planned to overthrow the government with the assistance of his fellow officers. His aims were the introduction of social reforms, which he believed would never be carried out by the existing régime, and the withdrawal of British forces from the area of the Suez Canal, *q.v.* In 1948 he fought with the Egyptian forces which unsuccessfully invaded Israel, and said afterwards that the inefficiency of the Egyptian government was responsible for a shortage of munitions. In the same year he formed the secret Free Officers' Movement which chose as its leader the much respected General Mohammed Neguib, *q.v.* Nasser led the *coup d'état* of 23 July 1952 which caused King Farouk to abdicate, and in June 1953 became Deputy Prime Minister. He replaced Neguib as Prime Minister in April 1954 after accusing him of seeking absolute power; the young officers who had become the new rulers also considered that at such an early stage social reforms were more important than the return to parliamentary government which Neguib desired. In July 1954 the discussions in which Nasser had been the chief Egyptian negotiator culminated in an agreement by which British forces were to withdraw from the Suez Canal zone. He became President of Egypt in June 1956 and of the United Arab Republic in February 1958.

National Labour Relations Act, 1935, also known as the Wagner Act. An Act passed by the U.S. Congress as part of President Franklin D. Roosevelt's New Deal, *q.v.* It declared the right of employees to form trade unions and to bargain collectively with their employers through representatives of their own choosing. Freedom of organization was granted under the Constitution, but many employers had refused to negotiate with unions and had discriminated against, or discharged employees who joined unions. The Act named certain 'unfair labour practices' by employers and employees which became punishable. In particular, employers were forbidden: (1) to interfere with employees in the exercise of their right to organize and bargain collectively; (2) to interfere with or dominate any labour organization or to contribute financial or other support to it; (3) to encourage or discourage membership in any labour organization by discrimination in regard to hire or tenure of employment; (4) to discharge or otherwise discriminate against an employee because he had filed charges or given testimony under the Act; (5) to refuse to bargain collectively with a representative chosen by his fellow employees. The National Labour Relations Board was created by the Act as an independent agency with the right to name the officially recognized unions, to conduct secret ballots to determine the exclusive representative of employees, to issue orders requiring employers and employees to cease and desist from any of the specified unfair labour practices, and to petition the courts for the enforcement of its orders.

Nationalization. The acquisition by the state of any property, such as the steel industry, the railway system, the chemical industry or the land. Nationalization has been a common practice in the twentieth century even in countries with private enterprise economies. Thus the French government has nationalized the Banque de France and holds fifty-one per cent of the shares in the national railway company, the Société Nationale des Chemins de Fer Français; the German Federal Republic owns eighty-five per cent of the shares in the Deutsche Lufthansa, its civil air line; and the Italian government monopolizes the production of salt and tobacco. Socialists and Communists tend to advocate nationalization as a general policy rather than as a remedy to be used in isolated cases. The constitution of the British Labour Party, q.v., states that the aims of the Party are to be achieved 'upon the basis of common ownership of the means of production, distribution, and exchange', but this general approach has now been abandoned in practice; unsuccessful attempts were made in 1960 by Hugh Gaitskell and others to amend this part of the constitution so that it would correspond with the actual policies of the Party.

N.A.T.O. North Atlantic Treaty Organization, q.v.

Nazis. Popular contraction of the name National-Socialists, the party led by Adolf Hitler. The term arose as a parallel to the word 'Sozi' (the first two syllables of 'Sozialisten'), with which the German

Socialists had been labelled by their opponents in earlier times. National-Socialists were first styled Nazi-Sozi, but the second half of the term was later abandoned. Today groups in the German Federal Republic sympathetic to the National-Socialists' aims are called neo-Nazis.

Neguib, General Mohammed. Born 20 February 1901 in Khartoum; educated at the Egyptian University, Cairo. He served on the General Staff during the Second World War, and afterwards became Sub-Governor of Sinai and Governor of the Red Sea Provinces. He served as a brigade commander with the Egyptian troops which attacked Israel in 1948. He became Director-General of the Frontier Corps in 1950 but was demoted for criticizing the corruption of those at King Farouk's palace who had engaged in wartime deals with Israel. He was elected President of the Cairo Officers' Club in 1952 in opposition to the royal candidate and then led the *coup d'état* which caused the abdication of King Farouk. He became Prime Minister, Commander-in-Chief, and Military Governor in 1952, and President in 1953. He was removed from these offices in 1954 when other officers decided that he was too cautious to institute the necessary social reforms.

Nehru, Jawaharlal. Prime Minister of India; born Allahabad, 14 November 1889. A high-caste Hindu of Kashmiri descent, he was educated in England at Harrow, Cambridge University, and the Inner Temple, where he qualified as a barrister in 1912. In 1920 he joined the nationalist, non-violence movement led by Gandhi and became a passionate advocate of Indian independence. Between 1920 and 1927 he was imprisoned eight times for his political activities. In 1929 he was General Secretary of the All-India Congress Committee and succeeded his father as President of Congress. In September 1946 he was appointed Vice-President of the Executive Council, or interim government, of India, set up by the Viceroy, Lord Mountbatten. Eleven months later he became the first Prime Minister, and Minister for Foreign Affairs, of the Dominion of India; from 1953 until April 1957 he was also Minister of Defence. In domestic affairs he has made the problem of India's over-population his special concern; he was the first Hindu politician publicly to declare his approval of birth control.

Nenni, Pietro. Italian Socialist leader; born 9 February 1891. He spent eleven years of his childhood in an orphanage. In 1911 he was imprisoned, with Benito Mussolini who later became dictator of Italy, for participating in Socialist riots against the Italo-Turkish war. His career in journalism, which began on the *Lucifero,* an Ancona newspaper, was interrupted by service in the Italian army from 1915 to 1918. After working on various other journals he became editor of *Avanti*, the official organ of the Italian Socialists, until its suppression by Mussolini in 1926 when he fled to France.

He was a political commissar of the Garibaldi brigade, which supported the government in the Spanish Civil War of 1936–9, and defeated a force of Italian Fascists sent to Spain by Mussolini to help the Spanish Fascist rebels under Franco. In February 1942, while in unoccupied France, he was arrested on the orders of Laval, the Vice-Premier of the Vichy government, and sent to Italy where he was imprisoned until 1943. In August 1944 he became Secretary-General of the Italian Socialist Party. He held government office as Vice-Premier and Vice-President of the Council of Ministers in 1945, was then Vice-Premier in the de Gasperi government until June 1946 and Foreign Minister from October 1946 to January 1947. In that month the right wing of the Socialist Party seceded, but Nenni continued to lead the left-wing Socialists.

Néo-Destour. The Nationalist (Constitution) Party of Tunisia; it has the support of the Arab trade union movement (U.G.T.T.) which is affiliated to the International Confederation of Free Trade Unions, *q.v.* Although the party, as opposed to the Vieux-Destour extremists, has always advocated moderation it was outlawed by the French, and its President, Habib Bourguiba, *q.v.*, deported. In May 1955 Bourguiba was called in by the French to advise on a new constitution for Tunisia. In the first all-Tunisian cabinet, formed on 17 September 1955, the Néo-Destour party members held six out of thirteen posts and all the most important offices other than that of Prime Minister. It remains the most powerful Tunisian political party.

Nepal. An independent kingdom in the Himalayas; population (1958) 8,473,478, of whom about ninety-one per cent are illiterate; area, including Mount Everest, 54,362 sq. m.; capital Katmandu. The aborigines are of Mongolian type, with a considerable admixture of Hindu blood from India. There were once many hill clans and small principalities, one of which, Gurkha, became predominant in 1769 and has since given its name to men from all parts of Nepal. In 1846 the power of the King was usurped by the Rana family who established for themselves the post of hereditary Prime Minister. The Kings became merely titular heads. The Rana Maharajas were in power until 1951, and took an annual revenue of £1,500,000 from Nepal, of which they kept ninety per cent for themselves, for investment in India, overseas, or in jewels. The other ten per cent was spent largely on an army, and on government information agents. The Ranas obtained the money from customs and from farming out the timber and rice resources to their relations.

In 1950 and 1951 there was a revolt against the Ranas, and in November 1951 the Prime Minister, Maharaja Mohun Shamsher, handed over his post to Matrika Prasad Koirala. Some supporters of the Ranas were eventually included in the new government. An Advisory Assembly of eighty members was formed and it was decided to hold an election. Governments were unstable in face of Rana opposition, however, and the promised reforms were not introduced. Political frustration produced twenty-nine political parties and a civil disobedience campaign by the Nepali Congress Party, which in January 1955 demanded general elections, an independent judiciary, control of inflation, and a properly organized police force.

On 2 March 1955 the Crown Prince, Mahendra Bir Bidran Shah (whose father, King Tribhuvana, died on 14 March), dismissed the Koirala cabinet, which had been defeated in the Assembly, introduced direct rule, announced the introduction of income tax, and decided to tax the large land holdings of the Ranas. He prepared a First Five-Year Plan, to cost £14,000,000.

King Mahendra dissolved the Assembly in June 1955, and subsequently announced that elections would be held in 1959. Amid the throng of competing politicians the most able and significant is probably Dr K. I. Singh, the left-wing former Nepali Congress leader, who led an abortive rising in Katmandu in January 1952, and subsequently escaped to Tibet and thence to Peking. The Chinese government agreed at the Afro-Asian Conference, *q.v.*, to repatriate him; he was handed over at the Tibetan frontier in September 1955 and given a royal pardon. He has his own party, the National Democratic Front, often known as the 'China lobby'. The King ended direct rule in January 1956 and reintroduced cabinet government, with the leader of the conservative Praja Parishad Party as Prime Minister of a cabinet which excluded the Nepali Congress Party. The Prime Minister resigned in July 1957 and Dr K. I. Singh formed a United Democratic Party government which lasted for two months. He encountered powerful opposition when he tried to abolish corruption in the civil service and when he opposed the acceptance of foreign aid. The King then announced plans for the drafting of a constitution and for the eventual holding of elections, which took place in February 1959, when the Nepali Congress Party won 74 of the 109 seats. A government was formed in May 1959 by B. P. Koirala, who is a half-brother of M. P. Koirala, and was largely responsible for the fall of the Ranas in 1951; he is also an anti-Communist and an advocate of land and tax reforms. In December 1960 he was dismissed and imprisoned by the King, who assumed full powers.

Nepal is poor; for years there were no industries but recently jute and sugar mills and some other factories, and three hydro-electric plants, have been established. There are few public utilities and the judicial system was only made uniform in 1956, while there was no taxation system until 1955.

Netherlands. Officially called the Kingdom of the Netherlands, an independent state on the North Sea and north of Belgium; area approximately 12,670 sq. m.; population (1958) 11,278,024; capital Amsterdam; seat of government The Hague. In 1815 William of Orange-Nassau was made King of the Netherlands which then consisted of the United Provinces in the north, which had been under French domination, and certain Belgian provinces in the south, which were subject, before the French Revolution of 1789, to Austria. This union was dissolved as a result of the Belgian Revolution of 1830.

The Netherlands is a constitutional and hereditary monarchy under Queen Juliana of Orange-Nassau (born 1909; inaugurated as Queen in 1948). The legislature is the States-General comprising a First Chamber of 75 members, elected for six years by the Provincial Diets, and a Second Chamber of 150 members elected for four years by universal suffrage. After the 1959 elections the position in the First Chamber (the upper house) was: Catholics 25, Labour Party 22, Anti-Revolutionaries 8, Christian Historicals 8, Liberals 7, Communists 4; and in the Second Chamber (the lower house): Labour Party 48, Catholics 49, Anti-Revolutionaries 14, Christian Historicals 12, Liberals 19, Communists 3, others 5. A coalition led by the Liberal Party and the Catholics was formed under Professor de Quay (Catholic) as Prime Minister. Since 1948 the Catholic Party has insisted on coalition cabinets embracing as many parties as possible, but the system became increasingly unworkable after 1954. The Catholics dislike government with the Labour Party in opposition because the Catholic workers might be inclined to vote for the Labour Party. This dilemma enabled the Labour Party to dominate the coalitions, until the 1959 government, which was the first administration since 1945 to have no Labour members.

The Netherlands is dependent on foreign trade and its government has accordingly adopted policies of deflation and restraint at regular intervals to improve the balance of payments position. The Dutch, like the Belgians, have ensured an adequate level of industrial investment. They have been able to abandon most of their former discrimination against dollar imports, and their exports (including dairy produce, horticultural produce such as bulbs, and manufactures) are highly competitive in price with those of other countries. There has been a customs union with Belgium and Luxemburg, known as Benelux, *q.v.*, since 29 October 1947. The overseas territories of the Netherlands are Netherlands New Guinea, *q.v.*, which is the subject of a dispute with Indonesia, and the Netherlands West Indies, *q.v.*

Netherlands New Guinea *or* **West Irian.** The western half of New Guinea, *q.v.*, and only remaining overseas territory of the Netherlands in Asia; area 160,000 sq. m.; population about 700,000, mostly Papuans, a different ethnic group from the inhabitants of the Indonesian islands to the west; capital Hollandia. Administration is exercised by a Governor assisted by a government council consisting of the heads of the general services. An advisory council, the territory's first elected and representative body, was inaugurated in April 1961. A mixed British, Dutch, and U.S. company produces petroleum, and several oilfields have been proved.

The area was not included in the transfer of sovereignty to Indonesia of Dutch Asian possessions on 27 December 1949, and it was agreed that its future should be decided by negotiation within a year from that date, but no agreement was reached, and discussions broke down in 1951. The Political Committee of the United Nations General Assembly has several times encouraged the Dutch and the Indonesians to resume discussions. In November 1954 the Netherlands government accused Indonesia of violating Netherlands territory by sending an armed landing party to Netherlands New Guinea, and Dutch reinforcements were sent there in January 1955. Moderate Dutch politicians have advocated a temporary condominium, until such time as the native peoples are able to decide their own future. Others favour an international conference devoted to the New Guinea problem, which could be attended by the Netherlands, Indonesia, and the S.E.A.T.O. countries, and as a result of which Dutch New Guinea might be placed under United Nations trusteeship. At the Afro-Asian Conference, *q.v.*, in April 1955, the Afro-Asian nations supported the Indonesian claim. The Dutch once hoped that some accommodation might be reached within the framework of the Netherlands-Indonesian Union, but the Union was dissolved in 1956. Indonesia has asked for a complete transfer of sovereignty.

Netherlands West Indies. The overseas territories of the Netherlands, and formerly its colonies, in South America and the West Indies. They are of great economic importance to the Netherlands and comprise:

(1) Dutch Guiana, or Surinam, in South America, bordered on the east by French Guiana, on the south by Brazil, on the west by British Guiana, and on the north by the Atlantic Ocean. It has an area of 54,000 sq. m., and a population of about 246,000. Surinam has some of the world's largest deposits of bauxite (the raw material from which aluminium is made), of which great quantities are exported to the U.S.A. (2) Netherlands Antilles, which are two groups of three islands each in the Caribbean Sea, 550 miles apart from each other. Their total area is 436 sq. m. and their population about 194,000. They consist of the Netherlands Windward Islands (Curaçao, Aruba, Bonaire) and the Netherlands Leeward Islands (St Maarten, St Eustatius, Saba). The economy of the Antilles is based on the refining of oil imported from Venezuela to Curaçao (where over half the population live) and Aruba. The oil refineries, controlled by companies affiliated to Royal Dutch-Shell and Standard Oil of New Jersey, are among the largest in the world.

On 15 December 1954 a law was approved by Queen Juliana by which the Netherlands and the Netherlands West Indies were constituted as a single realm under the House of Orange, the former colonial status of Surinam and the Netherlands Antilles being ended. The Statute of the Realm which enacted this provided that the three constituent parts of the realm would possess full autonomy in their domestic and internal affairs.

Neutrality. Non-participation in a war between other states. If a state wishes to be considered neutral and thus to have the rights enjoyed by a neutral, it must observe certain duties, and in particular must abstain from any interference with the war. It must neither favour nor hinder any belligerent, must prevent belligerents from making use of its territories, and must defend itself against any violation of its neutrality. No hostilities between belligerents may be undertaken or tolerated on neutral territory or in neutral waters. Public opinion, the press, and even the government of the neutral state may show sympathy with one belligerent, so long as these feelings do not find expression in actions violating impartiality.

Perpetual neutrality arises where a state, such as Switzerland, has been neutralized by a special treaty. Benevolent neutrality is a term used in some treaties which empowers a state to help a belligerent without actually going to war. Such help would usually be a violation of the modern duty of neutrality, but is consistent with the older, less precise, definition of neutrality. Partial neutrality exists where part of the territory of a state is neutralized, as are, for instance, the Åland Islands, *q.v.*

Neutrality, Treaty of. A treaty between states by which they agree that if any of them is attacked by a state not a party to the treaty, the others will remain neutral. Treaties of neutrality were concluded before the Second World War between Italy and Yugoslavia, 1933; Italy and the U.S.S.R., 1933; and between each of the Baltic states of Estonia, Lithuania, Latvia, and Finland, with the U.S.S.R., 1935.

New Deal. The policy inaugurated by Franklin Delano Roosevelt (born 1882, President of the U.S.A. from 1933 until his death in 1945) in 1933 in order to overcome the economic crisis which had arisen in 1929. It consisted of a series of far-reaching economic and social measures which differed greatly from previous attempts to end the depression by orthodox deflationary means. The National Industry Recovery Act and the Agricultural Adjustment Act, parts of which were later declared by the Supreme Court to be unconstitutional, gave to the executive wide powers in industrial and agricultural matters. The government assisted the recovery of industry by a programme of public works planned by the Public Works Administration, and by providing credit at low interest rates. Legislation was passed providing for an extensive house-building programme supported by government subsidies. A Works Progress Administration was set up to provide employment for workless persons in need of financial assistance. The rights of workers to form trade unions were codified and strengthened by the National Labour Relations Act, 1935, *q.v.*, which compelled employers to bargain with the group representing the free choice of the majority of the workers. A social insurance scheme was introduced by the Social Security Act. The New Deal policies did not end unemployment in the U.S.A., but helped to reduce the number of workless from 17,000,000 to 7,000,000. President Roosevelt's policies may be compared with those of the Democratic administration under President Truman, who in 1949 introduced the Fair Deal, *q.v.*

New Guinea. A large island to the north of Australia. (1) Netherlands New Guinea, *q.v.*, is that part, with various small islands, which lies to the west of the 141st meridian of east longitude, and was formally annexed by the Netherlands in 1884, after being controlled by Dutch interests for nearly three hundred years; area 160,000 sq. m.; population about 700,000; capital Hollandia. (2) New Guinea Territory, which is administered with Papua, is the northern portion of the eastern part of the island and was a German colony when Australia occupied it in 1914; it was entrusted by the League of Nations to Australia after the First World War to be administered as a mandated territory, and became a trusteeship territory after the Second World War; area 93,000 sq. m.; population (1958) 1,341,268, of whom 15,073 were non-indigenous; administrative headquarters Port Moresby, in Papua, but formerly at Rabaul, New Britain, a nearby island. (3) Papua, the remaining part of the island, was occupied by the Queensland government in 1883 and the Australian government took over the administration in 1906; area 90,600 sq. m.; population 487,150; capital Port Moresby.

New Zealand. A Dominion and member of the British Commonwealth; area of North and South Islands and a number of smaller islands, including the Island Territories, 103,939 sq. m.; population 2,326,129; capital Wellington. It was discovered in 1642 by Tasman and visited several times in the eighteenth century by Captain Cook; British sovereignty was ceded by the Maori chiefs by the Treaty of Waitangi and the islands became a British colony. Many Maoris later revolted against British rule, but in 1870 approximately half of the North Island was allotted to them, and peace was established. In 1907 New Zealand was given the status of a Dominion.

Executive authority is vested in the Governor-General, who must act on the advice of an Executive Council, appointed from a House of Representatives of 80 members, including 4 Maoris, elected by popular vote for three years. At the general election held on 26 November 1960, the Labour Party, in power from 1935 to 1949, and since 1957, and led by Walter Nash, was defeated, securing 34 seats; the National Party, led by Keith J. Holyoake, won 46 seats, thus increasing its representation by 7 seats. Holyoake then took office as Prime Minister. The Communist Party fought some industrial seats but was unsuccessful.

The economy is largely agricultural and pastoral, with important exports of wool, butter, beef, cheese, hides and skins, dried and condensed milk, lamb and mutton. The major trading partners are Australia and the U.K. As a member of A.N.Z.U.S., *q.v.*, New Zealand now concentrates its defence efforts on the Far East and is reluctant to undertake Commonwealth commitments involving responsibility elsewhere. In 1955, for example, it was released from its previous obligation to the U.K. to provide troops for service in the Middle East in the event of hostilities. It agreed, however, to send military aid to Malaya.

Newfoundland. A Province of Canada; area (exclusive of its Dependency, Labrador, which has an area of 110,000 sq. m.) 46,185 sq. m.; population (excluding Labrador which has 10,750 people) 438,250; capital St John's. Newfoundland is an island off the east coast of Canada and was England's first colony, having been occupied on behalf of Elizabeth I in 1583. It was constituted as a Dominion at the Imperial Conference of 1917, but encountered such grave financial difficulties that its Dominion status was suspended in 1933. A Royal Commission recommended that the island should be administered by a Commission of Government, comprising three members from Newfoundland and three from the U.K. A referendum in July 1948 decided by a narrow majority (78,408 to 71,464) in favour of confederation with Canada rather than a return to responsible government as it existed till 1933. Newfoundland accordingly became a Province of Canada on 1 April 1949. In the 1959 elections to the legislature the result was: Liberals 31; Progressive Conservatives 3; United Newfoundland Party 2. Most of the population are engaged in fishing and its subsidiary industries; there is a large newsprint output, and there are several mines, which produce copper, fluorspar, iron ore, lead, limestone, and zinc.

Ngo Dinh Diem. President of the Republic of South Viet-Nam; born 1901 near Hue, the third son of a Roman Catholic Mandarin at the Court of Annam. After graduating from the civil service school at Hanoi he became a district chief, in 1929 a provincial governor and, in 1932, Minister of the Interior in the French puppet government. He resigned this post after three months. During the war years he shunned Japanese, French, Viet-Minh, and Chinese alike. He paid for his neutrality in 1945 when the Viet-Minh held him under arrest for four months; they buried alive his elder brother. In April 1947 he founded the National Union Front—a political organization opposed equally to French and Communists and dedicated to the principle of non-violence. It was immediately banned by the French. In 1951 he left Viet-Nam for the United States where for two years he lobbied Congressmen to withhold support from French colonialism and to make American aid to Indo-China conditional on reform. He spent 1953 in a monastery in Belgium and hurried to Paris at the fall of Dien Bien Phu. The French offered him the Premiership of Viet-Nam on 15 June 1954, and, with an acceptable promise of complete independence, he returned to Saigon.

With the help of United States military and economic experts, who regard Diem as the only possible alternative to Ho Chi-Minh, he has restored some semblance of order to South Viet-Nam. In spite of efforts by French residents to depose him, he exiled the pro-French commander of the army, General Nguyen Van Hinh, closed down the gambling dens and brothels of Saigon, reorganized the currency and launched his country into international trade, and drafted proposals for land reform and for a national assembly. He finally established his authority over terrorist sects in the Saigon riots of September 1955. In a referendum held on 23 October 1955 he was chosen, by a large majority, to replace Bao Dai, *q.v.*, as head of state.

Nicaragua. The largest Central American state, bordering on the Pacific and Atlantic Oceans; area 57,143 sq. m.; population (1959) 1,423,511, with sixty-eight per cent of mixed Spanish and Indian extraction, fifteen per cent white and mostly of Spanish descent, fourteen per cent Indians, Negroes, and mulattos; capital Managua. Sixty-six per cent of the population are illiterate. Nicaragua was ruled by Spain from the sixteenth century until it became independent in 1821. Under the 1950 Constitution the President is elected by direct suffrage for six years; Congress consists of a Senate (of sixteen members and ex-Presidents of the republic) and a Chamber of Deputies (of forty-two members). From 1950 until his murder in 1956 the President and virtual dictator was General Anastasio Somoza. He was succeeded by his son, Luis Somoza, who took office in February 1957.

Agriculture is the principal source of national wealth and there are important exports of coffee, cotton, and sesame seed. Nicaragua has been in debt for many years; by an agreement between British creditors and the Nicaraguan government in 1911, renewed in 1917 and 1920, customs receipts and certain other revenues are collected by the Collector-General of Customs, who must be an American, and are applied to the payment of the external debt. The government is permitted to spend any surplus.

Until 1948 Nicaragua was on good terms with Costa Rica, since President Teodoro Picado of Costa Rica was a friend of President Somoza. In that year José Figueres, who later became President of Costa Rica, deposed Picado. Relations between the two countries deteriorated, in spite of a 'pact of amity' on 21 February 1949. Nicaragua moved troops towards the common border in April 1954, bought twenty-five fighter aircraft (P–51s) from Sweden in December 1954, and on 11 January 1955 gave either active or passive support to an invasion of Costa Rica (which had no standing army) by Costa Rican exiles. During the dispute President Somoza challenged the Costa Rican President to a duel on the frontier, but Figueres did not accept the offer. (*See* Organization of American States.) Nicaragua and Costa Rica signed a treaty of friendship in January 1956.

Niger. An independent republic; area 458,976 sq. m.; population 2,415,000 comprising Hausas, Djermas, Touareg, Peuls, Songhais, and 3,000 Europeans; capital Niamey. The Hausas (1,000,000) and the Djermas form a distinct ethnic group, being black and living in the south, while the Touareg (300,000) and the Peuls (300,000) are pale-skinned. The country is land-locked, with Mali, the Sahara departments of Algeria, and Libya to the west and north, Chad to the east, and Upper Volta, Dahomey, and Nigeria to the south. The French created the separate territory of Niger by decrees in 1922 and 1926 and it became one of the eight territories comprising French West Africa, q.v. It obtained self-government within the French Community, q.v., on 18 December 1958; and complete independence, after breaking with the Community in June 1960, on 3 August 1960.

Legislative powers are vested in an assembly of 60 members elected every five years by universal suffrage. At the 1958 elections the Rassemblement Démocratique Africain, led by Hamani Diori, obtained control; the other leading party is the African Regroupment Party, led by Djibo Bakary, which has opposed any participation by Niger in the French Community. Executive authority is vested in the Prime Minister (Hamani Diori) who is invested by an absolute majority of the Assembly.

The country is short of water and there are only two permanent waterways, the Niger (on which stands Niamey) in the extreme west, and the Kamadougou, which flows into Lake Chad, to the east. Beans, manioc, and millet are produced, and there are exports of decorticated groundnuts, livestock, furs, and gum arabic.

Nigeria. A Dominion and member of the British Commonwealth, it was, until 1960, the largest British colony; it is in West Africa, and its territorial divisions are the Northern, Eastern, and Western Regions, the Southern Cameroons, and the federal capital of Lagos; area 373,250 sq. m.; population 35,300,000. The Southern Cameroons (*see* Cameroons, British) is a trusteeship territory and belonged to Germany until 1918. Under the 1954 Constitution Nigeria became a federation: the federal House of Representatives has 312 elected members and the political parties are based largely on regional affiliations. At the elections held in December 1959, the Northern People's Congress (which opposed the trend towards unification and wished the status of the central government to be reduced to that of a managing agency) won, under the leadership of the Sardauna of Socoto, 150 seats (all in the Northern Region). The Congress derives its support from the northern aristocracy and is opposed by the Northern Elements Progressive Union, which won 8 seats. The National Council of Nigeria and the Cameroons (N.C.N.C.), then led by Dr Nnamdi Azikiwe, q.v., won 89 seats, mostly in the Eastern

Region, among the Ibo people, where its main power lies, and some, unexpectedly, in the Western Region. The Action Group, led by Obafemi Awolowo, *q.v.*, won 62 seats. It is an alliance between the rulers and chiefs of the west and the rising class of rich business and professional men. The N.C.N.C. campaigned in the west as 'the party of the common man'. A coalition government, under the premiership of Alhaji Abubakar Tafawa Balewa, *q.v.*, was formed, and it included 10 representatives of the Northern People's Congress and 7 representatives of the N.C.N.C. The country became independent on 1 October 1960 and Azikiwe became Governor-General in November 1960.

Nigeria has valuable deposits of manganese ore, silver, and monazite which contains the radio-active element thorium; mining rights are vested in the government. It exports considerable quantities of palm-kernels, groundnuts, palm oil, cocoa, and tin; the U.K. is its most important trading partner.

Nihilism. From the Latin word *nihil*, meaning nothing; an intellectual movement in Russia in the middle of the nineteenth century, which became famous through Turgenev's novel, *Fathers and Sons*, 1862. Nihilists recognize no authority, doubt every general principle and value, and stand for freedom of the sovereign individual. Nihilism has often been confused with anarchism. Though its rejection of authority paved the way for political revolutionaries, it is a philosophical and literary outlook rather than a political doctrine.

Nixon, Richard Milhous. U.S. politician; born 9 January 1913 in California and educated at Duke University, North Carolina. He practised law from 1937 to 1942, when, after a short period as an attorney in the government service, he joined the U.S. navy, with which he served until 1946. He was then elected as a Republican member for Los Angeles in the House of Representatives. He was responsible for the citation for contempt of Congress of Gerhard Eisler, who had refused to testify before the House of Representatives Committee on Un-American Activities. In 1948 he unsuccessfully proposed legislation which would have committed the U.S.A. to grant military aid to countries threatened with Communist infiltration. He was an active supporter of the Subversive Activities Control Act, 1950, *q.v.*, but has said that the U.S.A. must not, in its efforts to break up subversive movements, impair or destroy any fundamental rights. He became a Senator in 1950 and in 1952 was elected to the office of Vice-President. He was returned for a second term as Vice-President in 1956, and in 1960 was the unsuccessful Republican Presidential candidate, being narrowly defeated by John F. Kennedy.

Nkrumah, Kwame. President of Ghana; born 1909 and educated at a Roman Catholic mission school and Achimota College. He became a school master in 1931 and later, with financial assistance from his uncle, who was a diamond prospector, studied sociology at the all-Negro University of Lincoln in Oxford, Pennsylvania, and became President of the African Students' Association of America and Canada. At the end of the Second World War he attended the London School of Economics and Political Science where he published a magazine *New African*, which was banned in the Gold Coast. In 1947 he became General Secretary of the United Gold Coast Convention, a popular nationalist party, which he left in 1949 to found the Convention People's Party. Nkrumah attacked the new Gold Coast Constitution alleging that it impeded progress towards self-government, and was imprisoned for his political agitation. The Governor released him from jail in 1951, when his party won the Gold Coast General Election, and made him Prime Minister. He remained as Prime Minister when the Dominion of Ghana was established on 6 March 1957, and became President when Ghana became a republic, within the British Commonwealth, in July 1960.

Nobel Prizes. By the will of A. B. Nobel, a Swedish chemist and engineer who died in 1896, the bulk of the fortune which he amassed from the manufacture of explosives was left to establish five annual prizes. Four go to the persons who have done the most distinguished work in physics, chemistry, medicine or physiology, and literature. The fifth goes to the person who or society which has done the most outstanding work for peace.

Non-Aggression Pact. An agreement between two states to abstain from the use of force against each other and to settle any differences by negotiation and arbitration.

Nordic Council. Comprises representatives from Denmark, Finland, Norway, Sweden, and Iceland, who give advice to the governments of these five countries on measures to improve Scandinavian co-operation. It has urged the governments to take concerted action to establish the necessary conditions for a common market in certain goods, as a first step towards a customs union, but developments in this direction were arrested by the establishment in 1959 of the European Free Trade Association, *q.v.*, which included Denmark, Norway and Sweden. The first products to be included in the common market were to be agricultural machinery, chemicals, furniture, leather goods, paint, porcelain, radios, shoes, and textiles. The Council is also concerned with minor measures of co-operation, such as the rule that Scandinavians no longer need passports when visiting other Scandinavian countries.

North Atlantic Treaty Organization. Set up by the North Atlantic Treaty, 4 April 1949, between the members of the Brussels Treaty Organization, *q.v.* (Belgium, France, Luxemburg, the Netherlands, and the U.K.), and Canada, Denmark, Iceland, Italy, Norway, Portugal, and the U.S.A. Whereas the Council of Europe, *q.v.*, and the Organization for European Economic Co-operation, *q.v.*, are European organizations, this Treaty links the two North American powers to a group of European states. Under Article Five the parties declare that they will regard an attack on one of them as an attack on all, and that, if an armed attack occurs, each will assist the country attacked by 'such action as it deems necessary'. This is less strict than the duty imposed on members of the Brussels Treaty Organization and the Western European Union, *q.v.*, to give to each other 'all the military and other aid and assistance in their power'. Since 1949 the following states have joined N.A.T.O.: the German Federal Republic, Greece, and Turkey. The Treaty declares a determination by the parties 'to safeguard the freedom, common heritage and civilization of their peoples founded on the principles of democracy, individual liberty and the rule of law'.

It was inspired partly by west European fear of the U.S.S.R. and partly by disappointment with the United Nations, in which the work of the Security Council, which is responsible for dealing with threats to peace and aggression, was being hindered by the Russian use of the veto. The Treaty was declared to be a regional arrangement of the type contemplated by the United Nations Charter. It was more significant than the Rio Treaty, *q.v.*, or the Brussels Treaty, because it was the first treaty in which the U.S.A. had ever undertaken European commitments in peacetime. The wording of Article Five ensures, however, that there is no automatic obligation to fight; the U.S. Congress, for example, would still be able to decide whether or not the U.S.A. should go to war.

North Borneo. The northern part of the island of Borneo, *q.v.*, comprising the colony of British North Borneo, *q.v.*, the protected state of Brunei, *q.v.*, and the colony of Sarawak, *q.v.*

North Korea. The Democratic People's Republic of Korea, a state not recognized by the western powers, established after the partition of Korea, *q.v.*, in 1945; area 46,814 sq. m.; population (1939) 8,229,000, 1960 estimate approximately 10,000,000; capital Pyongyang. It was under Russian military occupation from August 1945 until December 1948. During this period a Communist-led provisional government was set up; from this evolved the Supreme National Assembly which adopted a Constitution modelled on that of the U.S.S.R., and on 12 September 1948 proclaimed a republic. The new state was immediately recognized by the U.S.S.R. and its satellites. It has since been governed by a coalition of three parties, the Communists, the Chendogyo, and the Democrats, represented on a Central Committee of five which includes the Prime Minister, Kim Il-sung, one woman, Pak Chong Ae, and the Foreign Minister, Pak Sung Chul.

Relations with South Korea, q.v., deteriorated steadily in 1947 and 1948. U.S. attempts to reunify the country were thwarted by the U.S.S.R., and the matter was referred to the United Nations who, in 1947, voted for unification under one freely-elected government and sent a commission to Korea to negotiate an agreement. Meanwhile an army of 200,000 was recruited in North Korea mainly from Korean repatriates who had taken refuge from the Japanese in Siberia and Manchuria and had been trained by the Chinese in guerrilla warfare. In 1948, prior to the holding of South Korean elections to an assembly in which 100 vacant seats were to be reserved for representatives from the North, North Korea cut off the supply of electricity from their hydro-electric power plants, thereby causing an industrial standstill, and considerable temporary unemployment, in the South. There were innumerable incidents along the 38th parallel in 1948 and 1949 which culminated, on 25 June 1950, in the invasion of South Korea by the army of the North. The United Nations declared North Korea to be an aggressor and sent troops to the aid of the South; China recruited 200,000 volunteers who entered the fighting on the side of the North in November 1950 when the United Nations forces reached the Manchurian border. The war continued until 27 July 1953 when an armistice was signed by which the line of division between North and South Korea remained in the neighbourhood of the 38th parallel; there has been no subsequent agreement on reunification.

Although much of its generating and industrial plant was destroyed in the Korean War, North Korea has a valuable industrial potential, and this has been developed considerably since the end of the war in 1953. There are considerable deposits of iron ore, and metallurgical, cotton-spinning, and hydro-electric power works are intensively developed by the Japanese. Korea's sole petroleum refinery, its major cement works, and the nitrogenous fertilizer works of the Chosun Chilso Company are all in the North. Trade is mainly with the U.S.S.R.

North Viet-Nam. The zone north of the 17th parallel allotted to the

Viet-Minh, *q.v.*, in July 1954 by the terms of the Geneva Agreements on the cessation of hostilities in Viet-Nam, *q.v.*; population 13,790,000; seat of government Hanoi. The Viet-Minh government, which controls the zone, is recognized as the government of Viet-Nam by China and the U.S.S.R. According to the Constitution of 1946, which proclaimed a Democratic Republic of Viet-Nam, all power is vested in the people and the legislature consists of a unicameral Parliament of the People elected by secret ballot. A Parliament was elected in May 1960 but the administration is in the hands of the President of the Republic, Ho Chi-Minh, *q.v.*, the Prime Minister (since 1955) Pham Van Dong, and the Deputy Premier and Commander of the Armed Forces, General Vo-Nguyen Giap who have governed through the Lien Viet (National Union Front) and the Lao Dong or Workers' Party. The Geneva Agreements stipulated that North Viet-Nam was to be reunited with South Viet-Nam in July 1956, and that a General Election was to be held then to determine the future government of Viet-Nam, but this part of the Agreements was not carried out.

Northern Cameroons. *See* Cameroons, British.

Northern Ireland. A part of the U.K., comprising the six Northern Irish counties of Antrim, Armagh, Down, Fermanagh, Londonderry, and Tyrone; area 5,242 sq. m.; population 1,407,700; capital Belfast. It is often referred to as Ulster, *q.v.*, of which it forms a part. Under the Government of Ireland Act, 1920, as amended by the Irish Free State Act, 1922, Northern Ireland has limited self-government exercised by a Parliament, comprising a Senate of 2 ex-officio and 24 elected members, and a House of Commons of 52 members elected for five years. The elected Senators are appointed by the House of Commons on a proportional representation basis. Certain legislative and fiscal powers are reserved to the government of the U.K. Northern Ireland also returns 12 members to the House of Commons in London; at the 1959 General Election 12 Conservative members were elected. Anti-Partition candidates obtained fifteen per cent of the total vote. The majority of the population in Northern Ireland is opposed to the unification of Ireland and wishes to remain within the British Commonwealth.

Northern Rhodesia. A British protectorate in Central Africa; area 288,130 sq. m.; population (1960 estimate) 2,460,000, including 2,340,000 Africans, 77,000 Europeans, and 6,000 Asians; seat of government Lusaka. On 1 August 1953 Northern Rhodesia, while retaining its status as a protectorate, joined Southern Rhodesia and Nyasaland to form the Federation of Rhodesia and Nyasaland, *q.v.*

The United National Independence Party, led by Kenneth Kaunda, demands full voting rights for Africans and the right of Northern Rhodesia to secede from the Federation.

Northern Tier. The group of Near and Middle Eastern Powers, Turkey, Persia, and Pakistan, which, with the U.K., are associated under the Central Treaty Organization, *q.v.*

Norway. An independent state in Scandinavia; area 124,525 sq. m.; population (1958) 3,510,199; capital Oslo. It was united with Denmark from 1397 to 1814, and from 1814 until 1905 its throne was united with that of Sweden, when it broke away and chose as sovereign a Danish prince who became King Haakon VII. It is a constitutional and hereditary monarchy; legislative power is vested in the Storting (parliament), with 150 representatives elected every four years. They choose one quarter of their number to form the Lagting (upper house), the other three quarters forming the Odelsting (lower chamber). Questions relating to laws are dealt with by each house separately; most other matters are discussed by both houses together. Executive power is vested in the King acting through the cabinet (Statsråd) comprising the Prime Minister and at least seven ministers.

The most powerful group in the Storting, since 1935, has been the Labour Party, which at elections held on 7 October 1957 secured an outright majority of the 150 seats, increasing its share of the total vote from 46·7 per cent in 1953 to 48·4 per cent. The Labour Party is divided from the four main opposition parties by its Socialist beliefs and its desire for a high degree of state direction and control over the economy. After the First World War the Labour Party had strong radical leanings, and until 1923 was a member of the Communist Third International, but later moderated its views and joined the Socialist Second International. The Party has brought Norway out of its traditional neutrality into full membership of the North Atlantic Treaty Organization. It is led by Einar Gerhardsen, Prime Minister from 1945 to November 1951 and since January 1955, and Halvard Lange, Foreign Minister since 1946. The opposition parties are the Conservatives, who are reluctant to accept any extension of state controls (29 seats), the Liberals, who are radical in outlook (15), the Agrarian or Farmers' Party (15), the Christian Popular Party (12), and the Communist Party (1).

Of the total area 73·9 per cent is unproductive and 22·8 per cent consists of forests, which are one of the chief natural sources of wealth. The principal exports are fish and its products, pulp and paper, iron ore and pyrites, and other minerals. The only coal deposits lie in the Spitsbergen Archipelago, *q.v.* Hydro-electric power production has doubled since 1945; the government plans to develop steel and aluminium industries and to expand the economy of north Norway. The country has the sixth largest merchant fleet in the world (11,203,000 gross tons in June 1960). Apart from the immense number of rocky islands around its coast, Norway exercises sovereignty over the Spitsbergen Archipelago, 550 miles to the north of the northernmost part of Norway, Jan Mayen Island, 300 miles north of Iceland, Bouvet Island, an uninhabited island in the Southern Atlantic Ocean, Peter I Island, in the Antarctic Ocean, and Queen Maud Land, in the Antarctic Continent, *q.v.*

Nuncio. From the Latin *nuntius*, herald, the title of the Papal envoy in foreign Catholic capitals. The Papal Nuncio is universally accepted as the doyen of the diplomatic corps.

Nyasaland. A British protectorate in central Africa; area 36,870 sq. m.; population (1960) 2,860,000, including 2,810,000 Africans, 8,510 Asians, and 9,500 Europeans; seat of government Zomba. On 1 August 1953 Nyasaland, while retaining its status as a protectorate, joined Northern and Southern Rhodesia to form the Federation of Rhodesia and Nyasaland, *q.v.* The Malawi Congress Party, led by Dr Hastings Banda, *q.v.*, and Orton Chirwa, formed in 1959 to succeed the proscribed Nyasaland African Congress Party, insists on the right of Nyasaland to secede from the Federation, as recommended by the Monckton Report, *q.v.*

Nyerere, Julius. Tanganyikan politician; born 1922, one of 26 children of a chief, he is a Roman Catholic; educated at the University College of East Africa, Makerere, and Edinburgh University, where he studied history and economics, he was a teacher at a Catholic school near Dar-es-Salaam until 1955 when he decided to give all his time to political activity, and became the leader of the Tanganyika African National Union (T.A.N.U.) which was overwhelmingly successful at the 1958 and 1960 elections to the Legislative Council. He became Prime Minister on 1 May 1961.

O

O.A.S. Organization of American States, *q.v.*

Oder-Neisse Line. The boundary between Eastern Germany and Poland established after the Second World War; it is marked by the river Oder which flows into the Baltic Sea at Szczecin (formerly Stettin), and its tributary the Neisse which has its source in Czechoslovakia. The line was accepted by the U.K., the U.S.A., and the U.S.S.R. as part of the Potsdam Agreement, *q.v.*, of 2 August 1945. All German territory east of a line from the Baltic coast immediately west of Swinemünde, and thence along the Oder and the Western Neisse to the Czech frontier, was placed provisionally under the administration of Poland and withdrawn from the authority of the Allied Control Council in Berlin. This territory formed nearly a fifth of Germany's 1938 area, and contained about a quarter of its arable land and between one sixth and one seventh of its 1938 population. It included the best land for growing potatoes, sugar-beet and wheat, much of which used to feed Western Germany. Poland was awarded Stettin (as it then was) and a small area west of the town.

Although the three powers stated that the final delimitation of the western frontier should take place later, the Oder-Neisse Line was accepted as permanent by the Polish government, which expelled large numbers of Germans who later comprised nearly a quarter of the West German voters. An agreement describing the line as the permanent frontier was concluded between the German Democratic Republic and Poland on 6 July 1950; the Poles were, in addition, granted the whole of the thirty-mile long island of Usedom and some land in Mecklenburg. The German Federal Republic, the U.K., and the U.S.A. did not recognize this agreement. On 6 July 1955 the East German and Polish governments declared that the Oder-Neisse Line was the permanent frontier. The U.K. and the U.S.A. have claimed that there was an understanding at Potsdam that the new frontier was conditional on the granting of free elections in Poland, and that in any event final agreement can only be reached when a peace treaty is concluded with a government of a united Germany.

O.E.C.D. Organization for Economic Co-operation and Development, *q.v.*

O.E.E.C. Organization for European Economic Co-operation, *q.v.*

Okinawa. Largest island of the Ryuku Islands, which lie 500 miles to the south-west of Japan, between the Japanese island of Kyushu and Formosa; they are nominally owned by Japan, but the peace treaty with the U.S.A., which came into effect on 28th April 1952, gave the U.S.A. 'the right to exercise all and any powers of administration, legislation and jurisdiction', though it recognized that Japan had a residual sovereignty. Japan is obliged to agree to any proposal made by the U.S.A. to the United Nations to make the Islands a trusteeship territory with the U.S.A. as the administering government. The most northern group of the Islands, the Amami-Oshima group, was returned to Japan in 1953. The parts of the Islands remaining under

U.S. control have an area of 848 sq. m. and a population of approximately 849,300; the capital is Naha, in Okinawa. U.S. military bases in Okinawa (on which 718,500 people live) occupy 12·4 per cent of the total area and 10·8 per cent of the arable area, and the island plays an important part in the U.S. military dispositions in the western Pacific Ocean. Among the most important issues in local politics are the date at which the Islands will be returned to Japan, the amount of compensation paid to dispossessed farmers, and the extent of the land area used by U.S. forces.

Ollenhauer, Erich. Socialist politician in the German Federal Republic; born in 1901 in Magdeburg. He spent the early part of his career in the German Socialist youth movement, which he joined in 1916, and of which he was an official from 1920 to 1928, and Chairman from 1928 to 1933, when he joined the executive committee of the German Socialist Party. After Hitler came to power Ollenhauer went to Prague and was deprived of his German citizenship in 1935; he was in Paris from 1938 to 1941 and in the U.K. from 1941 to 1946. After his return to Western Germany he became deputy chairman of the Socialist group in the federal legislature; in 1952 he succeeded Kurt Schumacher as chairman of the group and of the Socialist Party.

Oman. An area in the interior of the independent state and Sultanate of Muscat and Oman, *q.v.* Trucial Oman is the name sometimes applied to the adjacent area, further up the Persian Gulf, known as the Trucial Coast, *q.v.*

One Glass of Water Doctrine. A belief, held by Communist revolutionaries during the early stages of the Russian and Chinese revolutions, that a good Communist should regard sexual desire as being no more important than a glass of water. This doctrine was revoked by Lenin when the revolution achieved success in Russia, but it is still the rule in China where it is known as Pei-shui-chu-i. Communist revolutionaries in the west are not believed to adhere to this doctrine.

O.P.E.C. Organization of Petroleum Exporting Countries, *q.v.*

Open Door Policy. The policy of trading with all nations or individuals on equal terms, and not giving monopolies or preferences to any individual country.

Organization of American States (O.A.S.). A regional agency set up by the Ninth International Conference of American States at Bogota, Colombia, in April and May 1948, to co-ordinate the work of all the various inter-American organizations. It is a successor to the International Bureau of the American Republics set up by the First International Conference of American States in 1890. The twenty-one members (each with one vote) are: Argentina, Bolivia, Brazil, Chile, Colombia, Costa Rica, Cuba, the Dominican Republic, Ecuador, Guatemala, Haiti, Honduras, Mexico, Nicaragua, Panama, Paraguay, Peru, Salvador, Uruguay, the U.S.A., and Venezuela.

The O.A.S. is a regional organization within the framework of the United Nations of the type permitted by the United Nations Charter and is a stronger version of the Pan American Union, *q.v.* The most important provisions of the Charter of O.A.S. deal with the peaceful settlement of disputes between members, and lay down the procedure for mediation, arbitration, and the reference of legal questions to the International Court of Justice. Such matters as the recognition of *de facto* governments and of territories acquired by force, the propagation of doctrines leading to aggression, and the civil rights of women, are also covered in the Charter.

The organs of O.A.S. are: (1) the Inter-American Conference, meeting every five years, at which government representatives decide policy; (2) the Consultative Meeting of Ministers of Foreign Affairs, which considers urgent problems and takes decisions in matters covered by the Rio Treaty, *q.v.*, being helped by an Advisory Defence Committee; (3) the O.A.S. Council, comprising representatives of all members, to supervise the progress of O.A.S.; (4) the Pan American Union, the central and permanent organ of O.A.S.; (5) the Specialized Conferences, meeting to deal with special technical matters or to develop specific aspects of inter-American co-operation; (6) the Specialized Organizations, inter-governmental organizations established by multilateral agreements to discharge specific functions in their respective fields of action.

An example of the way in which O.A.S. operates in the military sphere occurred when Costa Rica was invaded from Nicaragua by Costa Rican exiles on 11 January 1955. The O.A.S. Council met in emergency session in Washington on the same day in response to an appeal by the Costa Rican government, which invoked the Rio Treaty. O.A.S. sent a fact-finding mission to Costa Rica which reported on 13 January that war material was flowing across the Nicaragua-Costa Rica frontier; the Council then called on Nicaragua to stop the supplies of war material and asked all American states to give 'prompt consideration' to Costa Rica's request for aircraft. The U.S.A. accordingly supplied five aircraft, this being the first occasion on which an American republic had received aid under the Rio Treaty to enable it to repel external aggression. O.A.S. later proposed a demilitarized zone on each side of the frontier, which was accepted by Costa Rica and Nicaragua.

Organization of Central American States. Was set up in 1951 by Costa Rica, Salvador, Guatemala, Honduras, and Nicaragua. Panama refused to join. Its aims are to promote economic, cultural, and social co-operation between its members. It encountered difficulties immediately after its formation when Salvador proposed that it should approve an anti-Communist resolution; this was opposed by Guatemala, which withdrew from the Organization in April 1953. After the revolution which overthrew the Arbenz régime, Guatemala rejoined the Organization, but its first meeting was further postponed as a result of the invasion of Costa Rica from Nicaragua on 11 January 1955. The first formal conference was held at Antigua, Guatemala, in August 1955. All five members attended and Panama sent observers. The conference passed a number of resolutions to promote economic, cultural, and social co-operation, agreed to set up a committee of jurists to study the codification of Central American legislation, and elected a Secretary-General.

Organization for Economic Co-operation and Development (O.E.C.D.). Was set up in 1961 by twenty nations (Austria, Belgium, Canada, Denmark, France, the German Federal Republic, Greece, Iceland, Ireland, Italy, Luxemburg, the Netherlands, Norway, Portugal, Spain, Sweden, Switzerland, Turkey, the U.K., and the U.S.A.) to succeed the Organization for European Economic Co-operation, *q.v.* Its members are the eighteen members of O.E.E.C., and Canada and U.S.A., which were associate members of O.E.E.C. Its tasks are: (1) to encourage and co-ordinate the economic policies of member countries; (2) to contribute to the expansion of countries in a state of development, whether members or not; and (3) to facilitate the development of world trade and settle trade problems.

Organization for European Economic Co-operation (O.E.E.C.). Was set up in 1948 by sixteen nations (Austria, Belgium, Denmark, France, Greece, Iceland, Ireland, Italy, Luxemburg, the Netherlands, Norway, Portugal, Sweden, Switzerland, Turkey, and the U.K.) in response to the Marshall Plan, *q.v.*, to co-ordinate the economic activities of European countries receiving aid under the European Recovery Programme, *q.v.* An annually elected President is in charge of the Supreme Council which represents all member nations; under the Council there is an Executive Committee of seven, with a Chairman, but any country interested in the subject under discussion can join meetings of this Committee. A permanent international secretariat under a Secretary-General is empowered to prepare agenda and submit proposals to the Council, to the Committee, and to expert technical committees set up by the Council, e.g. on manpower, coal, chemicals, and customs. The German Federal Republic and Spain joined O.E.E.C. as full members in 1955 and 1959 respectively; Yugoslavia has been allowed to participate to a limited extent; Canada and the U.S.A. are associate members. The members and associate members agreed in 1960 that O.E.E.C. should be replaced by the Organization for Economic Co-operation and Development *q.v.*

Organization of Petroleum Exporting Countries (O.P.E.C.). Constituted in January 1961 in Caracas by Iraq, Kuwait, Persia, Qatar, Saudi Arabia, and Venezuela, who resolved: (1) to demand that the oil companies should 'maintain their prices steady and free from all unnecessary fluctuations which affect the economic development of both producing and consuming countries'; (2) to formulate a system to ensure the stabilization of prices by regulating production; (3) not, in the cases of the other members, to accept beneficial treatment, in the form of increased exports or higher prices, from the oil companies if any one member should have sanctions applied against it by an oil company as a result of applying any unanimous decision of the Organization.

Organization for Trade Co-operation. An international agency, which the parties to the General Agreement on Tariffs and Trade, *q.v.*, agreed in 1955 should be set up to administer the General Agreement. It was originally hoped that the International Trade Organization, *q.v.*, contemplated by the Havana Charter, *q.v.*, would do this work, but the I.T.O. was never set up because the U.S.A. failed to ratify the Charter.

O.T.C. Organization for Trade Co-operation, *q.v.*

Outer Mongolia. *See* Mongolian People's Republic.

Outer Seven. A term often used to describe the members of the European Free Trade Association, *q.v.*

Over-Full Employment. Defined by Lord Beveridge in his *Full Employment in a Free Society* as a state of affairs in which, in the U.K., there was an unemployment rate of less than three per cent. A rate of three per cent would constitute Full Employment, *q.v.*

P

Pacific Security Pact. The tripartite security treaty concluded between Australia, New Zealand, and the U.S.A. on 1 September 1951 and more commonly known as A.N.Z.U.S., *q.v.*

Pakhtunistan. Land of the Pakhtuns or Pathans; a name used by the Afghan government to describe a mountainous area in the

Peshawar Division of Pakistan near the Afghan frontier; population approximately 2,500,000. In 1947 it was incorporated, with the consent of the inhabitants, most of whom are Moslem, into the Dominion of Pakistan, and administered by Pakistan political agents. In March 1955 the Pakistan government proposed to merge all the states and tribal areas of West Pakistan into a single administrative unit, giving each region representation in the Provincial Assembly in proportion to its population. The Afghan Prime Minister, Sardar Mohammed Daoud, denounced the move as an 'aggressive act,' and insisted on the formation of the separate, independent state of Pakhtunistan. Incidents occurred in Kabul, the Afghan capital, which resulted in the evacuation of all Pakistan residents, the Afghan consulate in Peshawar was attacked and a state of emergency was declared in Afghanistan, Egypt, Iraq, Saudi Arabia, and Turkey offered to mediate between the two Moslem countries; the offer was accepted, but on 28 June the Saudi Arabian envoys admitted their failure to reconcile the two governments. The dispute really concerns the exact delimitation of the Afghan-Pakistani frontier. Pakistan is ready to fight to maintain the Durand Line, the boundary agreed between Afghanistan and British India in 1892. On 5 May 1955 a British government spokesman declared that Pakistan's sovereignty over Pakhtunistan was undisputed. The U.S.S.R. and India have since declared their support for the Afghan claim.

Pakistan. A Dominion within the British Commonwealth comprising the following former territories of British India: Baluchistan, West Punjab, Sind, North-West Frontier, East Bengal, and thirteen princely states including Bahawalpur and Khairpur, all of which have a majority of Moslem inhabitants; area 364,737 sq. m.; population 93,812,000; federal capital Islamabad. The need for a separate association of Moslem states within India became apparent to Moslem leaders when the Hindu-dominated Congress Party, q.v., decided that in the political struggle for Indian independence there was no room for minority religious organizations. In the 1935 Provincial elections, Moslem League candidates won a substantial minority of the seats in the United Provinces Assembly; the Congress Party refused to admit them into a coalition unless they first dissolved their party organization. Moslem nationalists, led by Khaliquzzaman and Jinnah, left the Congress Party, united under the slogan 'Islam is in danger', and, in response to the Viceroy's offer of Dominion status in 1940, rallied Moslem support for the idea of 'Pakistan'. They made it clear to the United Kingdom government that there could be no peaceful withdrawal from India without partition.

In 1947 the right of self-determination was given to every state and principality in British India. As the Moslem population was concentrated in the north-west and in the extreme south-east the new state of Pakistan comprised two areas separated by a thousand miles of Indian territory. When the U.K. relinquished its authority to the Provincial governments the boundaries between East and West Punjab had not been defined, police and administrative services were in a process of transfer, and the Pakistan government of East Bengal had its headquarters in a girls' school in Dacca. In the fighting and pillage which accompanied the trek of Moslems to Pakistan, and of Hindus to India, the Punjab was ravaged and more than half a million people killed. Only the personal intervention of Gandhi prevented a similar massacre in Bengal. The assets of British India were divided in the proportion of 17½ per cent to Pakistan and 82½ per cent to India; India's reluctance to yield any share of the foreign sterling balances, or of arms and military equipment, provoked strong resentment. Subsequent disputes over the decisions by the states of Junagudh and Manavadar to accede to Pakistan (which were forestalled by Indian occupation on 8 November 1948), and by Kashmir, *q.v.*, to join the Indian Union, although most of its people are Moslem, have intensified hostility between India and Pakistan, and over sixty per cent of Pakistan's central government revenue is spent on defence. In consequence, political and economic evolution has been very slow; in 1955 the state had yet to enact a constitution. A decision taken in 1954 to accept U.S. military aid, ostensibly to protect the Afghan frontier against Russian penetration, exacerbated Indian hostility and further divided the militant western region from East Pakistan which resents the preoccupation of West Pakistan with Middle East affairs.

West Pakistan is an arid region, almost in the Middle East; its 42,968,000 people speak Urdu and eat wheat. The rice-eating Bengalis in East Pakistan export the jute and earn the foreign exchange which balances the Federal budget. There is a Hindu minority of 9,000,000 among the 50,844,000 inhabitants of East Bengal; in the national elections of June 1955 it sent nine non-Moslems out of a total of forty representatives to the Constituent Assembly. A crisis occurred in relations between East and West Pakistan at the 1954 Provincial elections when East Bengal rejected the Moslem League (government party) candidates and returned a majority for the United Front, *q.v.*, headed by Fazlal Huq, and supported by Shahid Suhrawardy, *q.v.* Although the government which they formed was dismissed as corrupt by Maj.-Gen. Iskander Mirza, who ruled alone in Bengal on behalf of the Governor-General, the crisis was then resolved only by the separation of the regions into two distinct administrative entities, so that Bengal could handle its own finances, and the inclusion in the Federal government of equal numbers of East and West Pakistanis.

In 1954 the Governor-General, Ghulam Mohammad, with the support of the army, dissolved the seven-year-old Assembly on the grounds that it was no longer representative and that it had not produced a constitution. He directed the Prime Minister, Mohammed Ali, to take into his cabinet three men, Major-General Mirza as Minister of the Interior, Shahid Suhrawardy as Minister of Law, and General Ayub Khan as Minister of Defence, who had not been elected to the Assembly. These actions were challenged in the Chief Court of Sind and declared unconstitutional; this decision was reversed by the Federal Court in April 1955 and the powers of the Governor-General were defined. He was thus enabled to order elections for a new Constituent Assembly, the representatives being elected by the Provincial Assemblies, which would appoint an Electoral Commission and draw up a constitution within six months. East Bengal made its participation in such an Assembly conditional upon the restoration of parliamentary government in the Province. The results of the elections were announced on 21 June 1955: Moslem League 25 seats; United Front 16; Awami League (led by Shahid Suhrawardy) 13; the non-Moslem parties (United Progressive Parliamentary Party, the Pakistan National Congress, and the Scheduled Castes Federation) 9; Azad Pakistan Party 1; Communist Party 1; Noon Group (a Punjab party opposed to the unification of West Pakistan) 3; Independents 4; representatives from the states and tribal areas 8. A coalition government was formed of Moslem League and United Front members, but this was replaced in September 1956 by a coalition, led by Suhrawardy, of the Awami League, and the Republican Party formed in 1956 by the then Chief Minister of West Pakistan, Dr Khan Sahib, who was murdered in 1958. The Republicans comprised former supporters of the Moslem League both inside and outside the Federal Assembly. When the Republicans withdrew their support from Suhrawardy, in October 1957, I. I. Chundrigar, of the Moslem League, became Prime Minister of a coalition which included the Republican Party. When Chundrigar brought in a Bill providing for communal electoral rolls (a scheme favoured by the Moslem League), the Awami League and some Republicans combined to overthrow him. Sir Malik Firoz Khan Noon led a mainly Republican ministry from December 1957 to October 1958, General Ayub Khan then became Premier and also succeeded Mirza (President since March 1956) as President, in

October 1958. Mirza had already abrogated the Constitution, and Ayub Khan therefore had full powers.

The Pakistan Constitution, providing that the country should be an Islamic Republic, and approved by the Constituent Assembly, became law on 23 March 1956; simultaneously the Assembly decided that Pakistan should remain within the British Commonwealth.

Economic stability will not be achieved until factories are built to manufacture the raw jute and cotton which are the principal exports, and agricultural production is improved. This is dependent on the success of irrigation schemes in the Punjab but agreement with India over the canal waters dispute, *q.v.*, in 1960, considerably improved the economic prospects. Economic, technical, and agricultural assistance is received from the U.S.A. Pakistan is a member of the Central Treaty Organization, *q.v.*, and of the South-East Asia Collective Defence Treaty, *q.v.*

Palestine. An area of 10,429 sq. m. on the eastern Mediterranean Sea which was part of the Ottoman Empire until the end of the First World War. The state of Israel, *q.v.*, occupies 8,048 sq. m. of Palestine. After 1918 Palestine was placed under British administration by a League of Nations Mandate which incorporated the Balfour Declaration, *q.v.*; the terms of the Mandate imposed on the U.K. the obligation to 'place the country under such political, administrative and economic conditions as will secure the establishment of the Jewish national home, while at the same time safeguarding the civil and religious rights of all the inhabitants of Palestine'. In accordance with this requirement Jews were admitted into Palestine, the population of which had in 1919 been almost entirely Arab, but only on limited annual quotas. Arab revolts in 1921 and 1929 were quelled by the British, but the Hope Simpson and the Passfield reports of 1930, following the second revolt, recommended the suspension of Jewish immigration and a Legislative Council which would have had an Arab majority. The plan was abandoned in the face of Zionist opposition. The persecution of Jews in Germany caused an increase in the flow of immigrants, both legal and illegal. In 1939 the British government declared that it was not a part of its policy that Palestine should become a Jewish state; it also rejected the Arab claim for an Arab state, and said that the objective was to be an independent Palestinian state, 'the two peoples sharing authority in government in such a way that the essential interests of each were secured'. A Palestinian state was to be set up in ten years.

After the Second World War there was strong opposition among Palestinian Jews to the continuance of British occupation. There were outbreaks of fierce fighting and the problem was referred by the U.K. to the United Nations in February 1947. The United Nations Special Committee on Palestine recommended partition of the area; this recommendation was accepted by the United Nations General Assembly. On 14 May 1948 the British High Commissioner left Palestine and the state of Israel was proclaimed. Arab forces from Egypt, Iraq, Jordan, Lebanon, and Syria then attacked Israel, but hostilities ceased in January 1949. Although partition had been recommended, Israel occupied various areas allotted to the Arab state, increasing its territory by forty per cent; Jordan acquired parts of Palestine west of the river Jordan, and Egypt occupied the Gaza Strip, *q.v.*, which had been allotted to the proposed Arab state.

Pan American Union. An organization of American states which arose out of the meeting on 14 April 1890, in Washington, D.C., of the First International Conference of American States. The Conference established the International Bureau of the American Republics, which later became the Pan American Union and held annual conferences. The aim of the Union was to foster political and economic collaboration between the American states and a feeling of solidarity between North and South America. The work of the Union was often made difficult by the reticent attitude of the South American states, which feared the economic and political hegemony of the U.S.A. In spite of this, a number of institutions was created to promote cultural and economic co-operation, and about forty agreements relating to inter-American trade, traffic, migration, and other questions were concluded. At a conference at Panama on 3 October 1939, the twenty-one American republics established a 'neutrality zone' of 300 miles, and in some places of 600 miles, around the whole American continent except Canada. This Declaration of Panama did not prohibit absolutely all warlike acts at sea or in the air in the zone, but provided for mutual consultation as to practical steps if hostilities should occur within it. The U.K. protested, claiming that the establishment of the zone was incompatible with international law and that it created a sanctuary for German vessels.

After the Second World War the need for even greater Pan American integration became apparent, and in 1948 there was created the Organization of American States, *q.v.*, of which the Pan American Union is the central and permanent organ and general secretariat.

The Union has four administrative departments which deal with: (1) economic and social affairs; (2) international law; (3) cultural affairs; (4) administrative services. It also acts as adviser to the

Council of the Organization of American States, and its organs, in the preparations for inter-American and Specialized Conferences; as a depository of instruments of ratification of inter-American agreements; and as a clearing-house for information on all the member countries.

Pan-Germanism. The belief that all German-speaking peoples should be brought together in one empire. Pan-Germanists have advocated particularly the absorption into Germany of the German-speaking provinces of Austria. Adolf Hitler, who was born in Austria, was brought up in an atmosphere of Austrian Pan-Germanism and realized some of its aims by his annexation in 1938 of Austria and the Sudeten territories of Czechoslovakia. In the west, strict Pan-Germanists would approve of the incorporation in Germany of Alsace-Lorraine, Luxemburg, and the German-speaking part of Switzerland, but claims of this sort have not been pressed since 1945. As for the territories to the east of Germany, many Germans openly demand the return of the lands awarded to Poland under the Potsdam Agreement, *q.v.*, of 1945, and reject the permanency of the Oder-Neisse Line, *q.v.*, as a frontier. Poland tried to forestall such demands by mass expulsions of Germans from these lands in 1945 and 1946.

Panama. An independent Central American state on the Atlantic and Pacific Oceans; population 1,000,000 (excluding those in the Panama Canal Zone); area 29,224 sq. m.; capital Panama. It was formerly one of the nine departments of the Republic of Colombia, but with U.S. encouragement it revolted and became independent on 3 November 1903. Fifteen days later Panama agreed to give facilities to the U.S.A. for the construction and maintenance of an inter-ocean canal, and granted to the U.S.A. in perpetuity the use, occupation, and control of the Panama Canal Zone (two strips five miles wide on each side of the Canal), and within the Zone the exclusive rights to exercise sovereign power and authority. The Canal was opened to commerce on 15 August 1914. In return the U.S.A. paid $10,000,000, and an annual sum of $250,000 to begin in 1912.

The treaty was revised in 1936 (the annual payment being increased to $430,000) and on 25 January 1955 when the annual payment was increased to $1,930,000, although Panama had asked for $5,000,000 yearly, or alternatively a fixed percentage of annual receipts from the Canal tolls. The 1955 revision (1) removed many discriminations against Panamanians employed in the Zone; (2) required Canal employees to make their purchases from local merchants instead of from tax free commissaries in the Zone; (3) gave Panama the right to tax the incomes of some 17,000 workers who were not U.S. citizens and who lived outside the Zone; they are mainly descendants of British West Indians employed as labourers on the construction of the Canal. The revision was negotiated for Panama by President José Antonio Remón, under whom Panama had made considerable economic progress since 1952, but he was assassinated on 2 January 1955. His Vice-President succeeded him but was later jailed for plotting the assassination. The Second Vice-President then completed the Presidential term which expired in 1956, when Ernesto de la Guardia was elected President. On the expiry of his term he was succeeded, in October 1960, by Roberto Chiari, leader of a coalition of four of the eight opposition parties, who had been President for a brief period in 1949.

Under the Constitution there is a single-chamber legislature elected every four years and consisting of fifty-three elected members, and a President and two Vice-Presidents, elected by direct popular vote. The soil is extremely fertile, but only a small part has been developed and Panama imports sixty per cent of its food requirements. The exports include bananas (grown by an associated company of the United Fruit Company and shipped to the U.S.A.), cacao, coconuts, and hides. Panama has the world's fifth largest oil tanker fleet.

The Panama Canal Zone is governed by the Canal Zone Government and operated by the Panama Canal Company, both set up on 1 July 1951. The Secretary of the U.S. Army holds all the shares of the Company. The area of the Zone, including the Canal itself, is 684 sq. m.; its population, excluding some 10,000 military personnel, is about 42,000. The Company's income is derived almost entirely from tolls levied on vessels using the Canal, which amounted to $45,529,000 in the year ending 30 June 1959.

Pandit, Vijaya Lakshmi. Politician; born 18 August 1900 into a prosperous Brahman family and educated privately. Already a Socialist, in 1928 she became a supporter of the non-violent non-co-operation movement led by Gandhi which opposed British rule in India. She was imprisoned in 1932, although she was a mother with three young daughters, for participating in the public observance of India Independence Day. She became a member of the Allahabad Municipal Board and later Chairman of the local Education Committee in 1935. She was the Minister of Local Self-Government and Public Health in the United Provinces Government, 1937–9, and as a member of the Congress Party was elected to the Legislative Assembly. In 1940 she was sentenced to four months' imprisonment for anti-war activities, and was detained under the Defence Regulations from August 1942 to June 1943. In 1946 she again became Minister of Local Self-

Government and Public Health; she led the Indian delegation to the United Nations in 1946, 1947, and 1948; was Ambassador to the U.S.S.R. in 1947–9, to the U.S.A. in 1949–51, and President of the United Nations Assembly in the 1953–4 session. In 1954 she was appointed High Commissioner for India in London and Indian Ambassador to Ireland. She is the sister of Jawaharlal Nehru, *q.v.*

Papua. A territory in south-east New Guinea, *q.v.*, administered by Australia.

Paraguay. An independent South American state without access to the sea, situated between Argentina, Bolivia, and Brazil; population 1,650,000 with a high percentage of Guarani Indian blood; languages Guarani and Spanish; area 157,039 sq. m.; capital Asuncíon. Paraguay was ruled by Spain from the sixteenth century until 1811, when independence was declared. During the nineteenth century the country suffered from a series of devastating wars, involving Argentina, Brazil, and Uruguay. From 1870 onwards there were grave disputes with Bolivia over the area known as the Chaco, lying between the rivers Paraguay and Pilcomaya, which led to war between the two countries from 1932 to 1935; the boundary was eventually fixed by arbitration in October 1938.

Agriculture is still primitive although the soil is productive and the climate suitable for many sub-tropical products, but only four per cent of the cultivable land is farmed. The staple diet is maize and manioc (an edible root, the source of tapioca). Wheat is imported from Argentina to feed the towns, and live cattle are imported. The principal exports are cotton, timber, and quebracho extracts used in tanning.

During the Second World War the U.S.A., anxious to have a strategic base on the borders of Argentina, supplied to Paraguay, then under the dictator Higinio Morinigo, goods, money, and technical assistance, improved the airport at Asuncíon, built roads, and assisted the development of agriculture, cattle-raising, forestry, and the health services. Morinigo, however, also contrived to remain on good terms with Argentina, being aware of his country's dependence on the Paraná river as an outlet to the Atlantic through Argentina, and on Argentine finance. Morinigo was overthrown by a military junta in 1948. There were then four Presidents in rapid succession, followed by Federico Cháves (1950–4) who joined the Argentinian–Chilean pact of economic union, by which Paraguay received considerable financial help. On 4 May 1954 Cháves was forced to resign by a section of the Colorado Party, the only political party permitted, and by a section of the army, led by General Alfredo Stroessner, commander-in-chief of the armed forces. The president of the Colorado

Party became President, but in July 1954 Stroessner, as the only candidate, was elected President. He was re-elected in 1958. There is continual competition between Argentina, Brazil, and the U.S.A. for predominance in Paraguay, which is reflected in dissensions within the Colorado Party. President Stroessner was sympathetic to the Perón régime in Argentina, and gave asylum to Perón when the latter was deposed in 1955, but the country has recently developed economic links with Brazil.

Parliament Acts, 1911 and 1949. Two British laws which define the powers of the House of Lords, *q.v.* All legislation needs the assent of both Houses of Parliament, as well as of the Queen, except in the circumstances described in the Acts. A Bill can be presented for royal assent without the agreement of the House of Lords if the House (1) fails in one month to pass a Bill which, having passed the House of Commons, *q.v.*, is sent up endorsed by the Speaker as a money Bill before the end of the session; or (2) refuses in two successive sessions to pass a public Bill (other than a money Bill) and if one year has elapsed between the date when it was read a second time in the House of Commons in the first session and a third time in the second session. A money Bill is one which only relates to the imposition, remission, repeal, and alteration of taxes, to charges on the Consolidated Fund, etc.; the power to shorten the period of delay by the House of Lords to six months in this way has only been used three times. The second part of the rule makes it impossible, in effect, for the House of Lords to delay a Bill for more than one year. The basic principle was established by the 1911 Act; the 1949 Act reduced the periods of delay to their present length. The 1911 Act exempted from its own provisions Bills to extend the life of Parliament; this is limited to five years, a period which cannot now be prolonged without the consent of both Houses.

Pathanistan. Pakhtunistan, *q.v.*

Pearson, Lester Bowles. Canadian Liberal politician; born 23 April 1897 and educated at Toronto University and St John's College, Oxford. After serving in the First World War he worked for the Armour Meat Company in Chicago for two years and then took an academic post at Toronto University. He left the University in 1928 to become First Secretary of the Department of External Affairs, and was in the Office of the Canadian High Commissioner in London from 1935 to 1941, when he became Assistant Under-Secretary of State for External Affairs. He was in Washington during most of the Second World War as Minister to the U.S.A., and was appointed Ambassador in 1945. He entered politics in 1946, was elected to represent an Ontario constituency, and became Under-Secretary of State for External Affairs. He was Secretary of State for External Affairs from 1948 to 1957. Since 1930 he has attended a large number of international conferences; he was President of the United Nations General Assembly in 1952 and was awarded the Nobel Peace Prize in 1957. He became the leader of the Liberal Party in 1958.

Pentagon. A five-sided building in Virginia, U.S.A., on the outskirts of Washington, D.C., occupied by the Department of Defence.

Persia. An independent state; area 628,000 sq. m.; population, according to 1956 census, 18,944,821; capital Teheran. Since 1949 foreigners have been permitted to call the country Persia, although the name had been previously altered to Iran. The despotic rule of the Qajar Shahs was modified in 1906 by the establishment of a National Assembly (Majlis) of 136 (now 200) members, elected for two (now four) years. Provision was also made for a Senate of 60 members, half elected and half nominated, but this was not constituted until 1950. In 1925 the reigning Shah of the Qajar dynasty was deposed by the National Assembly which elected Reza Khan Pahlevi, a Persian Cossack regiment officer, as Shah. He abdicated in 1941, when British and Russian armies invaded Persia to expel the German agents whom he had admitted and encouraged, and was succeeded as Shah by his son Mohammed Reza Pahlevi (born 1919). In 1942 the U.K. and the U.S.S.R. guaranteed the independence of Persia, which then declared war on Germany, Italy, and Japan. All allied forces were to be withdrawn after the end of the war, but Russian troops remained in Azerbaijan in north-west Persia, where an autonomous pro-Communist government was set up. The matter was referred to the United Nations and after direct negotiations between Persia and the U.S.S.R. the Russian troops withdrew. The government in Azerbaijan was led by a group sponsored by the Tudeh (Communist) Party, which had been founded in 1941 but was suppressed in 1949 after one of its members had tried to assassinate the Shah.

The principal product is petroleum. In 1901 William Knox D'Arcy was given a sixty-year monopoly of oil production in about five sixths of Persia. The Shah was to receive sixteen per cent of the profits. In 1909 D'Arcy founded the Anglo-Persian Oil Co., in which the U.K. bought substantial shares before the First World War in order to ensure adequate oil supplies for the Royal Navy. In 1933 the Company and the Persian government concluded a new agreement by which the concession was to run for sixty years from 31 December 1933, over about 100,000 sq. m. of Persia, and the Persian share of the royalties was increased. In 1951 the Majlis and Senate approved a Bill which nationalized the oil industry and took over the installations of the Oil Company, which had then become the Anglo-Iranian Oil Co. Oil exports and the Company's operations in Persia ceased. After internal disturbances, during which the Shah temporarily left the country, and Dr Mussadiq, the leading supporter of nationalization, was arrested, the dispute between the government and the Company was settled in August 1954. The agreement provided for the operation of the oil installations by the National Iranian Oil Co. and a consortium in which the interests were to be: British Petroleum Co. (formerly Anglo-Iranian Oil Co.) forty per cent, Royal Dutch-Shell fourteen per cent, Gulf, Socony Mobil, Standard Oil of California, Standard Oil of New Jersey, and Texas Co. seven per cent each, Compagnie Française des Pétroles six per cent, nine other U.S. companies five per cent. The joint operation was to continue until 1979, with a further fifteen years' option. The Persian government receives fifty per cent of the earnings.

Economic progress in Persia has been slow, in spite of a development programme drawn up by Overseas Consultants Inc., a group of U.S. experts, in 1949, under which the oil revenues were to be used for investment. The main exports are fresh and dried fruit, wool and hair, skins and leather, and raw cotton. Although there has been some redistribution of land, promoted principally by the Shah, most of the wealth of Persia remains in the hands of a small number of people, and there has been widespread corruption in central and local government. Opium-smoking is a major social problem. The United Nations Narcotics Bureau has expressed its concern at the effects of opium addiction in Persia; the Persian Minister of Health stated in 1955 that 100,000 persons died every year as a result of opium addiction, and that some 5,000 other addicts committed suicide each year, leaving their families destitute. The drug has a debilitating effect on over half the labour force. Opium-growing was banned in 1955.

Personality Cult. Encouragement of excessive adulation of individuals; a practice attributed by Nikita S. Khrushchev, *q.v.*, First Secretary of the Communist Party of the U.S.S.R., to his predecessor, Marshal Joseph Stalin, who died in 1953. At a secret session of the Communist Party Congress on 25 February 1956, Khrushchev stated that a cult of Stalin had arisen after Lenin's death, that Stalin had abused the prestige and popularity which he had gained by gradually abolishing collective leadership inside the Communist Party, and by using repressive measures against his opponents and later against everyone who did not share his views. On 28 March 1956 an article in *Pravda*, *q.v.*, stated: 'Stalin's disregard of the principle of collective leadership, and the frequent decisions taken by him personally, led to the distortion of party principles and party democracy, to the violation of revolutionary law, and to repression.'

Peru. An independent South American state on the Pacific Ocean; population 10,068,000, of whom nearly half are Indians; area 514,059 sq. m.; capital Lima. Spain ruled Peru from the sixteenth century until the revolutionary war of 1821–4. Under the 1856 Constitution (amended in 1860, 1919, 1933, 1936, 1939, and 1945) the President is elected for six years by direct popular vote; Congress comprises a Senate and a House of Representatives, each House being elected for six years.

Peru consists of an almost rainless coastal plain, which is divided from a vast and tropical interior by the Andean ranges. Economic progress is beset by many difficulties: in the interior the Indians cling to primitive farming methods, while development of the mineral resources in the mountains requires considerable capital investment. All three regions face the problem of transport. Agriculture and mining occupy more than seventy per cent of the inhabitants. The chief agricultural products are cotton, sugar, wool, hides, and skins. Minerals produced include antimony, bismuth, copper, gold, lead, silver, vanadium (of which Peru is the world's largest producer), and zinc. Efforts are being made to develop the interior; these include the establishment of more railways, hydro-electric plants, and smelting plants and refineries for the minerals.

From 1945 to 1948 Peru was ruled by President J. L. Bustamante, who strove to hold the balance between the Alianza Popular Revolucionaria Americana (A.P.R.A.), the only Latin American movement with mass Indian support, and the conservative groups (sometimes called the Forty Families) who owned businesses in Lima. The Apristas had a majority in Congress and were anxious to carry out the sweeping social reforms which they had planned, but were prevented from doing so by other interests. In October 1948 General Manuel Odría and a military junta overthrew Bustamante, and in 1950 Odría was elected President for six years in an election at which he was the only candidate and from which A.P.R.A. was banned. A small Socialist Party provided almost the only opposition in Congress. The Minister of the Interior was entitled to take any measures to safeguard order, and the law provided that the courts should not interfere with such measures. The leader of A.P.R.A., Víctor Raúl Haya de la Torre, took refuge in the Colombian Embassy in Lima, and after spending several years in the building was permitted to leave Peru.

The Odría régime tried to improve the economic situation. It built roads and irrigation works, induced foreign capital to increase its investments in the mines, passed a law (in 1952) to encourage oil companies to expand their operations, and achieved substantial budget surpluses. However, the government enjoyed little active support: this may have been due to its failure to carry out land redistribution.

In June 1956 Dr Manuel Prado y Ugarteche, a moderate conservative who was President from 1939 to 1945, was elected to succeed Odría as President, easily defeating the government's official candidate. Prado then legalized A.P.R.A. and released many political prisoners. Haya de la Torre was allowed to return in March 1961.

Philippines. An independent state in the western Pacific; total land area 114,830 sq. m., comprising eleven important islands, of which the largest are Luzon and Mindanao, and 7,089 others, mostly unnamed; population 24,000,000, mostly of Malay stock with a strong Chinese and Spanish admixture, and including 300,000 Chinese; capital Manila, in Luzon. The islands were ceded by Spain to the U.S.A. for $20,000,000 after the Spanish-American War of 1898. The Filipinos agitated for independence and the U.S.A. introduced various home rule measures, including a 1934 Act of Congress which established a Philippine Commonwealth. The islands were occupied by Japan during the Second World War but after their liberation the independent Republic of the Philippines came into existence on 4 July 1946.

Under the 1935 Constitution, amended in 1940 and 1946, a President and Vice-President are elected for 4 years; the legislature consists of a Senate of 24 members (elected for 6 years) and a House of Representatives of 102 members (elected for 4 years). At the 1953 elections Ramon Magsaysay, formerly a member of the Liberal Party and Minister of Defence, was elected President as the leader of the Naçionalista Party, defeating Elpidio Quirino, who had been President since 1949. The Naçionalistas were supported by business interests but also attracted a large popular following. They have absolute majorities over the Liberals in the Senate and the House of Representatives. A Naçionalista programme of social and economic reform weakened the Communist-led Hukbalahap movement. Magsaysay, who was regarded by the Liberals as a puppet of the U.S.A., was killed in an aircraft accident in March 1957. He was at once succeeded by his Vice-President, Carlos P. Garcia, also a Naçionalista, who was subsequently (on 12 November 1957) elected President.

The country is predominantly agricultural, with important exports of coconut and manila hemp (sixty-eight per cent of all exports since the war), sugar, gold, zinc, and silver. The 1946 Philippine Trade Act, passed by the U.S. Congress, provided for duty-free trade between the two countries for nine years (except for rice, sugar, and tobacco) and gradually increased payments of duty thereafter, rising to tariff duty on U.S. goods at the ordinary level by 1 January 1974.

Relations with Japan were embittered after the Second World War by memories of the occupation and of the Japanese withdrawal from Manila, when approximately 40,000 Filipinos were killed. The total war damage was estimated in 1946 at $8,000,000,000; after years of negotiations the Japanese agreed to pay to the Philippines $800,000,000 in capital goods, services, cash, investment funds, and development loans.

Pinay, Antoine. French politician and former Prime Minister; born 30 December 1901. He was first elected to the Chamber of Deputies in 1936 as an Independent Radical. As the Senator for the Loire department he voted with the 568 Members of Parliament who conferred special powers on Marshal Pétain in 1940. In January 1941 he was appointed to the short-lived Conseil-National set up by the Vichy government but he subsequently took a courageous stand against the German occupation authorities and was freed in 1945 from the 'ineligibility restrictions' imposed on former supporters of Pétain. He joined the right-wing Independent Republican Party and was elected in 1946 to the second Constituent Assembly and then to the first National Assembly. He was Secretary of State for Economic Affairs in the Queuille cabinet, 1948–9, and in July 1950 joined the Pleven government as Minister of Transport and Public Works, a post he held in all successive administrations until he became Prime Minister (March–December 1952). He served as Minister of Foreign Affairs in the brief 1955 government of Edgar Faure. He is representative of French business interests in his opposition to increased taxation. In his 1952 budget he attempted to curb inflation by government saving and investment, which he described as 'technical steps', and not left-wing or right-wing policies; at the same time he offered an amnesty to tax evaders. He still considers himself to be a business man (he is a leather manufacturer) rather than a politician. He was Minister of Finance in the Debré government from January 1959 until his resignation in January 1960 after differences as to economic policy.

Poland. An independent state in eastern Europe; area 120,360 sq. m.; population about 29,527,000; capital Warsaw. After achieving considerable military successes between the fourteenth and sixteenth centuries Poland declined, and there were three partitions of the country in the eighteenth century (in 1772, 1793, and 1795) in which Austria, Prussia, and Russia shared. Though Napoleon created a small independent state, the Congress of Vienna, 1815, re-partitioned Poland except for the Republic of Krakow which was later seized by Austria.

Poland was declared independent in 1918 and power was assumed by Josef Pilsudski who recruited Polish soldiers to fight the Russians during the First World War; from 1926 onwards government was by a semi-Fascist dictatorship, at first under Pilsudski and after his death in 1935 under a group of officers loyal to the Pilsudski tradition. Nearly forty per cent of the budget was spent on armaments owing to the fear of invasion by Germany or the U.S.S.R. Both powers invaded and partitioned Poland in 1939. During the Second World War about 3,000,000 of the 3,500,000 Polish Jews were murdered by the Germans. More than one half of the population of Warsaw was killed and the capital was almost completely destroyed. By March 1945 the Russian Army, supported by Polish forces, had liberated Poland. In June 1945 the Polish Provisional Government of National Unity was formed, comprising the anti-Communist government-in-exile in London under Mikolajczyk and the pro-Communist Polish Committee of National Liberation, which had been formed in Moscow and moved to Lublin. Elections were held in January 1947 in which the government bloc obtained 382 out of the 444 seats in the Sejm (Parliament) but there was an atmosphere of Communist and secret police terror. Mikolajczyk fled to London in October 1947.

In 1948 and 1949 the Socialists and Communists merged into the United Workers' Party, and the Peasants' and Polish Peasants' Parties merged into the United Peasants' Party. Under the 1952 Constitution supreme power is vested in the Sejm, which is elected every four years on the basis of one deputy for every 60,000 people. It elects a Council of Ministers which is the supreme executive organ. At the 1961 elections a single list of National Unity Front candidates was offered to the electorate (of whom 95·5 per cent voted), the United Workers' Party obtaining 255 seats, United Peasants' Party 117, Democratic Party 39, and non-party deputies 49. Real power lies in the central committee of the United Workers' Party, led by Wladyslaw Gomulka, the Party Secretary, who was in disgrace from 1949 to 1956 for supporting Tito, q.v. His return to power in October 1956 coincided with anti-Stalinist demonstrations throughout Poland and these enforced resignations from Polish government posts of many Russian officers, including Marshal Rokossovsky, the Minister of Defence. There has been extensive industrialization and the key industries have all been nationalized or put under government control.

By the agreements at Potsdam, *q.v.*, and Yalta, *q.v.*, Poland was in effect moved to the west. 70,000 sq. m. were yielded to the U.S.S.R., and in return Poland received 44,231 sq. m. of Germany, including Silesia, part of the Baltic coast, and most of East Prussia. About 8,500,000 Germans were expelled from these areas; West Germans refuse to accept this frontier, the Oder-Neisse Line, *q.v.*, as permanent.

Popular Front. The collaboration of Communist, Socialist, and other political parties against Fascism, originally suggested by the Communist International in 1935. The French Popular Front government, under Léon Blum, was in office from 1936 to 1937 and for a short period in 1938. The Spanish government appointed in May 1936 by the President of Spain, who was the Popular Front leader, is normally described as a Popular Front government, but although it believed in radical social reforms it contained no Socialist or Communist members; it was eventually overthrown by Fascist rebels.

Portugal. An independent state in the western part of the Iberian peninsula; area 34,500 sq. m.; population, of whom in 1950 40·4 per cent of those over seven years old were illiterate, 8,654,436 (1953); capital Lisbon. From the eleventh century it was a monarchy and became a great imperial power, sharing in the division of the New World with Spain in 1493. It ruled the greater part of South America, including Brazil, until the beginning of the nineteenth century. An armed revolt in 1910 forced King Manuel II of Braganza-Coburg to flee to England, and a republic was declared. Between 1910 and 1926 there were twenty-four revolutions and *coups d'état*, and no real progress was made towards a democratic form of government. The parliamentary régime was finally overthrown by a military *coup* in May 1926, but the Army officers who came to power had no solution for the country's economic difficulties; in 1928 the President, General Carmona, invited Dr Oliveira Salazar, *q.v.*, to reform the economy as Minister of Finance. He has been the virtual dictator of Portugal ever since.

Under the 1933 Constitution, based largely on the Constitution of Fascist Italy, parliament consists of two houses, the National Assembly and the Corporative Chamber. The National Assembly has 120 members elected for four years by a direct but limited suffrage, and exercises legislative and financial powers. At the elections in November 1953 the União Nacional, the only authorized party in Portugal, secured all 120 seats; the 28 opposition candidates, the first to be permitted since 1928, received 43,000 of the 258,000 votes cast, but were all defeated. There was a similar result at the elections in November 1957, when the União Nacional won all 120 seats, while the 5 opposition candidates were defeated. The Corporative Chamber consists of representatives of commercial, cultural, industrial, and religious interests and local authorities. All Bills introduced in the National Assembly must be submitted to the Corporative Chamber. So far the President has been elected for seven years by a direct but limited suffrage; Rear-Admiral Américo Tomás, the government candidate, was elected President on 8 June 1958, defeating General Humberto Delgado, whose supporters demanded the restoration of fundamental democratic liberties. The substantial size of the minority vote received by Delgado was one of the factors which caused the government to amend the Constitution in 1961, so that henceforth the President is to be appointed indirectly, by an electoral college.

The remnants of Portugal's former overseas possessions constitute the fifth largest empire in the world and are of considerable economic importance, providing in 1953 sixteen per cent of Portugal's imports, taking twenty-seven per cent of its exports, and yielding large dollar returns. The Azores (nine islands in the Atlantic) and the Madeiras (an island group 520 miles west of Lisbon) are part of metropolitan Portugal. The Portuguese overseas territories (which ceased to have the status of colonies on 11 June 1951) are: in Africa, Angola (Portuguese West Africa), *q.v.*, sending coffee, diamonds, maize, and sugar to Portugal; Portuguese Guinea, producing palm-oil, rice, and seeds; Mozambique (Portuguese East Africa), producing cotton, copra, maize, sisal, and sugar; S. Tomé and Principe Islands, producing cacao, coffee, and copra; and Cape Verde Islands, producing coffee; in Asia, Portuguese India (Goa, *q.v.*, Angediva, Sâo Jorge, Morcegos, Damão, and Diu), producing iron ore, manganese, and cashew nuts; Macao in China, with a valuable transit trade; and Portuguese Timor, producing coffee and copra.

Portugal's domestic resources are meagre, though it has important exports of cork and cork products, cotton goods, wine (including port), sardines, and wolfram and pyrites. Competition for wolfram and pyrites between the allied powers and Germany during the Second World War, and a renewed demand during the Korean War, produced record prices for these minerals. The central feature of the economy, and therefore of Portugal's attitude to its empire (*see* Goa), is that Portugal only achieves a satisfactory trade balance as a result of the contributions from the overseas territories. If these contributions were suddenly to cease, Portugal would be in serious economic difficulties. At home, the government is generally reluctant to speed up industrial development although recently several large hydro-electric plants have been constructed, railway lines electrified, and a thermal power station built.

Potsdam Agreement. Was concluded by the U.K., the U.S.A., and the U.S.S.R. at the Cecilienhof Palace at Potsdam, the residence of the former German Crown Prince, in the course of discussions between 17 July and 1 August 1945. The three powers reaffirmed their policy towards Germany, outlined at the Yalta Conference, *q.v.*, in February 1945, and agreed that for the time being no central German government should be established. The German economy was to be decentralized to eliminate excessive concentration of economic power as exemplified by cartels, syndicates, trusts, and other monopolistic arrangements, but Germany was to be treated by the occupying powers as a single economic unit, common policies being established in regard to its industries and economic life generally. Production of metals, chemicals, machinery, and other items directly necessary to a war economy was to be restricted to Germany's approved post-war peacetime needs.

It was agreed that the city of Königsberg and the area adjacent to it should be transferred to the U.S.S.R., and that the Polish western frontier, about which no final decision had been made at the Yalta Conference, should be on the Oder-Neisse Line, *q.v.* The three powers agreed that the transfer to Germany of many Germans remaining in Czechoslovakia, Hungary, and Poland would have to be undertaken, but should be effected in an orderly and humane manner. France, which had been promised an occupation zone in Germany when the three major powers met at Yalta, was excluded from the Potsdam discussions.

Poujade, Pierre. French politician; born in 1920. After leaving school at the age of thirteen he took a number of casual jobs and joined the French Fascist youth movement. From 1940 to 1942 he worked in government youth camps, but went to Africa in 1942 when the Germans occupied southern France; he became a sergeant in the Free French Air Force. After the war he opened a stationery shop in the small town of St Céré in Central France. In 1954 he formed the Union for the Defence of Small Shopkeepers and Artisans, saying that France needed a less complicated inland revenue system, with reduced taxes for retailers. His followers assaulted tax inspectors, bought back at public auctions the goods of bankrupted shopkeepers, and provided legal aid for shopkeepers unable to pay their taxes. The Poujadistes attracted many supporters, including anti-semites, former Fascists, and dissident Gaullists as well as those who objected to the tax structure. The movement received financial support from the North African settler lobby.

Pravda. A newspaper which is the official organ of the Central Committee of the Communist Party of the U.S.S.R. Its opinions on Communist policy are sometimes more authoritative than those expressed by *Izvestia*, *q.v.*, although there is rarely any difference in outlook between the two journals. The word *pravda* means truth; the newspaper was founded in 1912 with Joseph Stalin as editor and Vyacheslav Molotov as his secretary.

Présence Francaise. A right-wing French settlers' group in Algeria. Its methods have included the lobbying of Gaullist and other right-wing deputies in the French National Assembly, the production of newspapers and pamphlets, bribery of the police force and the intimidation of French settlers who betrayed any sympathy for the Algerian nationalist cause.

Privy Council. Originally an advisory Council to the British sovereign. As a body the Privy Council is not now asked to give advice. Orders in Council and Proclamátions are approved by the Queen in the presence of three Privy Councillors (enough to constitute a quorum), after which it is announced that the Queen held a Privy Council. The matters considered, however, will have been previously recommended by the responsible departments of government. The Cabinet itself is in origin an informal committee of the Privy Council, and Cabinet Ministers (and some other Ministers) are Privy Councillors. Individuals retain the title of Privy Councillor even after resignation from the Cabinet. Sometimes the title of Privy Councillor (P.C.) is an honorary title bestowed for distinguished services to the state. Privy Councillors are addressed as 'Right Honourable'. There are various committees of the Privy Council, such as the Board of Trade, which seldom meet. An important committee which does meet is the Judicial Committee of the Privy Council, composed of Privy Councillors who are or have been in high judicial office (usually Law Lords and ex-judges). It sits to hear appeals from parts of the British Commonwealth. It also, among other matters, hears ecclesiastical appeals from Church courts and any problems referred to it by the Crown.

Proletariat. From the Latin word *proles*, meaning offspring (alluding to the number of children of the poorer classes): the class of wage-earners with little or no property of their own who depend on the sale of their labour. Definitions of the limits of the proletarian class vary; at one time only manual workers were included, but a process of 'proletarianization' of the middle class is discernible in some countries, particularly where (as in the U.K.) many manual workers earn more than professional or white-collar workers.

Propaganda. Statements of policy or facts, usually of a political nature, the real purpose of which is different from their apparent purpose. In this sense propaganda existed before the twentieth century, but its importance has increased in an age when communication is easier and when it is more important to influence ordinary people. The term is used to describe a statement by a government or political party which is believed to be insincere or untrue, and designed to impress the public at large rather than to reach the truth or to bring about a genuine understanding between opposing governments or parties. People do not usually admit that they are issuing propaganda and the word is much misused. Propaganda by one's own government or political party is described as a policy statement or as part of its news service; genuine approaches and statements of policy by another government or party are frequently dismissed as mere propaganda.

Proportional Representation. An electoral system under which a legislature reflects the strength of the various political parties among the electorate at large. It has several forms, the simplest being one in which a country is divided into large constituencies each returning several members; those candidates are elected who obtain more than a certain fraction of the vote, and their surplus over that fraction is distributed among the other candidates according to the second and later choices indicated on the ballot-papers. Other candidates whose votes then reach the required quota are also elected. This is the method of the transferable vote. Under another method the votes given to a party in any constituency which are not sufficient for the election of a candidate are reserved for a second sorting, in which these remainder votes from various constituencies are added up. If the total is sufficient for the election of one or more candidates, these are taken from a national list of the party, and they become Members of Parliament without a constituency. Supporters of proportional representation say that it would satisfy the large numbers of citizens who might otherwise be unrepresented in Parliament, that the large parties would moderate their views, and that the system is inherently fair. Its opponents say that the electors do not want a Parliament which photographically represents each party and that the system makes for unstable coalition governments. The Labour Party advocated proportional representation until it became the second largest party in the U.K. in 1922, when the cause was taken up by the Liberal Party. It should not be confused with the Alternative Vote, *q.v.*

Protected State. A territory, with its own ruler, controlling its internal affairs but under the protection of another state which usually manages its foreign relations. A protected state is a special type of protectorate, *q.v.*, differing from most protectorates which generally contain groups of tribes with few acknowledged rulers, whereas a protected state resembles more closely a unified state. The powers of a protected state depend on its arrangement with its protector. Tonga, with its own Queen, is an example of a British protected state.

Protectorate. A territory, not formally annexed, over which the protecting state has power and jurisdiction but not full sovereignty. There are almost as many types of protectorate as there are protectorates and a detailed description of a protectorate is therefore impossible; in every case it is important to examine the way in which the protection began (by treaty, grant or usage, for example) and not simply to accept the title protectorate as a description of the particular territory. In the case of British protectorates the inhabitants are not citizens of the United Kingdom and Colonies and the territories are treated as foreign territories, but, although the inhabitants do not owe allegiance to the Crown, they owe an almost unlimited duty of obedience in return for its protection. A protecting state does not usually permit other states to enter into relations with the peoples of the protectorate. There are British protectorates (in some cases adjacent to colonies) in Aden, Gambia, Kenya, Northern Rhodesia, Nyasaland, the Solomon Islands, Uganda, and Zanzibar. The term is often confused with the terms 'colony', *q.v.*, and 'protected state', *q.v.*: the latter may best be regarded as a special type of protectorate.

Puerto Rico. A group of islands in the West Indies belonging to the U.S.A.; area 3,475 sq. m.; population (1959) 2,340,000, three quarters of whom are of Spanish descent; capital San Juan. It was ceded by Spain to the U.S.A. in 1898 as a result of the Spanish-American War; its name was changed from Porto Rico to Puerto Rico by an Act of the U.S. Congress in 1932. Although its foreign relations are in the hands of the U.S. State Department, the 1952 Constitution, establishing the Commonwealth of Puerto Rico, gave it extensive powers of local self-government. In 1953 President Eisenhower told the United Nations General Assembly that if the legislature of Puerto Rico, which is elected by universal suffrage, should adopt a resolution in favour of absolute independence he would immediately recommend to the U.S. Congress that such independence be granted; the legislature decided in January 1954 not to take up this promise. The standard of living is among the highest in Latin America. An increasing measure of investment from the U.S.A. has brought prosperity to the islands. The inhabitants are American citizens and liable for military service in the U.S.A., but do not have to pay American federal taxes.

Q

Qatar. An independent state in the Persian Gulf; area 8,000 sq. m.; population 40,000; capital Doha. Under a treaty of 3 November 1916 its relationship with the British government is similar to that of the states on the Trucial Coast, *q.v.* It was ruled from 1949 to 1960 by Shaikh Ali bin Abdullah bin Jasmin al Thani; he then abdicated in favour of his son, Shaikh Ahmad. Oil production began in 1949 and the revenue derived therefrom is the principal source of income, which has been used to build a hospital, schools, and water distillation and electricity plants. A concession is held by Qatar Petroleum Co., the ownership of which is the same as that of the Iraq Petroleum Company, *q.v.*

Quai d'Orsay. An embankment of the river Seine in Paris, where the French Foreign Office is situated.

Quemoy. An island which, with three smaller ones, is six miles from Amoy, on the mainland of China, but is occupied by Chinese forces loyal to the government of Formosa, *q.v.*; area 70 sq. m.; population approximately 47,000 civilians and 60,000 troops; capital Quemoy City. It is surrounded on three sides by the mainland.

R

Rahman, Tunku Abdul. Prime Minister of Malaya since it became independent on 31 August 1957. Born 8 February 1903, he is the son of the Sultan of Kedah and was educated at St Catherine's College, Cambridge; he returned to England in 1947 to complete his Bar examinations. As President of the Alliance Party, he has insisted on independence for Malaya and 'Malayanization' of the public services. In spite of his nationalist views he has taken pains to encourage foreign, and especially British, investment.

Rakosi, Matyas. Hungarian politician; born 14 March 1892, of Jewish origin; educated at the Eastern Commercial Academy, Budapest. He joined a workers' political movement in 1910, became a clothing store clerk in 1912, and then spent a year in England where he was employed in a London bank. He served as an officer in the Hungarian army in the First World War, and was taken prisoner while fighting on the Russian front. He played a leading part in the Hungarian Communist revolution led by Bela Kun and in 1919 became the Assistant Commissar of Finance of the short-lived Hungarian Republic. He took refuge first in Austria and, from 1920 until 1924, in Moscow where he was appointed Secretary to the Third International's Executive Committee. He returned to Hungary to reform the Communist Party which was, at that time, an illegal organization, but he was soon arrested and saved from execution only by protests organized from abroad. He remained in prison, having been detained for six years after his sentence had expired, until 1940 when he was exchanged, with the Russians, for captured Hungarian trophies from the Leningrad Museum. After a further four years in the U.S.S.R. he returned once again to Hungary as First Secretary of the Hungarian Communist Party. He was Deputy Prime Minister from 1945 to 1952, and Prime Minister from 1952 to 1953 when he was removed from office and a new policy was adopted. In 1955 his policies, which stressed the need for heavy industry and collective farms, came once more into favour, but he was not re-appointed Prime Minister and in July 1956 he resigned from the post of First Secretary of the Hungarian Communist Party. In March 1958 the Socialist Workers' Party (as the Communist Party had been re-named) announced that it had decided to permit Rakosi to rejoin the Party.

Rapacki Plan. A proposal for a central European zone free of nuclear weapons. It was contained in a memorandum delivered in Warsaw by the Polish government to representatives of nine foreign states on 14 February 1958. The Plan took its name from the Polish Foreign Minister, Adam Rapacki. The zone was to include Poland, Czechoslovakia, and Eastern and Western Germany. The memorandum stated: 'In this territory nuclear weapons would neither be manufactured nor stockpiled; the equipment and installations designed for their servicing would not be located there; the use of nuclear weapons against the territory of this zone would be prohibited.' These obligations were to apply to the states in the zone, to France, the U.K., the U.S.A., and the U.S.S.R., and to the other states (which then included Belgium, Canada, Denmark, and the Netherlands) with forces stationed in the zone.

The memorandum recommended control by a system of aerial and ground inspection, supervised by representatives from the member states of the Eastern European Mutual Assistance Treaty, *q.v.*, and the North Atlantic Treaty Organization, *q.v.* The Polish government expressed the hope that the establishment of such a zone would lead to the reduction of conventional forces within the zone, and that the system would be a useful precedent for a broader agreement on disarmament, *q.v.*

The U.S.S.R. supported the Plan, while the U.K. and the U.S.A. objected to it, partly because it would favour the eastern powers, with their predominance in conventional weapons, and partly because it did not provide for German reunification.

Rapallo, Treaty of. A treaty of friendship signed in 1922 by Germany and the U.S.S.R., at Rapallo, near Genoa, where an international conference on economic questions and reparations was being held. The terms were unimportant but the Treaty was significant as it secured for the U.S.S.R. its first official recognition by a major power. It offended the other major powers, but was a direct result of their policy of treating Germany and the U.S.S.R. as inferior states.

Rapprochement. A diplomatic term meaning the re-establishment of good relations between states.

Ratification. The formal adoption by a state of a treaty signed by its representatives. It is effected by an exchange of documents, embodying their formal adoption of the treaty, between the states concerned. This gives an opportunity, particularly in democratic countries, for public opinion to express itself, although most representatives today are careful not to sign a treaty unless they are certain that it will be ratified. It is an essential process in countries in which the treaty-making power is, under the Constitution, vested in some organ which cannot itself carry on negotiations with other states; thus in the U.S.A. the treaty-making power is vested in the President, subject to the advice and consent of the Senate. In the U.K. treaties are ratified by the Sovereign. A discussion in the Houses of Parliament of the contents of a treaty has no effect on its binding force as between the U.K. and the other contracting states. However, no treaty concluded by the U.K., whether or not it has been ratified, can affect the private rights of British citizens until its provisions have been put into the form of a statute and passed by Parliament.

Minor matters of an international nature are frequently agreed by the government departments of various states. These are not considered to need ratification. Under the category of 'executive agreements', for example, arrangements are sometimes made by representatives of the U.S. State Department with representatives of other states, and these are not subject to the constitutional rules about treaties.

Reciprocal Trade Agreements Act. A U.S. law empowering the President to reduce import tariffs in return for concessions granted to U.S. exports. The U.S. Tariff Commission reports to the President if such tariff reductions, proposed or actual, injure, or threaten to injure, domestic producers. If the President rejects the advice of the Commission he must give his reasons for so doing to Congress.

Redistribution. A reorganization of electoral districts, involving their creation, abolition, merging, and alteration, to ensure that each representative speaks for approximately the same number of voters. The districts represented by the members of the U.S. House of Representatives, *q.v.*, and the British House of Commons, *q.v.*, are subject to redistribution. In the U.K. the House of Commons (Redistribution of Seats) Act, 1949, provides for four permanent Boundary Commissions (for England, Scotland, Wales, and Northern Ireland) which have to report to the government at intervals of not less than three nor more than seven years, so that revision of parliamentary boundaries can be made by Order in Council. Each House of Parliament must approve of such Orders in Council before they can take effect. The distinction between redistribution and gerrymandering, *q.v.*, should be noted.

Referendum. A reference of a particular political question to the electorate for a direct decision by popular vote. In some countries alterations to the constitution can be made only with the consent of the electorate obtained by a referendum. The Australian Constitution, for example, which is contained in the Schedule to the Commonwealth of Australia Act, 1900, can only be altered by a referendum. This device need not be confined to constitutional matters. In Switzerland a referendum must be held not only on constitutional amendments but on any law if 30,000 citizens so insist. The referendum is not used in the U.K.

Republican Party. One of the two great political parties in the U.S.A.; the other is the Democratic Party, *q.v.* The name was once an alternative title for the Democratic Party until in 1828 the advocates of high tariffs, led by John Quincy Adams and Henry Clay, broke away and were called National Republicans or Whigs. The present Republican Party emerged in 1854 out of an alliance between the National Republicans and the northern Democrats, both of whom opposed slavery. It came to power when Abraham Lincoln became President in 1861 and ruled (except for the administrations of Cleveland, 1885-9, 1893-7, and of McKinley, 1897-1901), until 1912. At the close of the nineteenth century it believed in high tariffs, U.S. imperialism, and the strengthening of the federal administration. It comprised an alliance of the industrial east and the agricultural west, giving tariff protection to the east and free land to the farmers of the west. After the second Woodrow Wilson administration, the Republicans came to power again in 1920, prevented U.S. ratification of the Versailles Treaty, *q.v.*, and supplied three successive Presidents, Warren Gamaliel Harding, Calvin Coolidge, and Herbert Hoover. It was defeated in 1932, largely as a result of the world economic slump, and replaced by a Democratic majority in Congress. The party was once isolationist in outlook but is now committed to an active U.S. foreign policy, though it has placed more emphasis on the significance of Asia and less on that of Europe than has the Democratic Party. It is often regarded as the more right-wing of the two parties, though it has members who are more progressive in outlook than most members of the Democratic Party. Among its most important members are: Richard M. Nixon, *q.v.*, Nelson Rockefeller, *q.v.*, Henry Cabot Lodge, *q.v.*, and Dwight D. Eisenhower, *q.v.*, President from 1953 to 1961. The Party emblem is an elephant.

Reuther, Walter. A Vice-President of the American Federation of Labour and Congress of Industrial Organizations, *q.v.*, the combined trade union organization formed in 1955, and in charge of its Industrial Union Department; born in 1908 in West Virginia, the grandson of a German emigrant and the son of a trade union organizer. He left school at sixteen and became an apprentice machinist. He went to Detroit in 1927 where he worked for the Ford motor firm and at the same time attended a high school and Wayne University. He was dismissed after trying, against the firm's rules, to organize his fellow-workers, and spent his savings on a world tour during which he worked with other Americans for sixteen months in a factory at Gorky in the U.S.S.R. However, he remained unsympathetic to American Communists whom he described as 'the colonial agents of a foreign power'. On his return to Detroit he did much to improve the organization of the automobile workers in Michigan and to ensure that their strikes were successful, and was attacked and beaten up by Ford's private police in 1937. In 1941 the Union of Automobile Workers became the most important union in its field when Ford at last agreed to negotiate with organized labour. Reuther became President of the U.A.W. in 1946 and of the Congress of Industrial Organizations in 1952. In 1955 he won the agreement of Ford and General Motors to a scheme for supplementary unemployment benefits paid by the employers for all employees laid off who had completed at least one year's service. Reuther described the new principle embodied in the agreements as a guaranteed annual wage.

Rhee, Syngman. Former Korean leader; born 26 March 1875 and educated at a Methodist mission school in Seoul in Korea and at George Washington, Princeton, and Harvard Universities, in the U.S.A. He was imprisoned and tortured by the Japanese from 1897 to 1904 for leading student demonstrations, and on his release went to the U.S.A. for six years where he completed his education. He returned to Korea in 1910 as a Y.M.C.A. official, speaking in favour of Methodism and resistance to the Japanese occupation, but was forced to flee to Hawaii, where he founded the Korean Methodist Church. From 1919 to 1941 he was recognized by Koreans in exile as the President of their provisional government. He returned to Korea in 1945 as Chairman of the Representative Democratic Council of South Korea, and in 1948 was the first Chairman of the National Assembly. He became President of the Korean Republic in 1948 and was re-elected in 1952, 1956, and 1960, but was forced to resign in April 1960, and retired to Hawaii.

Rhodesia and Nyasaland. *See* Federation of Rhodesia and Nyasaland.

Rio de Oro. An area to the west of Morocco and on the Atlantic Ocean; it was a Spanish colony until on 14 January 1958 the Spanish government announced its amalgamation with Saguia el-Hamra (to the north, between Rio de Oro and Spanish Southern Morocco, *q.v.*) into the province of Spanish Sahara, *q.v.*

Rio Treaty. The Inter-American Treaty of Reciprocal Assistance, signed at Rio de Janeiro, Brazil, on 2 September 1947, by representatives of all the states of the western hemisphere except Canada, Ecuador, and Nicaragua. Under the Treaty every signatory has, when an aggression has been committed against any American state, the obligation to intervene. An armed attack against any one of the American states is considered to be an attack against all. The nature of the intervention required to bring the Treaty obligations into force is not clearly defined; nor, if a conference of American states is summoned, does a decision of such a conference (which must be passed by two thirds of all the signatories) bind a state to use its armed forces without its consent. If U.S. forces, for example, are attacked in areas outside the security zone of the Americas (which stretches from the North Pole to the South Pole) the other American countries are not automatically involved.

Some Latin American states wished the Treaty to include 'economic aggression' as a type of aggression; others wanted the U.S.A. to make proposals similar to the Marshall Plan, *q.v.*, which had just been put to the European states. The Treaty, however, was eventually confined to military matters, the U.S.A. arguing that European needs were greater than those of Latin America and that the latter would benefit more from individual arrangements with each state. Detailed provisions for the peaceful settlement of disputes between American states were later agreed at the Conference of Bogota, 1948, which set up the Organization of American States, *q.v.* (*See* under this last heading a description of the first occasion on which an American republic received aid under the Rio Treaty to enable it to repel external aggression.)

Rockefeller, Nelson Aldrich. U.S. politician; born 8 July 1908 and educated at Dartmouth College. In 1931 he joined the foreign department of the Chase National Bank, and from 1931 to 1938 he was a Director of the Rockefeller Centre, of which he was also Chairman from 1945 to 1953 and 1956 to 1958. He was Co-ordinator of Inter-American Affairs in Washington from 1940 until 1944, and Assistant Secretary of State from December 1944 to August 1945. From 1950 to 1951 he was Chairman of the International Development Advisory Board, and he was later Under-Secretary of Health, Education and Welfare (1953 to 1954) and Special Assistant to the President (1954 to 1955). He succeeded in his first attempt to win an elective office when, as a Republican, he unseated the Democratic Governor of New York in 1958. He was unsuccessful in his efforts to secure the Republican nomination as Presidential candidate in 1960.

Rome Treaties. Two agreements, signed in Rome on 25 March 1957 by the representatives of Belgium, France, the German Federal Republic, Italy, Luxemburg, and the Netherlands, and providing for the establishment of the European Atomic Energy Community, *q.v.*, and the European Economic Community, *q.v.*

Ruanda-Urundi. A trusteeship territory under Belgian administration, situated in east Africa, with the Congo Republic (formerly Belgian), Uganda, and Tanganyika to the west, north, and east respectively; area 20,540 sq. m.; population (1958) 4,689,065 natives, comprising the Bahutu (83 per cent), Batutsi (15 per cent), and Batwa (2 per cent) tribes, 7,105 Europeans, and 2,320 Asians; capital Usumbura. The kingdoms of Ruanda (in the north) and Urundi (in the south) became part of German East Africa shortly before the First World War but Belgian forces entered the area in 1917 and Belgium took over the administration, under a League of Nations mandate, in 1923; the area became a trusteeship territory after the Second World War, when the United Nations succeeded the League of Nations and, on 13 December 1946, the trusteeship agreement was approved by the United Nations General Assembly. The territory was united economically and administered with the Belgian Congo until the latter became independent in 1960. There are few natural resources and agriculture and cattle-breeding are the main sources of income.

Rumania. An independent state on the Black Sea; area 91,671 sq. m.: population (1960) 18,360,000; capital Bucharest. It became independent as a result of the Treaty of Berlin, 1878, which united the Danubian principalities of Wallachia and Moldavia with part of southern Bessarabia and northern Dobrudja. In 1881 it became a kingdom under the family of Hohenzollern-Sigmaringen. As a result of

291

the First World War Rumania gained the rest of Bessarabia, *q.v.*, from the U.S.S.R., Transylvania and the Bukovina from the old Austro-Hungarian Empire, and southern Dobrudja from Bulgaria. Between 1919 and 1939 there was much political and social unrest, during which there were at least six different dictatorships. Although there were rich resources of oil (of which one third was owned by British companies), grain, and timber, large numbers of the agricultural population were ruined by the activities of extortionate urban money-lenders who encouraged over-production and charged interest rates as high as fifty per cent. Although there were free elections governments frequently altered the electoral laws in their own favour. There were strong links with Germany, Rumania's largest customer, and considerable sympathy among the Rumanian ruling classes for Nazi anti-semitic policies.

In 1940 the U.S.S.R. demanded the return of Bessarabia and northern Bukovina and these were given up; southern Dobrudja was returned to Bulgaria. In November 1946, after the Russian army reached Rumania, a coalition government was formed by the Communists, Liberals, Ploughmen's Front (a pro-Communist Peasant Party), and Social Democrats (who were later absorbed by the Communists), which compelled King Michael to abdicate and proclaimed a 'People's Republic' on 30 December 1947. A Popular Democratic Front, comprising the four remaining parties (the Workers' or Communist Party, the Ploughmen's Front, the National Popular Party, and the Hungarian Popular Union) won overwhelming majorities at subsequent elections to the Grand National Assembly, which is elected for four years with one member for every 40,000 of the population. There is now complete Communist control. Russian troops were allowed to be stationed in Rumania under the Rumanian Peace Treaty to maintain lines of communication between the U.S.S.R. and Austria; when the Russians left Austria these troops remained in Rumania under the 1955 Eastern European Mutual Assistance Treaty, *q.v.*, but in July 1958 the Russian government announced that they had all been withdrawn.

The economy is mainly dependent on petroleum, though there are also resources of coal, gold, iron, lignite, mica, and silver. The petroleum industry produced about 11,438,000 tons of oil in 1959–60, as compared with an annual pre-war output of 8,700,000 tons. Approximately 60 per cent of all exports go to the U.S.S.R.

Agricultural collectivization is less advanced than in other East European countries, partly owing to a lack of machinery. There has been considerable development of heavy industry.

The leading figure in the Communist Party after the Second World War was Gheorghe Gheorgiu-Dej, First Secretary from 1945 to 1954 and Prime Minister from 1952 to October 1955; he was succeeded by Chivu Stoica, a trade unionist who had played an important part in the industrialization of Rumania. Gheorgiu-Dej resumed the post of First Secretary, becoming President in March 1961, when Stoica was succeeded as Prime Minister by Gheorghe Maurer.

Rusk, David Dean. U.S. politician; born in 1909 on a small farm in Cherokee County, Georgia, the son of an ordained Presbyterian who was also a teacher and cotton farmer; educated at Davidson College, North Carolina, and, as a Rhodes Scholar, at St John's College, Oxford, and then at Berlin University and the California Law School. He was Assistant Professor of Government and Dean of Faculty at Mills College, Oakland, California, until 1940. He then joined the army, and at the end of the Second World War was deputy chief of staff in the China – Burma – India theatre of operations. He joined the State Department in 1946 as assistant chief of the international security affairs division and succeeded Alger Hiss in 1947 as director of the Office of Special Political (United Nations) Affairs, becoming Deputy Under-Secretary of State in 1949, and assuming responsibility for far eastern affairs in 1950. He was appointed President of the Rockefeller Foundation in 1952, and in 1961 he became Secretary of State.

Russia. The name often used to describe the Union of Soviet Socialist Republics, *q.v.*, but also used with reference to the Russian Soviet Federal Socialist Republic (R.S.F.S.R.), which is the largest of the fifteen constituent Republics.

Ryuku Islands. A group 500 miles to the south west of Japan, nominally belonging to Japan but controlled by the U.S.A. which has substantial military forces in the Islands and particularly in Okinawa, *q.v.*

S

Saarland. A highly industrialized area of 800 sq. m. on the river Saar; population (1958) 1,040,200; capital Saarbrücken. In language and habits the people are German; the territory became a *Land* of the German Federal Republic on 1 January 1957. The area is part of the Middle Kingdom between France and Germany which was set up in A.D. 843 when Charlemagne's domains were divided among his three grandsons; it has been the subject of disputes between the two countries ever since. The Saar was ruled by France in Napoleon's day, but in 1815 most of it, including Saarbrücken, was included in the new Prussian province of the Rhineland. After the First World War it was placed under the control of the League of Nations, which permitted it to be administered by France for a fifteen-year period. At the end of that time a plebiscite was to decide whether the inhabitants wished to belong to France or Germany. They decided in 1935 to be re-incorporated in Germany.

In 1945 it was occupied by the French who demanded its annexation; the Constitution of 8 November 1947 provided for complete economic union with France, and made defence and foreign relations French responsibilities. On 23 October 1954 France and the German Federal Republic agreed (1) that the economic and customs union should be maintained, (2) that the Saar should continue to have internal autonomy, (3) that a High Commissioner appointed by the Western European Union, *q.v.*, should represent the Saar in matters of foreign affairs and defence, and (4) that a referendum should be held on this proposed arrangement. This plan did not contemplate the complete economic Europeanization of the Saar, which had been recommended as a solution by the Council of Europe's Committee on General Affairs, through its *rapporteur* Van der Goes van Naters. The van Naters solution emphasized the fact that the Saar is part of the coal and steel community which covers Belgium, Luxemburg, the Ruhr, and eastern France. The Germans regarded Europeanization as a French device to secure hegemony and to deprive Germany permanently of the Saar. The French thought that it would leave the way open for a future German conquest.

By the referendum held on 23 October 1955 a majority of more than two to one of the electorate of 670,000 rejected the Franco-German plan, which was strongly opposed by the pro-German parties in the Saar.

In June 1956 the French Prime Minister and the German Federal Chancellor agreed (1) that the Saar should become a German Land on 1 January 1957; (2) that the Saar would be economically integrated with the German Federal Republic by stages over a three-year period to be completed by 1 January 1960; and (3) that after 1960 the Saar would have a special economic status in order to maintain Franco-Saar commercial exchanges on a high level. The economic integration was in fact completed by 5 July 1959.

Salazar, Dr António de Oliveira. Portuguese Prime Minister; born 28 April 1889 at Santa Comba, the son of a poor smallholder. He studied law and economics at the University of Coimbra, where he became Professor of Economics in 1918. After the military *coup d'état* of 28 May 1926 he was appointed Minister of Finance but resigned after a few days. He was recalled in the same capacity in 1928, reorganized the Portuguese budget, was offered the Premiership in 1932 and has held it since, becoming virtually dictator of Portugal. Salazar is probably the only European dictator who came to power not by struggle but by invitation. He set out to rebuild Portugal on the lines of what he termed the 'Estado Novo', the New State. He drafted a new constitution, authoritarian and corporate; it was accepted by plebiscite in 1933. He then carried out a programme of reforms, including the improvement of living conditions, industrial development, public works, and education. After he came to power he organized the União Naçional (the only authorized political movement in Portugal), the Portuguese Legion, and the Youth Movement. His administration is Fascist in character, both in concept and in execution.

Salvador, *or* El Salvador. An independent Central American state on the Pacific Ocean, area 8,058 sq. m., mostly mountainous; population (1958) 2,475,665, mainly illiterate, Spanish-speaking, and Roman Catholic; capital El Salvador. It was ruled by Spain from the sixteenth century to 1821, became part of the Federation of Central American States in 1821, and has been independent since 1839. After the 1948 revolution a new constitution was introduced in 1950 with many social welfare provisions. Universal suffrage was permitted for the first time in the 1950 elections to the Constituent Assembly. The number of members in the Legislative Assembly depends upon the population, there being one deputy for each 38,000 inhabitants. The Assembly is elected for two years. Lt.-Col. José María Lemus was elected President in 1956 for six years, but in November 1960 there was a bloodless *coup d'état* in which he was exiled and replaced by an army junta who were supplanted by another junta in January 1961.

Coffee accounts for eighty-five per cent of the value of Salvador's exports, which also include cane sugar, cotton, and sisal, and are nearly all sold to the U.S.A. Salvador is so densely populated that there is continuous emigration to neighbouring countries.

San Francisco Conference. A meeting of delegates from fifty nations held at San Francisco, California, U.S.A., from 25 April to 26 June 1945, which drafted the Charter of the United Nations, *q.v.*, and the Statute of the International Court of Justice, *q.v.*

San Marino. Officially the Most Serene Republic of San Marino. An independent state in Italy, near the Adriatic Sea; area 38 sq. m.; population 14,000; capital San Marino. It was founded in the fourth century; its present-day independence is guaranteed by a treaty, signed on 29 April 1953, with Italy, with whom there has been a customs union since 1862.

The state is ruled by a Council of sixty elected members of whom two are elected as regents for six months and are thereafter ineligible for office for three years. In the elections, which take place every four years, there is universal adult suffrage; women have been able to vote since 1959. One half of the electorate lives abroad, although many return to vote. Results in the election of 12 September 1959 were: Communists 16 seats; Left-wing Socialists 8; Christian Democrats 27; Democratic Socialists 9. The Communists and left-wing Socialists lost 11 seats as a result of the election. Government until 1957 was by a coalition of Communists and left-wing Socialists, who had been in office since 1943. In 1957 defections from the Communist and Socialist Parties enabled the Christian Democrats to come to power.

San Marino produces ceramics, cereals, cheese, olive oil and wine, and rears cattle; carved stone and white and hydrated lime are also exported. Further revenue is obtained from the licences granted to companies which register there to avoid foreign taxes, from the tourist trade, from picturesque postage stamps, and from an Italian government grant.

Sarawak. A British colony in north-west Borneo; area 47,000 sq. m.; population 750,000, including Sea Dayaks, Chinese, Malays, Land Dayaks, and Kayans; capital Kuching. For over one hundred years it was ruled by the Brooke family, known as the White Rajahs, after the Sultan of Brunei had granted governmental powers to Sir James Brooke in 1841. From 1888 onwards Sarawak was a British protected state, but it was ceded to the U.K. by the Rajah on 1 July 1946.

Satyagraha. A Sanskrit expression meaning 'faithful obstinacy' used to describe non-violent resistance to authority in India. It was practised by followers of Mahatma Gandhi against police and soldiers before the end of British rule in India, and more recently by opponents of Portuguese rule in Goa, *q.v.*

Saudi Arabia. An independent state occupying most of Arabia; area 927,000 sq. m.; population about 6,000,000; capitals Mecca and Riyadh. It comprises the Hejaz (an area of 112,500 sq. m. with a coast-line of 800 miles on the Red Sea, and the towns of Jedda and Mecca), Nejd (meaning 'plateau', an area of 800,000 sq. m. to the east and south of the Hejaz), and Asir (on the Red Sea coast between the Hejaz and Yemen). These three areas were unified to form the Saudi Arabian Kingdom by Ibn Saud (1880–1953) whose family had once ruled Nejd but had been deposed. The U.K. recognized, by treaty, the complete independence of the Kingdom in 1932.

The major source of revenue was once the tax imposed upon the Moslem pilgrims to Mecca, the holy city, but the discovery in 1936 of oil at Damman, in Nejd, transformed the Saudi Arabian economy.

The main concession, of approximately 440,000 sq. m., was granted under agreements in 1933 and 1939 to the Arabian American Oil Co. (Aramco), which is controlled by the Standard Oil Cos. of California and New Jersey, the Texas Co., and the Socony Mobil Oil Co. Inc. Aramco, whose most important oilfields are at Abqaiq, Ain Dar, and Damman, has had its head office at Dhahran since 1953, and is the only major oil company with headquarters in the Middle East. The oil reserves are among the highest in the world, and the government's revenues increased from about £3,000,000 in 1938 to some £125,000,000 in 1960. Aramco was the first oil company in the Middle East to concede the principle of a fifty-fifty division of profits between company and government.

Apart from the oilfields the country is still undeveloped, in spite of the money which flows into the Treasury. About 15 per cent of the expenditure in 1959–60 was on health, education, social services, agriculture, and communications, 15 per cent on development, and 35 per cent on armaments. An unknown amount was spent on subsidies for tribes in the interior and on the 325 Saudi Arabian princes of the realm. Aramco has set up an Arab Industrial Development Division to promote the growth of light industries. In May 1958 King Saud published a decree introducing the cabinet system, but this decree was cancelled in December 1960 when he relieved his brother, Emir Faisal, of the office of Prime Minister, and assumed the task himself.

Saudi Arabia is a member of the Arab League, *q.v.*, although this group was weakened by the decision of Iraq, with which there was a traditional dynastic rivalry, to join the Baghdad Pact, *q.v.* In 1955 it decided to accept armaments from, and to establish diplomatic relations with, the U.S.S.R., although it had previously obtained some military supplies from the U.S.A.; it also concluded a defence pact with Egypt on 27 October 1955 which provided for joint command of the armed forces in war and peace and that neither country would conclude a separate agreement without the consent of the other.

Schäffer, Hermann Rudolf. Christian Democratic politician in the German Federal Republic; born 1892. After serving in the First World War he took an administrative post on the staff of a professional association; he was an active member of the German State Party until 1933. In 1945 he joined the Free Democratic Party, and has been one of its representatives in the federal legislature since 1949. In 1953 he was appointed Minister without Portfolio in the coalition government led by Konrad Adenauer, *q.v.* He then became Minister of Finance and, in 1957, Minister of Justice.

Schleswig-Holstein. A province in the northern part of the German

Federal Republic; area about 6,125 sq. m.; population 2,275,800, of whom approximately 40,000 are of Danish extraction; capital Kiel. Schleswig and Holstein were taken from Denmark by Prussia in 1864. The Danes in North Schleswig asked to be returned to Denmark, and in 1920 a plebiscite was held (under the Versailles Treaty) which resulted in their demands being fulfilled. The Danes have since renamed the area South Jutland. South Jutland includes a racially-conscious German minority of 9,700 which returns one member to the Danish Parliament.

In South Schleswig, which had since 1920 remained a part of the German province of Schleswig-Holstein, differences emerged after the Second World War. The Danish voters were deprived of all their four seats in the Landtag (provincial parliament) in 1954 by an electoral law which required a party to obtain five per cent of the aggregate vote before it was entitled to a seat. Under a Danish-German agreement in 1955 the Schleswig-Holstein government supported modification of the electoral law to give Danes in South Schleswig representation similar to that enjoyed by the Germans in North Schleswig. Both governments agreed to give equal status to minority schools. Danish extremists demand administrative separation of South Schleswig from Holstein, removal from the province of recently settled refugees who comprised twenty-eight per cent of the population, and eventual self-determination for South Schleswig.

S.E.A.T.O. The organization of the South-East Asia Collective Defence Treaty, *q.v.*

Secession. Formal withdrawal from an organization, such as a party, church or state. A secession from a state is often preceded by a revolt. The fourteen colonies seceded from Great Britain and became the U.S.A. in 1776, Brazil seceded from Portugal in 1822, the former Spanish South American states from Spain in 1810, Greece from Turkey in 1830, Cuba from Spain in 1898, and Panama from Colombia in 1903.

Security Council of the United Nations. Consists of eleven members (including China, France, the U.K., the U.S.A., and the U.S.S.R. as permanent members) and has the primary responsibility for the maintenance of international peace and security. The six non-permanent members are each elected for a two-year term. The members of the United Nations agree, under the United Nations Charter, to accept and carry out the decisions of the Council. On procedural matters its decisions are made by an affirmative vote of seven members, but on all other matters this vote must include the concurring votes of the five permanent members. This is the device known as the 'veto', *q.v.*, which the U.K., the U.S.A., and the U.S.S.R. accepted in the Yalta Agreement, *q.v.*, in February 1945. When measures for the peaceful settlement of a dispute are being discussed a party to the dispute must abstain from voting.

The Security Council determines the existence of any threat to the peace, breach of the peace, or act of aggression. It makes recommendations or decides to take enforcement measures to maintain or restore international peace and security. It may take enforcement measures by calling on members either to apply measures not involving the use of armed forces (*e.g.* interruption of economic relations and of means of communications) or to provide air, sea or land forces to deal with the offending nation. Member states can defend themselves, either individually or acting together, until the Security Council takes action.

Various commissions and committees have been set up by the Security Council from time to time, such as the Disarmament Commission, the Committee on the Admission of New Members, and the United Nations Truce Supervisory Commission in Palestine.

Segni, Antonio. Italian politician, born in Sassaria, Sardinia, in 1891. He became Professor of Law at Perugia University at the age of 29, and was later appointed Rector of the University of Sassari. He took little part in politics while the Fascists were in power, but in 1942 he organized a secret Christian Democratic movement in Sardinia, and later led the local partisan organization. He was Under-Secretary for Agriculture in the Bonomi and de Gasperi governments of 1945–6, and served as Minister of Agriculture under de Gasperi between 1946 and 1951 when he introduced land reforms involving the redistribution of large estates, particularly those of absentee landlords. He was Minister of Education from 1951 to 1954, when he became Professor of Procedural Law at Rome University; in July 1955 he became Prime Minister of a coalition government of Christian Democrats, Democratic Socialists, and Liberals, but he resigned in May 1957 after losing the support of the Democratic Socialists. He was Prime Minister again from January 1959 to February 1960.

Senate. The upper house of a bicameral legislature. The most important Senate, which is the upper house of Congress, *q.v.*, is that of the U.S.A. It has ninety-six members (two from each of the forty-eight States, irrespective of the size of their populations) elected by popular vote for six-year terms, one third standing for election every two years. A member must be at least thirty years of age, must have been a citizen of the U.S.A. for nine years, and must be a resident of the State which he represents. A vacancy is usually filled by a temporary appointment by the Governor of the State in question. The Vice-

President of the U.S.A. is *ex officio* President of the Senate. Treaties made on behalf of the U.S.A. with other countries must be ratified by a two-thirds majority of the Senate.

Senegal. An independent republic; area 76,084 sq. m.; population 2,269,000, comprising Wolofs (approximately 700,000, mostly Moslems), Sereres, Peuls, Tukulers, and 47,000 Europeans; capital Dakar, the former capital of French West Africa, *q.v.* The country is on the west coast of Africa, with Mauritania and Portuguese Guinea to the north and south respectively, and Mali to the east; it completely surrounds (except for a narrow strip of Gambian coast) the British colony of Gambia. It became a French territory in 1840, when it consisted of a number of sultanates and territories controlled by chiefs; it later became one of the eight territories comprising French West Africa, and it achieved self-government within the French Community, *q.v.*, on 25 November 1958. On 4 April 1959 it entered into a federal union with the Soudanese Republic, known as the Mali Federation, *q.v.*, which itself achieved complete independence, still within the Community, on 20 June 1960. Senegal seceded from the Federation in August 1960.

Legislative powers are vested in an assembly of 80 members elected every five years by universal suffrage. At the elections held on 22 March 1959 all the seats were won by the Senegalese Progressive Union (U.P.S.). The other main parties contesting the elections were the African Regroupment Party (led by Abdoulaye Ly) which was opposed to any participation by Senegal in the French Community, and the Senegalese Solidarity Party, led by Ibrahim Seydou N'Daw. Executive power is exercised by the Prime Minister or President of the Council (Mamadou Dia, leader of the African Federalist Party) who is invested by an absolute majority of the Assembly.

The principal exports are groundnuts, groundnut oil, phosphates and oilcake, while millet, maize, and rice are cultivated. The economy is predominantly agricultural. Nearly all the foreign trade of Mali and Mauritania passes through the port of Dakar.

Separation of Powers. The custom, common in democratic countries, of dividing the powers of government into three – legislative, executive, and judicial. It implies that none of these three powers is able to control or interfere with the others (*e.g.* that judges should be independent of the executive), or that the same individuals should not hold posts in more than one of the three branches (*e.g.* that civil servants should not sit in Parliament), or that one branch of government should not exercise the functions of another (*e.g.* that ministers should not be allowed to make laws). The principle was outlined in the eighteenth century by the French writer, Montesquieu, who stated that the stability of English government was due to the separation of powers. In its first sense, that the powers should not control each other, it was rigidly applied in the Constitution of the U.S.A., where executive power is vested in the President whose departmental heads are responsible to him and not to Congress. In the U.K., however, the executive gradually became directly responsible to the legislature; the judiciary is still independent of the executive, but it must obey the laws passed by the legislature, although there can be no interference by Parliament with its day-to-day activities.

Separatism. A belief that a particular group or area should be separated from the larger organization of which it forms a part. It is applied to political movements which advocate independence; for example, those in Newfoundland who wish to sever all ties with Canada are separatists.

Sharett, Moshe. Israeli Socialist politician and first Foreign Minister of Israel; born October 1894 in Russia; educated in Russia, Tel-Aviv, Istanbul, and at the London School of Economics and Political Science. He moved to Israel in 1906 and in the First World War was an officer in the Turkish Army. He was a member of the Poalei Zion Executive in England from 1920 to 1925, and worked on the Palestine Labour daily paper, *Davar*, from 1925 to 1931. From then until the establishment of the state of Israel he was employed by the Jewish Agency, *q.v.* During the Second World War he was mainly responsible for the formation of the Jewish Brigade Group serving with the British forces. He was chief delegate of the Jewish Agency to the United Nations and helped to bring about the United Nations decision made on 29 November 1947 to create an independent Jewish state in Palestine. In May 1948 he became Foreign Minister in the provisional Israeli government; in February 1949 he was elected as a Mapai member to the Knesset and became Foreign Minister in the elected government. On the retirement of David Ben-Gurion, *q.v.*, in December 1953, Sharett became Prime Minister as well as Foreign Minister; he allowed Ben-Gurion to resume the post of Prime Minister in November 1955 when relations with Egypt and other Arab states became exceptionally strained. In June 1956 he resigned from the post of Foreign Minister and was succeeded by Mrs Golda Meir, the Minister of Labour.

Siam. An independent state in south-east Asia known since 1949 as Thailand, *q.v.*

Sib, Treaty of. An agreement signed in 1920 by the Sultan of Muscat and Oman, *q.v.*, and a group of sheikhs from Oman, an area in the interior of Muscat and Oman. The Sultan had exercised authority over Oman for over two hundred years and, as Imam, had also been a spiritual functionary. The latter office was in abeyance for over a hundred years until, in 1913, the tribes in Oman elected an Imam. The Treaty, of which few details have been published, states that the Sultan is not to interfere in the internal affairs of the Omanis. The present Imam Ghalib has claimed that the Treaty recognized that Oman was an independent sovereign state, and he has issued Omani passports. He has also alleged that the oil concession granted in 1937 by the Sultan to a subsidiary of the Iraq Petroleum Company, and purporting to give rights to the Company over Oman, was a breach of the Treaty, as the Imam and the Omanis were not consulted. In December 1955 the Sultan led an expedition against Nizwa, in central Oman, as a result of which the Imam and his supporters were temporarily dispersed. Another rising in Oman in July 1957 was suppressed with the aid of British forces.

Sikkim. An Indian protectorate to the east of Nepal and to the south of Tibet; area 2,818 sq. m.; population (1951 census) 137,158; capital Gangtok. The relationship with India is governed by a treaty concluded on 5 December 1950, by which India was given special responsibility for communications, defence, and foreign affairs. The protectorate produces corn, millet, rice, and apples and oranges. The ruler (His Highness Maharaja Sir Tashi Namgyal, born 1893, succeeded in 1914) governs with the assistance of a council of which more than two thirds of the members are elected. Chinese spokesmen have claimed that Sikkim, with Bhutan (to the east), and Ladakh (part of Kashmir) are part of Tibet and thus part of China.

Singapore. A British colony at the southern end of the Malayan peninsula; area, comprising Singapore Island and adjacent islets in the Indian Ocean, 224 sq. m.; population (1959) 1,581,600, of whom approximately 1,190,100 are Chinese, 217,300 Malayans, 134,600 Indians and Pakistanis, 13,900 Europeans, and 12,000 Eurasians. Singapore is an important British naval base and commercial centre. It has full powers of internal self-government; the 1959 Constitution established a Legislative Assembly of 51 members, elected by universal suffrage. The U.K. retains responsibility for defence and external affairs; in the event of a breakdown of internal security which seriously affects British defence responsibilities, the constitution can be suspended. On the Internal Security Council Singapore is represented by the Prime Minister and two other Ministers; the U.K. is represented by the High Commissioner, who is Chairman, and two others; Malaya has one representative. The Head of State, as representative of the Queen, must be of Malayan birth, and is chosen on the advice of the Prime Minister; he is known as the Yang di Pertuan Negara.

At the first elections held under the new constitution, on 30 May 1959, the People's Action Party (P.A.P.), led by Lee Kuan Yew, and with a left-wing outlook and multiracial support, won 43 of the 51 seats. The People's Alliance, led by Lim Yew Hock, a former Chief Minister, won 4 seats; the United Malays National Organization (U.M.N.O.) 3 seats; and one independent was returned.

Most politicians favour the proposal that Singapore should be merged with Malaya, but the Federation has not so far reciprocated this desire. Singapore lives by its entrepôt trade and handles large quantities of rubber, tin, and oil, but attempts are being made to increase investment in industry.

Slump. A fall in prices or demand, usually the result of some failure in spending. A boom may be converted into a slump when wages do not rise enough to enable consumers to spend on a scale that will satisfy the producers, or when business firms do not embark on sufficient new capital outlay.

Social Credit. A movement based on the theories of the late Major C. H. Douglas, who believed that permanent prosperity could be achieved through a reform of the monetary system. He ascribed social and economic evils to the insufficient supply of money and its control by banks. He proposed the 'A + B theorem', saying that all prices are made up from two classes of payments: A, payments made to individuals as wages, salaries, and dividends, and B, payments made by producers (for raw materials, bank charges, etc.) to other firms and which are, properly speaking, working capital. Only A payments create purchasing power, while B payments, being capital, cannot be consumed by the payee. As national income is equal to the total of A payments, and as the total of prices is determined by A + B, purchasing power for the extra amount must be provided for the proportion of the product equal to B. This supplementary purchasing power has hitherto been supplied by new money created by the banks which has been used to grant loans which had, in due course, to be repaid. Thus a constant flow of money to the banks has been lost as purchasing power. This has led to the total of prices exceeding the total of incomes, or to what is called over-production.

Douglas suggested that the banks should place the new money which, under the present credit system, they create every day, in the hands of the consumer. The retailer would have to sell the goods below cost, and his loss, plus a commission, would be credited to his account at the bank. The prices would be arranged so that the total wages, salaries, and dividends would be sufficient to buy all the goods. Another method of increasing purchasing power was the 'national dividend', payable to everyone according to the prosperity of the country.

Orthodox critics say that the system would lead to inflation, despite all safeguards, and that it neglects the need for the formation of fresh capital and unduly stresses the interests of consumption. Socialist critics say that the system seeks the remedies for social evils in the sphere of circulation only, instead of tackling the problem of re-organizing capitalist production; Hugh Gaitskell has criticized the obscurity and dogmatism of Douglas, calling him 'a religious rather than a scientific reformer'.

The only places where the Social Credit Party has gained power are in Canada, in Alberta in 1935 (where Douglas condemned his Party's activities) and in British Columbia in 1952. In both cases the Party's success resulted from popular discontent with the provincial government rather than positive belief in Social Credit.

Socialism. A political and economic theory according to which the means of production, distribution and exchange should be owned and controlled by the people, everyone should be given an equal opportunity to develop his talents, and the wealth of the community should be fairly distributed.

Solid South. An American political term referring to the fact that the southern States of the U.S.A. have for a very long time invariably voted for the Democratic Party. The majority in this political group-ing are loyal Democrats, but in recent years there has emerged a considerable number of dissident right-wing Democrats, sometimes called 'States' Righters' or 'Dixiecrats'. Their recent support of the Republicans has arisen partly out of a hope that a Republican administration would have greater respect for States' rights, and in particular that the Federal Government would intervene less to pro-tect the civil liberties of the Negroes and to insist on social welfare measures. Southerners are easily discouraged from supporting the Republican Party by any decline in farm prices, and look to a Democratic administration to provide the farmers with subsidies.

Somalia. An independent republic, also known as the Somali Republic, in north-east Africa on the Gulf of Aden and the Indian Ocean, with French Somaliland to the west, Kenya to the South, and Ethiopia inland; area 288,000 sq. m.; population 2,140,000; capital Mogadishu. The country, which became independent on 1 July 1960, was created by uniting the protectorate of British Somaliland, *q.v.*, and the territory of Somalia; the latter had been ceded by the U.K. to Italy in 1925, occupied by the U.K. in February 1941, and returned to Italy as a trusteeship territory under a trusteeship agreement concluded in December 1950. Many Somalis support a scheme for a Greater Somalia which would include French Somaliland (with its deep-water port of Djibouti) and parts of Kenya and Ethiopia. At the first elections ever held in Somalia, in February 1956, 43 out of the 60 elective seats were won by the League of Somali Youth. The country receives subsidies and technical advice from Italy and the U.K. There are disagreements with Ethiopia as to the demarcation of the border, particularly between the former British Somaliland and Ethiopia where the Haud and Reserved Area is the subject of dispute (*see* British Somaliland). Somalia is a poor country, and the main occupations are agriculture and cattle-rearing.

Soudanese Republic. The name given to the French overseas territory of Soudan, in French West Africa, *q.v.*, when it achieved self-government within the French Community, *q.v.*, on 24 November 1958, until, on the collapse of the Mali Federation, *q.v.*, it declared, on 22 September 1960, that it would thenceforth be known as the Republic of Mali, *q.v.*

Soustelle, Jacques. French politician, born 1912 into a working-class Protestant family. He has had a distinguished career as an anthropologist and ethnologist, specializing in the Aztec civilization, and, at the age of twenty-five was appointed assistant director of the Paris Musée de l'Homme. His political activities began in left-wing circles. He agitated against the Munich Agreement, rallied support in Latin America, where he was on a diplomatic mission, for de Gaulle in 1940 and in 1942 became Commissioner for Information for the Free French. When the Free French headquarters were moved from London to Algeria in 1943 he was made director of secret services and of counter-espionage. After the Liberation Soustelle became Minister of Information and then Minister for the Colonies in de Gaulle's government. He was later chief organizer of the Gaullist political party, the Rally of the French People, launched in 1947. In 1951 he was elected as a U.A.R.S. (Social Republican) Deputy for the Rhône but refused to enter any government until January 1955, when he accepted the invitation of his wartime colleague, Pierre Mendès-France, to be Governor-General of Algeria.

He was then known to favour colonial federalism and equal rights for Algerian Moslems, so that his appointment was not acceptable to the French Algerian settlers. After studying the methods of the F.L.N., however, he decided to annihilate the Nationalist movement. On his return to Paris he founded the Union for the Salvation and Rebirth of French Algeria, and pursued a policy of uncompromising hostility to Algerian independence. He was primarily responsible for the successive downfalls of the Bourgès-Maunoury government in November 1957, on a Bill to give Algeria limited self-government, and the Gaillard government in April 1958, for accepting Anglo-American proposals for a reconciliation with Tunisia, following the French aerial bombardment of Sakiet. He helped the French officers and settlers in Algeria to organize their coup in May 1958, and was appointed Minister of Information by de Gaulle in July 1958. In the Debré government, formed in January 1959, he became Minister Delegate to the Prime Minister, with responsibility for the two Sahara departments of Algeria (Saoura and Oasis), atomic research, and various other overseas departments and territories. There was an insurrection in Algiers on 24 January 1960, in protest against the Algerian policy of de Gaulle; the insurrectionists surrendered on 1 February but Soustelle, who was believed to favour them, was dismissed from office by de Gaulle on 5 February 1960.

South Africa. A republic, once member of the British Commonwealth; area 472,359 sq. m.; population (1960) 15,841,128, comprising 10,807,809 Bantus (Zulu, Basuto, Xhosa, Pondo, etc.), 3,067,638 whites, 1,488,267 coloured people (the Cape Malays and the descendants of slaves from the east and of the now nearly extinct Hottentots, with a strong infusion of Dutch blood), and 477,414 Asians (mostly Indians or descendants of Indians); capital Pretoria. The Union of South Africa consists of the provinces of Cape of Good Hope, Natal, Transvaal, and Orange Free State.

A settlement was established at the Cape of Good Hope by the Dutch East India Company in 1652, and in the eighteenth century the settlers began to encounter, and to defeat in war, the various Bantu tribes which were moving southward from Central Africa. In 1814, after the Napoleonic Wars, the British Cape Colony was established; resentment at the British intrusion and at the amount of compensation offered when slavery was abolished in 1833 incited the Dutch-speaking settlers (the Boers or Afrikaners) to trek northwards into the interior and found the South African Republic or Transvaal, and the Orange Free State. Boer hatred of the English increased when in 1895 Cecil Rhodes (Prime Minister of the Cape Colony and Managing Director of the British South Africa Company which controlled Rhodesia) organized an unsuccessful invasion of Transvaal, later called the Jameson Raid, in order to assist British exploitation of the Rand goldfields in Transvaal. War broke out in 1899 and in 1902 the Boers had to surrender and become British subjects, but were promised self-government; this was granted and a constitution was enacted by the U.K. in 1909 when the South Africa Act was passed. The Union of South Africa came into being in 1910.

The result of the South Africa Act and the Statute of Westminster of 1931 (see Westminster, Statute of) had been to give South Africa the independence of a sovereign state with full power to amend its constitution, but only in the manner laid down in the entrenched provisions, q.v., of the 1909 Act. Legislative power was vested in the Queen, represented by a South African Governor-General, acting with a Senate of 86 members, some nominated and some elected, and a House of Assembly of 160 members elected for five years. There were 3 Native representatives in the House, elected by those whose names appeared on the Cape Native Voters' roll, but these members and 4 similar members of the Senate, were deprived of their seats in June 1960. In 1961 the National Party (a right-wing semi-Fascist group believing in white supremacy and apartheid, q.v., allied to the Dutch Reformed Church, with republican beliefs, and led by Verwoerd, q.v., Louw, and Dönges) held 103 seats; the United Party (which accepts the principle of racial segregation but not the civic disabilities imposed upon Africans or the unparliamentary and dictatorial approach of the National Party; its leader is Sir de Villiers Graaff) held 53 seats; the South African Labour Party held no seats, having lost all its 5 seats at the general election in April 1958. These figures included the 6 representatives of South-West Africa, q.v.

At a referendum in October 1960 the whites, by a majority of 52 per cent to 48 per cent, voted for a republic. The republic became effective on 31 May 1961, when South Africa also withdrew from the Commonwealth, under pressure from its members.

The Union's most valuable exports are wool, gold, diamonds, copper, and textiles. The development of stable manufacturing industries has been hampered by the reluctance of foreign financiers to invest in a country in which Nationalist policies may cause social unrest and economic disorder. The shortage of foreign currency has made it necessary for the government to impose import controls since 1948. Immigration in general and British immigration in particular have been opposed by the Nationalists, who believe in selecting citizens who will favour their party; this policy, combined with mining and industrial expansion and a rigid application of the colour bar, has led to a serious shortage of skilled labour which impedes development.

South Korea. The Republic of Korea, inaugurated on 15 August 1948 when U.S. military government came to an end, and officially recognized by the western powers but not by the U.S.S.R. and its satellites; area 38,452 sq. m.; population (1958) 21,909,742; capital Seoul. While the country was under U.S. military occupation, from August 1945 until August 1948, an attempt was made to establish some form of democratic government in which North Korea, *q.v.*, could participate as soon as the U.S.S.R. permitted the reunification of Korea, *q.v.* Accordingly, a general election was held on 10 May 1948, under the observation of a United Nations Commission, at which ninety per cent of the electorate voted for 203 members of a National Assembly; 100 more seats were reserved for the one third of the population living north of the 38th parallel. A Constitution (the first in 4,000 years of Korea's history) was adopted and a republic declared; Dr Syngman Rhee, *q.v.*, was elected President.

When North Korea invaded South Korea on 25 June 1950 the South was totally unprepared for war. U.S. policy had been to restrain the belligerent President Rhee; in order to avoid the charge that it was building a military base on the Asian mainland it supplied only light arms, and no tanks, to deal with local unrest, threatened cessation of economic aid should there be any movement of South Korean troops north of the 38th parallel, and withdrew all its military forces, except for an advisory mission of five hundred, by June 1949. When the Security Council of the United Nations asked all member nations to render assistance to the Republic of Korea the U.S. provided the commanders of the United Nations army, most of the men and practically all the equipment. There were 142,000 U.S. casualties in the war; British casualties numbered 4,451. An armistice was concluded on 27 July 1953 by which a demilitarization zone between the two states was established roughly along the 38th parallel and a Neutral Nations Supervisory Commission was appointed to see that the armistice terms were observed and to arrange for the exchange of prisoners.

South Korea was devastated as a result of the war. Although the Sangdong mine has one of the world's largest deposits of tungsten, and there is an abundance of amorphous graphite, the state is insolvent and dependent on economic aid from the west which amounted to $2,468,200,000 between 1945 and 1958. Further relief is in the hands of the United Nations Korean Reconstruction

Agency (U.N.K.R.A.) which is financed by voluntary contributions from governments.

At the elections held on 2 May 1958, to fill 233 seats in the National Assembly, the President's party, the Liberals, retained power with a reduced majority. They won 122 seats while their main opponents, the Democrats (led by Vice-President Chiang Myun or John M. Chang, a Roman Catholic, born in 1899 and educated in the U.S.A.) won 77 seats. Although Rhee secured re-election as President in March 1960 and also engineered the defeat of Chang in the Vice-Presidential election, the corruption and repressive measures of his government resulted in his enforced resignation in April 1960. At the elections held on 29 July 1960 under the new Constitution of that year, the Democrats won 172 seats, and Chang became Prime Minister, while another Democrat, Yoon Bo Sun, was elected President. Chang was ousted by a military junta in May 1961.

South Tirol. The portion of Tirol south of the Brenner Pass, formerly part of the Austro-Hungarian Empire, which was acquired by Italy in 1919; it was known as Bozen but since its cession to Italy it has been called Alto Adige or Bolzano; population 350,000, of whom 220,000 are German-speaking South Tirolese, 116,000 Italian-speaking, and 1,400 Ludin-speaking inhabitants; capital Bolzano. By the Grüber–de Gasperi agreement of 5 September 1946 between Austria and Italy the South Tirolese were to be given 'complete equality of rights with the Italian-speaking inhabitants, within the framework of special provisions to safeguard the ethnological character and the cultural and economic development of the German-speaking element'; the agreement also stated: 'the populations of the above-mentioned zones will be granted the exercise of autonomous legislative and executive regional power'. The agreement was later incorporated in the Paris Peace Treaty of 10 February 1947 (ratified on 15 September 1947) and made part of the Italian constitution by statute on 26 February 1948.

By the same statute there was established the autonomous region of Trentino – Alto Adige, comprising the two provinces of these names. Trentino (of which the capital is Trento or Trent) has a population of approximately 400,000, all Italians, so that the autonomous region has a total population of 750,000 and an Italian majority, whereas the South Tirol itself has a German-speaking majority. The Austrian government has demanded a greater degree of autonomy for the South Tirol and has accused the Italian government of breaking the 1946 agreement; the Italian government denies that there has been a breach, and argues that the statute of 1948 gave to each province in the region a council to handle matters reserved to the provinces, and that some 17 aspects of government are by law and in fact left to the provincial council of South Tirol, where the Conservative and Catholic South Tirolese People's Party (S.V.P.) is supported by the German-speaking majority. The S.V.P. insists that autonomy in all matters should be transferred from the regional council to the provincial council.

South Viet-Nam. The zone south of the 17th parallel allotted to the government of Viet-Nam in July 1954 by the terms of the Geneva Agreements on the cessation of hostilities in Viet-Nam, *q.v.*; population 13,000,000; capital Saigon. The government in Saigon is recognized by the U.K. and the U.S.A. as the legal government of Viet-Nam. A republic was declared in 1955 by the President, Ngo Dinh Diem, *q.v.*, who replaced the former head of state, Bao Dai, *q.v.*, as a result of a popular referendum. Diem governed by ordinance through a cabinet chosen largely from his own relations. Until 1956 he had difficulty in establishing authority throughout South Viet-Nam owing to the existence of several terrorist organizations with private armies. These included the Hoa Hao sect, the Cao Daists, who were religious fanatics, and the Binh Xuyen whose leader, General Van le Vien, controlled the Saigon police and many of its brothels. The remaining French residents lent support to these organizations in the hope of discrediting the nationalist, anti-French government and creating such disorder that the French expeditionary force would not be withdrawn; the last French troops in fact left in 1956. Diem has launched a literacy campaign and a programme of social reform, which has closed Saigon's opium dens, and he has introduced financial measures designed to improve the country's trade position. He receives over $100,000,000 a year in U.S. aid.

At the general elections held on 30 August 1959 the results were: National Revolutionary Movement 74; Independents 43; Viet-Nam Socialist Party 3; Social Democratic Party 1; opposition candidates 2. Although 86 per cent of the electorate voted and there was considerable freedom of speech, the details of the campaign were closely supervised by the government, which financed and controlled the printed publicity of all the candidates. Approximately 120 of the successful candidates were known to support the policies of Diem.

South-East Asia Collective Defence Treaty. Agreed by Australia, France, New Zealand, Pakistan, the Philippines, Thailand, the U.K., and the U.S.A. at Manila in the Philippines on 8 September 1954. The Treaty set up the South-East Asia Treaty Organization (S.E.A.T.O.) with headquarters at Bangkok and provided for a Council and

Secretariat. The eight signatories agreed to take collective action in the event of either external aggression against any one of them or internal subversion. They also agreed to co-operate in economic matters, but the main emphasis has been on military and anti-Communist rather than on economic measures. The area involved has been so defined in the Treaty that an attack on Formosa or Hong Kong would not bring the Treaty obligations into operation.

South-West Africa. A territory controlled by South Africa and once a German colony; area 317,887 sq. m.; population (1951 census) 467,716, of whom 49,612 are Europeans; capital Windhoek. It was a German possession from 1884 until the end of the First World War when it was entrusted by the League of Nations to South Africa to be administered as a mandated territory. No trusteeship agreement was concluded by South Africa with the United Nations after the Second World War, and the International Court of Justice therefore held in 1950 that the area was still under an international mandate and that South Africa was obliged to submit it to the supervision and control of the General Assembly and to render annual reports on it. It is the only one of the areas which were under League of Nations mandate which has neither become independent nor been placed under trusteeship. Under the South-West Africa Affairs Amendment Act, 1949, the territory is represented by six members in the House of Assembly and by four members in the Senate of South Africa. This Act involved a closer association between the territory and South Africa but stopped short of incorporation. The South African government has thus obeyed the Court ruling which forbade incorporation, but has refused to submit reports on the territory. When the chiefs of the Herero tribe, which had suffered expropriation of its reserves by white settlers, attempted to make their own report to the United Nations, they were prevented from leaving South-West Africa. Their case was taken up by the Rev. Michael Scott, who gave evidence on their behalf at the United Nations.

In the elections for the South-West African Legislative Assembly held in March 1961 the Nationalist Party, which has the same aims as its parent organization in South Africa, secured 16 seats and the United Party 2. Of the 28,000 voters in the territory, all of whom are white, seventy per cent are Afrikaners, twenty-two per cent German-speaking, and eight per cent English-speaking.

Southern Cameroons. *See* Cameroons, British.

Southern Rhodesia. A British self-governing territory to the south of Northern Rhodesia and to the north of the Union of South Africa; area 150,333 sq. m.; population (including 2,885,000 Africans and

225,000 Europeans) 3,110,000; capital Salisbury. Since 1 August 1953 it has formed part of the Federation of Rhodesia and Nyasaland, *q.v.* The United Federal Party, supporting the continuance of the Federation and the control of the Southern Rhodesian territorial government by educated and responsible people, won 17 out of 30 seats in the Legislative Assembly at the election held on 5 June 1958; its leader, Sir Edgar Whitehead, is Prime Minister. The right-wing Dominion Party, favouring the retention of the Land Apportionment Act, 1930, which in effect apportioned more than half the land to the white population, won 13 seats. The National Democratic Party, led by Joshua Nkomo, demands full voting rights for Africans and the right of Southern Rhodesia to secede from the Federation.

Soviet. Russian word meaning 'council'. Workers' councils, under the name of Soviets, emerged first in the Russian Revolution of 1905. They reappeared in the 1917 Revolution, and became the organs of the Communist revolution and later of the national administration. Until 1936 the lower Soviets chose the higher Soviets (district, regional, and state Soviets) by means of indirect election. Features of the original Soviet system were unity of legislative and executive power, and of local and state authorities. It was claimed that the system ensured the participation of the masses in the administration. In 1936 the Constitution was amended and the system of indirect election abandoned, though the name was retained. All Soviets of whatever degree are now elected directly by the people and the lower Soviets do not control the higher ones, such as the Supreme Soviet, *q.v.*

Soviet Union. Union of Soviet Socialist Republics, *q.v.*

Spain. An independent state in south-west Europe; area 196,700 sq. m.; population (1958) 29,784,019; capital Madrid. It was ruled by monarchs of the Aragon, Bourbon, and Habsburg families until 1931 when the dictatorship of General Primo de Rivera was overthrown, a republic was proclaimed, and King Alfonso XIII left the country. A provisional government of Republicans and Socialists was formed and ruled Spain, with strong opposition from the right wing, until a general election was held on 16 February 1936, in which the left-wing parties secured a clear majority over the right and centre parties. Manuel Azaña, the leader of the Popular Front, was elected as President on 10 May 1936. The government formed by Azaña, which contained neither Socialists nor Communists, initiated a land reform (at that time one per cent of the population owned fifty-one per cent of the land) and other social reforms which aroused the opposition of conservative circles, and particularly of the large land-owners. A revolt, led by Franco, *q.v.*, and supported and financed by the officer class, the feudal aristocracy, the bulk of the politically-minded Roman Catholics, and the monarchists, began on 18 July 1936 in Spanish Morocco and then spread throughout Spain. By August Germany and Italy had intervened to help the Fascist rebels. The U.S.S.R. later assisted the Spanish government. After nearly three years of disorder and bitter civil war fighting ended in March 1939 with the success of the Fascist rebels.

In 1942 Franco, as President, reinstituted the Cortes (Assembly) which comprises 441 members, 103 National Counsellors of the Falange, 145 from the Courts and National Syndicates, 102 Mayors, 16 Ministers, 25 representatives of the professions, and 50 other eminent people appointed by Franco. The Cortes is the supreme organ of the state for the preparation and enactment of laws.

During the Second World War Spain was continually in touch with the German and Italian governments but, though anxious to seize Gibraltar, *q.v.*, from the U.K., remained officially neutral. In 1946 the United Nations resolved that Ambassadors should be withdrawn from Spain; however, most of the major powers have since resumed diplomatic relations, although refusing until 1955 to admit Spain to the United Nations. The U.S.A. appreciated its strategic importance and on 26 September 1953 concluded an agreement at Madrid for military and economic aid, to cover a twenty-year period, during which air and naval bases were to be leased to the U.S.A.

Spain is technically a monarchy, under a law passed in 1947, and it is possible that on the death or retirement of Franco, Prince Juan Carlos de Bourbon (born 1938), son of the Count of Barcelona (Don Juan de Bourbon) and the grandson of Alfonso XIII, would become King. Under the 1947 Succession Law, however, Franco was given complete power to choose his successor, who must not be less than thirty years old when he succeeds to the throne.

Spanish Morocco. The name formerly given to the northern portion of Morocco, *q.v.*, about fifty miles wide, lying between the Rif Mountains and the Mediterranean, which from 1912 to 1956 was recognized as a Spanish sphere of influence; area approximately 11,236 sq. m.; population 1,082,000 of whom nearly 1,000,000 are Moslems; capital Tetuan. It included the free ports of Melilla and Ceuta, which became Spanish possessions in 1496 and 1581 respectively. The division of Morocco into French and Spanish spheres of influence took place as a result of a Protectorate Treaty between France and the Sultan at Fez on 30 March 1912 and a Convention between France and Spain at Madrid on 27 November 1912. The Sultan's powers in Spanish

Morocco were delegated to a Khalifa, whose administration was controlled by a Spanish High Commissioner. The frontier with French Morocco, *q.v.*, was never properly defined and the Spaniards, who considered that they had a prior claim to protect Morocco, tended to push southwards. In 1934 they occupied Ifni, *q.v.*, and obtained treaty rights south of the river Draa, in the areas later known as Spanish Sahara, *q.v.*, and Spanish Southern Morocco, *q.v.*

Spain followed the example of France in April 1956 by recognizing the sovereign and independent status of Morocco, and agreed that the Convention of Madrid no longer governed relations between Spain and Morocco. The Spanish government accordingly handed over the administration of Spanish Morocco to the representatives of the Sultan, Sidi Mohammed ben Youssef. In January 1958 Spain reorganized Ifni and Spanish Sahara so that they became **provinces.**

Spanish Sahara. A province of Spain to the west of Morocco and on the Atlantic Ocean; area 105,448 sq. m.; population approximately 14,000. It comprises the two former colonies of Rio de Oro and Saguia el-Hamra, to the south of Spanish Southern Morocco, *q.v.* Its establishment as a province was announced on 14 January 1958, when the enclave of Ifni, *q.v.*, was also made a province. It is administered by the Director-General of African Provinces in Madrid. There are believed to be substantial oil reserves, especially in the northern coastal area near Cape Bojador, south of the capital, Aaiun.

Spanish Southern Morocco. Also known as Tarfaya, this mostly desert area of nearly 10,000 sq. m. was administered as part of the protectorate of Spanish Morocco, *q.v.*, from 1912 until the emergence of Morocco as an independent state in 1956. It lies on the Atlantic Ocean between the parallel of 27°40′ North latitude and the River Draa. On 10 April 1958 it was returned by Spain to Morocco. To the north and south respectively are the Spanish provinces of Ifni, *q.v.*, and Spanish Sahara, *q.v.*

Special United Nations Fund for Economic Development (S.U.N.F.E.D.). A fund proposed by the Economic and Financial Committee of the United Nations General Assembly, and unanimously recommended by the Assembly in December 1954. The Committee said that from the fund long-term, low-interest loans, or outright grants, could be made to finance basic development works, such as roads or harbours, which offered too little return on the investment to qualify for a loan from the International Bank for Reconstruction and Development, *q.v.* The U.K. and the U.S.A. stated that the extent of their financial contributions to S.U.N.F.E.D. must depend on the progress of disarmament. Other countries made their support conditional upon that of the U.K. and the U.S.A.

Specialized Agencies. Inter-governmental organizations with wide responsibilities in economic, social, cultural, educational, health and other fields, whose work is co-ordinated by the Economic and Social Council, *q.v.*, of the United Nations.

Spheres of Influence. Certain countries, or parts of countries, in which another state, without annexation, desires to exert exclusive influence. For many years after 1907 Persia was divided into British and Russian spheres of influence. The U.S. government regards it as vital that no pro-Communist régime should come to power in Central or South America, which it regards as one of its spheres of influence. Eastern Europe, with the exceptions of Finland, Yugoslavia, Greece, and Turkey, can be regarded as a sphere of influence for the U.S.S.R.

Spitsbergen Archipelago. Also known as Svalbard, a commercially important group of Norwegian islands about 550 miles north of the northernmost part of Norway; total area about 24,300 sq. m.; population approximately 3,500. It comprises a main island, West Spitsbergen, North East Land, Edge Island, Barents Island, and some smaller islands. There were Dutch, British, and Norwegian claims to sovereignty in the seventeenth century when there was much lucrative whale-hunting, but the hunting ended and the claims lapsed until the twentieth century when rich coalfields were discovered. Once more there were disputes, but on 19 February 1920 Norwegian sovereignty was recognized by the Treaty of Paris between Norway and other interested states, and the Archipelago was officially taken over by Norway on 14 August 1925. The Treaty provided that the economic exploitation of the Archipelago should be open equally to all the signatory powers. After 1930 only Norway and the U.S.S.R. (Russia having annexed a coalfield in 1912) carried on mining there; in 1941 British, Canadian, and Norwegian forces dismantled or destroyed most of the mining plant to prevent the Germans from benefiting from the mines in case they arrived in the Archipelago. By 1958 coal production was over 600,000 tons annually; there were approximately 1,900 workers in the three Russian camps, and about 1,300 in the three Norwegian camps, one of which was not being operated. Though earnings are high there is a heavy turnover of labour. The islands are ice-blocked for most of the year and there is total darkness from October to February. The mines, however, are a valuable source of supply for north Norway, and the Norwegian government has tried to increase production and to reopen the closed mine. Neither

Russian requests, which were rejected, to discuss the defence of the Archipelago, nor Norway's commitments under the North Atlantic Treaty have altered its non-military status, for the 1920 Treaty provided that no military bases or fortifications of any kind should be established.

Stakhanovite. A worker who exceeds the quota of work allotted to him. Alexei Stakhanov was a Russian miner who regularly exceeded his quota, or 'norm', and who was held up to other Russian workers as an example to be followed. Stakhanovites were given higher wages, rewards in kind and special social privileges. Penalties were imposed for the under-fulfilment of norms. The system was sometimes abused, for propaganda purposes, by the establishment of very low norms which would clearly be exceeded by a wide margin. Norms would sometimes be raised, however, in order to disguise a reduction in wages. The U.S.S.R. is now less interested in individual record-breaking than in an all-round increase in production, and piece-rates have been found to be adequate incentives for skilled workers.

State Department. The branch of the U.S. government responsible to the President for the conduct of foreign affairs. It is the oldest department, having been established (as the Department of Foreign Affairs) on 27 July 1789 by the fourth Act of Congress passed after the adoption of the Constitution. Its head is the Secretary of State.

Statute of Westminster, 1931. *See* Westminster, Statute of.

Sterling Area. A group of countries which decided in 1931, when the U.K. went off the gold standard, to tie their currencies to sterling rather than to gold and to hold their currency reserves in the form of balances with the Bank of England. During and after the Second World War the acute shortage of gold and dollars compelled sterling area members to impose exchange control; this means that, although there is freedom of exchange within the sterling area, the territories that earn a net surplus of dollars sell their excess dollars to the British Treasury for sterling, and those that spend more dollars than they earn can buy dollars for sterling from the British Treasury. In 1961 the territories in the sterling area, described in the Exchange Control Act of 1947 as the 'scheduled territories', were: the U.K. and its colonies; all British Commonwealth countries with the exception of Canada; and Burma, Iceland, Ireland, Jordan, Libya, and the seven independent states on the Trucial Coast.

Stevenson, Adlai Ewing. Born 5 February 1900 at Springfield, Illinois, the son of Lewis Green Stevenson, Secretary of State for Illinois, and the grandson of Adlai Stevenson who was Vice-President of the U.S. under President Cleveland. After graduating from Princeton University in 1922 he was employed on the family newspaper in Illinois. He took a law degree at the North-Western University School, Chicago, was called to the Illinois bar in 1926 and in 1933 became special counsel to the Agricultural Adjustment Administration (A.A.A.), one of the organizations instituted by President Roosevelt as part of the New Deal, *q.v.* He was also assistant general counsel to the Federal Alcohol Control Administration. In 1935 he resumed his legal practice until the American declaration of war in 1941 when he became special assistant to the Secretary of the Navy. In 1943 he followed the Allied Armies into Italy as head of the Foreign Economic Administration, which was responsible for the first programme of relief and reconstruction. He was later attached to the Air Force Mission to Europe until 1945 when he was appointed special assistant to the Secretary of State. In 1946 and 1947 he was a U.S. delegate to the United Nations, in the inauguration of which he had played a prominent part. In 1948 he stood, as a Democrat, for the post of Governor of Illinois, pledged to establish an honest State administration, and won by the largest margin in the State's history. He received the Democratic nomination in the Presidential election in 1952 and increased the Democratic vote, but was beaten by Dwight D. Eisenhower, *q.v.* He married Ellen Borden, from whom he is now divorced; they have three sons. He was chosen as Democratic Presidential candidate again in 1956 but was again defeated by Eisenhower. In January 1961 he became U.S. Ambassador to the United Nations.

Strategic Trusteeship Territory. Any territory among the Trusteeship Territories, *q.v.*, which is designated by the administering country as a 'strategic area'.

Subversive Activities Control Act, 1950. An Act passed by the U.S. Congress, it set up the Subversive Activities Control Board, which can decide whether any organization is a 'Communist action organization', a 'Communist front organization', or a 'Communist-infiltrated organization'. If the Board so decides, the organization can be required to file with the Department of Justice a list of its members, the sources of its funds, and a detailed account of how the funds are spent; it must also state on all its propaganda that the Board has made a finding against it. Members of 'action' groups and officers of 'front' groups cannot apply for, or use, a U.S. passport, seek any office or employment under the government, or apply for a job in a defence industry without revealing their status. Offences against this rule are punishable with a fine of $10,000 and imprisonment for five years; a person is considered to have committed a fresh offence every day that he breaks the law. The aim of the Act was to bring Communists and their supporters into the open rather than to declare their organization illegal.

Succession States. The independent states which, after the First World War, either were set up on, or obtained a share of, the territory of the former Austro-Hungarian Empire. They included Austria, Czechoslovakia, Hungary, Italy, Poland, Rumania, and Yugoslavia. Succession to territory usually involves succession to the international rights and duties of the former sovereign. The peace treaties made express provision, for example, for the apportionment between the states concerned of the pre-war debts of the Austro-Hungarian Empire.

Sudan. An independent state to the south of Egypt which was an Anglo-Egyptian condominium from 1899 to 1 January 1956; area 967,500 sq. m.; population (1955–56 census) 10,262,536, partly Arabs and partly Negroes; capital Khartoum. Its status as a condominium administered by a Governor-General on behalf of the U.K. and Egypt was confirmed in the Anglo-Egyptian Treaty of 1936, but on 12 February 1953 the two governments signed an agreement approving of proposals for Sudanese self-government.

A crucial factor in Sudanese politics is the difference in outlook between the Islamic Arab-speaking north and the non-Islamic and more primitive south, which fears northern dominance and has clear memories of rapacious northern slave-traders. The National Unionist Party (N.U.P.), which won an absolute majority at the elections held in November and December 1953, was supported by some, such as the Ashigga Party, who advocated a close union with Egypt, by some who favoured a less direct link, and by orthodox (Khatmi) Moslems who voted N.U.P. because their religious rivals, the heterodox Mahdists (the Ansar sect), voted for the opponents of the N.U.P. The Umma Party opposed the N.U.P., demanded independence for Sudan, and was associated in the minds of many voters with British policy. After the elections the N.U.P. suffered from its internal differences, but its leader, Sayed Ismail el Azhari, who became Prime Minister in January 1954, eventually accepted the principle of complete independence, while the Khatmia and the Mahdists reached a measure of agreement on the methods by which self-government could be achieved. El Azhari resigned in July 1956 in favour of the Secretary-General of the Umma Party, Abdullah Khalil, who was better able to secure the support of both rival sects.

On the completion of the Sudanization of the administration in 1955, the legislature asked for the departure of the British and Egyptian troops and for arrangements for self-determination to be put in hand forthwith. There were mutinies in the province of Equatoria in south Sudan by units of the Sudan Defence Force which dreaded the consequences of rule from Khartoum. Some southern politicians suggested that south Sudan should be federated rather than united with the north. The Sudanese government then declared the independence of Sudan; Egypt and the U.K. accepted this and the country became independent on 1 January 1956.

At the general election in February and March 1958 for 173 seats in the House of Representatives the results were: Umma Party (conservative in outlook, pro-western) 63 seats; N.U.P. (strongly supported in the three towns of Khartoum, Omdurman, and North Khartoum, and favouring a defence pact with Egypt) 45; People's Democratic Party (Khatmi dissidents from the N.U.P.) 27; Liberals (non-Arabs and mainly non-Moslems from the south) 20. Abdullah Khalil continued as Prime Minister.

On 17 November 1958 the Army assumed control; the Constitution was suspended and the House of Representatives was dissolved, and a Supreme Council was vested with full powers, but its close connexions with the Umma Party and the west made it the subject of criticism and on 4 March 1959, under military pressure, it was reorganized. The leader of the revolt of November 1958, General Ibrahim Abboud, continued in office as President of the Supreme Council and Prime Minister.

The economic development of Sudan depends largely upon the proper use of the waters of the Nile Valley, which has created the cotton fields which yield Sudan's most valuable export. Most of the cotton is produced by the Gezira Scheme, irrigated from a dam on the Blue Nile. Recent developments have included the El Managil Scheme which will double the area of the Gezira estate.

Suez Canal. The Canal, 101 miles long, connecting the Mediterranean and Red Seas. It was opened for navigation in 1869; the Suez Canal Company, an Egyptian company which owned the Canal and was managed largely by Frenchmen, was granted a concession to levy fees on all ships (48 per day in 1958) passing through. The concession was due to expire on 17 November 1968 when the ownership of the Canal would have reverted to the Egyptian government. The British government owned 353,504 of the Company's 800,000 shares and one third of the transit tonnage was British.

Under the Convention of Constantinople, signed in 1888, the Canal was exempted in perpetuity from blockade and all vessels, whether armed or not, must be allowed to pass through in peace and war. The Anglo-Egyptian Treaty of October 1954 provided for the withdrawal of British forces from the Suez Canal Zone, as originally suggested by the British Labour government in 1946.

On 26 July 1956 the Egyptian government nationalized the Company, stating that the resulting revenue would be used to build the High Dam, *q.v.* Suez Canal Company shareholders were to be paid the Paris Stock Exchange closing prices (as on 26 July) for their shares. During the subsequent conflict with France, Israel, and the U.K. (*see* Egypt), the Egyptian government blocked the Canal; by April 1957 the obstructions had been removed by a United Nations mission and by April 1958 the daily average of ships in transit was greater than before nationalization. On 13 July 1958 an agreement was signed by representatives of the former shareholders and of the United Arab Republic, by which the latter agreed to pay approximately £29,000,000 as compensation for nationalization. The basis of the compensation was, as originally suggested by the Egyptian government, the value of the shares at the date of nationalization.

Suhrawardy, Husain Shahid. Pakistan lawyer and politician, and once Awami League Prime Minister; born 1892 in West Bengal; educated at Oxford. A former Chief Minister in undivided Bengal, he had, since the partition of British India in 1947, advocated more control for East Pakistan in federal affairs. His party joined with the United Front, *q.v.*, to defeat the Moslem League, *q.v.*, in the 1954 Bengal provincial elections. In an individual capacity he entered the non-party administration of Mohammed Ali on 20 December 1954, and as Minister of Law he was instrumental in legalizing the summoning of a new Constituent Assembly and in supervising the appointment of an electoral commission. His party emerged as the third largest in the Assembly after the elections of July 1955 and he was invited to head a government of Moslem League, United Front, and Awami League supporters; however, the terms on which he was prepared to take office, complete autonomy for East Pakistan, recognition of Bengali as a state language, and the exclusion of the United Front, were unacceptable to the Moslem League. After the League's parliamentary débâcle in September 1956 he formed a government coalition of his own party and the Republicans which continued until October 1957 when the Republicans withdrew their support, forcing him to resign. He was widely regarded by Pakistanis as their only politician of comparable stature to Nehru. With all other political parties, the Awami League was abolished on 7 October 1958. Suhrawardy was on 15 July 1960 disqualified by the Elective Bodies (Disqualification) Tribunal at Lahore from seeking any elective posts in Pakistan for six years, as he was found guilty of charges of misconduct during his tenure of office.

Sukarno, Ahmed. President of the Republic of Indonesia; born 6 June 1901 in Java. After participating in an unsuccessful revolt against the Dutch in 1926 he fused the native parties of the Netherlands East Indies into one nationalist organization modelled on the Indian Congress Party, *q.v.* He was imprisoned three times by the Dutch and exiled to Sumatra in 1940. When the Japanese invaded the islands in 1942 he negotiated with them on the future status of Indonesia. They appointed him President of the Java Central Council, and when a Republic of Indonesia was proclaimed in 1945 he became its first President. After the Japanese surrender the Dutch accused him of collaboration; he had difficulty in maintaining his position against Sjahrir, the Socialist-Nationalist, but regained political supremacy in 1947 and supervised the transfer of sovereignty on 28 December 1949 from the Netherlands to the Republic of Indonesia, *q.v.*

S.U.N.F.E.D. Special United Nations Fund for Economic Development, *q.v.*

Supreme Court. The highest Court in the U.S.A., described in the Constitution as follows: 'The judicial power of the United States shall be vested in one Supreme Court, and in such inferior courts as the Congress may from time to time ordain and establish.' It hears appeals from lower courts in civil and criminal cases and is empowered to interpret all laws and treaties passed by Congress and to decide whether they are constitutionally valid. The Chief Justice and his eight Associate Justices are each paid $35,000 annually. The choice by the President of persons to become Supreme Court Justices must be approved by the Senate. Many cases decided by the Court have been of fundamental constitutional significance. In 1954, for example, it decided that racial segregation in schools violated the constitutional rule relating to the equality of U.S. citizens; there could be no such thing, it ruled, as separate but equal educational facilities. The decision affected the education of some 12,000,000 children in twenty-one States.

Supreme Soviet, *or* Supreme Council. The legislature of the U.S.S.R., comprising the Council of the Union and the Council of Nationalities. These Councils have equal powers and are elected for a term of four years. The Council of the Union is elected on the basis of one deputy for every 300,000 of the population; the Council elected on 16 March 1958 had 738 members. The Council of Nationalities comprises 640 deputies elected by the fifteen constituent Republics and by various autonomous Republics, autonomous regions, and national areas within the constituent Republics. Voting, which is on the basis of universal suffrage with the exception of the insane and those deprived of civil rights, is by secret ballot. The electors vote for or against a single list, and the important part of the election is the preliminary decision in each constituency as to who should be included on the list. The Communist Party is the only legal political party, but non-members may be entered on the list.

The Supreme Soviet usually meets twice a year for about a week. It delegates most of its power to its elected Presidium, which acts on its behalf between the sessions. The Chairman of the Presidium since May 1960 has been Leonid I. Brezhnev; the post is equivalent to that of President in other countries. The Supreme Soviet also elects the Council of Ministers, which is the highest administrative and executive organ in the U.S.S.R.; its Chairman is Nikita S. Khrushchev, q.v. The First Vice-Chairmen are Anastas Ivanovich Mikoyan and Alexei Kosygin.

Svalbard. Spitsbergen Archipelago, q.v.

Swaziland. A British Protectorate and one of the High Commission Territories, q.v.

Sweden. An independent state in Scandinavia; area 173,436 sq. m.; population (1958) 7,436,066; capital Stockholm. It was involved in many international struggles from the sixteenth to the eighteenth century, and once dominated Finland and much of Germany, extracting a large income from the north German coastal ports. Its power declined and it has not been involved in a war since 1814. Under the 1809 Constitution, with its amendments, the throne is hereditary in the House of Bernadotte, the family of Marshal Bernadotte, one of Napoleon's Marshals, who became King in 1818. King Gustav VI Adolf (born 1882) ascended the throne in 1950. There is a Riksdag (parliament) of two elected Chambers. The First Chamber of 151 members, appointed for eight years, one eighth being replaced every year, is elected by the County and Town Councils, which are elected every four years by direct election. The Second Chamber has 232 members, who are directly elected for four years by universal suffrage. The Council of State (Cabinet), headed by the Prime Minister, is responsible to the Riksdag. The 1958 First Chamber comprised 79 Social Democrats, 29 Liberals, 24 Agrarians, 16 Conservatives, and 3 Communists. The 1960 elections, held on a basis of proportional representation, gave to the Second Chamber 114 Social Democrats, 40 Liberals, 39 Conservatives, 34 Centre Party, and 5 Communists. The Social Democrat Party has been in office since 1932, except for three months in 1936. During their years of office they introduced one of the world's most highly-developed schemes of social insurance, encouraged the growth of co-operatives, and exercised state control over the railways, public utilities, air transport, many bus routes, and some industries, (e.g. iron ore, wood-pulp, sugar, alcohol, oil refining) but did not interfere on any large scale with the manufacturing industries. They are led by Dr Tage Erlander, the Prime Minister. The Agrarians, or Centre Party, with whom the Social Democrats formed a coalition in 1936–9, as well as since 1951, find most of their supporters in the rural districts and look to the Social Democrats to protect agriculture from foreign competition, but often feel that this alliance loses them votes to the Conservatives, particularly in southern Sweden. The Liberals, who were of far greater importance during the struggle for a universal franchise, believe in a 'social-liberalism' rather than Socialism, and advocate a reduction in housing subsidies and technical adjustments to the health services. The Conservatives oppose government intervention in trade and industry; they find support among industrialists and landowners. The Communist Party was formed in 1919 by some dissident Social Democrats. The four main parties oppose all foreign alliances, while the Communists would welcome closer relations with the U.S.S.R.; all five parties have rejected Swedish adherence to N.A.T.O.

Half of Swedish manufacturing production and nearly all Swedish exports are accounted for by the engineering, iron, steel, and timber industries. There are huge deposits of iron ore in Lapland, north of the Arctic Circle, and smaller deposits farther south; most of the ore is exported to the U.K. and to the German Federal Republic. Sweden produces over ninety per cent of its own food requirements. The U.K., although still one of the principal trade partners of Sweden, has been replaced since 1952 by the German Federal Republic as Sweden's largest supplier of goods.

Switzerland. A federal republic in Central Europe; area 15,950 sq. m.; population (1961) 5,400,000; capital Berne. The Swiss Constitution is one of the most democratic in the world. The historical division of the country into twenty-five cantons (16 were federated by 1513) each of which has its own parliament and government, has produced a high degree of regional autonomy within a federal state. There is frequent use of plebiscites; in the smaller cantons the male citizens gather in the open air to vote on local issues; any group of 30,000 citizens, or the representatives of eight cantons, may demand a referendum on a law already passed by the federal parliament. Although the franchise is restricted to men this is by the deliberate choice of the women themselves. The Constitution, most of which dates from 1848, stresses the principle of equality between the various racial and religious groups in Switzerland regardless of their numerical strength. German is the dominant language in nineteen of the cantons; however French, Italian, and Romansch, the language spoken by most of the people in the canton of Graubünden (Grisons), are also recognized as the official national languages. Protestants number fifty-six per cent of the population and Catholics approximately forty-two per cent but there is complete religious toleration and state education is undenominational. In accepting a proposal to abrogate certain articles of the Constitution which banned the Jesuit Order, the Head of the Swiss Department of Justice stated: 'the decisive principles of Switzerland's democratic order, freedom of religion and conscience, freedom of religious expression and the denominationally neutral character of public education are so firmly rooted in the Constitution that any attempt to alter them is [in 1955] certain to fail'.

The country is of great strategic importance. Through its railway system it controls communications between north and south Europe; it acts as a buffer state between France, Italy, and Germany; its mountain defences are almost impregnable. Since 1815 its neutrality has never been violated. The absence of war, together with low taxes and a well-ordered economy – the harnessing of hydro-electric power to provide cheap fuel, heavy investment in specialized industries, *e.g.* locomotive construction and grinding machinery, and intensive dairy-farming and afforestation – have brought economic stability which has, in turn, attracted foreign currency. Banking is one of Switzerland's most profitable industries.

The Swiss Federal Assembly consists of two Houses; the National Council (Nationalrat) of 196 members who are elected by direct vote every four years; and the Council of States (Ständerat) to which the cantons each send two representatives. The Federal Assembly elects the Federal Council (Bundesrat), or government, of seven members, all of whom must be from different cantons; and the Prime Minister, who also acts as head of state, is elected annually from the members of the government. In practice the government is always a coalition.

At the elections held in October 1959 the Social Democratic Party (Socialist) won 51 seats; the Radicals (a progressive bourgeois party inclined to centralism) 51 seats; the Catholic Conservative Party (right-wing) 47 seats; the Peasants' Party 23 seats, and the Communists 3 seats.

Syndicalism. A form of Socialism, *q.v.*, aiming at the ownership and control of all industries by the workers, as opposed to the type of Socialism which involves ownership and control by the state. It has also been called anarcho-syndicalism, owing to its close relationship to Anarchism, *q.v.* Syndicalists have preferred to improve the conditions of the industrial workers by direct action, such as strikes and the practice of working to rule, rather than by political and parliamentary effort. Under Syndicalism the state would be abolished and replaced by a federation of units. There would be a functional economic organization instead of representation of geographical units. The syndicalist movement had followers in the U.K., France, Germany, Italy, Spain, Argentina, and Mexico, but dwindled away after the First World War, losing many of its members to the Communists. Its ideas also influenced the Fascist conception of a corporate state, *q.v.* Syndicalists had some influence in the British Labour Party, *q.v.*, when it was founded, but this declined after 1918 in the face of opposition from the parliamentary and reformist wing, and from trade unionists such as Ernest Bevin who was once a member of the Social Democratic Federation but who came to fear that Syndicalism would involve the workers in responsibility for their industries and put them at a disadvantage when bargaining for more wages.

Syria. One of the two regions (the other is Egypt, *q.v.*) which since 1 February 1958 have comprised the United Arab Republic, *q.v.*; area 72,234 sq. m.; population 4,420,587, mainly Moslems; capital Damascus. It was part of the Ottoman Empire until 1920, when it became a mandated territory of the League of Nations; the British approved of the proclamation as King of Syria of Emir Feisal, son of King Hussein of the Hejaz and supporter of the allied cause in the First World War, but when the French objected he had to leave, and later became King of Iraq. France was entrusted with the Mandate, but insisted on treating Syria as a colony until the French Popular Front government under Léon Blum agreed in 1936 to grant independence after a probationary period of three years. Thus, after many years of insurrection, the French became popular; however, French officers in Syria organized rebellions to prove that there was local opposition to the agreement and the right wing in Paris prevented its ratification. Allied forces (including the Free French) occupied Syria in 1941 to prevent the Vichy French administration from admitting the Germans, and independence was immediately proclaimed. In 1945 French forces tried to retain power by shelling Damascus; they were forced to leave under threat of bombardment by British troops.

In 1949, after a period of unrest, an army dictatorship, led by Brigadier Adib Shishakly, obtained real control of Syria. The outward forms of democracy were preserved and Shishakly was elected President in July 1953. His party, the Arab Liberation Movement, obtained 72 out of 82 seats in subsequent parliamentary elections by advocating a welfare state and armed neutrality, but his government was overthrown by an army uprising in February 1954, when a former President, the nonagerian Hashem Bey Atassi, was restored. Atassi retired in 1955 and Shukri el-Kuwatli, another former President who lived in Egypt during the Shishakly régime, was elected President.

The Syrian political parties were then the Arab Socialist Baath Renaissance Party, led by Akram Hourani, which favoured close co-operation with Egypt and opposed the Baghdad Pact between Turkey, Iraq, Persia, and Pakistan; the Parti Populaire Syrienne (P.P.S.), a Fascist group which advocated the union of Syria and Iraq but was dissolved in 1955; the pro-Egyptian National Party, whose leaders were Faris el-Khury and Sabry Assali, and the Independents, led by Dr Khaled el-Azem, a former Prime Minister. In the 1955 elections none of the parties secured a majority in the Chamber of Deputies, and in 1956, after a succession of inconclusive coalitions, the three leading groups found themselves looking to Egypt for leadership. Sabry Assali became Prime Minister in June 1956, and in January 1957 Dr Khaled el-Azem (a landowner and businessman with considerable influence, who supported the banning of the P.P.S.) joined the government as Minister of Defence. The three main parties then agreed to join Egypt in the creation of the United Arab Republic, and after its establishment in February 1958 political parties were dissolved and replaced (as in Egypt) by a National Union.

On 21 October 1959 President Nasser appointed Field-Marshal Abdel Hakim Amer, Vice-President of the U.A.R. and Chief of the Armed Forces, as supervisor of general policy in Syria, and put him in charge of the Syrian branch of the National Union.

Syria is essentially agricultural and poor in proved mineral resources although there is a continual search for oil. The government receives revenue from the pipe-lines of the Iraq Petroleum and Trans-Arabian Pipeline Cos., originating in Iraq and Arabia. The textile industry at Aleppo and Damascus has been considerably expanded but there is insufficient capital available for the improvements in irrigation and communications that would greatly increase Syrian prosperity.

T

Taft-Hartley Act, *or* Labour Management Relations Act. Passed by a U.S. Congress which had a Republican majority, against the veto of President Truman; it became law on 23 June 1947. By altering the law as established by the Norris-La Guardia Act, 1932 (which outlawed injunctions against strikers except where the government was a party to the dispute) and the National Labour Relations Act, 1935, *q.v.* (which guaranteed the right of unions to bargain collectively for employees, provided machinery for the certification of bargaining units by the National Labour Relations Board, and restricted unfair labour practices by employers), it constituted an important departure from the labour policies of the New Deal, *q.v.* The Act (1) empowered the President, in the case of an actual or threatened strike which he considered prejudicial to public safety or welfare, to appoint a board of enquiry, and, after hearing the report of the board, to direct the Attorney-General to petition a Federal District court for an injunction restraining the strike for a 'cooling-off' period of 75–80 days, during which employees would vote secretly on their employers' proposals; if no agreement was reached the strike could then be resumed; (2) extended the list of unfair labour practices; (3) prohibited 'closed shop' agreements, under which membership of the appropriate union is made a condition of employment; (4) prohibited employers and employees from terminating or modifying a contract unless they gave sixty days' notice to the other party and offered to negotiate a new contract; (5) prohibited union expenditures in connexion with federal elections.

The President said that he opposed the Act because it would lead to increased governmental interference in economic life, it would encourage distrust between employers and employees and it was unworkable. Organized labour bitterly attacked the law.

Taiwan. The island of Formosa, *q.v.*

Tammany Hall. An important U.S. political organization, officially the New York County Democratic Party Committee; Chairman: Carmine de Sapio. It began as a club, the Society of Tammany, in 1789, but since about 1825 the club has been the official organization of the Democratic Party in one of the counties (Manhattan) of the State of New York. In the nineteenth century the Society was often corrupt, but made itself responsible for the welfare of European immigrants, receiving their votes in return. There are four other counties in New York City: The Bronx, Queen's, King's (Brooklyn), and Richmond (Staten Island). Each county has a similar Democratic Party Committee but Tammany Hall is the most powerful and usually controls the votes of the New York State representatives when the Democratic Party presidential candidate is chosen.

Tanganyika. A German colony from 1884 to 1918; later administered by the U.K. under United Nations Trusteeship, a League of Nations

Mandate having terminated in 1946; area 361,800 sq. m.; population (1957 estimate) 8,329,000 Africans, 20,619 Europeans, 103,000 Asians, Arabs, and others; capital Dar es Salaam. Slavery was abolished in 1922. The territory is largely agricultural, the most important products being sisal (Tanganyika is the world's principal exporter of this kind of fibre and produces approximately one half of the world's supply), coffee, cotton, and beans. There are also important diamond and gold exports. The 1955 Constitution provided for the appointment of 10 Asians, 10 Africans, and 10 Europeans as members of the unofficial side, and 34 members of the government side, of the Legislative Council. In 1955 a United Nations visiting mission recommended more multiracial primary, secondary, and higher education, economic development, and more political evolution, with a guarantee of self-government within fifteen years. The Constitution was further modified and in September 1960 elections were held to return 71 members, 50 representing ordinary constituencies, the Asian and European communities having 11 and 10 reserved seats respectively. The Tanganyika African National Union (T.A.N.U.) led by Julius Nyerere, *q.v.*, won 70 seats; this party has demanded a federation of Tanganyika, Kenya, Uganda, and Zanzibar, with the possible eventual addition of Northern Rhodesia and Nyasaland. On 1 May 1961 internal self-government was granted and Nyerere became Prime Minister; complete independence was to follow on 28 December 1961.

Tangier. A city in Morocco, *q.v.*, which was an integral part of Spanish Morocco, *q.v.*, from 1912 to 1923. By the Tangier Convention of 18 December 1923 and 8 July 1925, Tangier and some land surrounding it (with a total area of 225 square miles) became a neutralized and demilitarized International Zone, under a committee of control on which were represented Belgium, France, Italy, the Netherlands, Portugal, Spain, Sweden, the U.K., and the U.S.A. A Legislative Assembly of 27 members, with a European majority, was set up to represent the native and foreign communities; it was to be presided over by a Mendoub, representing the Sultan of Morocco who in theory remained sovereign after 1912. Spanish forces re-occupied the Zone on 14 June 1940, when German and Italian armies were conquering Europe, but had to withdraw in October 1945, when the Zone was again internationalized. When Morocco achieved independence in March 1956, the Sultan stated that the Zone should again become part of Morocco proper, and this principle was accepted by the committee of control. On 29 October 1956 a declaration was signed in Tangier by representatives of Morocco and the member states of the committee of control, terminating the international status of the area. On 19 April 1960 the zone was once more incorporated financially and economically in Morocco.

Teheran Conference. A meeting between President Franklin D. Roosevelt of the U.S.A., Winston Churchill, Prime Minister of the U.K., and Marshal Stalin of the U.S.S.R., at Teheran in Persia between 28 November and 1 December 1943. The joint statement issued after the meeting said that plans for the destruction of the German forces had been concerted and that agreement had been reached as to the scope and timing of the operations to be undertaken against Germany from the east, west, and south.

Tennessee Valley Authority. A federal agency established in the U.S.A. in 1933 by Act of Congress. It is concerned primarily with the generation, sale, and transmission of electric power, with flood control, with the development and production of fertilizers, and with the maintenance of navigation. It operates in an area of some 41,000 sq. m., embracing parts of the States of Alabama, Georgia, Kentucky, Mississippi, North Carolina, Tennessee, and Virginia, which are all in the valley of the Tennessee river. The Authority has built twenty dams. Its activities have for many years been strongly opposed by business interests, which believe that projects of this sort should be developed by private enterprise, and which resent the refusal of the T.V.A. to make profits as large as those which private enterprise would make. The T.V.A. was financed at the outset by the U.S. Treasury, and has been able to make regular repayments of the sums lent to it. It was authorised by Congress in 1959 to borrow money from private investors.

Terms of Trade. The relationship between the demand for a country's exports and the cost of its imports. If the demand for its exports increases, or the cost of its imports decreases, or if both these things happen, then a country's terms of trade are said to have improved; if the converse happens, the terms of trade are said to have worsened. A favourable movement in the terms of trade, which may only be temporary, will improve a country's balance of payments position, but may conceal a decline in its real power as a seller of exports. In the case of a manufacturing country, such as the U.K., a typical example of an unfavourable movement of the terms of trade would be an increase in the cost of primary products which was not accompanied by a corresponding increase in the price of manufactured goods.

Terrorist. One who resorts to violence and terror to advance his political aims, which frequently include the overthrow of the established order. The word is often used by the supporters of a particular régime to describe and to vilify any of its opponents who resort to acts of violence. The opponents of a régime, however, would wish to be called partisans, nationalists or resistance workers rather than terrorists.

Thailand (formerly Siam). An independent state in South-East Asia bordered by Laos and Cambodia in the east, by Malaya in the south, and separated from Burma by a 200-mile stretch of the river Salween; area 198,247 sq. m.; capital Bangkok; population 22,811,701, of whom fifteen per cent are Chinese. Buddhism is the principal religion. By the Conventions of 1896 and 1904 the U.K. and France agreed to regard the country as a neutral zone between their Burmese and Indo-Chinese possessions, and although it became involved in frontier disputes with Cambodia and, more recently, with Laos, Thailand has not since been invaded. As the ally of Japan in the Second World War it was ceded in 1945 the two Shan states and the four Malay states, which were all returned to the U.K. in 1946.

Under the Constitution of 1951 the King ruled with the advice of the Assembly of the People's Deputies of 283 members, 123 of whom were nominated by him and the rest elected by indirect election. The present King, Bhumibol Adulyadej (born 1927), succeeded his brother King Ananda Mahidol, whose assassination in 1946 was followed by the return to power, and the appointment as Prime Minister, of the former dictator Field-Marshal Pibul Songgram. In practice the country was governed by Songgram (until a bloodless *coup d'état* in September 1957) with a Council of Ministers all of whom held commands in the armed services. After the general election on 15 December 1957 the balance of power remained with the 123 nominated members who supported the military junta, led by Marshal Sarit Thanarat, which had overthrown Songgram. In October 1958 the Constitution was abrogated and an interim Constitution, introduced in January 1959, provided for the establishment of a nominated Constituent Assembly of 240 members to draft a new Constitution and to legislate. Thanarat, however, continued to act as Prime Minister and to rule by decree and the majority of the Assembly were officers of the armed services.

The chief product and export is rice. The rise in the world price of rice has made it increasingly difficult to sell and Thailand relies on foreign loans for all internal investment and development.

Third Reich. The Nazi régime in Germany from 1933 until 1945. The term was coined by Möller van den Bruck, a nationalist German writer, in his book *Das Dritte Reich*, published in 1924. Nazis said that the First Reich was the Holy Roman Empire (962–1806) and that the Second Reich was the German Empire, established by Bismarck in 1871, which came to an end when Kaiser Wilhelm II abdicated in 1918. The Nazi leader Adolf Hitler hoped that the Third Reich would survive for a thousand years.

Thorez, Maurice. French Communist politician, born 28 April 1900 in Pas-de-Calais. He went to work in a coal mine when he was twelve, soon joined the French Socialist Party and became an active trade unionist. He was one of the two-thirds majority of the Socialist Party congress of 1920 which decided to secede and to form the Communist Party. He became General Secretary of the Communist Party in 1930 and was elected to the Chamber of Deputies in 1932. He has been one of the most significant politicians in France since 1936, when a General Election increased sixfold the Communist representation in the Chamber of Deputies. In the Second World War he was conscripted into the French army, from which he deserted and fled to the U.S.S.R.; he was sentenced *in absentia* to a six-year prison term and deprived of his citizenship. After a general amnesty had been declared in 1944 he returned to France and took his place as a member of the Constituent Assembly. While the Communist Party was represented in the government, between 1944 and 1947, Thorez exerted considerable influence in French politics. He was Minister of State from 1945 to 1947 and was thought a possible successor to General de Gaulle as President of France in 1946. Although he still leads the Party, ill-health and prolonged absences from the political scene have diminished his authority.

Tibet. An autonomous western region of China, north of the Himalaya mountains; area 470,000 sq. m.; population about 6,000,000, of whom one fifth are Lamas (Buddhist monks); capital Lhasa. The area is governed ultimately by China, but the nominal ruler is the fourteenth Dalai Lama. When a Dalai Lama dies an infant born at the moment of his death is sought and brought up as the successor as he is deemed to be a reincarnation of the dead man. A successful military power in the ninth century, Tibet was overrun by the Chinese Manchu Empire in the eighteenth century, but the latter's authority was not exerted until the end of the nineteenth century. Following the overthrow of the Manchu dynasty in 1911, the Chinese garrisons were driven out in 1912. Between 1931 and 1933 China began once more to assert her power, in 1950 reoccupied eastern Tibet, and later reoccupied Lhasa. A rival deity, the Panchen Lama, was for some time supported by China in opposition to the Dalai Lama, but the Dalai Lama then appeared to support the régime, and both deities attended the meeting of the National People's Congress of China in 1954. In

March 1959 there was an unsuccessful armed uprising against the Chinese, and the Dalai Lama fled to India.

Tito, Marshal. President of Yugoslavia; born Josip Broz, the son of a peasant, near Zagreb, Croatia, in May 1892. He left school at twelve and worked as a farm labourer, dishwasher, and mechanic until he joined the Austro-Hungarian army, rising to the rank of regimental sergeant-major. In 1915 he was captured on the Russian front and sent to various prison camps. He was freed during the Russian Revolution, fought for three years with the revolutionaries and then returned to Yugoslavia. Eventually he became a full-time political organizer; from 1927 to 1928 he was the district secretary of a metalworkers' union and was active in the illegal Yugoslav Communist Party. He then spent over six years in jail, as a political undesirable, and on his release in 1936 left the country and helped to recruit Yugoslavs for the International Brigade in the Spanish Civil War. After the invasion of Yugoslavia by Germany in 1941 he organized the National Liberation Front of partisan forces and proved to the western powers that his army was the only effective anti-German movement in Yugoslavia; the troops of General Draja Mihailović, who were supported by the Royal Yugoslav government in London, fought no major battle after the autumn of 1941. Although the leadership was largely Communist, the majority of Tito's partisans had other, or no, political affiliations. He was acclaimed as the national leader.

He became Marshal of Yugoslavia and President of the National Liberation Committee in November 1943, when he demanded that the allies should cease to recognize the exiled Yugoslav government. From 1945 until 1953 he was Prime Minister and Minister of National Defence. He carried through a policy of extensive nationalization of industry and living accommodation, and of investment in hydroelectric schemes and railroad construction. However. land reform was restricted to the breaking-up of large holdings and redistribution of plots in excess of four and a half acres. Tito has resisted all persuasion by the U.S.S.R. to force through collectivization of agriculture against the wishes of the peasant small-holders who represent eleven twelfths of the population and on whom he relies for political support.

In 1953, under Yugoslavia's new Constitution, he was elected President of the Republic, Chairman of the Federal Executive Council, and Supreme Commander of the Armed Forces. He claims that Yugoslavia represents in Europe the same independent, neutral, Socialist position that India holds in Asia.

Togo. An independent Western African state between Ghana and Dahomey; area 20,404 sq. m.; population approximately 1,091,000; capital Lomé. Under the name of Togoland, *q.v.*, the land was part of a German colony from 1894 to 1914, and administered by France until independence was achieved on 27 April 1960. Government is by a council of ministers, responsible to a Chamber of Deputies of 46 members, elected by universal suffrage every five years. The Prime Minister appointed when independence was granted was Sylvanus Olympio. Togo exports cocoa, cotton, and coffee, and there are substantial deposits of bauxite and phosphate.

Togoland. Name of an area in West Africa which was a German colony from 1894 to 1914, was divided between France and the U.K. on the outbreak of the First World War and placed under League of Nations Mandates after the war, and became a trusteeship territory in 1946; the British portion became, under the name of the Volta Region, a Region of Ghana, *q.v.*, upon the establishment of that Dominion on 6 March 1957, and the French portion became an independent state on 27 April 1960, as the republic of Togo, *q.v.* The trusteeship territory comprised 34,934 sq. m., of which France administered approximately two thirds. The decisions that British Togoland should enter Ghana, and that French Togoland should become independent, were taken by plebiscites in May 1956 and October 1956 respectively.

Tory. A word often used to describe a supporter of the British Conservative Party. In the seventeenth century the 'Tories' were the robbers who roamed Ireland in plundering bands after the Irish rebellion. The name was applied derisively after 1680 to those who approved of the succession of a Catholic heir to Charles II, by people who wanted to suggest that they were a set of 'Popish thieves'. Most Tories favoured the Stuart cause after 1689, but later became supporters of the established monarchy. After 1832 they called themselves Conservatives.

Totalitarian. A term denoting a single-party, dictatorial system of government, based on the 'totality of the state', as opposed to the liberal conception which allots to the state only certain functions, reserving others to the free decision of the individual. The totalitarian state extends its influence over the whole of life, private as well as public, and exacts full submission of the individual to its demands. The term has been used to describe the Nazi and Fascist governments which were headed by Hitler and Mussolini respectively in Germany and Italy. Examination has shown that although individuals and groups were subjected to treatment and laws which they could not oppose and which were often cruel and illiberal, there was not the complete centralization of power and authority that would exist in a truly totalitarian state. The term is widely used, however, to describe political systems which aim at, even if they do not achieve, the 'totality of the state'. In this wider sense it may be correctly applied to the U.S.S.R., China, Nazi Germany, and Fascist Italy.

Trade Disputes and Trade Unions Act. A British law enacted in 1927 after the General Strike and wholly repealed in 1946 by the Labour government of 1945–51. It declared sympathetic strikes to be unlawful, if conducted on a scale calculated to coerce the government, and, by the 'contracting-in' clause, made it illegal to require any member of a trade union to make a contribution to the political fund of a trade union unless he had declared in writing his willingness to do so.

Trade Unions. Associations of workers for the common representation of their interests. They try to secure higher pay, better working conditions, shorter working hours, and other advantages, for their members. On these matters they aim to conclude with the employers collective agreements which will apply to non-members as well, although sometimes it is part of their policy to prevent employers from employing non-members. If negotiations fail they sometimes withdraw their labour. Trade unions were frequently suppressed and persecuted in the first half of the nineteenth century, but achieved general recognition in Europe by the end of the century. In the U.S.A. the National Labour Relations Act, 1935, q.v., legally recognized the rights of workers to organize trade unions. There are national trade union organizations in most countries; since the Second World War there have been attempts to create a genuinely international trade union movement, in the course of which the World Federation of Trade Unions, q.v., and the International Confederation of Free Trade Unions, q.v., have been established.

Trades Union Congress. An association of approximately 186 British trade unions with a membership of over 8,176,000, founded in 1868 when the Manchester and Salford Trades Council took the initiative in calling the first Congress. The primary function of the T.U.C. is to bring union representatives together each year to consider matters of common concern to their members. Its elected General Council keeps in touch with government departments and takes an interest in all legislation affecting organized labour, but the affiliated unions remain autonomous, the T.U.C. having no control over their actions in wage negotiations.

Transport House. An office block in Smith Square, Westminster, London, used as a headquarters by the Labour Party. The building is owned by the Transport and General Workers' Union.

Transylvania. The mountainous western region of Rumania. It was part of the Turkish Empire until 1699 when it was ceded, with Hungary, to Austria after the Turks had been defeated in battle. The majority of its inhabitants are Ruman peasants and not of Magyar stock; they welcomed the transfer of Transylvania to Rumania after the First World War when the Austro-Hungarian Empire collapsed. The territory was formally awarded to Rumania by the Treaty of Trianon in 1920. In the Second World War Germany rewarded the Hungarians for their help by returning Transylvania to them, but the region was restored to Rumania under the Paris Peace Treaty of 10 February 1947.

Treaty. A formal agreement between two or more states. Other terms, such as convention, pact, act, and declaration are sometimes used, but the binding force of such arrangements is the same as that of a treaty. The Final Act of the Congress of Vienna, 1815, the Declaration of Paris, 1856, the Geneva Conventions on the Protection of Civilians in Wartime and on the Treatment of Prisoners of War, 1949, and the Balkan Pact, 1954, were all treaties which bound their signatories. A treaty differs from a contract between two individuals because it is valid even where the parties have not freely entered into it; duress does not invalidate consent as it does in the ordinary law of contract. A treaty is really a type of international legislation, which binds those concerned irrespective of their wishes; treaties which prescribe general rules of conduct for a number of states are often called law-making treaties. The two stages in the making of a treaty are usually its signature by plenipotentiaries on behalf of the contracting states, and its later ratification by or on behalf of the heads of the states. Ratification is not essential in all cases, and is frequently omitted in minor agreements.

Trieste. An important port and legally a Free Territory from 1947 to 1954; area 285 sq. m. The port was a product of the railway age. In the 1840's it was developed by the German Baron Bruck from a Slovenian fishing village into the main port of the Austro-Hungarian Empire. Italian merchants settled in, and later controlled the commerce of the city, thereby providing an ethnic justification for Italy's claim to sovereignty. France and the U.K. recognized this claim in 1915 in order to bring Italy into the European war against Germany, and in spite of American protests that the port rightly belonged to the new Yugoslavia, which embraced Slovenia, the Treaty of Rapallo, in 1920, confirmed Italy in possession of Trieste.

Under the terms of the Paris Peace Treaty of 10 February 1947, Italy gave up the city of Trieste and the Istrian peninsula and these were constituted a Free Territory. This was divided, temporarily, into two zones: Zone A (which included the city of Trieste) was administered jointly by a U.K. and U.S.A. Military Government, and Zone B (south of Trieste) was placed under Yugoslav Military Government. In 1948 the western powers proposed to restore the entire territory to Italy, but changed their policy when Yugoslavia left the Cominform, *q.v.* Ill-feeling which resulted in riots was provoked between the two countries. Military Government in both zones was terminated by a Memorandum of Understanding which was signed by the U.S.A., the U.K., Italy, and Yugoslavia on 5 October 1954. Yugoslavia agreed only after strong pressure had been exerted by the U.S.A. The administration of Zone A (population 297,000 of whom ninety per cent are Italian) was handed over to the Italian government which undertook to maintain Trieste as a free port, *q.v.*, and to rent to Yugoslavia docks and wharves; Yugoslavia retained Zone B (population approximately 70,000 of whom fifty-five per cent are Slovene) to which a 200-yard strip of territory from Zone A was added. However, since 1947, Yugoslavia has concentrated on expanding Rijeka (formerly Fiume) as the main port for itself and for the Austrian and Hungarian hinterland, with such success that by 1959 Rijeka was dealing with more cargo than Trieste.

Tripartite Declaration of 1950. A guarantee of the *status quo* in Palestine. France, the U.K., and the U.S.A. bound themselves in May 1950 'should they find that any of these states [Israel or the Arab states] was proposing to violate frontiers or armistice lines . . . immediately to take action, both within and outside the United Nations, to prevent such violations'.

Trotskyite. A Communist who supports the view advanced by Leon Trotsky (a leading Russian revolutionary who, in 1924, was ousted by Stalin in the struggle for power and was later exiled) that excessive Russian nationalism is incompatible with true international Communism. Stalin believed in concentrating on the economic development of the U.S.S.R. to an extent which, in Trotsky's opinion, was bound to produce a bureaucracy with a predominantly national outlook.

Trucial Coast. A coastal strip on the Persian Gulf and the Gulf of Oman, in which are the seven independent states of Abu Dhabi, *q.v.*, Ajman, Dubai, Fujairah, Ras al Khaimah, Sharjah, and Umm al Qaiwain, all under British protection; total area about 32,300 sq. m.; population approximately 86,000, of whom between one fifth and one tenth are nomads. Their relationship with the U.K. is governed by a Treaty of 1820, by which they agreed to abstain from plunder and piracy, a Treaty of Perpetual Peace in 1853, and the Exclusive Agreement of 1892, by which they agreed not to enter into any treaty or correspondence with any power other than the British government. The recognized arbiter and adviser of the seven sheikhdoms is the British Political Resident in the Persian Gulf at Bahrein, *q.v.* Revenue is derived from customs dues and oil concession payments, and to a small extent from pearls. All mainland concessions are held by Petroleum Development (Trucial Coast) Limited, the ownership of which is the same as that of the Iraq Petroleum Co., *q.v.* Sea-bed concessions are held by the I.P.C. and the D'Arcy Exploration Co., a subsidiary of the British Petroleum Co.

Truman, Harry Swinomish. President of the U.S.A. from 1945 to 1952; born at Lamar, Missouri, 8 May 1884. He worked on the *Kansas City Star* in 1901, as a timekeeper for a railroad contractor in 1902, with the National Bank of Commerce and the Union National Bank in Kansas City from 1903 to 1905, and then returned to the family farm. He served in the U.S. army in France in the First World War. From 1922 to 1924 he was a judge at the Jackson County Court, and studied at the Kansas City School of Law; he was the presiding judge from 1926 to 1934 when he was elected as a Democrat to the U.S. Senate. He was re-elected in 1940 and was elected Vice-President of the U.S.A. on 7 November 1944, taking office on 20 January 1945. On the death of President Franklin Delano Roosevelt on 12 April 1945 Truman became President; he was responsible for deciding that atomic bombs should be dropped on Hiroshima and Nagasaki. At the end of his term he stood for election as President on 2 November 1948 and was successful. During his second term he formulated the Truman Doctrine, *q.v.*

Truman Doctrine. A policy expounded by President Harry S. Truman on 12 March 1947 when he said that the U.S.A. ought 'to support free peoples who are resisting attempted subjugation by armed minorities or outside pressure. If we falter', he said, 'we may endanger the peace of the world and we shall surely endanger the welfare of our own nation.' The occasion of this statement was his speech to Congress asking for the appropriation of $400,000,000 worth of aid to Greece and to Turkey as an emergency measure. Shortly afterwards, on 5 June 1947, the Marshall Plan, *q.v.*, was put forward.

Trusteeship Territories. Areas which have been placed under the international trusteeship system, by which the administration of certain non-self-governing territories is supervised by the United Nations.

The Trusteeship Territories are: (1) in East Africa: Ruanda-Urundi, *q.v.*, administered by Belgium; Tanganyika, *q.v.*, administered by the U.K.; (2) in West Africa: the Cameroons, *q.v.*, administered by the U.K.; (3) in the Pacific area: Nauru Island, administered by Australia on behalf of Australia, New Zealand, and the U.K.; New Guinea, *q.v.*, administered by Australia; Western Samoa, administered by New Zealand, and the Trust Territory of the Pacific Islands, administered by the U.S.A.

Each Territory is the subject of a Trusteeship Agreement between the United Nations and the administering country. The country must agree to encourage respect for human rights and fundamental freedoms within the Territory, and to prepare its people for self-government and independence; it must submit annual reports to the United Nations, which sends out visiting missions to inspect the conditions in the territories. The Trusteeship Council, one of the six main organs of the United Nations, helps the General Assembly to supervise the Trust Territories. The Council is composed of: (1) member countries administering Trust Territories; (2) permanent members of the Security Council which are not administering Trust Territories; and (3) as many other members (elected for three-year terms by the General Assembly) as may be necessary to secure equality in numbers between administering and non-administering members.

Until a Trusteeship Territory becomes independent or self-governing the administering country has full rights of legislation and administration under the Trusteeship Agreement. In the Agreement all or part of a Territory may be designated by the administering country as 'strategic', in which case the Security Council supervises the Territory with the help of the Trusteeship Council. This device was not used in the case of the mandated territories, which were the equivalent of Trusteeship Territories when the League of Nations was in existence. The Trust Territory of the Pacific Islands (which comprises a number of islands, formerly German possessions, which were administered by Japan as a mandatory power between the two world wars) has been designated as a strategic area by the U.S.A., which can by its Agreement close certain areas for strategic reasons. Under this power the U.S.A. has closed the areas around Bikini and Eniwetok atolls, in the Marshall Islands, for nuclear fission experiments.

T.U.C. Trades Union Congress, *q.v.*

Tunisia. An independent state on the North African coast lying between Algeria and Libya and extending southwards to the Sahara; area 48,195 sq. m.; capital Tunis. It has an Arab population of 3,430,000 and a European colony of 280,000 of whom 180,000 are French. It was occupied by France in 1881 because the French authorities considered that an independent Tunisia threatened the security of their rule in the neighbouring territory of Algeria, *q.v.* Although the French appropriated half of the cultivable land, thereby driving many peasants into migrant, seasonal, agricultural work (which now absorbs more than one third of the population) and causing severe unemployment, the country has a substantial middle class, a land-holding peasantry, few nomads, and the only real trade union organization in the Moslem world. The largest unions are the General Union of Tunisian Agriculturalists (U.G.A.T.) and the U.G.T.T. which organizes the labourers and is affiliated to the International Confederation of Free Trade Unions, *q.v.* These have lent support to the Néo-Destour, *q.v.*, the moderate nationalist party of Habib Bourguiba, *q.v.*, who, with Tahar Ben Ammar, successfully negotiated an agreement with the French, signed in Paris on 3 June 1955, which was a prelude to independence.

The Prime Minister, Tahar Ben Ammar, then gave his resignation to the Bey, Sidi Mohammed el-Amin, who invited him to lead the government under the new Constitution. The first all-Tunisian cabinet since 1881 was formed on 17 September 1955 and consisted of six members of the Néo-Destour Party, five Independents, including the Prime Minister, and one Socialist. The Vieux-Destour, which maintained an unco-operative attitude to the French, and the Communist Party, were excluded. The granting of self-government considerably improved relations between France and Tunisia; it also had repercussions in Algeria where the French authorities were embarrassed by nationalist demands for similar concessions.

A further period of unrest forced the French government to accelerate the process of transferring power to the Tunisians, and on 20 March 1956 France recognized Tunisia as an independent sovereign state. The treaty concluded in 1881 was abrogated, as were all such provisions of the protocol of 3 June 1955 as might be inconsistent with the new status of Tunisia. At Tunisia's first general elections, held on 25 March 1956, the National Front (comprising the Néo-Destour, the U.G.T.T., and other organizations) won all 98 seats in the Constituent Assembly. Tahar ben Ammar resigned and Habib Bourguiba formed a new government consisting largely of Néo-Destour members. On 25 July 1957 the Constituent Assembly abolished the monarchy and Habib Bourguiba became President as well as Prime Minister. He was re-elected by popular vote on 8 November 1959, when the National Front won all 90 seats in the Legislative Assembly established by the Constitution of 1 June 1959.

The fact that most Tunisian trade is with France has not prevented the country from pursuing an independent foreign policy. This has included the giving of assistance to the Algerian rebels (in spite of French retaliation by bombing in February 1958 the Tunisian village of Sakiet) and the adherence of Tunisia to the Arab League. There are exports of wheat, oranges, lemons, citrus fruits, dates, phosphates, and iron and lead ore.

Turkey. An independent state partly in Asia Minor and partly in eastern Europe; area 296,185 sq. m.; population (1960) 27,776,000, of whom ninety-eight per cent are Moslems; capital Ankara. The Ottoman Empire, which once extended from Morocco along the North African coast to Cairo, included eastern Europe as far as the Adriatic Sea and had its eastern boundaries on the Caspian Sea, collapsed after the First World War. A Turkish Republic was set up in 1923 under the Presidency of Kemal Ataturk (1881–1938). Ataturk assumed dictatorial powers, separated Church and State, banned polygamy, the veil, and the fez, ordered Turks to wear European clothes, abolished titles, abandoned Arabic in favour of Latin script, suppressed Communism, took the first census, developed industries, and generally westernized Turkey.

The People's Republican Party, founded by Ataturk, with a policy of nationalism, laicism, and étatisme (state control of the economy), was virtually the only political party for many years, but after some encouragement from the government the Democratic Party was created. It first came to power in 1950. At the elections for the Grand National Assembly on 27 October 1957 the results were: Democratic Party, led by Adnan Menderes, 421 seats (48 per cent of the votes); People's Republican Party, led by Ismet Inönü, 173 (41 per cent); the right-wing Republican National Party 4; Freedom Party 4. Elections were held every four years on a basis of universal adult suffrage, and the cabinet was responsible to the Assembly for its actions. A President was elected by each Assembly for its own life; in 1950, 1954, and 1957 Celal Bayar (born 1884) was appointed.

On 27 May 1960 there was a *coup d'état* led by General Cemal Gursel, Commander-in-Chief of the Turkish land forces, who formed a Committee of National Union, consisting entirely of officers, to rule Turkey, and abrogated the Constitution of 1924. Bayar and Menderes were arrested and in September 1960 the Democratic Party was dissolved. The leaders of the revolt believed that the Menderes régime had betrayed the tradition of Ataturk and placed too much emphasis on conservatism and the Moslem religion.

Turkey received approximately forty-five per cent of all foreign aid to the Middle East between 1945 and 1958, during which period there was a rapid increase in production. Eighty per cent of the population work on the land, where there has been extensive mechanization of agriculture; there are considerable exports of grain, tobacco, cotton, and dried fruit. The output of Turkish metals (iron, chrome, copper, and manganese), which find a ready market for hard currency, has also been greatly expanded. There may be large oil resources, as yet unlocated, but so far Turkey has found it hard to pay for its oil imports. The increase in productivity, the liberal distribution by the government of agricultural credits and subsidies, and the devotion to defence of sums equal to half of the budget, have combined with the post-Korean War rise in world prices to produce inflation and budget deficits.

In the Second World War Turkey, whose active support of the allied powers would probably have involved occupation by Germany and liberation by the U.S.S.R., chose to remain neutral. Its present commitments are to Yugoslavia and Greece (under the Balkan Pact, *q.v.*), to Pakistan, Persia, and the U.K. (Central Treaty Organization, *q.v.*), and, as a member of N.A.T.O., to the North Atlantic Treaty powers. There is a long-standing fear of the U.S.S.R.; in 1945 the Russians denounced their Treaty of Neutrality, Non-Aggression, and International Co-operation which had been signed in 1925. The Dardanelles, *q.v.*, which are part of the straits connecting the Mediterranean with the Black Sea, are of strategic significance.

T.V.A. Tennessee Valley Authority, *q.v.*

U

U Nu. Burmese politician; born 25 May 1907 and educated at Rangoon University; he is a devout Buddhist and a Socialist. He was a school teacher before the Second World War and a member of the We Burmans nationalist society which demanded independence. The British government rejected his offer to help them to fight the Japanese in 1941, and imprisoned him; the Japanese released him and made him Foreign Minister of a Burmese government. After the war he was Vice-President of his party, the Anti-Fascist People's Freedom League, Speaker of the Constituent Assembly in 1947, and became Prime Minister when Burma became independent in January 1948. He was succeeded as Prime Minister by U Ba Swe in June 1956, when he decided to devote a year to reorganizing the Anti-Fascist People's Freedom League. He was Premier again from March 1957 to

October 1958, resigning in favour of General Ne Win, but became Premier once more in April 1960.

Ubangi-Shari. A territory of French Equatorial Africa which on 1 December 1958 achieved self-government within the French Community under the name of Central African Republic, *q.v.*

Uganda. A British protectorate in East Africa, bounded by the Congo Republic (formerly Belgian), Sudan, Kenya, Tanganyika, and Ruanda-Urundi; area 93,981 sq. m.; population 5,593,000, including 8,400 Europeans and 54,300 Asians; capital Entebbe. It comprises the Province of Buganda, *q.v.*, and the Eastern, Western, and Northern Provinces. The territory came under British influence in 1890 and a protectorate was declared in 1894. Buganda and three of the four districts of the Western Province (Bunyoro, Ankole, and Toro) have native monarchs and a special relationship with the British government. The rest of Uganda is ruled indirectly by native chiefs and subchiefs. In 1955 the Governor reconstituted the Legislative Council for a period of six years. The Council's elected members, after the election of March 1961, comprised 43 Democratic Party and 35 Uganda People's Congress members, 2 Independents and 1 Uganda National Congress member. The protectorate is agricultural, with exports of cotton and coffee; agricultural production is almost entirely in African hands. It was announced in 1950 that land would not be taken for development without consultation with the local African governments. Hydro-electric plants are being built, and considerable sums are being spent on education and capital development. The government is trying to encourage a national outlook among the provincial tribes, and does not wish the increase in local responsibility to result in tribal separatism.

U.K. United Kingdom of Great Britain and Northern Ireland, *q.v.*

Ukraine, formerly known as South Russia. One of the fifteen constituent Republics of the U.S.S.R.; area 225,000 sq. m.; population 41,900,000; capital Kiev. It is inhabited by Slavs speaking a language different from but akin to Russian; it is situated in the south-western part of the European area of the U.S.S.R. Tsarist Russia regarded the Ukrainians as a branch of the Russian people, calling them 'Little Russians', as compared with the 'Great Russians' of North Russia, and forcing the Russian language upon Ukrainian officials and teachers. After the Russian Revolution of 1917 the Ukraine was occupied by German and Austrian armies and then became a theatre of civil war until December 1919 when the Ukrainian Soviet Socialist Republic was formed. It joined with the other Soviet Socialist Republics in Russia in July 1923 to form the U.S.S.R. From 1920 until 1939 Western Ukraine, an area of some 34,400 sq. m. with 6,000,000 Ukrainian inhabitants, was ruled by Poland, which had rejected the Curzon Line, *q.v.*, a line proposed by the U.K. and largely following the ethnical border between Poles and Ukrainians. This territory was re-incorporated in the Ukraine on 1 November 1939, after the U.S.S.R. and Germany had partitioned Poland. Ukraine also acquired Northern Bukovina and parts of Bessarabia, *q.v.*, from Rumania in 1940, and Ruthenia (Sub-Carpathian Russia) from Hungary in 1945. These areas all contained substantial numbers of Ukrainians. The Ukrainian Soviet Socialist Republic is, like Byelorussia, *q.v.*, a member of the United Nations Organization.

Ulbricht, Walter. Communist politician in the German Democratic Republic; born 30 June 1893 in Leipzig. He became an active trade unionist in 1910, while employed as a woodworker; he joined the Socialist Party in 1912 and left it in 1919 to join the Communist Party. After five years as a member of the German parliament (Reichstag) he fled from Germany to escape from the Nazis. In 1946 he was elected to the Central Secretariat of the Communist-controlled Socialist Unity Party (S.E.D.), and in 1949 was appointed Deputy Premier of the German Democratic Republic. He held this post until September 1960, when he became Chairman of the Council of State which was formed to replace the office of President.

Ulster. A province of Ireland before the Government of Ireland Act of 1920. It comprised nine counties: Antrim, Armagh, Down, Fermanagh, Londonderry, Tyrone, Cavan, Donegal, and Monaghan. Under the 1920 Act the first six of these counties, described collectively as Northern Ireland, *q.v.*, elected a Parliament on 24 May 1921. The southern Irish ignored the Act and in 1922 the Irish Free State Act created a Dominion called the Irish Free State, from which the six counties expressed their desire to be excluded.

U.N.E.S.C.O. United Nations Educational, Scientific, and Cultural Organization, *q.v.*

U.N.H.C.R. United Nations High Commissioner for Refugees, *q.v.*

U.N.I.C.E.F. United Nations International Children's Emergency Fund, *q.v.*

Union of Soviet Socialist Republics (U.S.S.R.). Area 8,707,870 sq.m.; population (1960) 212,400,000; capital Moscow. It comprises fifteen constituent Republics, of which the largest (covering seventy-seven per cent of the total area) and most important is the Russian Soviet Federal Socialist Republic (R.S.F.S.R.), which occupies most of the European part, and most of the northern sector of the Asiatic part, of the U.S.S.R. The Emperor Nicholas II, Tsar of Russia, was forced to abdicate as a result of the revolution which broke out in Russia in March 1917, and the R.S.F.S.R. was set up after the Communists seized power in November 1917. The U.S.S.R. was formally established in 1923, and the constituent Republics were then the R.S.F.S.R., Byelorussia, *q.v.*, the Ukraine, *q.v.*, and the Transcaucasian Soviet Socialist Republic. These were joined by Uzbekistan and Turkmenistan in 1925, and by Tadjikistan in 1929. In 1936 the Transcaucasian S.S.R. was split up into the three Republics of Armenia, Azerbaijan, and Georgia; Kazakhstan and Kirghizia were proclaimed as Republics. In 1940 Estonia, *q.v.*, Latvia, *q.v.*, Lithuania, *q.v.*, and Moldavia were added; the Karelo-Finnish S.S.R., set up in that year, was merged with R.S.F.S.R. in 1956.

The 1936 Constitution states: 'The economic foundation of the U.S.S.R. consists of the Socialist economic system and the Socialist ownership of the tools and means of production, firmly established as a result of the liquidation of the capitalist economic system. . . . The economic life of the U.S.S.R. is determined and directed by a state plan of national economy in the interests of increasing the public wealth, of steadily raising the material and cultural standard of the working people, and of strengthening the independence of the U.S.S.R. and its capacity for defence. Work in the U.S.S.R. is a duty and a matter of honour for every able-bodied citizen, on the principle: "He who does not work shall not eat".'

Legislative authority is vested in the Supreme Soviet, *q.v.*, which acts between sessions through its Presidium, and is responsible for electing the Council of Ministers, the highest administrative and executive organ. Most of the real power in the U.S.S.R. is exercised by the Presidium of the Central Committee of the Communist Party, of which the First Secretary is Nikita S. Khrushchev, *q.v.* The Communist Party pervades every representative body and all other Russian organizations. Its members are a small minority, varying in size, but usually about four per cent of the population.

After the 1917 Revolution British, Japanese, Polish, and other forces attacked Russia in an attempt to overthrow the new Communist government, but their efforts proved unsuccessful, and by 1920 the civil war had come to an end. For many years relations between the U.S.S.R. and the western powers were marked by hostility and mistrust. In 1939 the U.K. abandoned its policy of appeasement of Nazi Germany and tried to conclude a treaty with the U.S.S.R., but instead a Russo-German pact was signed on 23 August 1939. Germany's invasion of Poland on 1 September 1939 was followed by a declaration of war on Germany by France and the U.K. on 3 September; on 17 September Russian forces entered Poland from the east by arrangement with Germany and the country was partitioned. On 23 June 1941 Germany, helped by Finland, Hungary, and Rumania, invaded the U.S.S.R., which thus entered the Second World War in alliance with the U.K. Since 1945, and particularly since 1947, when the Marshall Plan, *q.v.*, and the Truman Doctrine, *q.v.*, were put forward by the U.S.A., relations between the U.S.S.R. and the western powers have been strained. The western powers have been concerned about: (1) Russian domination of the countries of eastern Europe (Poland, the German Democratic Republic, Hungary, Bulgaria, Rumania, and Czechoslovakia) which have pro-Russian governments; (2) Russian influence over countries in the Middle and Far East which the western powers have previously regarded as subjects for western colonial or economic expansion or as western military strongholds; and (3) the possibility that the U.S.S.R. may launch an aggressive war.

Since 1917 the U.S.S.R., then primarily an agricultural country, has become one of the world's foremost industrial producers. Since 1920 the economy has been developed by a series of plans, and particularly by the five Five-Year Plans of 1928–32, 1933–7, 1938–42 (interrupted in 1941), 1946–50 and 1951–5. In 1960 the volume of production of coal, petroleum, electricity, pig iron, and crude steel was in each case more than double that of 1940. Production of coal, steel, and electricity in each case exceeded the combined amount produced by the U.K. and the German Federal Republic. There were also remarkable increases in agricultural production. The sixth Five-Year Plan (1950–60) was replaced in 1959 by a Seven-Year Plan for 1959–65, under which industrial output is to increase by 80 per cent and agricultural output by 70 per cent.

Uniscan. An agreement concluded in 1950 by Denmark, Norway, Sweden, and the U.K. to develop closer economic co-operation. It envisaged the mutual exchange of privileges, such as the raising of tourist allowances, permission for Scandinavian countries to repatriate sterling capital and to borrow in the London market, and concessions as to royalty payments. There is no international staff but periodic discussions take place between the four governments.

United Arab Republic. The state created on 1 February 1958 by the union of the two independent sovereign states of Egypt, *q.v.*, and Syria, *q.v.*; area 458,432 sq. m.; population 30,045,000; capital Cairo. A plebiscite held on 21 February 1958 confirmed the union and the election of Gamal Abdel Nasser, *q.v.*, as President.

Executive authority is vested in the President, assisted by Ministers responsible to him and appointed by him. The cabinet announced by the President on 7 October included 14 Egyptian and 7 Syrian Ministers. On 9 March 1958 the Republic formed a federation with Yemen, *q.v.*, known as the United Arab States, *q.v.*

United Arab States. A federation established on 9 March 1958 by the United Arab Republic, *q.v.*, and Yemen, *q.v.* Article One of the charter signed by President Nasser and the Crown Prince Al Badr of Yemen said that the federation was to include 'the United Arab Republic, the Kingdom of Yemen, and those Arab states which will agree to join this union'. The charter provides for unified defence and foreign policies, for a supreme council consisting of the heads of the two states and any others which join, and for a federal council comprising equal numbers of representatives from each state. The permanent seat of the federal council is the Yemeni port of Hodeida, although meetings may also take place in Cairo and Damascus.

United Front. A coalition of East Pakistan political parties which originally included the Krishak Sramik Party led by Fazlal Huq, and the Awami League, led by Husain Shahid Suhrawardy, *q.v.*, In the East Pakistan provincial elections held in April 1954 it obtained eighty-six per cent of the total vote, thereby defeating the government party, the Moslem League, *q.v.*, on a twenty-one point manifesto which demanded the release of political detainees, recognition of Bengali as a state language and the maximum possible autonomy for East Pakistan. A United Front government was formed under Fazlal Huq but was not approved by the Federal Prime Minister who refused to accept the resignations of members of the outgoing government. In May 1954 parliamentary government was suspended for a period of thirteen months. In February 1955 Awami League members of the United Front moved a resolution of no confidence in Fazlal Huq's leadership; the League subsequently contested the elections of July 1955 as a separate party, winning 13 seats against the Moslem League's 25 seats and the United Front's 16 seats.

The United Front formed an East Pakistan ministry which remained in office until August 1956 when they were replaced by a coalition led by the Awami League.

United Kingdom of Great Britain and Northern Ireland. Area 93,053 sq. m.; population 52,675,094. The U.K. consists of the Kingdoms of England and Scotland, the Principality of Wales, and Northern Ireland. Except for Northern Ireland, *q.v.*, the constituent parts of the U.K. are not autonomous, although Scotland has a separate legal system. The rules of the British Constitution are to be found not in any single document but in a large number of parliamentary enactments, judicial decisions, and generally accepted conventions. The most important enactments are Magna Carta (1215), the Act of Union with Wales (1536), the Petition of Right (1628), the Habeas Corpus Act (1679), the Bill of Rights (1689), the Act of Settlement (1701), the Union with Scotland Act (1707), the Union with Ireland Act (1800), partly repealed in 1921, and the Parliament Acts, 1911 and 1949, *q.v.*

Supreme legislative power is vested in the Queen, acting with the advice and consent of the House of Lords, *q.v.*, and the House of Commons, *q.v.*, and legislative proposals (Bills) do not become laws (Acts of Parliament) until they have received the royal assent. The Queen has in theory a right to veto Bills by refusing her assent, but the veto is never used. Although the legislature is bicameral, the power of the House of Lords to prevent or impede legislation has been strictly limited by the Parliament Acts. In her executive capacity the Queen acts only on the advice of her Ministers, except in certain minor matters, such as the granting of personal honours. Her Ministers are in turn collectively responsible to the House of Commons, which by an adverse vote on a serious matter could force the Prime Minister to advise the Queen to dissolve Parliament, when a General Election would ensue. A number of senior Ministers (nineteen out of thirty-nine in 1961) are members of the Cabinet, an inner group which decides government policy.

The U.K. has one of the most comprehensive schemes of social welfare in the world. The National Insurance Act, 1946, provides for unemployment, sickness, maternity and widows' benefits, guardians' allowances, retirement pensions, and death grants. The National Insurance (Industrial Injuries) Act, 1946, provides a system of insurance against personal injury by accident arising out of, and in the course of, employment and against certain diseases due to the nature of the employment. The Old Age Pensions Act, 1936, provides for the payment of non-contributory old age pensions, and the National Assistance Act, 1948, provides for grants of financial assistance to all persons without resources or whose resources (including national insurance benefits) need to be supplemented. The National Health Service Act, 1946, established a health service free (except for certain small basic charges introduced later for prescriptions, dental treatment, etc.) to all in the U.K. This service extends to foreigners, who are also favoured by the British immigration laws, which for many hundreds of years have imposed no political tests on refugees who have sought admission. Under the Education Act, 1944, full-time schooling is compulsory for all children from the age of five, and free in publicly maintained primary and secondary schools.

The most valuable physical exports of the U.K. are electric and non-electric machinery, road vehicles and aircraft, chemicals, cotton yarns and woven fabrics, and iron and steel. The chief buyers of British goods are Australia, South Africa, the U.S.A., Canada, New Zealand, India, the Netherlands, Sweden, and the German Federal Republic.

The foreign policy of the U.K. is conditioned by its desire to co-operate with the United Nations, its firm friendship with the U.S.A., its alliance with France concluded in 1904 and re-affirmed in 1946 by Ernest Bevin and Léon Blum, and its membership of the North Atlantic Treaty Organization, *q.v.*, the Central Treaty Organization *q.v.*, and the South-East Asia Collective Defence Treaty, *q.v.*

United Nations. An international organization which came into existence on 24 October 1945 as a result of decisions made at international conferences during the Second World War, and as a successor to the League of Nations, *q.v.* At the Moscow Conference on 1 November 1943 the representatives of China, the U.K., the U.S.A., and the U.S.S.R. declared that they recognized 'the necessity of establishing at the earliest practicable date a general international organization, based on the principle of the sovereign equality of all peace-loving states, and open to membership by all such states, large or small, for the maintenance of international peace and security'. The Dumbarton Oaks Conference, *q.v.*, which ended on 7 October 1944, made proposals for the structure of the world organization, and delegates of fifty nations met at San Francisco between 25 April and 26 June 1945 to draft the United Nations Charter and the Statute of the International Court of Justice, *q.v.* Membership of the United Nations is open to all peace-loving states which accept and, in the judgment of the organization, are able and willing to carry out the obligations of the Charter. New members are admitted by a two-thirds vote of the General Assembly, *q.v.*, upon the recommendation of the Security Council, *q.v.* There have been disputes as to the admission of new members and several states are still excluded. North Korea, South Korea, Outer Mongolia, North Viet-Nam, and South Viet-Nam, for example, have been unsuccessful in their applications. Some non-members have been admitted to certain specialized agencies.

The Secretariat consists of a Secretary-General and such staff as the United Nations may require. The Secretary-General is the chief administrative officer of the United Nations and is appointed for five years by the General Assembly on the recommendation of the Secretary Council. Dag Hammarskjöld, *q.v.*, was first appointed Secretary-General in 1953 in succession to the first Secretary-General, Trygve Lie. He submits an annual report to the General Assembly on the work of the United Nations. The permanent headquarters of the United Nations is in New York City on land provided partly from money given by John D. Rockefeller, Jr, and partly by the City of New York.

The United Nations has six principal organs: the General Assembly, *q.v.*, the Security Council, *q.v.*, the Economic and Social Council, *q.v.*, the Trusteeship Council, the International Court of Justice, *q.v.*, and the Secretariat. In all these organs, other than the International Court of Justice, the official languages are Chinese, English, French, Russian, and Spanish, and the working languages are English and French. In the General Assembly, Spanish is also a working language. The official languages of the International Court are English and French.

The aims of the United Nations are declared in the United Nations Charter to be 'to save succeeding generations from the scourge of war . . . to reaffirm faith in fundamental human rights, in the dignity and worth of the human person, in the equal rights of men and women and of nations large and small, and to establish conditions under which justice and respect for the obligations arising from treaties and other sources of international law can be maintained, and to employ international machinery for the promotion of the economic and social advancement of all peoples'. The activities of the United Nations are discussed under the title of the appropriate organ, *e.g.*, General Assembly, or under the titles of the areas in question, *e.g.*, Indo-China, Kashmir, Korea. One of the most important functions of the United Nations is its quasi-diplomatic task of assessing world opinion, and urging its decisions on the governments concerned.

United Nations Educational, Scientific, and Cultural Organization (U.N.E.S.C.O.). Came into existence on 4 November 1946 with the object, according to its Constitution, of contributing 'to peace and security by promoting collaboration among the nations through education, science, and culture in order to further universal respect for justice, for the rule of law, and for the human rights and fundamental freedoms which are affirmed . . . by the Charter of the United Nations'. Its three bodies are: a General Conference, comprising one representative from each member state, which meets every two years to approve the programme and budget; an Executive Board of twenty-four members which meets at least twice a year and is responsible for the execution of the programme adopted by the Conference; a Secretariat under a Director-General and with headquarters in Paris. U.N.E.S.C.O. is one of the specialized agencies, *q.v.*, of the United Nations.

The activities of U.N.E.S.C.O. fall under the following eight broad headings: (1) Education: eliminating illiteracy and encouraging fundamental education, raising educational standards, promoting through education greater respect for human rights, making available information on educational techniques. (2) Natural Sciences: creating greater collaboration between scientists and encouraging the popularization of science. (3) Social Sciences: encouraging the study of the psychological and social problems involved in the development of mutual understanding, such as racial prejudice and religious differences. (4) Cultural Activities: developing cultural exchanges between member states and giving people access to works of art, literature, and philosophy. (5) Exchange of Persons: providing information as to the opportunities for work and study abroad, and providing travelling fellowships. (6) Mass Communication: keeping the public informed about the work of U.N.E.S.C.O. and significant events in the fields of education, science, and culture, and campaigning to help people to obtain easier access to knowledge. (7) Rehabilitation: assessing and making provision for the educational needs of schools, libraries, and scientific institutions in war-devastated areas and under-developed countries. (8) Technical Assistance: providing expert advice in the fields of fundamental education, teacher training, technical and general education, scientific research, and scientific advisory services. Member states are advised in such matters as their literacy campaigns, school building programmes, surveying of mineral resources, teacher training, and development of electrical engineering.

United Nations High Commissioner for Refugees (U.N.H.C.R.). Appointed on 1 January 1951, he has two main tasks: (1) to provide international protection for refugees, and (2) to promote activities designed to establish refugees economically, socially, and legally, either in countries where they are living or in new communities. The work of the Commissioner and his Office (which is in Geneva) covers all refugees, except those who have been given full rights of citizenship by their country of asylum or for whom other arrangements have been made, as in the case of the Palestine refugees. The small administrative expenses of the Office are financed by the United Nations, but the members of the United Nations decided in 1950 that the size of the remaining refugee problem did not warrant the expenditure of official international funds, and the work itself therefore has to depend on voluntary contributions, from governmental and non-governmental sources. In 1954 the office was awarded the Nobel Peace Prize.

United Nations International Children's Emergency Fund. Was established by the United Nations General Assembly on 11 December 1946; it functions under the supervision of the Economic and Social Council, *q.v.* It was originally responsible for helping child health and welfare programmes in countries devastated during the Second World War, but since 1950 it has extended its interests to the children of the under-developed countries. The Fund, which has its headquarters in New York, is dependent on voluntary contributions from members of the United Nations and from the public. One example of its work is the assistance that it has given, by supplying emergency supplies of milk, to the mothers and children of the Arab refugee population in Jordan.

United Nations Relief and Rehabilitation Administration (U.N.R.R.A.). Was the first large agency to work on behalf of the people in Europe and the Far East who had become refugees as a result of the Second World War, and to attempt to reconstruct the industry and agriculture of those nations, irrespective of political ideology, whose economies had been damaged by the war. It was established on 9 November 1943 and officially ceased its activities on 31 March 1949. It spent approximately $2,500,000,000, of which the U.S.A. contributed nearly three quarters, on food, clothing, textiles and footwear, agricultural and industrial rehabilitation material, and medical supplies. It prevented starvation in Albania, Czechoslovakia, Greece, Italy, Poland, and Yugoslavia. By 1946 the industries of most European countries had reached their pre-war production levels, whereas the same point was not reached until ten years after the First World War.

Much of the work of U.N.R.R.A. was taken over by other international organizations, its health work by the Interim Commission of the World Health Organization, *q.v.*, its child welfare work by the United Nations International Children's Emergency Fund, *q.v.*, its agriculture work by the Food and Agriculture Organization, *q.v.*, and its work on behalf of refugees and displaced persons, which continued until 30 June 1947, by the Preparatory Commission of the International Refugee Organization, *q.v.* The activities of U.N.R.R.A. as a grantor of large-scale financial aid were taken over by the U.S.A. in the spring of 1947, when Congress appropriated $400,000,000 as emergency aid to Greece and Turkey, and in June 1947 when the Marshall Plan, *q.v.*, was put forward.

United Nations Relief and Works Agency (U.N.R.W.A.). Is responsible for the resettlement of the Arab refugees from Palestine.

United States of America. Continental area 3,022,387 sq. m.; area including outlying territories of Alaska, *q.v.*, Guam, Hawaii, Panama Canal Zone, Puerto Rico, *q.v.*, Samoa, Virgin Islands, etc., 3,619,655 sq. m.; population of continental U.S.A. (1960) 179,323,175 (an increase of 18½ per cent between 1950 and 1960); capital Washington, in the federal District of Columbia. There are fifty States, of which thirteen were the original members after the Constitution was drafted in 1787. The Constitution is federal in character, a substantial part of the administration being carried on by the States. The legislative power is vested in Congress, consisting of the Senate, *q.v.*, and the House of Representatives, *q.v.* The two political parties are the Democratic Party, *q.v.*, and the Republican Party, *q.v.* After the 1960 elections the state of the parties was: Senate, 65 Democrats and 35 Republicans; House of Representatives, 262 Democrats and 175 Republicans.

Executive power is exercised by the President who is elected for a four-year term by indirect election. The Constitution provides that each State shall appoint a number of electors equal to the combined number of its senators and representatives in Congress; the framers of the Constitution thought that an inter-State convention, known as the Electoral College, of all these electors should choose a President. The electors are appointed directly by the people, who in effect choose either the Democratic group or the Republican group in each State. These groups do not decide independently who should be President, for the College never meets; the successful Presidential candidate is the one whose party has a majority among the electors. Since 1937 the President's term of office has begun on 20 January, two months after his election, which takes place in November every leap year. No President can serve more than two terms. The President has a right of veto over any measure presented by Congress for his approval, but the veto can be overridden by a two-thirds vote of Congress. He chooses his own Cabinet Ministers, who are responsible only to him.

Judicial power is vested in the Supreme Court, *q.v.*, which interprets the Constitution. The doctrine of the 'separation of powers', *q.v.*, is thus part of the U.S. Constitution, and the legislature has not the sovereign authority that it has in the U.K.

There is an elected Governor, a group of executive officials, a judicial system and a bicameral legislature in each State (except Nebraska, which has had a unicameral legislature since 1937). A

State legislature is empowered to deal with all matters not reserved to Congress by the Constitution nor prohibited by the State Constitution. It can, for example, enact its own rules as to the right to vote, the criminal law, marriage and divorce, labour and education. In some States one must pay a tax (poll-tax) to qualify for the suffrage. The State Governors are chosen by direct vote, and their terms of office vary from two years to four years.

The most valuable exports of the U.S.A. are motor vehicles, grains, electrical machinery, petroleum and its products, metals and manufactures from iron and steel mills, textile fibres and manufactures, and construction and mining machinery. Its chief customers are Canada, Japan, Mexico, the U.K., Venezuela, Cuba, the German Federal Republic, the Philippines, France, Brazil, Netherlands, and Italy. Its most valuable imports are coffee, non-ferrous ores and metals, non-metallic minerals, wood and paper, cane sugar, and crude rubber. It imports mostly from Canada, Brazil, the U.K., Colombia, Venezuela, Cuba, Mexico, the German Federal Republic, the Philippines, Japan, Chile, and France. The U.S.A. produces approximately one third of the goods and services and one half of the factory products of the world. Under the Reciprocal Trade Agreements Act the U.S.A. pursues a policy of reducing trade barriers, but this policy is qualified by rules which give protection to many U.S. industries which fear foreign competition.

Since the attack by Japan on Pearl Harbour in the Hawaiian Islands on 7 December 1941, the U.S.A. has abandoned its pre-war isolationism and has intervened directly in Asian and European affairs. The Monroe Doctrine, *q.v.*, still forms an integral part of U.S. foreign policy, but both Democratic and Republican Parties have accepted the need for positive commitments, and approve of U.S. membership of the North Atlantic Treaty Organization, *q.v.*, the South-East Asia Collective Defence Treaty, *q.v.*, and the United Nations, *q.v.* The country was one of the original members of the United Nations, although it had refused to join the League of Nations set up by the Versailles Treaty, *q.v.*, after the First World War. The U.S.A. regards itself as the leader of a world-wide struggle against the advance of Communism, and has sought, by military and economic aid to threatened countries, to prevent China and the U.S.S.R. from extending their influence.

U.N.R.R.A. United Nations Relief and Rehabilitation Administration, *q.v.*

U.N.R.W.A. United Nations Relief and Works Agency, *q.v.*

Untouchables. The lowest group in the Hindu caste system. There are over fifty-five million Untouchables in India who have hitherto been treated as a lesser race by high-caste Hindus and have suffered such disabilities as being refused admission to shops and restaurants, and access to public wells and bathing *ghats*. Under the Indian Constitution of 1950 untouchability was abolished and its practice forbidden. However, cases were continually being reported, and in May 1955 the Indian Parliament passed a Bill making discrimination against Untouchables a legal offence punishable by six months' imprisonment and a fine of £37 10s. The Indian government has been embarrassed in its campaign to improve the status of Asiatics in East and South Africa by the practice of caste discrimination at home.

Upper Volta. An independent republic; area 106,011 sq. m.; population 3,473,000, comprising Mossis (approximately 1,600,000), Bobos, and 3,700 Europeans; capital Ouagadougou. It is land-locked, being surrounded by the republics of Mali and Niger to the north, and those of Ivory Coast, Ghana, Togo, and Dahomey to the South. Its port is Abidjan, the capital of the Ivory Coast, with which Ouagadougou is linked by railway. It consists largely of lands which were part of the Mossi Empire. The French created the separate colony of Upper Volta in 1919 out of the colony of Upper Senegal and Niger, which had itself been created in 1904. It was divided between adjacent colonies in 1932 but brought into existence again in 1947 as one of the eight territories comprising French West Africa, *q.v.*, and it achieved self-government within the French Community, *q.v.*, on 11 December 1958, the constitution coming into force on 15 March 1959, and complete independence, after breaking with the Community in June 1960, on 5 August 1960.

Legislative powers are vested in an assembly of 75 members elected every five years by universal suffrage. In 1960, 62 seats were held by the Voltaic Democratic Union (the local section of the Rassemblement Démocratique Africain) and 5 seats by the Voltaic Regroupment Movement. Executive powers are exercised by the President of the Council (Maurice Yameogo).

Millet, maize, rice, and yams are produced, and there are meagre exports (mostly to Ghana) of livestock, fish, and karite.

Uruguay. The smallest South American state, situated between Argentina and Brazil and on the Atlantic Ocean; population about 2,800,000, mostly white and predominantly of Spanish and Italian descent; area 72,172 sq. m.; capital Montevideo. Uruguay was ruled by the Portuguese during the seventeenth century, and from 1726 to 1814 by Spain. After several wars it was declared an independent state in 1828 and a Republic was inaugurated in 1830.

From 1880 to 1958 the Batlle family played a dominant part in the development of the country, and led the governing party, the Colorados ('reds' or liberals). Since 1900 there has been a number of constitutional innovations designed to protect Uruguay from the emergence of a dictatorship. Under the 1951 Constitution the presidency was abolished and all executive power was vested in a bipartisan National Council (of nine men), modelled on the Swiss Federal Council. This Constitution took effect on 1 March 1952. Parliament consists of the Senate, with 31 members elected for four years, and the Chamber of Representatives, with 99 members, elected on a district basis for four years. The Senate seats are divided between the two political parties obtaining the highest number of votes, providing that they poll an absolute majority; if they do not, there is proportional representation.

At the election held in November 1958 the Blancos, or National Party, led by Luís Alberto de Herrera, defeated the Colorados, who thus lost power, when the change of office took place on 1 March 1959, for the first time for 94 years. Of the 9 seats on the bipartisan National Council 6 were awarded to the Blancos and 3 to the Colorados. The representation in the legislature is – Senate: 17 Blancos (9 from the Herrerista group and 8 from the Uníon Blanca Democrática), 7 Lista-15 and 5 Lista-14 Batllistas, 1 Catholic, and 1 Socialist; Chamber of Representatives: 51 Blancos, 38 Batllistas, 10 others. Although the Colorados had nationalized industries and conferred many social benefits on Uruguay, a system of intricate exchange rates, equivalent to export duties, had damaged the export trade in wool and beef, and those who supported the Blancos in 1958 included farm labourers, the middle class, and landowners.

Uruguay, the most stable South American democracy, has a high standard of living, no personal income-tax, and a well-developed system of old age pensions, maternity and child welfare centres, accident insurance, and education. Its wealth is obtained from its pastures, which support large herds of cattle and sheep. There is a number of commercial connexions with Argentina which the Herreristas in particular have been anxious to foster, but dislike of the Perón régime made the Batllistas reluctant to enter into closer relations with Argentina.

U.S.S.R. Union of Soviet Socialist Republics, *q.v.*

V

Vatican City State. This is the smallest independent sovereign state in Europe (0·16 sq. m.). After the incorporation of the former Papal States of Central Italy into the Italian Kingdom in 1870, the sovereignty of the Pope was limited to the palaces of the Vatican. The Popes refused to acknowledge Italy's action, and as a sign of protest no Pope left the Vatican after his election. This continued until 1929 when the Lateran Treaties were concluded between the Vatican and Italy, owing to the Italian Fascist dictator Mussolini's desire to settle the 'Roman question'. The Pope's sovereignty over only the Vatican palaces, the Lateran palace in Rome, and the Papal villa at Castel Gandolfo was confirmed, and the Vatican, thenceforward known as Vatican City, assumed external signs of sovereignty such as a coinage, police, radio station, and a postal system of its own. A large sum was paid to the Vatican as compensation for its territorial claims. In Italy the Vatican owns the controlling interest in thirty-one industries with a capital of over 300,000,000 pre-war lira, and has holdings in banks, shipping and insurance companies, chemical, textile, mining, and hydro-electric industries.

The Vatican is governed by the 263rd Pope, John XXIII, *q.v.*, elected on 29 October 1958 to succeed Pius XII. The present Pope (born 25 November 1881) is Angelo Giuseppe Roncalli, formerly Patriarch of Venice. Full legislative, executive, and judicial power is vested in the Pope. Nuncios are posted in many capitals and Apostolic Delegates in others. As the centre of the Roman Catholic Church, it commands the spiritual allegiance of more than 434,000,000 Roman Catholics, and is a political power of great importance. Its policy is to promote Catholicism all over the world. Catholic parties usually belong to the moderate right; before the Second World War they occasionally supported the extreme right, and Catholic Bishops blessed both the Italian legions which invaded Ethiopia and the Franco rebels in the Spanish Civil War. The Catholic Church opposed Nazism when Hitler attacked the Church in Germany and confiscated its properties. During the Second World War many priests supported left-wing underground movements in France and Italy. Roman Catholic political parties today are strongly opposed to Communism.

Venezuela. An independent state in the north-western part of South America; population (1958) 6,412,891; area 352,143 sq. m.; capital Caracas. Venezuela was ruled by Spain from the sixteenth century until the revolt led by Simon Bolivar, a native of Caracas, who defeated the Spanish forces in battle in 1813 and 1821. Venezuela became part of the Federal Republic of Colombia in 1822, and achieved complete independence in 1830.

Petroleum, discovered in 1922, accounts for over ninety per cent of the total value of the exports of Venezuela, which has the largest oil exports in the world. The government receives over fifty per cent of the gross profits from petroleum under its agreement with the Gulf, Shell, Creole (an affiliate of Standard Oil of New Jersey), and Texas Oil Companies. Most of the crude oil is refined in the neighbouring Netherlands West Indies, *q.v.*, but the percentage refined in Venezuela is increasing. In south Venezuela there are rich iron ore deposits which are being developed by the United States Steel and Bethlehem Steel Corporations. Other exports include coffee, gold, and cocoa.

In 1948 Colonels Carlos Delgado Chalbaud and Marcos Pérez Jiménez, at the head of a military caucus, overthrew a government led by the left-wing anti-Communist party, Accion Democratica (A.D.). Chalbaud became President, the A.D. was outlawed, and a strike among oil-workers was suppressed. In 1950 Chalbaud was assassinated; after a period of confusion Jiménez seized power in December 1952, but he was deposed by a military junta, backed by a popular rising, in January 1958. Rear-Admiral Wolfgang Larrazábal Ugueto was then appointed President. He resigned in November 1958 and in the following month stood for election as President, with the support of the left-wing Democratic Republic Union, but was defeated by Rómulo Betancourt (born 1908), leader of A.D., who had spent 21 years in prison or in exile.

Versailles Treaty. Concluded on 28 June 1919 between the victorious powers of the First World War and Germany. The first part of the Treaty concerned the structure of the League of Nations, *q.v.* As a result of the second part of the Treaty Germany ceded Alsace-Lorraine to France, Eupen-Malmédy to Belgium, part of Upper Silesia (after a plebiscite), Posen, and West Prussia to Poland, the port of Memel and its hinterland to Lithuania, Hulchin to Czechoslovakia, and part of Schleswig (after a plebiscite) to Denmark. Germany had to renounce its sovereignty over Danzig, *q.v.*, to abstain from union with Austria except with the unanimous consent of the League Council, to disarm, to abolish conscription, to maintain an army of not more than 100,000 men and a navy of six battleships with a corresponding number of cruisers and destroyers, to possess no submarines, no military aircraft, no heavy guns, and to build no fortifications. The Rhineland was to be occupied by the victorious powers for fifteen years and the Saar (now Saarland, *q.v.*) was to be internationalized; German rivers were to be internationalized and the German colonies were shared out among the victors and administered under League mandates. Germany was obliged to 'accept the responsibility of Germany and her allies for causing all the loss and damage to which the Allied and Associated Governments and their nationals have been subjected as a consequence of the war imposed upon them by the aggression of Germany and her allies' and had to pay reparations, fixed in 1921 at £6,600,000,000. Most of the territorial concessions were the subjects of disputes between the First and Second World Wars; in particular Upper Silesia, Posen, West Prussia, Memel and its hinterland, the Saar territory, and the Rhineland had all been re-acquired by Germany by the end of 1939. All the military prohibitions were disobeyed by the Nazis who came to power in 1933, while the sum due as reparations was gradually reduced, and entirely abrogated in 1932.

Verwoerd, Hendrik Frensch. South African Nationalist Party politician; born 1901 in the Netherlands and taken to South Africa as a child when his Dutch father emigrated there; educated at Stellenbosch University, where he studied psychology, and later at the Universities of Hamburg, Leipzig, and Berlin. At Berlin he was a lecturer in applied psychology and later head of the sociology department. After his return to South Africa and to Stellenbosch University he was one of the six members of the staff who protested against the admission into South Africa of German Jewish refugees. In 1937 he became editor of the Johannesburg Nationalist newspaper, the *Transvaler*. When (as editor) he brought an action against the Johannesburg *Star* for criticizing his treatment of war news, the judge dismissed his action and held that Verwoerd had knowingly given moral support to the enemy, i.e. to Germany. Shortly after his election to the Senate he was, in 1950, appointed Minister of Native Affairs, in which office he was able to put into practice his uncompromising belief in the principles of apartheid, *q.v.* He was elected as leader of the Nationalist Party, and so automatically to the vacant Premiership, on 2 September 1958, in succession to Johannes Gerhardus Strijdom, who died in August 1958. On 9 April 1960 an attempt was made to kill him, but he recovered from the serious gunshot wounds which he received.

Veto. The right to reject. The word is commonly used to describe the right of any of the five permanent members of the United Nations Security Council, *q.v.*, to prevent the Council from making a decision on non-procedural matters. The right is given by the Charter which states: 'Decisions of the Security Council on procedural matters shall be made by an affirmative vote of seven members. Decisions of the Security Council on all other matters shall be made by an affirmative vote of seven members including the concurring votes of the permanent members.' The formula was agreed at the Yalta Conference, *q.v.*, in February 1945 between the U.K., the U.S.A., and the U.S.S.R., and was a modification of the Russian view that the Security Council should take no action at all without the unanimous consent of the major powers. One exception was allowed; a party to a dispute should not vote when it was a matter of seeking a solution by peaceful means. When peaceful means of settling a dispute fail, every member of the Security Council can vote, even though it is a party to the dispute, and the majority required to take action to stop aggression must in theory include all the permanent members (China, France, the U.K., the U.S.A., the U.S.S.R.). In practice, a permanent member's abstention from voting on a substantive question is not regarded as a Veto, although a strict reading of the Charter would suggest that it should be regarded as a Veto.

The United Nations Charter declares: 'The organization is based on the principle of the sovereign equality of all its members'; but the allocation of permanent seats has given to five powers a privileged position, from which they could only be removed by an amendment of the Charter; this would itself require the concurrence of the Security Council and of the power or powers which it was sought to remove.

Vichy France. The central and southern parts of France which were not occupied by the Germans after the defeat of France in 1940, and which were ruled by a French administration from Vichy. The government was led by Marshal Pétain, to whom the National Assembly (by 569 to 80 votes) gave absolute powers when it brought the Third Republic to an end on 10 July 1940.

Viet-Minh. A political organization, founded by Ho Chi-Minh, *q.v.*; it was created in 1941 to resist the Japanese in Indo-China and transformed in 1951 into the Lien Viet Front. Since 1945 it has controlled the rural and jungle areas of Viet-Nam, *q.v.* The party is Communist and commands an efficient, politically-educated army which decisively defeated the French at Dien Bien Phu in 1954, and dominated the assembly of the Democratic Republic of Viet-Nam. Its authority north of the 17th parallel was recognized by the Geneva Agreements of 1954.

Viet-Nam. A French consolidation of the three ancient provinces of Annam, Tonkin, and Cochin-China; area 127,000 sq. m.; population 26,790,000, most of whom are Taoists or Buddhists, but including nearly 2,000,000 Roman Catholics; capital Hanoi. The French occupied Cochin-China in 1858 and established a colony there; Annam became a protectorate in 1874 and Tonkin in 1892. The mineral resources of the area – zinc, tin, iron, and coal – the rubber, and the two 'rice-bowls' of the Red river and Mekong river deltas, attracted French capital, and private investment was encouraged by government bounties and preferential tariffs. In 1940 the country was occupied by the Japanese and used as a military base for the invasion of Malaya. Resistance groups were active in Annam and Tonkin, and in August 1945 a Republic of Viet-Nam (an old Chinese name meaning 'Farther South') was declared, the Emperor of Annam, Bao Dai, *q.v.*, overthrown and a government was formed which comprised various nationalist, anti-Japanese, and Communist revolutionary parties, of which the Viet-Minh, *q.v.*, was the most important. The French negotiated with this government, through its leader, Ho Chi-Minh, *q.v.*, for an Indo-Chinese federation of Laos, *q.v.*, Cambodia, *q.v.*, and Viet-Nam. Their proposals were rejected because Cochin-China was excluded; apart from its economic value it belonged to the Union of the Three Ky, or Annamite peoples, and was considered to be an integral part of Viet-Nam. In December 1946 Viet-Minh forces attacked Hanoi; hostilities continued for eight years.

The successes of the Viet-Minh forced the French to conciliate nationalist opinion in the areas they still controlled. In 1949 Cochin-China was incorporated in Viet-Nam, Bao Dai was installed as head of state, and a union of the three Associate States of Indo-China was created which gave Cambodia, Laos, and Viet-Nam a measure of self-government. The defeat of the French at Dien Bien Phu in 1954 brought the war to an end. An armistice was agreed at Geneva between the French government and the Viet-Minh leader, General Giap, which the Viet-Nam foreign minister refused to sign, by which Viet-Nam was temporarily divided along the 17th parallel into two zones of North Viet-Nam, *q.v.*, and South Viet-Nam, *q.v.* It was also agreed that partition should end in July 1956 when free elections for a government of reunified Viet-Nam would be held. The partition did not end, nor were the elections held, in July 1956. The Geneva Agreements completed the transfer of sovereignty from France to Cambodia, Laos, and Viet-Nam.

Von Brentano, Dr Heinrich. Appointed Foreign Minister of the German Federal Republic when the Federal Chancellor, Dr Adenauer, gave up the post in June 1955; born in 1904, he is a lawyer, a Roman Catholic, and unmarried. He was imprisoned by the Nazis in July

1944, and after the war helped to found the Christian Democratic Party in Hesse, becoming leader of the Christian Democratic Party in the Bundestag in 1949. He has been actively concerned with the movement for European integration, and became a Vice-President of the Consultative Assembly of the Council of Europe in 1950.

W

Wagner Act. *See* National Labour Relations Act, 1935.

Wall Street. The site of the New York Stock Exchange. The term is used as a synonym for U.S. banking and financial interests.

War Crimes. Those acts of an enemy soldier or civilian which may be punished when the offenders are captured. They consist of breaches of the laws or customs of war. An act may be a war crime even though committed on superior orders; this was a basic principle of the Charters of the International and Far Eastern Military Tribunals set up in 1945, although it was conceded that the fact that a person had acted on the order of a superior could be considered in mitigation of punishment if the Tribunal decided that justice so required. In practice the war crimes tribunals mitigated the punishment where the defendant would have suffered a dire penalty for disobedience, but did not reduce it in the case of senior officers who faced no such penalty and should have refused to carry out their orders.

During the Second World War there were large numbers of war crimes, of which the vast majority was committed by Germany and its allies. On 8 August 1945 France, the U.K., the U.S.A., and the U.S.S.R. concluded an Agreement for the Prosecution and Punishment of the Major War Criminals of the European Axis. The Agreement provided for the creation of an International Military Tribunal to try those accused of war crimes. Article Six of the Charter annexed to the Agreement stated that the crimes coming within the jurisdiction of the Tribunal were: '(*a*) Crimes against Peace: namely, the planning, preparation, initiation, or waging of a war of aggression, or a war of violation of international treaties, agreements, or assurances, or participation in a common plan or conspiracy for the accomplishment of any of the foregoing; (*b*) War Crimes: namely, violations of the laws or customs of war. Such violations shall include, but not be limited to, murder, ill-treatment or deportation to slave labour, or for any other purpose, of civilian population of, or in, occupied territory, murder or ill-treatment of prisoners of war or persons on the seas, killing of hostages, plunder of public or private property, wanton destruction of cities, towns, or villages, or devastation not justified by military necessity; (c) Crimes against Humanity: namely, murder, extermination, enslavement, deportation, and other inhumane acts committed against any civilian population, before or during the war, or persecutions on political, racial, or religious grounds in execution of, or in connexion with, any crime within the jurisdiction of the Tribunal whether or not in violation of the domestic law of the country where perpetrated.' A similar International Military Tribunal was set up in the Far East, and the governments of the various allied states established tribunals in countries where war crimes had been committed.

An objection made on behalf of the defendants at the International Military Tribunal held at Nuremberg, Germany, was that the victorious states did not define the jurisdiction of the Tribunal so that it could deal with war crimes committed by their own subjects, although there was no doubt that some such offences, however few in comparison with those of the enemy, had taken place.

Warsaw Pact. The Eastern European Mutual Assistance Treaty, *q.v.*, signed at Warsaw in May 1955.

Weimar Republic. A description given to the Republic established in Germany, *q.v.*, after the First World War and the abdication of the Emperor Wilhelm II. Its Constitution, which was characterized by centralizing and socialistic tendencies, was adopted in July 1919 by a National Assembly which met at Weimar. Its Presidents were Friedrich Ebert (1919–25) and Field-Marshal Paul von Hindenburg (1925–34); the Republic virtually came to an end in 1933 with the appointment of Adolf Hitler as Chancellor or Prime Minister and the institution of the Third Reich, *q.v.*

Welensky, Sir Roy (Roland). A leading politician in the Federation of Rhodesia and Nyasaland; born 20 January 1907 in Salisbury, Southern Rhodesia, the son of a Jew born near Vilna. In 1923 he moved to Northern Rhodesia where he became an engine-driver and organized trade unions, opposing the Fascist trend which had become apparent in the Broken Hill area; he has been a member of the National Council of the Rhodesia Railway Workers' Union since 1933. From 1925 to 1928 he was the heavyweight boxing champion of Rhodesia. He was a member of the Northern Rhodesian Legislative Council from 1938 to 1953 and formed and led the Northern Rhodesia Labour Party. During that period he won for the elected members on the Council the right to be appointed to offices though he never accepted one himself. During the Second World War he was Director of Manpower and responsible for ensuring that there were adequate supplies of labour for the copper mines. He favoured federation and when it came he was knighted and appointed Minister of Transport and Communications. He became Prime Minister in November 1956.

West Indies Federation. An association of British colonies in the West Indies which came into existence as a federation on 3 January 1958; land area approximately 8,030 sq. m.; population approximately 3,152,500, of whom over 70 per cent are of African negro origin; seat of government, Trinidad. Detailed proposals for its establishment were made in 1947 when the proposed association was known as the Caribbean Federation, *q.v.* It comprises Barbados, Jamaica; *q.v.*, Trinidad, the Leeward Islands (except the Virgin Islands which decided not to join), and the Windward Islands. Negotiations for the inclusion of British Guiana, *q.v.*, in South America, and British Honduras, *q.v.*, in Central America, were unsuccessful.

Under the 1958 Constitution, contained in an Order in Council approved by the United Kingdom Parliament in July 1957, the Governor-General must act on the advice of the Council of State (the Cabinet) except in matters concerning defence, the financial stability of the Federation, and foreign affairs. In respect of these three matters the Crown may legislate by Order in Council, and the Governor-General may, with the approval of the British Colonial Secretary, act against the advice of the Council of State. The Federation is therefore not an independent sovereign state.

Legislative powers are vested in a Senate of 19 members appointed on a territorial basis by the Governor-General, and a House of Representatives of 45 members elected, on a population basis, by adult suffrage. At the first elections held in March 1958 the results were: Federal Labour Party (led by Norman Manley, *q.v.*, of Jamaica, Eric Williams, leader of the Trinidad People's National Movement, and Sir Grantley Adams, leader of the Barbados Labour Party) 25; Democratic Labour Party (led by Sir Alexander Bustamante, *q.v.*, of Jamaica, and Albert Gomes of Trinidad) 19; Barbados Independent Party, 1. At the first meeting of the House of Representatives in April 1958 Sir Grantley Adams was elected Prime Minister of the Federation.

The chief product and export is sugar, grown in each of the five groups of the islands; Cuba and the Philippines, however, have preference in the U.S.A. The other principal exports are molasses (Barbados and Leeward Islands), oil (Trinidad), rum (Barbados and Jamaica), bananas (Jamaica and Windward Islands), alumina and bauxite (Jamaica), and asphalt (Trinidad).

West Irian. Netherlands New Guinea, *q.v.*

Western European Union. Created on 5 May 1955, it is essentially an expanded version of the Brussels Treaty Organization, *q.v.*, which came to an end on that day. Its members are the Brussels Treaty powers (Belgium, France, Luxemburg, the Netherlands, and the U.K.), Italy, and the German Federal Republic, which became sovereign on the same day. There is a council of the seven Foreign Ministers, an Assembly consisting of the representatives of the seven members of the W.E.U. in the Consultative Assembly of the Council of Europe, *q.v.*, an Armaments Control Agency, various committees, and a secretariat. Its Standing Armaments Committee works in conjunction with the North Atlantic Treaty Organization, *q.v.*

Western Germany is the part of Germany which, under the Berlin Declaration of June 1945 and under the Potsdam Agreement, *q.v.*, of August 1945, became the Occupation Zones of France, the U.K., and the U.S.A. at the end of the Second World War. In December 1946 the U.K. and the U.S.A. agreed to an economic fusion of their Zones (which became known as Bizonia); this union, which came into effect on 1 January 1947, was later joined by the French Zone. These economic moves were largely the results of disputes with the U.S.S.R., particularly over the Russian demand for reparations. Under the Marshall Plan, *q.v.*, announced in June 1947, Western Germany received economic aid from the U.S.A. After the currency reform of June 1948 industrial production, which had made only a slow recovery after the heavy wartime bombing, increased rapidly from approximately forty per cent to over seventy per cent of the 1936 level by the end of 1948. A Constituent Assembly, elected by the *Länder* of the three Zones, met in Bonn on 1 September 1948 to draft a Constitution (known as the Basic Law) for Western Germany. The Law became effective on 23 May 1949 upon receiving the approval of a two-thirds majority of the parliaments of the *Länder*, and on that date the German Federal Republic, *q.v.*, came into existence.

Westminster, Statute of. An Act of Parliament of the U.K., passed in 1931, defining the legislative powers of the Dominions of the British Commonwealth, *q.v.*, and giving statutory effect to resolutions passed by the Imperial Conferences held in 1926 and 1930. No Act of Parliament of the U.K. passed after the Statute of Westminster was to extend to a Dominion as part of the law of that Dominion, unless the Dominion requested, and consented to, the Act. Each Dominion was given full power to make laws which applied beyond its boundaries, and to repeal or amend Acts of Parliament of the U.K. in so far as they formed part of the law of that Dominion, and no Dominion law was to be void on the ground of its repugnancy to the law of the U.K.

Nothing in the Statute was to give any new power to alter the Constitutions of Australia and New Zealand. The relationship between the central government and the provinces of Canada was to remain unchanged and as stated in the British North America Acts, 1867 to 1930. As a result of the Imperial Conferences and of the Statute of Westminster most of the Dominions then in existence passed constitutional measures which emphasized their independent sovereign status within the British Commonwealth.

W.E.U. Western European Union, *q.v.*

W.F.T.U. World Federation of Trade Unions, *q.v.*

Whig. A member of the English political group which, from 1680 onwards, wished to limit the power of the monarch and to give more power to Parliament. The original Whigs were the rebels who held out in the Scottish lowlands after the failure of their insurrection of 1679, and who opposed any attempt to bring Scotland into ecclesiastical uniformity with England. In 1680 those English politicians who wanted to exclude from the throne any Roman Catholic monarch were derisively called Whigs. The Whig nobles dominated the anti-Tory forces until the appointment of Gladstone as Prime Minister in 1868. From that date it is correct to describe these forces as Liberals rather than Whigs. The name is still used to describe the political parties in Liberia, *q.v.*

White Army. The Russian anti-revolutionary army in the civil war of 1917–21, so called in contrast to the Red Army of the Communists and in allusion to the royalist forces of the Vendée which attempted an insurrection against the republicans during the French Revolution, and which had as their badge a white lily, the emblem of the French monarchy.

White House. The official residence of the U.S. President in Washington, the capital of the U.S.A. Building began in 1792, but President Washington died before the house was ready for occupation. The first President to live in it was John Adams, who took up residence there in 1800. The building was partly destroyed in the course of a war with the British in 1814. Its grey walls were painted white to cover the smoke marks, and thereafter it was known as the White House.

White Russia. One of the fifteen constituent Republics of the U.S.S.R. and otherwise known as Byelorussia, *q.v.*

Whitehall. A street in London in and near which a number of important government ministries (including the Foreign Office, Home Office, Ministry of Health, War Office, Treasury, and Admiralty) are situated.

W.H.O. World Health Organization, *q.v.*

Wilson, James Harold. British Labour Party politician; born 11 March

1916 and educated at Jesus College, Oxford. He became a Lecturer in Economics at New College in 1937 and a Fellow of University College in 1938. During the Second World War he held a number of civil service posts as an economic adviser. He was elected to the House of Commons as the Member for Ormskirk in 1945 and was Parliamentary Secretary to the Ministry of Works, 1945–7, Secretary for Overseas Trade in 1947 and President of the Board of Trade from 1947 to 1951. Since 1950 he has represented the Lancashire division of Huyton in the House of Commons.

World Bank. The International Bank for Reconstruction and Development, *q.v.*

World Federation of Trade Unions. An international organization established in the autumn of 1945 by labour organizations from fifty-four countries, including the Congress of Industrial Organizations, *q.v.*, the Trades Union Congress, *q.v.*, and the Russian trade unions. The American Federation of Labour, *q.v.*, declined to participate in the formation of the W.F.T.U. on the ground that the Russian unions did not constitute a free and democratic trade union movement. In January 1949 the C.I.O., the T.U.C., and several other national groups withdrew from the W.F.T.U. Later that year there was formed the International Confederation of Free Trade Unions, *q.v.*

World Health Organization (W.H.O.). Came into being on 7 April 1948 as a result of proposals made at the San Francisco Conference, April–June 1945, and the International Health Conference at New York (convened by the United Nations Economic and Social Council), June–July 1946. The New York Conference set up an Interim Commission of W.H.O., pending ratification of the W.H.O. Constitution by members of the United Nations. When a cholera epidemic broke out in Egypt in September 1947 the Interim Commission appealed to all countries, and considerable quantities of vaccines and medical equipment flowed in from all parts of the world. W.H.O. organized the distribution and use of the materials and the epidemic was mastered in six weeks.

The legislative organ of W.H.O. is the World Health Assembly, meeting yearly and comprising representatives of all member states. It determines policy and votes on the budget. The Executive Board, representing eighteen member states, meets twice yearly to give effect to the decisions of the Assembly. Current work is entrusted to the Secretariat under the Director-General. The permanent headquarters are at Geneva. W.H.O. is one of the specialized agencies of the United Nations.

W.H.O. has two main groups of activities: (1) Advisory services which help countries to develop their health administration. Public health teams explain how to combat such maladies as malaria, tuberculosis, the venereal diseases, plague, typhus, cholera, and diphtheria, and how to improve maternal and infant hygiene, sanitation, and nutrition. Training is given so that countries will eventually have sufficient skilled personnel to apply modern techniques. (2) Central technical services, such as the administration of health conventions, biological standardization, establishment of an international pharmacopoeia, and publication of health statistics. It has an annual expenditure of about $16,900,000.

Y

Yalta Conference. A meeting between President Franklin D. Roosevelt of the U.S.A., Winston Churchill, Prime Minister of the U.K., and Marshal Stalin of the U.S.S.R., at Yalta, a Crimean health resort, between 4 and 11 February 1945. Final plans for the defeat and occupation of Germany were agreed; it was decided that the German surrender must be unconditional and that each of the three powers would occupy a separate Zone of Germany, while co-ordinated administration would be ensured through a central Control Commission consisting of the supreme commanders of the occupation forces, with headquarters in Berlin. France was to be invited to take an Occupation Zone and to participate as the fourth member of the Control Commission.

The three powers said that Germany should never again be able to disturb the peace of the world; that all German armed forces would be disbanded; that all German military equipment would be removed or destroyed; that all war criminals would be brought to justice and swift punishment; that all German industry that could be used for military production would be eliminated or controlled; that reparation would be exacted in kind for the destruction wrought by the Germans; and that all Nazi and militarist influences would be removed from the life of the German people. The U.S.A. abandoned its previous proposal, known as the Morgenthau Plan, that Germany should have a pastoralized economy, stripped of all heavy industry.

It was agreed that an international organization to maintain peace and security should be established. The foundations for such an organization had already been laid at the Dumbarton Oaks Conference, *q.v.*; a preliminary conference of the United Nations (the San Francisco Conference, *q.v.*) was arranged for April 1945 to prepare a United Nations Charter, and to discuss voting procedure, on which there had been no agreement at Dumbarton Oaks. The three statesmen agreed on a formula suggested by Roosevelt that (1) each member of the Security Council should have one vote; (2) decisions of the Security Council on procedural matters should be made by an affirmative vote of seven members; (3) decisions of the Security Council on all other matters should be made by an affirmative vote of seven members, including the concurring votes of the permanent members, provided that a party to a dispute should abstain from voting. The words 'including the concurring votes of the permanent members' permitted the device known as the Veto, *q.v.*, or the Yalta formula. It was agreed that the U.S.S.R. should have three seats in the United Nations, in respect of the Russian Soviet Federal Socialist Republic, the Ukrainian Soviet Socialist Republic, and the Byelo-russian Soviet Socialist Republic; the U.S.S.R. abandoned its request, made at Dumbarton Oaks, that each of its constituent Republics (there were then sixteen) should have a seat.

The three powers affirmed their belief in the principles of the Atlantic Charter, *q.v.*, and said that they would jointly assist the people in any liberated European state or former Axis satellite state in Europe to carry out emergency measures for the relief of distress, and to form interim governments broadly representative of all democratic elements and pledged to the earliest possible establishment through free elections of governments responsive to the will of the people. The U.K. and the U.S.A. discontinued their support of the Polish government in exile in London but insisted that the Polish government in Poland should hold free elections; the eastern frontier of Poland was to follow the Curzon Line, *q.v.*, and Poland was to receive substantial accessions of territory in the north and west.

Yemen. Independent state in Arabia, at the southern end of the Red Sea; area 75,000 sq. m.; population 4,500,000; capitals Taiz (the residence of the Imam, Ahmad bin Yahya Muhammad Hamid Ud Din, born 1891), and San'a. The Imam Ahmad, head of the Zeidi sect of the Shiah Moslems, succeeded to the throne on 14 March 1948 after the murder of his father on 17 February 1948. He defeated the forces which had seized power upon his father's death, and which were opposed to the feudal rule of the Imams, who for many years have monopolized all government posts and most businesses. In April 1955 the Imam put down another revolt, led by two of his brothers, one of whom, Abdullah, was Foreign Minister, and by army officers. He had his brothers executed, but then abandoned the traditional policy of isolating Yemen from the outside world, and in April 1956 concluded a tripartite military alliance with Egypt (which had already agreed to supply aircraft, guns, and tanks) and with

Saudi Arabia. The 1927 Treaty of Friendship with the U.S.S.R. expired in 1954, but in 1955 it was decided to renew it and to strengthen economic relations with the U.S.S.R. On 9 March 1958 Yemen entered into a federal union with the United Arab Republic, *q.v.*, known as the United Arab States, *q.v.*

The boundaries of Yemen and Saudi Arabia are fixed by the Treaty of Taif, 1934; the boundaries with Aden Protectorate, *q.v.*, have not been completely delimited, and agreements between Yemen and the U.K. (which came into force in 1934 and 1951) provide for a joint commission to undertake this task. The Imams claim that the establishment by the U.K. of a federation of tribes in the Western Protectorate amounts to a breach of the 1934 agreement. Yemen, which lies in the most fertile part of Arabia, exports coffee, grain, hides, and raisins. In 1955 the Imam granted an oil concession to a privately-owned U.S. company, the Yemen Development Corporation of Washington.

Yugoslavia. A Federation of the People's Republics of Serbia, Croatia, Slovenia, Montenegro, Bosnia and Herzegovina, and Macedonia: area 96,265 sq. m.; population (1958) 18,189,000; capital Belgrade. Yugoslavia achieved nationhood in 1918; Serbia and Bosnia were removed from Turkish influence and Slovenia and Croatia were separated from Austria-Hungary and a Kingdom of Slovenes, Croats, and Serbs was established under the rule of the Serbian king, Alexander Karageorgević. Unity was imperilled by religious quarrels (the Slovenes and Croats were mainly Roman Catholic, the Serbs Serbian-Orthodox, Bosnia had a large proportion of Moslem converts, and the Macedonians belonged to the Greek Orthodox Church), and the indifference of a Serbian king to the interests of his other subjects. As a result of uproar in the Constituent Assembly in 1928, during which the Croat Peasant Leader, Stepan Radić, was shot dead, King Alexander abrogated the Constitution and assumed dictatorial powers. After his assassination in 1934 his brother, Prince Paul, acting as Regent for the young King Peter, continued to rule with the support of the army and the ruling caste.

When the Germans invaded they met resistance from two partisan organizations: the Chetniks, led by General Mihailović, who operated in Serbia, and the National Liberation Front, led by Marshal Josip Broz Tito, *q.v.*, which recruited followers in Bosnia, Croatia, Montenegro, and Slovenia. When it was discovered that Mihailović had co-operated with the Germans the Serbian partisans joined Tito. His forces, in 1945, numbered 800,000 – the largest and most effective resistance movement in Europe – and had immobilized forty Axis divisions. On the liberation of Belgrade in 1944 a People's Republic was proclaimed and King Peter deposed. In elections held the following year ninety per cent of those who voted supported the new régime and Tito was made President.

Under the Constitution of January 1953 supreme federal authority is vested in the People's Assembly which comprises a Federal Council of 371 deputies, some of whom are elected by eight local Councils and others by universal and direct suffrage, and the Council of Producers, which consists of one deputy for every 70,000 workers engaged in production, transport, and commerce. The People's Assembly elects the President, and a government of thirty-four, the Federal Executive Council, from the Federal Councillors. The Constitution separates Church and State, gives equal rights to women, and provides for the distribution of land among the peasants.

Between 1918 and 1941 the Karageorgević family dominated the national economy: it controlled most of Yugoslavia's industry, opposed land reform, discouraged national investment, and allowed the economic assets of the country to pass into foreign ownership. In 1941 ninety-eight per cent of the copper, lead, timber, and cement industries were owned by foreigners. A decree of 1945 which confiscated, without compensation, the property of enemy nationals, war criminals, and collaborators, brought into state ownership nearly eighty per cent of the country's industry without affecting Yugoslav property.

Between 1946 and 1948 Yugoslavia pursued an aggressively independent Communist policy. Tito antagonized the western powers by (1) threats of refusal to sign the Italian Peace Treaty (*see* Trieste), (2) giving assistance to Communist troops in Greece, (3) shooting down U.S. planes flying from Vienna to Trieste. Although he concluded military and economic agreements with the east European bloc and with the U.S.S.R., he refused to accept direction from Moscow, and purged the Yugoslav Communist Party of its pro-Russian elements. He carried out land redistribution but would not forcibly collectivize agriculture, and by encouraging investment in peasant small-holdings he prevented the alliance of industrial workers and poorer peasants against the rich peasants (or *kulaks*), which occurred in the U.S.S.R., claiming that the peasants, who outnumber industrial workers by twelve to one, were 'the most stable foundation of the Yugoslav state'. For this 'fundamental error in Marxist-Leninist theory' he was expelled from the Cominform, *q.v.*, in January 1948. A *rapprochement* then took place with the western powers as a result of which Yugoslavia obtained credit from the Export-Import Bank, and loans from the International Monetary

Fund and the International Bank. In the first ten years of the Federation more than forty per cent of the national income was invested in heavy industry: since 1955 greater emphasis has been placed on the development of secondary industries and consumer products. The tourist industry has been encouraged as a valuable source of foreign exchange.

Yugoslavia is a party to the Balkan Pact, *q.v.*, with Greece and Turkey. Although normal relations with the U.S.S.R. were resumed in May 1955, Yugoslavia remained the only Communist country in Europe not committed to a military alliance with Russia.

Z

Zanzibar. A Sultanate and British protectorate off the coast of Tanganyika, comprising the islands of Zanzibar and Pemba, and several much smaller islands; area of the two main islands 1,020 sq. m.; population (1958 census) 299,111; capital Zanzibar. There is a strong Arab influence in the protectorate, originating from the seventeenth century when Omani Arabs helped the inhabitants to expel the Portuguese. The Sultanate became independent of Oman in 1856, and at that time it included a substantial part of the East African coast. Much of this was ceded to Germany and Italy outright in 1890, 1904, and 1924, but there remains a coastal strip, administered as part of Kenya, for which the Sultan receives £10,000 annually. Zanzibar and Pemba came under British protection in 1890.

Government is administered by the British Resident, and legislation consists of decrees by the Sultan, which become effective when counter-signed by the British Resident. The Sultan H. H. Seyyid Sir Abdullah bin-Khalifa (born 1910) succeeded his father in October 1960.

The general elections, held in January 1961, for 22 elective seats on the Legislative Council, resulted in 10 seats being won by the Afro-Shirazi Party (dominated by Africans, and looking to their fellow-Africans in Tanganyika for inspiration), 9 by the Zanzibar Nationalist Party (dominated by Arabs) and 3 by the Zanzibar and Pemba People's Party. There are also 3 officials and 5 appointed members on the Legislative Council. The majority leader is chief minister.

Zionism. A belief in the need to establish an autonomous Jewish community in Palestine, *q.v.* Many movements have tried to satisfy the desire of the Jewish people to return to the Holy Land. Modern Zionism was conceived by Theodor Herzl (1860–1904), a Hungarian-born journalist, working in Vienna, who, though an assimilated Jew, believed as a result of his own experience and particularly the lessons of the Dreyfus case that there was no security for the Jewish people unless they had a state of their own. His ideas were opposed by assimilated Jews who felt themselves secure in the countries in which they lived, but today Zionism is supported by the vast majority of the Jewish community. Although the original object of Zionism has been attained in the creation of the state of Israel, *q.v.*, it is still an active international force engaged in protecting the welfare, and extending the influence, of Israel.